Thomas D. Hamm
Read in February, 1980
for L. Perry's colloquium

FIRST SERIES.—No. 12.

THE

BOOK OF THE SEA;

FOR THE INSTRUCTION OF

LITTLE SAILORS.

NEW YORK:
KIGGINS & KELLOGG,
123 & 125 William St.

THE SAILOR.

SAILORS pass most of their time on the water. They become so used to living on the water, that when they are on land they sometimes do not know what to do with themselves to pass away their time. And after a few days or weeks they are very glad to be on board their ship again, and on the wide, blue sea. Sailors are kind and brave; and if you are kind to them they will do everything in their power to show that they feel it, and will repay it. They are a class of men who are very much needed, and do us great good by going

THE BRIG.

THE brig is next in size to the ship. It has but two masts —but is otherwise like a ship. The ship and the brig are called square-rigged vessels because nearly every sail is square. Like the ship, the brig too is used mostly in long voyages.

SCHOONER AND SLOOP.

THE schooner has two masts, and the sloop but one. The sail is fastened at the bottom to a long stick, called the boom, to the mast at the side, and to the gaff at the top. The vessel in the picture is a sloop.

upon the sea, and risking their lives in storms, to bring us the good things of countries afar off. They amuse one another on long voyages by telling long stories. This they call spinning yarns.

THE SHIP.

THE ship is the largest kind of vessel that sails upon the water. It has three masts, made of the trunks of pine trees, that have pieces of timber called yards put across them on which are spread the sails. Ships are used for long voyages, being often months out of sight of land.

THE SKIFF.

THE skiff is a small boat, made of boards or thin planks. It is used about rivers and on ponds and lakes, and is pushed through the water with a paddle, like a canoe. The canoe is made sometimes out of the trunk of a tree, and sometimes out of bark or skins.

LIKE prisoned eagles sailors pine
On the dull and quiet shore;
They long for the flashing brine,
The spray and the tempest's roar.

To shoot through sparkling foam,
Like an ocean bird set free—
Like the ocean bird their home
They find on the raging sea.

THE INTELLIGENCE OF A PEOPLE

THE INTELLIGENCE OF A PEOPLE

DANIEL CALHOUN

PRINCETON UNIVERSITY PRESS
PRINCETON, NEW JERSEY

L.C. Card: 72-9945
ISBN: 0-691-04619-0

Printed in the United States of America
by Princeton University Press

For J.N.M., who had but a single nature

PREFACE

THE ESSAY that follows is the first result of what started out differently, as a venture into the economic side of educational history. As once planned, the study would have explored one strand in the modernization of American education from about 1750 to 1870, would have examined the population pressures, economic needs, and social forms that affected modernization, and would thus have sought some answer to the question of whether the development period in American history has anything to say for the problems of nations that are seeking to promote economic—and educational—development in the twentieth century. The strand chosen for examination was the educational history of New York State over this period, when authorities created an increasingly complex school pattern for the state and also chose to invest larger amounts of the state's economic resources in that pattern.

But this project posed one embarrassing question. What if all this reorganization and investment made no difference to the quality of the human beings for whom the effort was being spent? Did educational modernization actually improve the ability of people to think about their world and to perform in it, or did it simply reshuffle the practices of schooling to fit into the changed institutional pattern of modern life? Schools became different, they were given better support, and they were presumably better; did this make any difference in the intelligence, in the mental capacity of the people? If it did not, then educational modernization may have been merely a great administrative chore, and no policy achievement at all.

When this question emerged, it began to seem that the

project should consider three successive questions. First, was there any significant change in American intelligence over the period studied? Second, what part did the schools play in bringing about any change? And third, on the assumption that modernization of the schools did contribute a significant part of any change in intelligence, what parts did the various social determinants of modernization contribute to the things that made a difference for intelligence? An organized set of answers to all these questions is still desirable. But the object of the following essay is only to suggest an answer to the first question. More modestly yet, it seeks to suggest how that question might be answered if scholars had done all the kinds of research that are needed.

The attempt to answer this question may seem foolhardy to two kinds of perfectly sane scholars: to those who know the uneven state of the art in American cultural history, and to those who have been trying to measure intelligence in the present, with living subjects and with all the advantages of controlled test conditions and refined psychological technique.

The problems of what intelligence is, and of how to measure it, create serious difficulties for the best-trained of psychologists and measurement specialists. From their many-sided work I have extracted certain more restricted assumptions, which may permit me to translate the concept of intelligence into historical terms. First, I assume that intelligence—whatever it is—varies according to the psychological and social experiences of individuals and that it may therefore vary over periods of history, in whole populations, if the experiences of those populations change. Repeated studies have pointed to wide changes in the measured intelligence of children, black or white, who undergo changes in the conditions in which they are growing up. These indicate that it is not foolish to look for historical changes in intelligence. Second, I assume that intelligence, whatever its genetic and physiological base, is ultimately a function of the whole experience of the individual, of the family conditions in which he is raised, of the formal learning he meets in schools, and of the public ideas that surround, sustain, and even express his mind. Third, I assume that the speculations and researches that psychologists have done on the cognitive development of individuals, and on the origins of both learning skills and learning problems, can provide a guide for the necessarily more intuitive inferences of the historian. Fourth, I assume that one of the distinctions psychologists often make between kinds of intelligence is simple enough to apply to historical materials: that between analytic and global, or between analytic and synthetic, or among quantitative, verbal, and spatial types of intelligence. (These three distinctions are of course not the same, but they are sufficiently similar to be played with in the same contexts.) Fifth, I assume that because intelligence—the ability to learn—is itself partly learned, it must be partly a result of what teachers expect. In other words, intelligence is partly the result of what happens when the older generation communicates certain ideas about the intellectual behavior the young should display, and the young then respond to those expectations in whatever ways their own needs suggest.

If these assumptions hold, then the historian may make some informed guesses about the level of intelligence that a population achieved in a particular period. He needs "simply" to examine what he can find about the ways individuals learned their mental capacity. The particular lines of exploration that I have selected for my own effort are three. The opening inquiry is negative: what problems did teachers report in the ways that pupils learned basic skills —the diffuse skills of perception, the verbal skill that is reading, and the quantitative skill that is arithmetic? If teachers left really adequate accounts of how pupils learned, and of how pupils were distributed among various kinds of success and failure at learning, then there would be no need to proceed further. In fact, teachers' descriptions of pupil behavior have always varied widely in quality.

Though the teachers and other school observers of the mid-nineteenth century left a plentiful number of descriptions, the teachers of the colonial period left very few descriptions at all. Therefore I have moved on to two other lines of inquiry. In matters close to private life, how did child-raising attitudes express basic expectations about the intellectual behavior and motivation of children? Even in the twentieth century, parental attitudes seem to make as much difference as specific parental practices, and there exists from the colonial period some definite testimony about how parents felt. Then, in the matter of men's public lives, the whole culture becomes evidence about intelligence. The process of education gave skills to writers, preachers, lawyers, or builders; such men, as they worked, learned how much response or understanding they could expect from the public. How did what these men produced express both their own skills and the ability of the general population? Along these two lines —child-raising attitudes and cultural products—I feel that I have found enough evidence to justify a speculative answer to the major question: did American intelligence change over the years from 1750 to 1870, and, if so, in what ways?

In carrying out my own trial at assessing changes in American intelligence, I have selected evidence in a way that reflects the project from which this study diverged. This limitation may serve some function of giving focus. Evidence about learning problems, about child-raising, and about preaching and shipbuilding and bridge-building, I have taken from descriptions of behavior in the New York area and from prescriptions that were probably influential with people who either lived there or moved there in large numbers (especially from New England). I have tried to avoid using material that seemed peculiarly Yankee, or peculiarly Southern, or peculiarly Western, or even peculiar to one of the sectarian cultures of Pennsylvania. Despite all this selecting, I have nevertheless presumed to talk about "American" intelligence as the phenomenon about which the evidence used might have something to say. For the early nineteenth century, this is a fair generalization, because New York did serve as a central channel for much of the settlement of the country, because the state combined some characteristics of Yankee New England with stolid, hierarchical patterns suggestive of farther south, and because it combined also much of the spirit of eastern urbanization with some of the process of westward extension and homogenization. As other workers have argued before in justifying their selection of New York as a test area, I hope that the area is narrow enough to permit description as a single, somehow coherent society, and yet central enough and broad enough to serve as an emblem of ways American. It was certainly, then and in its own terms, a place where men were learning how to argue passionately about the techniques of intelligence.

In using these materials, I have adopted methods that move from hint and surmise toward a sense of what an observer might have asserted about earlier thinking if he had walked in with some twentieth-century ideas on childhood, language, and technology. Of course, present-day psychologists often offer only tentative suggestions about how, say, family experience influences kinds of intelligence. They also disagree. So do writers about rhetoric and construction. From their cautions and dilemmas I have extracted whatever principles would suggest a consistent picture for the whole of my own material. Certainly the psychologists are free to deny that they intended any such arrogant coverage —although I suspect that many of them are willing to convert limited research findings into universal hunches when they respond to thinking in the society around them now. Still, I admit to laying rough, greedy hands on the ideas of certain scholars who have achieved great clarity and coherence in treating of encounters between the human mind and the external world. Their works that have reached to the needs of this study are: Howard I. Chapelle, *The Search for Speed under Sail, 1700-1855*; Neil Harris, *The Artist in*

American Society; Eleanor E. Maccoby and Lucy Rau (with Elizabeth Bing), *Differential Cognitive Abilities*; Erwin Panofsky, *Gothic Architecture and Scholasticism*; and Stephen Timoshenko, *History of Strength of Materials.* Each of these has demonstrated the possibility of making connections between otherwise isolated pieces of experience. I lean on them for license, as much as I draw on them for ideas. There come times when an inquirer asks not What can we prove? but What if it should be true that all these threads do hang together?

During several years of this puzzle work, many persons and organizations have given me support and encouragement. Grants have been made by the Committee on the Role of Education in American History, by the Senate Committee on Research of the University of California, Davis, and by the Guggenheim Foundation. Great amounts of help and advice have been given by librarians, curators, and photographers, at: the Harvard University Libraries; the Huntington Library and Art Gallery; the University of California, Berkeley; the New York Public Library; the New-York Historical Society; the Columbia University Libraries; the University of California at Los Angeles; the Stanford University Library; the G. W. Blunt White Library at Mystic, Connecticut; the Mariners' Museum at Newport, Virginia; the Admiralty Library, London; the Maritime Museum, Greenwich; the Scheepvaart Museum, Amsterdam; the Smithsonian Institution; and the Maritime Museum, San Francisco. At this last institution I must single out the late Albert Harmon, who provided an improbable, necessary link between the world of preaching and the world of shipbuilding.

Comments on one version or other of these essays have been made by many people: Oscar Berland, John T. Blake, Oscar Handlin, P.M.G. Harris, Michael Katz, David Riesman, Polly Calhoun Roddy, David Rothman, Charles F. Rozema, and Wilson Smith. From their criticisms I have tried to accept what I could, but have certainly not accepted enough to do justice to their understanding. The readers of any manuscript form a highly specialized audience. Often, though, a specialized audience can stand as representative of qualities in the larger population from which it comes. If that is true in this case, the American population is in better shape than I would have thought.

CONTENTS

ILLUSTRATIONS

THE INTELLIGENCE OF A PEOPLE

ONE

CHANGE IN INTELLIGENCE: NOW AND THE PAST

"INTELLIGENCE" is an evil word for Americans who are trying to understand each other in these last decades of our century. Even when we leave aside the second meaning that identifies intelligence with spying, or with conspiracy, we suspect that anybody who wants to talk about intelligence has invidious, possibly racist aims. If someone insists that there is such a thing that can be given this psychological label, he must believe that he and his kind of people have plenty of this quality, and that other groups have less. Even if he comes speaking in the guise of a humanitarian teacher, he must be one of those who would categorize children and serve them according to their label, not according to their individual character.

We have good reason to be suspicious. For about a hundred years now, a very large part of the men who have talked seriously about mental abilities have assumed that those abilities are a stable trait of the human body: inherited from parents, and not really subject to being changed by influence from outside the body. True, most educated Americans now no longer believe that abilities are determined by strict heredity. But "most educated Americans now" still do not represent the main drift of opinion over a long century. The longer-term weight of opinion—and much thinking even recently—has been pretty strictly hereditarian.

It had not always been so. Before the Civil War, even though most Americans and Europeans held to conventional notions about the superiority of the white race, they did not extend this belief to include rigid notions about the abstract nature of intelligence. Their flexibility on the subject showed in the way that early nineteenth-century visitors to America commented on the mental condition of the local inhabitants.

A common theme of the scribbling travelers was the high "intelligence" of the average American. Not that all agreed on this point. Basil Hall, who had been told that he would find American farmers to be "intelligent citizens," reported in 1829 that he never found "any thing of that peculiar intelligence, or that peculiar high-mindedness, so much insisted upon by American writers." But he admitted that schools succeeded in teaching elementary subjects to large masses of the population, even if these schools did not produce what he considered real education. And he yielded his point almost completely when he wrote in terms of what the twentieth century would consider the distinction between intelligence and achievement: "In one word, there is abundant capacity, and abundant desire to learn in America, but by no means any adequate reward for learning."[1] More commonly, observers did not distinguish between ability and achievement, though almost all made the same distinctions as Hall's between average and individual achievement. Tocqueville, for instance, wrote that the society could produce a tremendous quantity of mental accomplishment, even though perhaps little of individual greatness.[2] And Captain Marryat made the same kind of observation about the differences between American language and English language: "If their lower classes are more intelligible than ours, it is equally true that the higher classes do not speak the language so purely or so classically as it is spoken among the well-educated English."[3] The stereotyped qual-

[1] Basil Hall, *Travels in North America, in the Years 1827 and 1828* (Edinburgh, 1829), II, 69-73, 168-171, 175.

[2] Tocqueville, *Democracy in America*, tr. Henry Reeve, II (orig. 1840), Book I, chapter IX.

[3] Frederick Marryat, *A Diary in America, with Remarks on Its Institutions* (Philadelphia, 1839), II, 30.

ity of this response was indicated by the overtones of quick moral judgment that it included, as in Thomas Cather's summary description: "They possess great intelligence, energy, enterprise, and perseverance, all the elements necessary to make a flourishing commercial people, but they lack the qualities of a noble and generous nation."[4] The literacy of the average American, the ingenuity of Yankee workmen, the superficiality of most American instruction, the shoddiness of most American artisanship—these became the conventional rhetoric of observation.

But if the observations had any value at all, they depended on two assumptions. First, they assumed that it makes sense for social commentators to talk about the intellectual level and style of a population. Second, they assumed that this level can change over time, that it is a historical phenomenon. The Americans they were writing about were not originally much different from the observers who were describing them. Their culture had originally been quite European in tone. Explicitly to Tocqueville, and implicitly to many others, Americans were interesting precisely because they were Europeans who had changed over time, and in ways that Europeans might now find themselves experiencing. "We have seen the future" is the final cause of political travel. In intellectual matters, the future

[4] *Voyage to America: The Journals of Thomas Cather*, ed. Thomas Yoseloff (New York & London, 1961), 144. See also: Frances Anne Butler (Fanny Kemble), *Journal of a Residence in America* (Paris, 1835), 54*n*-55*n*, 89*n*, 142*n*-143*n*; William Cobbett, *A Year's Residence, in the United States of America*, 3rd edn. (London, 1828), 208-210; Isaac Fidler, *Observations on Professions, Literature, Manners, and Emigration, in the United States and Canada, Made During a Residence There in 1832* (New York, 1833), 39-44; Edouard de Montulé, *Travels in America 1816-1817*, tr. Edward D. Seeber (Bloomington, Ind., 1951), 181; Charles Augustus Murray, *Travels in North America* (London, 1854), 282, 291. Frances Wright, *Views of Society and Manners in America*, ed. Paul R. Baker (Cambridge, Mass., 1963), 18, 22, 216-217. And see Richard L. Rapson, "The American Child as Seen by British Travelers, 1845-1935," *American Quarterly*, XVII (1965), 520-534.

that travelers saw in America seemed to justify a modest optimism.

Alongside this outlook, Europeans and Americans alike soon developed more pessimistic arguments that appealed to a genetic, hereditarian logic. These arguments had been latent within the terms of some anti-American prejudice, and they were given new respectability by the evolutionary swell within nineteenth-century thinking. Although some Europeans had earlier put down America as a physically debasing environment, this had never been so convincing as the simple notion that the American population had been recruited out of European criminality—or in exceptional cases out of the Bible-reading wing of European religiosity. Brightness, as any intelligent gentleman knew from observing dogs and horses, was one of the traits of particular breeds. It was in the blood. When psychologists began measuring intelligence, toward the end of the nineteenth century, they both accepted and "demonstrated" the stability of intelligence as a physiological trait in the human animal.[5] There was only one way it could be changed: by natural selection or induced selective breeding. But only "natural" selection would encourage the fit (intellectually fit as well as physically). If Teutonic forests were the battlefield origin of the German graduate school, then free food and medicine for the indigent would only keep alive those too stupid to keep themselves alive. During the early part of the twentieth century, this logic picked up massive objective support from repeated studies of the relation between measured intelligence and family size. Children with higher I.Q.s came more often from small families; if these differences were fed into a straightforward model of population mechanisms, they predicted a steady decline in the intelligence of the population. This logic had, of course, long been implicit in the old English liberal arguments

[5] Joseph Peterson, *Early Conceptions and Tests of Intelligence* (Yonkers, 1925). Edward L. Thorndike and others, *The Measurement of Intelligence* (New York, 1926).

against outdoor relief: feed the incompetent and leave them at large, and they will only out-breed their betters.

In the twentieth century, many people who favored broader social services nevertheless accepted much of this evolutionary logic. Social workers and educators often assumed that the lower orders had lower innate intelligence, for which special educational systems should be designed. This pessimism was strong enough that it made the intelligence of *whole* populations a sensitive subject. It would not do to label one's clientele as stupid (not to their faces, anyway), and it would never be comfortable to think about one's whole population group, insiders and outsiders together, going down the mental drain. The subject of whether intelligence levels might be changing became acceptable only to elitists, eugenicists, and those among the nice types who enjoyed a self-lacerating pessimism. When major studies were finally mounted to measure whether intelligence levels were changing, they were sponsored by men whose principles led them to anticipate a decline.

Eventually one geneticist of more optimistic outlook, Lionel S. Penrose, devised a mathematical model within which it was *possible* for a population to gain in intelligence. The eugenicists dismissed his logic as oversimplified and unrealistic. He had to argue that there existed a group of least intelligence that was virtually sterile, and the obvious application of this to institutional defectives did not involve enough of the population to make much difference in any long run.[6]

The largest-scale efforts to measure changes in intelligence were made in Europe just after World War II, with pre-war measurements as base-lines. In one case, a Dutch study, the results showed a decline. But repeated studies made in Scotland and England produced either a mixed

[6] Lionel S. Penrose, "The Supposed Threat of Declining Intelligence," *American Journal of Mental Deficiency*, LIII (1948), 114-118. L. S. Penrose, "Genetical Influences on the Intelligence Level of the Population," *British Journal of Psychology*, XL (1950), 128-136.

pattern of change or—in one of the most careful studies—a distinct if modest shift upward. And when a repeat measurement was made in the Dutch study, it suggested that further changes in the post-war period had moved the level of measured intelligence back up. In the case of the Scottish Mental Survey of 1947, pessimists who had looked forward to the study were forced to shift their ground. They, who had long believed that test I.Q. was a genetic reality, now fell back on environmental arguments. They pointed out that the population might have been gaining over the years in physical health and test sophistication, so that the results could easily conceal a real decline in mental level.[7] But this argument, quite aside from the fact that it was contrived, was further weakened by demographic developments. In both Europe and America, the negative correlation between family size and child intelligence, or between family size and father's occupational level, grew weaker after World War II, to the point of nearly disappearing in some test situations. And when new studies took as their group to be measured not the families of school children, but populations including the unmarried and the childless, then it appeared that the intellectual level of those who produced no children had already been low enough to approach the supposedly unrealistic genetic model for a population that

[7] Scottish Mental Survey, *The Trend of Scottish Intelligence; a Comparison of the 1947 and 1932 Surveys of the Intelligence of Eleven-Year-Old Pupils* (London, 1949); and *Social Implications of the 1947 Scottish Mental Survey* (London, 1953). A. D. de Groot, "Effects of War upon the Intelligence of Youth," *Journal of Abnormal Psychology*, XLIII (1948), 311-317; and XLVI (1951), 596-597. W. G. Emmett, "The Trend of Intelligence in Certain Districts of England," *Population Studies*, III (1950), 324-337. Raymond B. Cattell, "Fate of National Intelligence: Test of a Thirteen-Year Prediction," *Eugenics Review*, XLII (1950), 136-148. Cyril Burt, Review of *The Trend of Scottish Intelligence*, in *British Journal of Educational Psychology*, XX (1950), 55-61. A. H. Halsey, "Genetics, Social Structure and Intelligence," *British Journal of Sociology*, IX (1958), 15-28. Cyril Burt, "The Trend of National Intelligence: Review-Article," *ibid.*, I (1950), 154-168.

would gain or remain stable in intelligence, through social selection.[8] Even before World War II, one of the key assumptions of the evolutionary pessimism may have been invalid. Now, after World War II, partial changes made it clear that the demographic process was not constant. The different reproductive behaviors of the parts of a population might conceivably produce either a trend of declining intelligence or a trend of increase. The actual pattern would depend very much on particular circumstances.

Meanwhile, back in the western hemisphere, workers had made two attacks, at first indirect, on measuring changes in intelligence over generation-long periods. One attack grew out of the clinical problem of finding norms for the word-association tests in which individuals were asked to say quickly what other word was suggested by each in a series of stimulus-words. The second grew out of the problem of classifying the abilities of United States Army recruits.

Psychologists had begun working with word-association tests before World War I, rather as if to learn whatever they could from a procedure that was easy to administer. They found, among other things, that the kinds of responses individuals gave varied with age, making the tests a rough measure of intelligence. Older subjects gave more standardized, less idiosyncratic responses than did children; and older subjects gave less frequent functional responses ("color" to "red"), more frequent opposite responses ("green" to "red"). The tendency for children to give the "correct"

[8] J. W. Thompson, "Genetics, Social Structure, Intelligence and Statistics," *ibid.*, XI (1960), 44-50. Jean Floud and A. H. Halsey, "Intelligence Tests, Social Class and Selection for Secondary Schools," *ibid.*, VIII (1957), 33-39. G. Thomson, "Intelligence and Fertility: the Scottish 1947 Survey," *Eugenics Review*, XLI (1950), 163-170. F. W. Warburton, "Relationship between Intelligence and Size of Family," *ibid.*, XLIII (1951-52), 36-37, 188. John D. Nisbet, "Family Environment and Intelligence," *ibid.*, XLV (1953), 31-40. Nisbet, "Level of National Intelligence," *Nature*, CLXX (1952), 852. Anne Anastasi, "Intelligence and Family Size," *Psychological Bulletin*, LIII (1956), 187-209.

function or logical responses for a word reached a peak just before adolescence, then declined during the later years of development. And when workers after World War II began redoing the norms of forty-five years earlier, they found that their whole groups, young separately or adult separately, had moved along the directions in which mature had earlier differed from pre-adolescent.[9] The apparent oddity, of course, was that maturity involved more of automatic, stereotyped responses, less of careful logic.

Along the second line, men who doubted that the genetic argument applied to large populations had been attacking the pessimistic approach with the weapons of environmentalism. Their immediate quarrel was with a racial finding that appeared in many measurements, especially in mental tests that the Army administered to draftees in World War I. These had shown lower levels in immigrants and Negroes than in the native white population. Here, the first step in re-analysis was simply to introduce an additional classification, by regions within the United States. This produced the now familiar indication that regional differences among native whites, and notably between South and North, were of the same order as racial differences inside any one region.[10] Although tests of local school populations continued to show gross differences in measured intelligence between white and Negro, Otto Klineberg initiated the more sophis-

[9] James J. Jenkins and Wallace A. Russell, "Systematic Changes in Word Association Norms: 1910-1952," *Journal of Abnormal and Social Psychology*, LX (1960), 293-304. Robert H. Koff, "Systematic Changes in Children's Word-Association Norms 1916-63," *Child Development*, XXXVI (1965), 299-305.

[10] Robert M. Yerkes, ed., *Psychological Examining in the United States Army*, National Academy of Sciences, *Memoir*, XV (1921), 681-683. John B. Miner, *Intelligence in the United States* (New York, 1957), 74-76, 98. Thelma G. Alper and Edwin G. Boring, "Intelligence-Test Scores of Northern and Southern White and Negro Recruits in 1918," *Journal of Abnormal and Social Psychology*, XXXIX (1944), 471-474. Henry E. Garrett, "A Note on the Intelligence Scores of Negroes and Whites in 1918," *ibid.*, XL (1949), 344-346.

ticated studies of black children that began to classify them according to how much of their own experience had been spent in the favorable environments of the North; the results showed that family migration could increase child intelligence.[11] Although a margin of difference continued to appear in measurements that compared Northern white and nonmigrant Northern Negro, the obvious deficits of the slum or ghetto environment could not be ignored, and this fact intersected with a growing awareness that ordinary intelligence tests discriminated against children from outside the bourgeois European tradition.

Up to this point in the arguments, the environments that were presumed to affect mental ability were understood in diffuse terms, much the same as the ordinary distinction between "good background" and "bad background." Then Europeans working with displaced populations during World War II began to reconsider the effects of institutional life on children. They brought in findings that children separated from their mothers in infancy suffered many psychological deficits, including intellectual loss as well as emotional disturbance. Around this idea there grew a massive literature on the consequences of maternal deprivation. The general correlation between inadequate mothering and retarded development was so plain that serious issues could arise only with respect to interpretation. On the American scene, for example, this finding did not fit mechanically into the investigations that attributed various ill effects to the mother-oriented families common in Negro slums. One way out was to analyze parental influence into many items more particular than the mother's nurturing. Another way out was to revise "maternal deprivation" to read "sensory deprivation." This certainly made sense for many of the studies on the effects of institutional environment, and it meshed

[11] Otto Klineberg, *Negro Intelligence and Selective Migration* (New York, 1935). Everett S. Lee, "Negro Intelligence and Selective Migration: A Philadelphia Test of the Klineberg Hypothesis," *American Journal of Sociology*, XVI (1951), 227-233.

also with many studies on laboratory animals. Young animals that were not given adequate physical stimulation while they were growing not only failed to develop much in problem-solving behavior; they also failed to develop neurological or biochemical structures that were associated with maturity. And when investigators found that removing massive amounts of brain tissue from an adult did not necessarily impair ability, they began to suspect that the physical basis of intelligence derives less from gross or original mechanical structures than from fine characteristics that develop redundantly in various parts of the brain.[12] Just where this leaves the argument between genetic and environmental conceptions is less important than the reconciliation it offers between the two old attitudes. In part, the old argument had been one between temperaments. The genetic side had appealed to men who wanted to be scientific by reducing phenomena to positive, particular, and especially physical explanations. The environmental understanding of intelligence had seemed nebulous, diffuse, and sentimental. But after the middle of the twentieth century, it was more and more the old hereditarian view that seemed to require metaphysical assumptions and categories from outside the sphere of serious genetics.

As soon as one began to think about the development of intelligence within the individual, over the life span, all that could save the strict hereditarian view was a faith that the whole course of development was a merely mechanical unfolding of a genetic pattern determined at conception. That such unfolding worked within some processes seemed likely enough, but most of the development schemes that scholars

[12] John Bowlby and others, *Maternal Care and Mental Health . . . Deprivation of Maternal Care* (New York, 1966). Sylvia Brody, *Passivity: A Study of Its Development and Expression in Boys* (New York, 1964). D. O. Hebb, *The Organization of Behaviour: A Neuropsychological Theory* (New York and London, 1949), 275-303. Leon J. Yarrow, "Research in Dimensions of Early Maternal Care," *Merrill-Palmer Quarterly*, IX (1963), 101-114.

suggested seemed to spill over into ideas about environment. Probably the most rigid scheme that attracted wide interest was that of Jean Piaget—and its attractiveness in America depended in part on the fact that Piaget was himself a humane, patient worker with children. His biologism carried no real odor of racial thought. He did argue that intelligence developed within the human organism according to a pre-established sequence of stages. Though this sequence allowed for little modification by environment, it also allowed for relatively little variation from individual to individual, or from group to group. Furthermore, although Piaget believed in an invariant sequence, he also believed that the child progressed to each higher stage by means of working with the materials of his environment. When Americans who worked along Piaget's lines considered whether his stages could be accelerated, their desire to intervene brought environmental effect back within his approach. In outcome, the Piaget approach merged with the direct environmentalist approach to form an "interactionist" conception of intelligence that became the normal and even orthodox one in the 1960s.[13]

Piaget argued that a child's progress from one mental level to another depended on his acquiring certain basic categories or concepts with which to think about his world. But this notion of concepts with which to think involved another possibility. Operational concepts, or ways of solving problems, or "cognitive styles," might differ in kind as well as in level or vigor. In a way, this could be read as more of the romantic, condescending idea that each individual or group was gifted "in its way." Suggestions of the rhythmic darky lurked within the notion of cognitive style, for those who wanted to use it that way. But the idea also

[13] J. McV. Hunt, *Intelligence and Experience* (New York, 1961). Shephard Liverant, "Intelligence: A Concept in Need of Re-examination," *Journal of Consulting Psychology*, XXIV (1960), 101-109. Jean Piaget, *The Language and Thought of the Child* (Cleveland and New York, 1955). Piaget, *The Psychology of Intelligence* (Paterson, N. J., 1963).

carried with it certain possibilities for analyzing environmental effects on intelligence, much as did the idea of sensory deprivation. Intelligence tests had long included a plurality of dimensions, the importance of which was recognized even by those who argued that a single "general factor" operated within most of the scales. These dimensions did not always reach the complexity of what anyone called cognitive style, but they did turn on such common distinctions as those among the verbal, the quantitative, and the spatial aspects of ability. From outside the technical tradition of testing, there also developed an interest in whether "creativity" was a real trait distinct from intelligence. This too was sometimes read as a difference between kinds of intelligence, specifically between "convergent" ability (that toward finding definite correct solutions to problems) and "divergent" ability (that for producing variety and fluency of ideas). Partly because the older romantic condescension had been acceptable even to many who took a "hard" line on the nature of intelligence, environmental explanations of differences in intellectual style gained ground quite easily.

For one thing, some of the categories in which psychologists discussed motivation bore obvious analogy to the conception of types of intelligence. The distinction between a "need for Achievement" and a "need for Affiliation" bore enough likeness to that between quantitative and verbal styles of intelligence to suggest plenty of hypotheses to the theory-builders, especially when they considered the notorious male-female differences between quantitative and verbal scores on tests. Investigators did not get very far when they tried to show that infant-raising practices were linked to the development of oral or anal or genital personality types, and thus to later intellectual styles. But they did produce a growing body of findings around the relations between child-raising attitudes, the learning of sex identification, the development of ego-strength, and the development of types of ability. Although the whole pattern of these relations was not clear, attempts to find some connections between emotional experience and intellectual development were producing positive results. And there kept turning up indications that parts of this cluster were changing over time. One change was the obvious shift in male and female roles that was taking place in as well as around the measuring sociologists. To the many studies that showed change in how people thought children should be handled, and to the long-standing but suspect belief of parents that they were handling children in ways different from those their own parents had used, there now began to be added studies that showed objective change in what people actually did with children, at least over the period during which social scientists had been collecting data.[14] On the motiva-

[14] Alice Ryerson, "Medical Advice on Child Rearing, 1550-1900" (Harvard Ed.D. thesis, 1960). Martha Wolfenstein, "Trends in Infant Care," *American Journal of Orthopsychiatry*, XXIII (1953), 120-130. Evelyn Miller Duvall, "Conceptions of Parenthood," *American Journal of Sociology*, LII (1946), 193-203. Daniel R. Miller and Guy E. Swanson, *The Changing American Parent* (New York, 1958). Lawrence D. Haber, "Age and Integration Setting; a Re-Appraisal of *The Changing American Parent*," *American Sociological Review*, XXVII (1962), 682-689, with reply by Miller and Swanson, p. 854. A. Davis and R. Havighurst, "Social Class and Color Differences in Child Rearing," *ibid.*, XI (1946), 698-710. Martha Sturm White, "Social Class, Child Rearing Practices, and Child Behavior," *ibid.*, XXII (1957), 704-712. Gerald R. Leslie and Kathryn P. Johnsen, "Changed Perceptions of the Maternal Role," *ibid.*, XXVIII (1963), 919-928. John E. Anderson, chairman, *The Young Child in the Home: A Survey of Three Thousand American Families* (New York, 1936). Urie Bronfenbrenner, "Socialization and Social Class through Time and Space," in E. Maccoby, T. M. Newcomb, and E. L. Hartley, *Readings in Social Psychology*, 3rd edn. (New York, 1958), 400-425. Paul J. Woods, Kathleen B. Glavin, and Caroline M. Kettle, "A Mother-Daughter Comparison on Selected Aspects of Child Rearing in a High Socioeconomic Group," *Child Development*, XXXI (1960), 121-128. Ruth Staples and June Smith, "Attitudes of Grandmothers and Mothers toward Child-rearing Practices," *ibid.*, XXV (1954), 91-97. Elinor Waters and Vaughn J. Crandall, "Social Class and Observed Maternal Behavior from 1940 to 1960," *ibid.*, XXXV (1964), 1021-1032. Martin Heinstein, *Child Rearing in California* (Berkeley, [ca. 1965]). Lilian Cukier Robbins, "The

tional side, a barrage of studies professed to show that the "need for Achievement" could be measured in cultural products as diverse as children's stories and elements of pottery design—and that these measures could be used to assess changes over time in this need as felt by whole societies. Again, the individual pieces of this barrage were often bizarre and unconvincing, but the pattern was suggestive.

But if interest in types or styles of mental activity directed some attention away from the genetic and toward the emotional bases of intellectual development, it also helped men look away from the individual, toward the cultural and social aspects of intelligence. Some of this was explicit even in Piaget, who insisted that a child needed to interact with other individuals as he acquired mental structures. In the hands of workers whose main interest was in group process as such, this idea turned into the notion that problem-solving activity is just as much a characteristic of groups as of individuals. In the "brain-storming" pushed by glorified personnel managers, in the "sensitivity training" that developed out of that, in the theoretical argument that democratic political organizations could produce decisions of quality beyond any apparent ceiling set by individual ability, in the argument that scientific progress entails the creation of consensus more than it does the achievement of logical finish, in complex studies on the relation between in-

Accuracy of Parental Recall of Aspects of Child Development and of Child Rearing Practices," *Journal of Abnormal and Social Psychology*, LXVI (1963), 261-270. Celia B. Stendler, "Sixty Years of Child-Training Practices," *Journal of Pediatrics*, XXXVI (1950), 122-134. Anne Louise Kuhn, *The Mother's Role in Childhood Education: New England Concepts, 1830-1860* (New Haven, 1947). Robert Sunley, "Early Nineteenth-Century American Literature on Child Rearing," in Margaret Mead and Martha Wolfenstein, eds., *Childhood in Contemporary Culture* (Chicago, 1955), 150-167. Urie Bronfenbrenner, "The Changing American Child—A Speculative Analysis," *Merrill-Palmer Quarterly*, VII (1961), 73-84. Nathan Maccoby, "The Communication of Child-Rearing Advice to Parents," *ibid.*, VII (1961), 199-204. Robert R. Sears, Eleanor Maccoby, and Harry Levin, *Patterns of Child Rearing* (Evanston, Ill., 1957).

dividual intellectual styles and the problem-solving behaviors of the groups to which men belong—in all these ways there grew up a willingness to see group action in the immediate working of intelligence, not just in causes or origins.[15]

And if the interest in group mentality foreboded a tolerance for social pressure against individuals, men whose assumptions were traditional or formal could look instead to language as the supra-individual structure of thought. If this led sometimes to the extravagancies of McLuhan, it included also the sober arguments of the Soviet psychologist Vygotsky, who saw language as the principal aspect of social life governing the development of individuals. A similar outlook worked in the arguments of Benjamin Whorf and his followers—that language categories defined the channels along with individuals could most effectively act. This particular kind of linguistic relativism enjoyed a considerable fashion for a few years, then seemed discredited by the inconclusive results of efforts to demonstrate it experimentally. It did not turn out that a people who had the same word for red hues and orange hues could not tell the difference between the two. This, of course, was a simplistic test, and it fitted well the interests of those scholars who preferred to study either racial differences in ability or social effects upon language. But when the relativists began to turn their attention from single words to whole repertories of vocabulary and phraseology—to the differences in whether individuals could devise *any* kinds of description to distinguish natural things—the Whorfian hypothesis be-

[15] Charles E. Lindblom, *The Intelligence of Democracy* (New York, 1965). George Herbert Mead, *Mind, Self, and Society* (Chicago, 1934). Gardner Murphy, *Human Potentialities* (New York, 1958), 113-128. R. Bruce Raup and others, *The Improvement of Practical Intelligence: The Central Task of Education* (New York, 1950). Harold M. Schroder, Michael J. Driver, and Siegfried Streufert, *Human Information Processing: Individuals and Groups Functioning in Complex Social Situations* (New York, 1967). J. M. Ziman, *Public Knowledge: The Social Dimension of Science* (Cambridge, 1968).

gan to look plausible again. The individual who found words to differentiate between two hues could actually work more effectively with the perceptual difference.[16] The increased sophistication here was comparable to that involved in the shifting conceptions of the physical basis of intelligence—from the simplisms of the early eugenicists to the complex interactive approach of a physiological psychologist like D. O. Hebb.

But this new linguistic relativism makes large areas of humanistic study relevant to the task of "measuring" whether and how intelligence has changed in whole populations. It shifts attention away from the mechanics of vocabulary, to the problems of rhetoric, style, and medium. Historically, it directs attention back not only to the growth of linguistic variety during the Renaissance, but to the deliberate efforts that academies and scientific societies have made at crucial times to change the cognitive style of language as used. And it leaves the student of popular culture free to consider either of two relations between cultural products and popular ability: the product as symptom of intelligence, or the product as guide and determiner of intelligence.

Suppose that all these ways of looking at human ability do describe the same, real world. How do they hang together? What does our knowledge about family life, about linguistic usage, about techniques of communicating, about patterns of group organization, about changes in cultural style, and even about the actual results of psychological testing, tell us about popular ability, understood in a general, average, or collective way? Specifically, although much that is said

[16] Delee Lantz and Eric H. Lenneberg, "Verbal Communication and Color Memory in the Deaf and Hearing," *Child Development*, XXXVII (1966), 765-779. Joseph Church, *Language and the Discovery of Reality* (New York, 1961). Roger W. Brown and Eric H. Lenneberg, "A Study in Language and Cognition," *Journal of Abnormal and Social Psychology*, XLIX (1954), 454-462. L. S. Vygotsky, *Thought and Language* (Cambridge, Mass., 1962).

may apply to industrial society generally, how has American intelligence changed in the recent past, and how is it changing now?

The first thing to be realized is simply that the whole subject is open. Once we recognize that a social group has gained in intelligence during some period, because of improvements in its environment, then the way is open to find either increases *or decreases* in *that* group's intelligence, or *any* other group's. And once we recognize that change in any direction is possible, for any group, we must recognize that the abstract base-line for any group might have been "high" or "low," if it could be measured. The natural history of mental ability in American populations could have taken many different courses. For example, there is no a priori reason not to suppose: that the average black who migrated to the New World was more intelligent than the average white; that the conditions of life in America depressed intelligence among black slaves but facilitated it among white workers; and that environmental changes in the twentieth century then began to brake or reverse this discriminatory pressure. That particular pattern, with something offensive in it for everyone, makes as much sense as any historical reconstruction made up by feeding twentieth-century test results into formal models of population change.

But then, so far as it makes sense to talk about a "standard" American population, abstract from racial or class distinctions, there is no particular reason to think that the intelligence of that standard population has been stable, in *either* genetic *or* environmental terms. Even now, the standard American has no reason to feel confident that he is one of an unchanging, reliable mental type.

During the twentieth century, ordinary intelligence has probably increased somewhat, at first for environmental reasons, more recently also for demographic or genetic reasons. As long as there remained a substantial farm population that was willing to move away from an environment that it found unsatisfactory, cityward migration was bringing people into a new life of stimulus, regularity, and formal discipline. This general influence was only implemented and illustrated by the growth of "test sophistication" among the parts of the population actually being measured. The standardized test was one more part of the process by which industrial techniques were applied to the personnel as well as to the materials of the modern economy; but the plasticity of human subjects meant that they became more and more like the standard being set for them, simply because they were being measured. The grosser aspects of this urbanizing of the mind were largely completed when the proportion of the population that was needed to produce a food supply began to approach a lower limit—by the 1930s, to put a rough figure on this process. The urbanizing of personal life often worked by means of reduction in family size: couples restricted the numbers of their children in order to achieve the flexibility needed for social mobility, in order to achieve progressive standards of living in the increasingly monetary city world, and also in order to train children better for urban roles. Although the smaller families of middle-class and intellectual couples might have meant a reduction in the numbers of the most intelligent in the following generation, this would have been true only to the extent that intelligence-in-parents was the cause, and small families the result. Actually, small family size promoted better physical and emotional attention to children, and therefore strengthened intelligence. When, after World War II, middle-class couples began raising slightly larger families than they had during the years of active transition to city life, then any genetic pressure against intelligence became at least ambiguous, even nil, and the small family became less critical as a nursery of brightness.

Another possible component of a modest increase in intelligence was an increase in the average level of schooling that Americans achieved, multiplied by the changing style of operation in public education. Early in the century, the average complete education extended through the eight grades of grammar school. Partly because it was an education in the rudiments, partly because American schools used formalistic methods, this training was mostly an imprinting of predefined formulas, definitions, associations, and habits. But even then, and even when high-school and higher education were themselves still largely formal, further mental development in an individual was associated with an ability to transcend the formal mental set assumed in grammar-school education. However modest were the achievements of progressivism in education, they certainly included a softening in the rote processes of the system. This was one meaning of the paradox in word-association tests: good little schoolchildren, prompt to dispose words into obvious logical categories, turned into more flexible adolescents and adults, willing to take care of the immediate stimulus with some trivial, automatic response, but reserving explanatory thought for the times when it would be appropriate.

At the same time, basic emotional roles in the society, such as male or female, or old and young, were becoming less rigid, more flexible in the way they were defined. Long before the splashy developments in the second half of the century, people were taking much less seriously the things that were supposed to show that a woman had an unfeminine mind, or the things that marked an impertinent tongue in a child. The sex and age categories that might channel mental style were becoming more diffuse (or perhaps simply more subtle). Many people, conservatives of a sort, feared this process. After all, these categories were part of the structures that individuals learned as they acquired strong, mature egos. Roles and labels seemed to ease minds over some of the pains in development, and they became an actual part of secure ego-functioning—meaning that these categories were in a sense part of intelligence itself. If the category boundaries were to fade, what would keep personalities from regressing to infantile, less competent levels?

It is partly in this context that we can interpret fears about the mass media. Stimuli from presses, lights, and loudspeakers were becoming more rapid, whether or not more intensive. At some point, communications were approaching the speed at which individuals really had only two choices—either to pay less attention, or to cut back on the complexity of their responses to each stimulus. Again, the situation was much like that which word-association tests indicated for the start of adolescence. An individual did not have time to spin out an elaborate learned formula in response to each stimulus. Among the middle-class groups whose earlier generations had taken to the school formulas, the discarding of these learnings looked like a loss of mental equipment and variety—as in part it was. Variety and complexity of thought were lagging, even while the elaborate kinds of conformity were also declining. Since social and technical problems were hardly becoming less complex, this meant that the culture, and the people within it, were driven toward building up complex products out of extremely simple elements. The ultimate emblem of this process was the replacement of the decimal by the binary number system in computer technology. Extreme rapidity of on-and-off responses was used in order to build up massive solutions to problems—an intellectual strategy that was accidentally of a piece with psychological changes taking place in the population at large.

This change in intellectual style—from the formula-bound to the informal but automatic—involved a dismantling of old attitudes and then a re-accumulating of new ones, a process that was largely carried out in the middle classes, but in a way that brought eventually greater continuity between working-class and middle-class intellectual styles.

At this point speculation begins to depend on controversial social ideas, at a level more subtle than any simple task of coping with old racist notions. The structure of the argument is simple enough: different social classes have raised their children quite differently; this has given their children different "cultural advantages," including different average levels of intelligence; therefore the growing similarity of child-raising practices, between middle-class and working-class families, has worked to make the base-line for intelligence more uniform through major groups of the population.

During the 1960s, of course, some commentators used this argument in racial terms, as when Daniel Moynihan argued that the Negro lower classes should become more like the middle classes in the way they handled children. To his argument, some of the defenders of the black family countered by denying one of the premises: that the ways in which the black family differed from the white made any difference to the quality of child mentality. And some of the more romantic defenders suggested that the special conditions of ghetto family life even promoted greater flexibility and early sophistication in the way children coped with the world.

The argument about the black family had proceeded on misleading assumptions, because nonracial arguments about the different effects of middle-class and working-class life had already built up a body of theory that neglected to take into account certain simple distinctions. Academic (therefore middle-class) observers had sometimes described working-class life as a longed-for contrast to the pains of middle-class morality: permissive, ebullient, sensual. Some had seemed to find these qualities confirmed by surveys of family life. But more skeptical academics reported surveys in which working-class parents came out as more authoritarian, not less; yet others reported surveys in which appeared no significant difference between middle-class and working-class child-raising practices.

These confusions arose from two things. First, there were two different things that "authoritarian" might mean. It might mean the imposing of arbitrary demands by parents, accompanied by an expectation that children be independent in the sense of not being a bother, and enforced by quickly decided physical punishment. This was usually what was involved when the working classes turned up as authoritarian, and it seemed to be an older or basic approach that underlay the behavior of all parents. But authoritarian might also mean the imposing of rigid schedules and impersonal disciplines, demanding great care and patience from the administering parent, but intended to produce greater independence and stronger ego-functioning in the child in the long run. This was usually what was involved when the middle classes turned up in studies as authoritarian.

Second, some kinds of parental behavior were actually changing over time. Middle-class parents had long been sensitive to whatever advice physicians or moralists might give. Their efforts to do as prescribed fluctuated uncertainly over the surface of whatever was constant in American family life. If parents were sometimes willing to take up a new prescription because the old did not seem to be making enough difference, they could also become dissatisfied when some child-raising strategy produced unintended effects. During the very early decades of the century, for example, the middle classes tried to adopt a strategy that was supposed to encourage independence and intellectual clarity in children—a strategy that may also have worked to undermine the security of important mental patterns. These were the years up to the 1930s when medical fashion called for imposing rigid, formal schedules on infants, in order to reduce the level of emotional dependency within the family. From that the inference should be simple: independence means strong ego; intelligence accompanies ego-strength; therefore the middle classes should have been producing more intelligent children, and the gap between them and the lower orders should have been widening—to the extent, of course, that economic improvement for working people might not have wiped out the psychological gap.

The scheduling prescribed in the literature was not just

firm; it was harsh, to the point that parents sometimes found it painfully difficult to impose. If these parents' diagnosis of the regime means anything, the scheduling might have come across to many children as plain rejection: the mere authoritarian instead of the authoritative. But one thing is clear in all the controversial literature about classes, races, and psychologies: that a harsh, rejecting behavior by parents hurts the mental development of children. Now energetic children may succeed in compensating for rejection, by moving out into fields away from the parent or teacher who presses for formal achievement. The child can take up challenges from the environment, relying partly on whatever symbolism he finds there. He can grow through physical performance, through action in the natural world, or through visual experience. As designed, the scheduling regime might have channeled children toward mental efficiency. As actually applied, it might have set up countercurrents in which children skipped the efficiency and opted for alternative *kinds* of intelligence.

During the generation after 1930, though, the scheduling fashion gave way before a strategy that journalists eventually identified with Dr. Spock: a desire to give children a nurturing, flexible family life, with much maternal attention that should foster mental security. This new attitude may or may not have had the social effects that moralists were later to worry about. But if it had any strictly intellectual effect, it should have done something to rearrange the middle-class family pressures of the 1920s. As against the scheduling regime, the newer way may have promoted less of strict intellectual ego-strength and order. But to the extent that the scheduling regime had worked harshly, the newer one might promote a more relaxed, anxiety-free intelligence. Some combination of these effects almost certainly worked within middle-class children, sometime between World War I and mid-century.

Finally, from about the 1950s, the psychologists and publicists who worked out lines of child-raising advice moved quite consciously to find some balance between earlier extremes. There are some indications that by these years, too, middle-class and working-class mothers were behaving much more alike in such matters as breast-feeding and weaning. With middle-class parents and physicians even conceding that parents should react spontaneously to defend their own peace of mind against children, some of the older or temporary class differences in family style were withering away. On the other hand, middle-class parents continued to press their children for intellectual achievement, and continued to have greater resources to help this achievement along. The new, more balanced and pragmatic approach, less faddish even if less based on principle, could mean creating fewer unintended obstacles to middle-class mental competition.

In all this, while effects certainly varied from family to family even within one "class," the mental effects of middle-class family life as a whole did fluctuate. The relationship between different class mentalities shifted. This was perhaps a matter of kind, not of degree. The general *level* of intelligence was probably increasing during the twentieth century, for pretty much the whole American population. But it was in intellectual *style*, or in such *types* of intelligence as verbal and mathematical and spatial, that the striking fluctuations may have occurred.

All this is familiar in the pathetic way that Americans, especially those we label the lower middle classes, strive to train and sponsor their children into the attitudes that will make them effective competitors in occupational mobility. But the same striving has appeared in different groups at different times—among eighteenth-century Quakers, and nineteenth-century Methodists, and twentieth-century Black Muslims. Because the methods that people have used in training their children to be bright have changed somewhat from fashion to fashion, and from generation to generation, the results that parents have achieved have also been subject to change. Most recently, if the self-blaming moralists of one older generation are to be believed, the "permissive" methods of one period helped create the unisex "confusions" of a succeeding period. But if those confusions reached deeply enough to be of any mental significance, then they must surely have worked to upset any simple typing or stylizing of intellectual behavior by sex. Whether such upset would raise or depress the general *level* of intellectual performance is of course a separate question.

The uncertain mental condition in which the standard American population found itself in the latter part of the twentieth century was not a new problem. For one thing, the whole process of modernization that that population had undergone a century earlier was quite similar to the experience black populations underwent when they migrated from the rural South to the urban North during the twentieth century. Clearly, too, when earlier Americans created the school system in which white middle-class children were to display competitive success, that act of creating a new institution was itself a major phase in the striving by families to improve the mentalities of their children.

These inferences about earlier education and earlier mentalities are speculative. There are real problems in applying diagnostic notions to a whole culture. For almost every stage of the learning cycle, the evidence about what was happening inside people is contaminated by the limitations on how observers examined the learning that was going on around them. The typical evidence is that given by the man who had, say, a certain kind of child-raising that he wanted to recommend, and who described existing practices and child behavior in a way to support his recommendations. But this contamination is unavoidable, given the impossibility of sending back observers who have even twentieth-century notions about clinical objectivity. What is more, the contamination is not wholly undesirable, since it directs attention to the real nature of what is sought: generalizations about mental change that may be applied usefully to a whole society.

Within the nature of history and historical evidence, how can measurable intellect be defined? Even in the present, it is hard to free the concept of intelligence from contamination. Intelligence tests are "culture-bound." Even when people who build tests eliminate as much as they can of items that refer to life within certain social groups (usually middle-class standard American), there remain the biases implicit in the testing process itself: in the notion that the rapid answering of formal questions is a meaningful activity, and in the blandly inquisitorial relation that prevails between questioner and subject. Even if emphasis is drained off from the questioner as an actual individual, the structure of the test remains as the jelling of thought patterns in individuals who test. While it may conceivably become possible to test mental performance objectively, this measuring has always tended to be not a mere recording but rather a relation between the measurer and the learner—that is, between the teacher and the learner. What looks at first like contamination turns out to have been a necessary part of any working definition of intelligence.

If it is true that for procedural purposes intelligence is first of all a kind of social relation, not a mere trait in the observed individual, then certain implications follow. A major part of educational development, so far as it changes the level of intelligence in a society, must be the training of people to participate in desired kinds of relations between communicating individuals and audience individuals. While the training of the communicators is part of this, the training of audiences touches larger parts of society, and much of the communicating skill that most individuals have is simply a projection of the ways they have learned to be an audience.

This creating of intelligence in the form of audience-participation is not an authoritarian process, not a mere imposing of ideas and passivity on individuals. The thing being communicated must itself be adjusted to the existing habits and needs of the audience. The communicator-audience relation, including the measurer-audience relation, must be culture-bound if it is to exist at all. And if it changes or improves, it can do so only through a process of mutual adjustment between the two parts, requiring perhaps always a sidewise process of dislocation, failed communication, and then readjusted contact. While there may have been some routine pedagogues who thought that they could improve the thinking of society by simply intensifying lessons already being taught, it is hard to conceive of growth in the mentality of a whole society except through some sequence of dislocations and renewals. Written educational history has noted that movements to improve men's minds have sometimes been schemes to cope with social disorder. But, though schools have been exploited by men with an opportunistic interest in social order, the real problem has not been one of conflict between pure teaching and wicked society. Quite aside from crude incursions made by ideologists from whatever camp, the social relation that is intelligence has itself been implicated in what happens to the larger society.

True, much of mental life is not public, is not obviously bound up in audience participation. There are moral grounds for objecting to any conception that denies individual autonomy. The individual does not use language for social purposes alone, but also to organize the experience that impinges upon him. His ability to understand the nonsocial aspects of reality may depend on the precision and subtlety of the words with which he describes that realty to himself. It may be important to the individual to solve quantitative problems that are of interest to him alone; even if these problems affect others, the process of solution is private. In either the verbal or the quantitative case, the individual who assumes that he has an audience may corrupt his own work.

But if audience-like behavior is sometimes corrupt, it is still powerfully usual. There are published from time to time diaries or meditations that the author is said to have written only for himself, without any reference to who might later read and judge his thoughts. To readers that such a performance then gets, the purity and the nonperformance quality of the diary may seem doubtful. The author seems to have an audience in mind, although he would have denied it, and even though he may himself have been unconscious of seeking response. Much of all verbal behavior makes ultimate reference to some conceivable audience, some persons who are both passive hearers and active judges.

There remains the problem of genuine creativity, which goes beyond the built-up interactions of any audience role even while it may still seek response. Because the scientist or writer may move beyond the existing audience roles, any exhaustive assessment of the mental level achieved by the society would, in principle, need to cover all the novel cultural products that men have turned out. This is especially true for a society in which intellectual achievement tends toward the unrelated and the unique. Societies have varied in the amount of solitary creation they support. The painter who works outside any contemporary school of vision, the monk who devotes himself to scientific labor, and the recluse who writes good verse are all part of their society. At least at the cliché level of intellectual history, situations like Renaissance Italy and Victorian England have excelled in the amount and quality of individual, autonomous work that flourished within them. Societies have varied, too, in the extent to which they were willing to leave the individual to himself.

Here is one difficulty in any argument that creativity transcends audience. At some times, the creative intellectual has appealed to a select audience composed of persons who all claim to be above audience appeal. Culture may claim to be individualistic but produce notable consistencies of style in scientific work or in the arts. At yet other times, the creative individual has appealed in his own thinking to an audience that has once existed but is now gone. Where the appeal to a past audience is more or less unconscious, it is probably efficient. Where conscious, it may carry the question, common and annoying in some comments on literature, "What has happened to the audience for____?" The blank may be filled with almost any genre, such as narrative verse or the multivolume novel. The question itself assumes that a form of creation, supposedly individual and private, would thrive if bound in a healthy audience relation. Although this assumption is at least arguable for the arts, it is valid for the sciences, where product has little meaning unless it can enter into the discourse shared by some collection of people. The growth of private skills feeds on the development of specialized audiences for the product of those skills.

This means that, in order to assess the intelligence of a society at large, one needs to make only two kinds of judgment. First: what is the level and nature of immediate audience response or audience-performer relation in the various audiences that are active within the society? And second: what structure of audiences does the society support?

If all audiences were separate and unrelated, this procedure would be problematic and difficult. Particular audiences do develop their own characteristics that can be assessed only in particular terms. At any time the assessing of what is happening to the mentality of a society may depend on a guess as to which of the current specialized audiences are likely to become more general in the future. But behavior does not flow simply from specialized groups out to the society. It is not valid to assume, without proof, that new kinds of audience role or learning are propagated outward from the innovations made by cultural leaders. It is one thing to call a particular standard of child-raising "Spockian"; it is another thing, and dubious, to assume that the physician Benjamin Spock was the effective source of that standard. Rather, individuals may bring into some specialized audience the behaviors that they have learned as participants in the general culture. Some politicians of 1870, and especially those who took themselves seriously as intellects, resented the popular appeal that Ulysses S. Grant exerted. Many other politicians, though, did not feel much resentment. Rather, they acted toward Grant as his supporters did and, presumably, as they wanted their own supporters to act toward them. The specialized audience of politicians as appreciators of each other's performances was not clearly distinct from the more general audience that was an activist society.

If the quality of general audience behavior may suggest much of what one wants to know about the behavior of those audiences that are special but not so special as they think, that quality may also indicate something about the structure of the audiences that the society does—or *can*—support. A population whose typical member has a short attention span, or at any rate little tolerance for sitting long in one place, is not going to foster the three-hour sermon or the five-hour political speech as an intellectual form. It is not, therefore, going to foster a structure of audiences in which the coordinating event is the occasional community-wide meeting, and it may foster both greater audience specialization and greater reliance on printed or electronic communication. Of course this particular kind of audience response in this case—the tolerance for listening to actual and protracted speech-making—may have developed because technology was providing new means for communication. But the trait may still serve as a symptom of the structure with which it is involved.

Finally, the overt structure of audiences is probably the one part of cultural life on which historians have done most work, tracing changes in the institutional aspects of culture: the schools, libraries, learned societies, newspapers, journals, licensing and censorship procedures, and meeting places. For most societies and many periods, the structure of audiences is not the problematic factor for the assessment of intelligence. Only to a somewhat greater degree is the character of response within special audiences a crucial point. What is really crucial is the kind of generalized audience response learned by "all" members of a society. Some impression of that response is the start of more complex assessment.

The primacy of audiences, and the fact that measured school intelligence is first of all an audience relation between teacher and pupils, determine the sequence of the chapters that follow. These chapters do not "start at the beginning" in any strict chronological sense. Rather, they attack first the obvious surface of the subject, as indicated by various definitions of intelligence. This means examining first of all the way Americans created in their schools a large audience for the care and training of intelligence. Many of the particular facts in this development may also be useful as preliminary or background to other problems. Close after the development of the school as audience there comes then the question of how teachers at different times actually observed what, for pedagogues, constituted the core of intelligence—the ability to learn.

Once these surfaces are examined, it becomes a little easier to look underneath, at the family attitudes that guided children through learning, or at the larger culture that supported learning and expressed its results. Neither of these areas has any simple chronological relation to intelligence as it appears in school learning. Family attitudes may help create the child mind that then tries to cope with material in school. But family attitudes also express the concentrated meaning of what is happening in the whole culture. The patterns that orators and technicians produce may express the outcome of what happened in the education of these particular men: such patterns may thus express the accomplishments of the whole system of educational audiences. But those same patterns establish an environment of words, objects, and images around the thinking of people. Specialized education determines professional products; but professional products suffuse the minds of a whole people. Family attitudes can point toward either past or future, and so can cultural products.

The effort to assess past intelligence is no simple tracing out of cause and effect from child-rearing through school experiences to professional training and adult competence. In fact, the cultural network is so complex and recursive that any strict attention to the causal links within it could interfere with the effort to identify the kinds of intelligence that were actually at work. The chapters that follow are not, then, efforts to trace successive steps in the causation of intelligence. They are like drillings sunk into different parts of the cultural landscape in an effort to establish some profiles for a kind of "geological survey" of what intelligence was like over a wide social area. For the whole inquiry, there are three main probings: into the school system with its formal learning problems, into the family as both focus and instigator of culture, and into the public culture within which men both created and attended. Within the particular area of the public culture, since it is impossibly wide and diffuse, three more particular drillings may suffice for the present: into the verbal work that was preaching, into the largely spatial work that was shipbuilding, and into the eventually mathematical work that was bridge building.

These particular points may show what happened. The larger world of explanation and purpose begins from there.

TWO

THE SCHOOLS AS TEST

A. The Course of Educational Development: New York and America, 1750-1870

The way nineteenth-century observers talked about "intelligence" did not always distinguish between intelligence as ability and intelligence as acquired information or skill. They talked, in fact, as if they assumed that schooling had been doing something not just to what people knew but to *how* they could go about knowing things.

At least in hope, schooling is one of the influences in the environment that can make a difference to the how of knowing. Though the inward, implicit aspects of schooling might make the most difference, the way the external pattern is arranged should offer some frame for the subtle workings of the culture on individual minds.

American education did grow strong and systematic over the century after 1750. So did the American economy. But that growth did not take off from a pure primitive or agrarian condition.

For every eighteenth-century community in which families subsisted on what they and their neighbors produced, and in which a plain ministration according to creed or Bible sufficed to state the relation between home people and the larger universe, there were many other communities that had complex ties with the larger world, and in which those ties required participation by many people. What gave scope for later growth was the fact that these ties, besides varying much from community to community, were in most places vital only to the margin of life. The average American family in the middle of the eighteenth century was a farm family that might enjoy its coffee or tea, its sugar and rum, just as it might enjoy sensing that its local pastor was retailing a discreet selection from recent theological and philosophical notions. But it did not expect the importers of tropical products to maintain a steady trade, offering dependably reasonable prices, nor did it expect every pastor to be fully engaged in what was happening in British or European thought. Under proper crisis conditions, Americans could even see tropical products and enlightenment ideas as symptoms of corruption.

Basic or literacy education, like the supply of basic sugars, was distributed somewhat evenly in the northern colonies, and that education could not be interrupted very long in any one place without setting up real discomfort or uneasiness. A community did not need to offer schooling every single year, but any very long omission of regular schools would interfere with economic and psychological functions vital to communities. Among these vital functions was that of fostering the ability of ordinary people to work and think with some sense of protection against the decisions made by authority, however benevolent.

In the ordinary rural community, an illiterate farmer could support a family at the level of bare subsistence without running into overwhelming difficulties. The moment he wanted more than subsistence, even if that margin was to be had simply by bartering his surplus with a local trader, he would run into trouble. Barter, at that time, was not a simple exchange of one substance for another, on the spot. It was usually a recorded credit transaction, a little like the workings in more recent times of a company store or of a planter's store for sharecroppers. Similarly, dealings in land were matters of written record, without nearly that basis of traditional understanding and obligation that sometimes governed land-dealing back in England. The American farmer could, if he had to, take the word of the local storekeeper on what was the condition of his account. He could, if he had to, take the word of substantial men, who held town or county office, on what were the terms of his deeds to land. In some parts of the country, he did just that. In the South, illiteracy ran high and so did deference to a local gentry in business and legal decisions. In northern and eastern areas, men of substance also enjoyed personal prestige, by twentieth-century standards, and were able to influence the day-to-day decisions that lesser men made. But there were also counterforces working to hold this influence in check, and one of these counterforces was literacy.

Literacy also helped to allay any fears men had that those in authority would impose ideas on their minds or aspirations on their souls. The overwhelming majority of men in the northern areas had come from Calvinist or Quaker backgrounds. They differed considerably in how much of religious authority they rejected, but they all rejected some of the upper layers of authority that had long decided what men should think or had determined who should be the personnel of the traditional intellectual apparatus—that is, "Church"—within society. Even when they continued to accord great authority to local or intermediate religious leaders, as did the Puritan groups, they tried to strengthen those leaders against outside authority by reinforcing the solidarity of leaders with local congregations and church members. In order for this solidarity to function, people had to understand the preacher. They had to be familiar with the forms in which he would speak to them, and they had to know something about the material that he would elaborate and expound. All this, of course, made literacy valuable.

At the same time, there were certain standards at work within local churches that limited the need for literacy. Churches held that it was un-Christian for members to go to law against each other. Instead, they should resolve their disputes (including many that were not covered by law) by moral arbitration within the church. Debts and land could be included in such arbitration. In many places, of course, the proportion of actual church membership was too low, or the level of religious seriousness too tepid, for such arrangements to have much force. But in any community where such standards governed, and where church membership set the standard for social relationship, direct face-to-face dealings could work as sanctions behind even credit and legal right, and literacy would be much less needed, except by those men who acted as intermediaries between the local society and the larger world. For communities in one of those streams of Calvinist action where intellectualism was not so strong as it was in high Puritanism, this kind of moral order did supplant some of the need for education. These streams included the Separatist, the Baptist, the Reformed Dutch (in their American version), and the Quaker.

In the northern and eastern parts of America, people were subject to some conditions that encouraged literacy, but also to some that made it less necessary. Depending on local traditions and leadership, and on access to the outside world, people in the middle of the eighteenth century lived in a fluctuating equilibrium between two styles of life—between a communal, personalistic style that did not require literacy except in its leaders, and a commercial, captious, argumentative style in which literacy was needed to maintain a standard of decision between men. Sometimes literacy, by quieting men's worst suspicions about other men, made it possible for a personal leadership to flourish up to the limits of the dogmas and individual rights about which men felt secure. At other times literacy served as a shelter behind which smaller groups, whose members trusted each other more than they did the community at large, could enjoy the warmth of a more personalistic life. The need for basic education was governed by the economic and moral organization of the local community.

The means of what the twentieth century would call basic education—that is, training in literacy and perhaps some simple figuring—were distributed widely, but in a sporadic and fluctuating way. Sometimes a community was required by province law to maintain a teacher. Sometimes it had a strong church that wanted to maintain a teacher. Sometimes that church was urged on by advice or requirements from some central religious organization. Sometimes outside religious organizations offered help to the community in its efforts to maintain a teacher. Sometimes groups of parents took the initiative. In each of these cases, including that in which a provincial law set a supposed requirement, what a community did depended on the balance between felt need and the practical problems of finding and paying a schoolmaster. In parts of New England, this balance worked out to favor the supporting of some kind of school, for some length of time, almost every year. In some parts of New York, the balance favored a more sporadic pattern.

In New York, the conditions of landholding sometimes favored a degree of gentry influence more like that of the South. There, the oldest churches in the area, the Dutch Reformed, were both more authoritarian and less intellectually active than many of the Calvinist churches of New England. Many parts of the Hudson Valley were, of course, in direct commercial contact with the outside world. In those places where this contact was less important, and local life was more self-contained, the balance of influences was such that people supported schools in only the most irregular way. Although some parts of New York belonged very much to the commercial, argumentative, literate style, other parts came as close as did almost any society in the North to the stolidity and personalism of an "undeveloped society." In some localities, the town and the Reformed church cooperated to maintain a school. In some, the Society for the Propagation of the Gospel, sending out funds and occasional agents from England, provided a little school support and made some not very successful efforts to induce local people to provide more. In others, local officials or family heads acted. In larger places like New York City or Albany, various of these authorities or agents acted at once, providing some choice among different kinds of schooling. In remote places, nothing at all might be done for long periods of time. Basic schooling was available some of the time in most places, but it was haphazard, irregular.

Beyond the basic level, the several parts of colonial America differed much in the quality and extent of the educational opportunities they offered. Only in some general ways did anything like a common system prevail.

It was the rare student who went past the fundamentals to seek a liberal education. Whether in its beginning stages in the schoolboy's struggling with Latin, or in its late stages in efforts to comprehend something of philosophy and science, liberal or general education served functions that did not call for recruiting into it more than a small fraction of the population. For many students, perhaps for most, liberal education served no functions of any specific use to society. Latin and Greek and philosophy, and the having attended some higher school, were marks of prestige and breeding. In a world where the few men of wealth did not always know what to do with their resources, the classics and college attendance were one of the less vulgar ways that a family could use its wealth.

But even if a student entered on liberal study expecting to serve nothing more than his own or his family's reputation, he found that much of the content of that study led toward less petty functions. This broadening was encouraged especially by the fact that classical and philosophical study did serve one practical, professional purpose: it did train the clergy of those groups that required a learned ministry. A minister needed classical and philosophical learning in order to expound the scripture, in order to maintain some contact with the world of European theology, and—perhaps most important of all—in order to defend on equal terms the views and interests of his own group, within and against the learning of an intellectual world that was international and therefore classical. Whether or not local people understood all the issues to which a minister addressed himself, they could sense in him a champion—whether in the feudal tourneying sense or the modern athletic sense.

The comparison to certain twentieth-century community functions is homely but not wholly inexact. Communities varied much in how well they supported schoolteachers, and they rarely acted as if they considered these teachers persons of great moment to them. They might also be captious and calculating about the kind of support they gave to a minister, but they were rarely indifferent to how they dealt with this man who represented them to the world in the combined functions of team and coach. It was this general sense of the educated man as representative and defender that gave to the man who was not entering the ministry a function larger than that of serving his own prestige. This was clear enough in the formal functions of colonial college education, as they had been stated in the seventeenth century: to raise up men for service in commonwealth as well as church. It became more complexly clear in the way American secular leaders used classical learning in the political struggles of the middle and latter part of the eighteenth century, when the content of classical allusion became a language by which persons from different parts of America communicated with each other, and in which Americans found a political example—the republican ideal—that they could present to Europeans as warranty for the prestige and acceptability of an emerging, whole American community. The boy who was put to liberal study for the sake of personal or family prestige might find in it, in addition, a source of private intellectual pleasure or a means of disinterested intellectual communion with other educated men. This was one way that the selfish aims of selective education could work to a pure end. But more important was the way liberal education linked the motives of individual prestige to the functions of community prestige and defense.

In the mid-eighteenth century, the ordinary members of a community might exercise an ultimate veto over unacceptable leaders, but it was common for leaders to choose their successors, or to give communities firm guidance in choosing new leaders. This meant, in the sphere of education, that general education had in most places the quality of sponsorship. A certain number of colleges and Latin grammar schools operated on a continuing, reliable institutional basis. Even within those provinces of New England that required some towns to maintain grammar schools, reliability depended often, though, on the interest an individual teacher took in receiving boys and preparing them for college. In many or most areas, there existed no intermediate school in institutional form. An individual schoolmaster or, especially, a minister would take time from other activities to train those few boys from the area who were seeking something more than basic education. The informal, personal quality of this teaching allowed opportunity for men of local influence to send in their own sons, if they chose, or to give encouragement to other local boys who fitted someone's conception of who were the deserving poor. If a particular area had no institutional schools beyond the basic ones, and could obtain college education for its boys only by sending them to college outside the area, the geographical structure of the process gave more strength to the sense of sponsorship. This was in fact the situation in New York just before the middle of the eighteenth century. There was one local institutional secondary school, but it was kept sporadically, and the nearest colleges were those at Princeton and New Haven, with Harvard and William and Mary more remote. On this level, then, the local institutional dearth tended to discourage further intellectual growth or, at best, to give strong weight to informal, personal, and private efforts.

In the training of professional men other than English-speaking Calvinist ministers, the whole of British America was in much the same condition that New York was in regard to intermediate or liberal education. For physicians, for lawyers, for the Anglican clergy, for the Dutch Reformed clergy, there were in 1750 no formal training institutions on the western side of the Atlantic. There were, of course, men at work as pastors, or lawyers, or physicians who could give advice and instruction to likely young men. Sometimes this instruction was arranged through a formal apprenticeship or period of office study, for which the young man paid in money or services. A kind of apprenticeship was used even by the Congregational clergy, who had facilities for formal training at Harvard and Yale: the recent college graduate, before he took a church himself, often continued to study for a time as a resident in the household of an experienced pastor.

Except for the Congregational and Presbyterian clergy, there was no professional group that offered both formal and in-service training within the limits of British America. Although some practitioners did without the formal training that was available only abroad, the prestige of that training hung over the plans men made. Ambitious would-be physicians did go to medical schools in Britain and Europe if they could. Aspiring lawyers or some men simply interested in public affairs did study at the Inns of Court in London. The ordination of Dutch Reformed clergy was controlled by authorities in the Netherlands, where candidates commonly went to study. Similarly with the Anglican clergy. In principle a man who wanted to take Anglican orders could study at William and Mary and then make the trip to England to be ordained by a bishop (there being no bishop in America), but this was not a satisfactory arrangement. William and Mary was not so clearly adapted for ministerial training as were Harvard, Yale, and Princeton. Although some men did study at one of the non-Anglican colleges, then convert to the Church of England before taking orders, many of the Anglican clergy in America were either colonials who had studied in England or priests who came out from England to take colonial parishes.

It was at this point, in the gap between British (or Dutch) and American institutions, that the motive toward educational development first became acute. Americans sensed their disadvantage as colonials, identified it with the feeling of inadequacy and cultural provincialism from which they often suffered, and began trying to bring their own thinking and their own educational institutions up to the British standard. Despite the fact that American society was not working up from an illiterate or even semiliterate state, despite the fact that much of American society was actually more commercial and open to the world than was the British rural society from which it derived, the pattern and style of the educational development that was beginning in America in the middle of the eighteenth century had much of the self-conscious, invidious, even snobbish tone that marked some developmental efforts in the newly ex-colonial world of the twentieth century.

Another characteristic of development was perhaps peculiar to America: it derived momentum from competition between localities and between religious denominations. When Samuel Bard returned from medical school in Edinburgh in 1766, hoping to organize a medical school and hospital in New York, he was working partly to give his community something it lacked in contrast with the home country, but he was working also to give New York the *first* medical school in America, by beating out the efforts of men working for the same object in Philadelphia. In this particular, he failed, since the Philadelphia school opened in 1765, the New York in 1767.

The efforts to establish a college in New York, in the same period, were overlaid by quarrels among Presbyterians, Anglicans and other religious groups, as also by a sense of competition with colleges in Massachusetts, Connecticut, and New Jersey. Each denominational interest had its own conception of the intercolonial competition. Those who wanted an Anglican-dominated college saw the colleges in the adjoining provinces as specifically Calvinist, so that it would be only fair to balance them off with a competing institution in between. Those who resisted that Anglican demand spoke of the competition as one between whole communities, and argued that a college in New York should represent all the groups in that community. Either view could seem equitable, depending on how one interpreted the relation between religious pluralism and the single local community. At the time, men were not able to settle on just how they conceived of the community. King's College was organized under generally Anglican control, but with some representation for other groups on the board of trustees, and with rules against the exclusion of non-Anglican students. As late as the 1850s, though, Columbia as the successor of King's was still suffering crises over the selection of unorthodox faculty members; the college accepted the idea of itself as a plural community only at about the time it made the transition from Columbia College to Columbia University. The old-fashioned or narrow views that were expressed during denominational controversy can give the impression that such controversy was irrational and destructive. Actually, during the years when King's was being organized, competition did as much as anything else to publicize the cause of educational development. It may have delayed for a few months or so the granting of the college's charter, but it did far more to diffuse through many groups the sense that community strength was desirable, that intellect was an important part of community strength, and that intellectual influence in a growing community was something worth working and fighting for.

For generations after that, general and professional education grew partly by means of the stimuli provided by intergroup competition. Denominational colleges multiplied gradually, then rapidly and in crowded haste during the early and middle years of the nineteenth century. Competing professional schools sprang up, sometimes one in any locality where a few practitioners could band together and persuade students to give them fees for lectures. Within New York, the competitive growth of general colleges began with Union in Schenectady, 1795, and continued in the establishment of dozens of other colleges in the generations to 1870. Professional competition within New York was most notable in medical education: groups in New York City tried to establish additional, competing schools in the 1790s, and in the years just after 1806 and in the late 1820s; they established lasting schools from the 1840s, and also succeeded in founding medical schools upstate. The same kind of competition gave vigor to the several phases in the growth of theological education. Denominations that had depended more or less on the supply of ministers from the home country (Anglican, Dutch Reformed, Presbyterian), established their own colleges and seminaries in America; groups holding to orthodoxy founded schools to counter declensions in the faith or seriousness of existing colleges. And denominations that had once been anticlerical or anti-intellectual founded schools to build the prestige and respectability that they needed in their struggles with rivals.

Something of the same drive for competitive development was expressed in the establishing of academies, first during the latter part of the eighteenth century. Leading men in a community, dissatisfied with the lack or unreliability of schooling past the elementary stage, disinclined to work through local governments that were not arranged to take on managerial tasks, and dissatisfied especially with the informal or narrow character of the teaching given by local ministers acting on their own, picked up a new form of organization that would give to their community a stable, institutionalized school for introducing local boys to the larger world of learning. They acted together as trustees to maintain a school, hiring a teacher or teachers on a regular basis. In those cases where they hired a strong individual, his style of work might provide continuity with the more obviously personal teaching of earlier years. But the academy was essentially a community-service institution, sponsored and controlled by a company of local leaders in much the same way that roads and bridges might be built and kept by companies of local men. It helped to train new representative leaders on a more continuing and reliable basis than had earlier been possible, and it helped to maintain community prestige at a time when many a locality was trying to win special advantage for itself. Although leaders continued to stand in a somewhat sponsoring relation to students, the formal institutional framework meant that a student's endeavor was becoming a little more businesslike and individualistic. The stages in that endeavor were not yet clearly defined, though. Some of the academies tried to give whole courses of classical or practical education, and it was not at first clear whether an academy was to be a local quasi-college or a school that prepared students for some centrally located college. Although most of the academies that survived became secondary schools, a few did become colleges.

During the organization of colleges, of new professional schools, and of those academies that came to function both as local quasi-colleges and as feeder schools for the firmly established colleges, men often tried to develop indigenous or up-to-date standards for what information and what ideas should be taught in the schools. In the initial stages of the organization of King's, as also in the later talk about other colleges and academies, spokesmen pointed to a variety of modern sciences or languages or vocational subjects that their particular schools would offer. Such studies would presumably give a training of practical use to young men who were going into commerce or politics or agriculture. But the underlying drive in the development of schools was not so much toward practicality as toward giving people a sense that they could cope on equal terms with outside authority, in a world in which commercial interdependence, imperial power, and intellectual innovation were penetrating to the needs of local people. Even in their competition among themselves, Americans needed to refer to some standard of success or excellence. Classical education and British ideas, supported by the inertia of teachers who did not want to lose the advantage of their own prior training, served as that standard.

New colleges that talked about offering modern subjects

settled back into offering a conventional, sometimes thorough classical course, spiced with minor concessions to the new. The legal profession, although its leading scholars after the Revolution lectured on American law, relied often on Blackstone's compendium as the handbook for educating young lawyers; and, even in the early years of independence, it sometimes tried to imitate the hierarchical social forms of the English profession. Medical teachers who tried to make botany and the materia medica central to the medical curriculum, thus giving special emphasis to the products and peculiarities of American conditions, soon settled back into offering a solid but more conventional anatomy-centered course, in effect leaving botanizing to the rising generation of quacks. Military education wavered between an Anglo-French pattern and a self-consciously republican, militia-oriented pattern. While the republican tone found a home in some local schools, it was the Anglo-French pattern that set the standard at West Point. Noah Webster's work to standardize distinctive American language and have it taught in the schools became, rather, a campaign to impose on Americans the rather priggish linguistic propriety toward which British English was tending in the early nineteenth century. The main outcome of the nationalistic educational development that gained strength from the mid-eighteenth century on was less to create new and peculiarly American forms of education than to give America as a whole, and many local leadership groups in particular, a more direct access to the formal, visible, prestigious levels of the educational system.

When educational nationalism did attempt to create new forms it usually failed, as it did in most of the attempts to import the university idea into the United States in the years immediately after the Revolution. The idea of a National University, often stated, found no support in the ways actual teachers wanted to live or actual students wanted to learn. Proposals for state universities, until well after the War of 1812, ran usually either to fanciful schemes on paper or to mere state-sponsored versions of the competing denominational colleges. The one kind of state university that amounted to much in the post-Revolutionary generation was that which was not an instructional institution itself, but a means by which leaders in state government attempted to exercise control over the growing variety of instructional institutions. As projected in Georgia and Michigan, and as carried out in New York in 1784, the state university was a supervisory body that had vaguely-defined powers over colleges, academies, and some other schools within the state. It could encourage and set standards, it was supposed to promote the cause of education generally, and it might be the agency by which politicians directed government approval or government money to particular deserving schools. The powers of the University of the State of New York were too vague and ill-coordinated to amount to much at first, but the institution itself survived and became a framework into which the state could gradually put some real educational functions.

On one level, of course, the resemblance between a supervisory institution like the University in New York and an instructional institution like, say, Jefferson's long-planned University of Virginia, was merely verbal. More largely, though, these different kinds of university were all attempts to bring some kind of order into an undirected educational development that was on the verge of becoming far more competitive and pluralistic than felt comfortable to most people then. Politics being what it was and is, some of these attempts to impose a restraining order were managed from the point of view of some one of the interests involved. This was what happened when various medical groups in New York tried to enlist the state university as backer for their own needs, and it was what happened when a New Hampshire government of one particular politico-religious complexion tried to assume control of Dartmouth College. In the outcome, the fecklessness of the University of the State of New York had about the same meaning as the difficulty men experienced in determining just what the Supreme Court's Dartmouth College decision of 1819 meant for the future of college development in the United States. They knew that the Supreme Court had prohibited a state from interfering with rights previous governments had granted out to private corporations, such as Dartmouth was; but they found it much easier to consider this a prohibition against state interference with corporations generally than to predict what it would mean for education.

The skills that were available for men to learn within higher education were also then too arbitrary to indicate any clear direction in which education might develop. In the professions especially, until the last two or three decades of the nineteenth century, formal curricula could contribute less to prevailing levels of ability than might the demands of practice, the diffuse educational influence of the press, or even the choices that the general population made among different kinds of service.

Christian ministers had to use or by-pass the low standards of college education, and many of their efforts to cope with this problem could only make it worse. As the general population worked hard to expand farms and develop cities, smaller proportions of people went to college, even while the number of colleges was increasing to serve the competitive needs of communities and denominations. College officials were under heavy pressure to make courses less difficult in order to keep up enrollments. Sometimes they tried to meet the situation by providing different *kinds* of courses instead of lower *levels* of instruction—as Union did with an engineering department in 1845, and as Harvard and Yale did with scientific schools after 1847—but such programs made little sense to employers before the Civil War. To the extent that nonliterary courses might attract students, they contributed to the apprehension of people who did worry about the quality of college training.

Among denominational leaders, some shared this worry; many more feared that their own colleges would lose their specifically religious character while trying to attract more students from the general population. During the eighteenth century, serious evangelical interests had tried to meet similar developments by organizing new colleges such as Yale and Princeton. While many groups continued to found new colleges during the following century, they relied on them largely as devices to hold their laity. In training the clergy, though, the new professional seminaries could do little to improve matters beyond offering a more specific training in Greek, theology, and some Hebrew. Since men entered the seminary direct from the academy or the revival meeting, and only infrequently after attending a general college, the seminaries took some men who might otherwise have attended college. Far from stimulating colleges to act as feeders, they probably weakened even further the demand for the regular college course. Two bureaucratic developments within denominations introduced new influences into the educational pattern. First with the American Education Society in 1815, then with other "education societies" in later decades, one religious group after another took measures to promote study by prospective ministers. To the extent that they recruited money to subsidize young men in their studies, these societies built up the level of support for education; but to the extent that they encouraged the founding of new colleges and seminaries, they diluted the concentration that new students might foster. Outside formal education, though, men in all denominations were establishing magazines and organizations that promoted a noncurricular religious education for laity and ministers alike. Religious philanthropies, such as missionary and tract societies, sent agents from place to place, begging money with specially arranged sermons. Periodicals gave scope to ministers whose talents lay more in writing than in speaking, and they distributed information that people might earlier have had to hear from their pastor in person. Again, by competing with the pastor as a needed intellectual authority, the religious press that grew up during the nineteenth century had uneven effects on the demand for colleges and seminaries that might make holy men into intellectual leaders. Since much religious literature went to laymen, it helped make them more critical and demanding, even while it made them less dependent.

In the long run, of course, the education of the clergy would become less important as the population turned away from religion to science. This shift in popular thought did not become dramatic, however, until quite late in the century. Darwinian ideas had little time to make much impact until after 1870, when semipopular lectures and books by men like Fiske and Huxley began to make the dogma of science insistent. Before that, science had spread in an informal, nondogmatic, even weak manner, as showed especially in medical and technical education.

Medical schools spread rapidly during the nineteenth century, much as did colleges. Even more demonstrably, their standards suffered. Few had any kind of endowment; not many, any sponsoring university. They relied on fees from students, including large fees paid for granting diplomas. Since most states abolished license requirements for both law and medicine during the generation before 1850, these medical diplomas became the only significant certificate of competence. Although the benefits of prestige encouraged individual medical professors to continue educating themselves at home and in Europe, the structure of the educational system did not encourage close study by students. Much as with religious denominations, the larger education of the medical profession stood to gain more from new kinds of development—from a medical press that grew rapidly more technical and modern in character, and from the growth of voluntary medical societies that strove to promote prosperity and learning among practitioners. As of mid-century, the most influential of these societies were local, such as the New York Academy of Medicine; on the national level, the new American Medical Association served only a vague umbrella function. The great difficulty lay not in organization, though, but in available knowledge. While the medical press of these years pointed with pride to the "scientific" advances of the profession, it really had little of concrete value to show except: vaccination, which was a preventive technique for one particular disease; anesthesia, which made surgical procedures more humane but not necessarily more effective; and an increasing boldness of surgeons in carrying off difficult feats. Many common treatments, such as purging, were either dangerous or pointless. The general population certainly demonstrated its basic intelligence by giving less and less patronage to regularly trained physicians during the early part of the nineteenth century. If they wasted some money on quacks, they still had little in the way of scientific treatment to buy until the germ theory of disease won gradual acceptance after 1880.

For different reasons, formal education also failed to make much contact with practice in the technical vocations, such as engineering. Here New York was the center of what little schooling was available, since West Point began active technical training after 1816, and Rensselaer after 1835. Neither of these furnished any great number of men for civilian engineering; and no other school trained even so many as they did, before the Civil War. Though a handful of important practitioners or technical teachers came from having been trained in Europe, most engineers had no school training different from that of the general population. For the building of canals, railroads, and other static structures, the typical engineer came out of the population of young men known to the promoters of transportation works in his neighborhood. He learned elementary techniques on the job, and proceeded from there. This meant that he was either a member of some prominent local family, or was the kind of "likely" young man whom merchants and gentry would be glad to pick up and promote. He came, that is, from much the same pool as did the student bodies of academies. For the construction of movable equipment, such as ships and steam engines, the typical builder came from a family that had already scored some success as master builders or master mechanics, following traditional techniques derived from earlier centuries. As these master-mechanic families rose in the world, they might give their sons additional general education for social prestige, but they did not put much store by college or school training in the mechanical techniques themselves. Although these families, like the local promoters of academies and canals, were free to promote any apprentices whom they personally liked, the system within which they operated did not concede any particular virtues to the outsider who had technical education. Again, things were to change after the Civil War, when more firms grew large enough to employ engineers without giving them authority, and when new kinds of industry moved rapidly into chemical and electrical work for which no traditional competence was available. Still, the first agricultural and mechanical colleges established under the land-grant system started in 1862 did not attract many students. As late as 1870, American technical performance hung at an uncertain overlap between local tradition and developing bureaucracy.

In general, the condition of the professions just after the Civil War meant that prevailing skills were closely tied to the preferences and practical experience available within local communities, while any leaven by formal training was either disorganized (as in verbal work) or not yet fully organized (as in scientific work). This unresolved state of professional training meant that the crucial educational developments of the period were those in primary education, over the several generations after the Revolution.

Even there, most of what politicians and school planners did during the earliest years of the nineteenth century took for granted the kind of basic education that was already available on the local level. The work they had done to bring American communities up to British standards, and the competition between communities to excel each other, affected the more public, prestigious parts of education but had less direct effect on how men began their learning within each community. Jefferson saw the poor condition of primary schools in Virginia as a black mark against his state, but he won little support for any concrete action on the local level, and in crises he gave his own political support to development programs that concentrated on the highest, the university level. Planners in New York, seeing the contrast between sporadic basic education and growing intermediate or professional education, in 1795 obtained a law that directed counties to support schools and offered state-aid money; but the legislature raised too little money to carry out the scheme, which enlisted the support of no administrators who were willing to make a cause out of enforcing and continuing the new law. When it expired in 1800 the project lapsed. State governments in various parts of the country did use public lands or special-purpose taxes or fiscal windfalls to create funds whose income would help local schools, but these moneys were usually simply transmitted to the localities as a form of tax relief or subsidy. By 1812, New York managed to put together such a fund, with which it reinstated on a more secure basis its earlier policy of distributing aid to local schools.

In fact, economic and educational development was already beginning to have unplanned repercussions on local life in both city and country. Some cities and some areas had natural advantages in competition, or created advantages for themselves. These areas grew rapidly and experienced the problems that accompany growth and mobility and increasing density of population. Other areas began to seem overcrowded or inhospitable, and their inhabitants began looking to the growing places as sources of profit or as new places to live. The growing areas were new agricultural lands or were the largest ports and centers of transportation, such as Boston within New England, or New York in relation to the whole Northeastern area. The lagging areas were the smaller ports and other towns, many of which had thrived in the eighteenth century, and the less adaptable agricultural areas within older states, such as those of eastern New York and northern New England.

The contrasting pressures and opportunities of a growing society began to erode that older set of adjustments between the individual and the larger world, within which a sporadic basic education had seemed adequate. The stimuli to new adjustment became obvious first in the growing cities, somewhat later in the lagging or isolated areas of the countryside. Both these situations stimulated innovations, which were then adopted in the newer agricultural areas in a derivative, less strenuous manner.

In cities like Boston and New York and Philadelphia, the growth of population began to transform the nature of poverty. Earlier, the children who could not or did not attend some simple school were relatively isolated within the social pattern of the city. Whatever their numbers, they seemed to be individual cases. They were the children of parents who did not save the few coins necessary to pay some woman who taught letters in a neighborhood garret school. Or they were the children of families that did not belong to any of the religious groups that maintained schools for their own children. The fact that their cases were isolated meant that they were visible to other people as exceptions, and that informal pressures or charities might keep down the numbers of children who never got into school. But as slums grew, the impoverished and demoralized people of society were no longer an interstitial presence; they became a well-defined group. At a time when the Catholic Church had not yet appeared as the immigrants' and workingmen's church, poverty might mean not belonging to any religious body; in some places this meant not having easy access to any kind of early schooling. Depending on what local custom and arrangements had been, different cities made different adjustments to this gap that was opening within society. Boston had long had public schools for all children, but had required that children know how to read before entering these schools, thus forcing children to get the very beginnings of instruction at home or at private neighborhood schools; in Boston, then, new adjustment meant the creating of public primary schools, putting many of the neighborhood teachers on the public payroll. In Philadelphia and in New York, new adjustment meant the creating of quasi-public charitable corporations that operated schools for children who would otherwise not be reached.

That corporation in New York City was the Free School Society, organized in 1805. Like the group in Philadelphia, the Society adopted the Lancasterian or monitorial system of instruction, which had been developed in England as a way to give cheap instruction to large numbers of poor children. Under it, one teacher would take scores or even hundreds of pupils in a single class. He himself taught only selected monitors within this large group; each monitor then transmitted the lesson, which was necessarily simple, definite, and formal, to a group of younger children. Although there was great flexibility of certain kinds within the system, since it permitted individual pupils to be advanced from monitor to monitor as they learned each lesson, the operation of the whole class as a social unit required that children respond and move with something like military precision. In practice, the Society's schools kept slipping back toward conventional classroom practices, with which teachers were familiar; but elements of the monitorial system persisted in New York schools through much of the early part of the century. Either because the Society's schools were actually economical, or because some other groups that maintained schools were willing to unload their responsibilities, the Society schools grew faster than others. In laws of 1813 and 1824 it was designated the principal recipient within New York City for state-aid funds that were being distributed to localities, and in 1826 it changed its name to Public School Society.

Up to a certain point, the Society school system gained

ground by yielding to its critics. Conventional teachers censured it as mechanical and unproductive, and it relaxed its strict emphasis on the monitorial technique. Some Protestant groups that were trying to maintain their own schools opposed its privileged position as recipient of state aid, and the Society responded by adopting a more broadly interdenominational stance, acquiring in the process an even nearer monopoly on aid funds. Similar conflicts occurred with Roman Catholic groups as immigration increased in the 1830s and 1840s, and in these conflicts the position of the Society became untenable. As a technically private organization, it could never argue convincingly that it made impartial, public-minded decisions on how to teach religion in the schools; the concessions that it did attempt became increasingly pointless as Catholic authorities worked toward what became their general stand against putting Catholic children into public schools. After many crises, the Public School Society gave way to a new system of "Ward Schools" that the city organized in 1842. These, which soon became a conventional public-school system, did not solve the problems of religion and state aid, but they did at least confine those problems within the ordinary terms that have characterized them in more recent argument.

As schools grew in the cities, and as schools elsewhere imitated some of the practices developed in large places, it became clear that the formality of the monitorial system was only a special case of a regularity that men wanted to bring to the schools. Much of the new urban population consisted of people from rural areas who had timed their daily activities by the sun and the processes of farm life. Even city business, on the smaller eighteenth-century scale, had been regulated by the flow of tides and household chores as much as by clock. The activities of larger populations, though, could be coordinated only by formal schedule. Habits of regularity and order, which had been marks of special diligence and puritanical virtue, now became mere necessities of city life. Schools became valuable as systems within which children would be accustomed to regularity. Silence and punctuality became more nearly standard in the list of schoolroom virtues, and teachers began caring more that children should behave in ways that would make the schools efficient productive systems.

In the cities, institutions for training leaders—that is, colleges and professional schools—multiplied as population grew, becoming more competitive and open in the way they operated; but elementary schools, as they multiplied in response to population pressure, set a more organized routine for pupils, who would have to fit into an urban life.

A similar disparity developed in rural areas, between academies as local leadership institutions and the common schools as sources of the skills with which people met the demands of the world around them. Population growth was one thing that facilitated the rise of the academies. But population growth put a strain on the ordinary farm family, especially in areas that were losing relative agricultural advantage. There seemed to be no land left to divide among numbers of sons. In household as well as field, work became harder as family size bore against the resources of worn, uneconomical farms. One solution was to migrate, and many families did just that. Another was for the family to take up industrial piece-work within the household; this put young children as well as parents to work, and it reduced the time parents could give to caring for children. Another solution, although it could hardly solve the larger economic problems, was to send some children out of the household, at least for some of the time, in order to reduce pressure on the wife. The school thus served as safety-valve for the household, as it has served in more recent families that have not even been subject to the kind of objective pressure that plagued many early-nineteenth-century farm families. Depending on the shifting balance of needs within the household, the same end of relieving pressure could be served by migration (either to the West or to a city), by household industry (during the brief period early in the century when that was often available as a way for families to make money), or by sending some children to school. Even westward migration eventually demanded some institutions more artificial and urban-like than what had been familiar in life on farms near the eastern seaboard—namely, canals and railroads to tie western farms to markets in the way that coasts and navigable rivers had once done for eastern farms. Many of the expedients that were open to rural families involved some increased acceptance of artifice and organization. Often, individuals who were rooted in some earlier mixture between organic and individualistic ways of life resisted the intrusion of more organization. But in the long run the new pressures did not favor a sentimental or even principled clinging to the less systematic ways of the past. If there was something fearful about the new adjustments, that was only more reason for providing country children with an orderly environment that would prepare them to be those members of the family who would eventually move to the city. During the generation after about 1810 there gradually developed support for improving and making more regular the schools in many parts of the countryside.

Some of the people who supported improvement found a point of attack in the academies—that is, in those institutions that had often appeared in the previous generation, establishing a prior claim on the resources that the local community had to invest in education. Once joined, the conflict between academies and common schools continued for many years. The academies seemed to siphon off the funds and the care that men of substance had to offer. They were geared to producing leadership for what the community had been, and were most acceptable to people who least felt the new pressures, or to people who could better their own lives through the particular kind of opportunity that the academies offered. Increasingly, too, the competition between the two kinds of schools became direct and invidious. Where once the academies had offered a preparatory or finishing education and had recruited students from among pupils who had spent some time at the local town or church schools, and where their function of training a representative leadership had therefore been plausible, they began to attract students from families who wanted to keep separate from the ordinary run of people. Sometimes such families sent children to local private elementary schools before sending them to the academy; sometimes they arranged to send children to the academies at earlier ages, so that what would have been community institutions tended to become pure private schools that took pupils in grades from elementary through the college-preparatory. During the same years, public high schools were developing in some places, as extension of the common schools. These high schools often required examinations for entering students, at a time when academies were often relaxing the distinction between elementary and secondary students. The competition between academies and public schools came to be one not only between two uses to which resources might be put, but also between two different conceptions of the pace at which education should operate, therefore two different conceptions of the social climate toward which education should be directed. The academies, even those that adopted a nominally military discipline, remained less regular, more flexible, even more familistic in their conceptions of how children should learn. The public schools tended toward a more formal, graded, departmentalized, regular organization of the learning process and the life cycle.

There were qualifications within this picture. In some states, a few academy teachers provided the leadership for the movement to support the common schools; in other states, and notably in New York, some academies undertook the task of training teachers for the common schools. But this was less a real deviation from what the academies meant than a realization by some individual teachers or principals that their own sympathies, or their own interests in recruiting a student body, should lead them to look outside the usual academy sphere. In 1868 the New York Regents took a position on the issues by requiring that academy students pass an entrance examination if they were to be counted in the allotting of state funds. By that time, academies in most parts of the country were headed for decline. By the end of another generation, they survived largely as an elite system overshadowed by the public high schools. In the meantime, the people who favored improving the common schools had organized into reform groups to support this cause. During the 1820s and 1830s these groups were mostly voluntary organizations, working outside and upon government. But it became clear that this kind of agitation was not the most promising way to overcome the resistance to change. In many localities the workers for improvement were not strong enough to control decisions made locally, and many of the people who had an interest in giving larger, more regular support to the schools had already begun their own adjustments to social pressure, by migrating from one area to another. Both the formal and the informal structures of local government made it difficult for such migratory people to have much influence on school decisions. Therefore central state agencies were needed to provide encouragement and to give local school supporters authoritative help that would overleap the heads of local conservatives. The school propagandists, aided by whoever might be interested in moralistic improvement or in centralization generally, worked successfully in the 1830s to persuade legislatures in the North to establish such agencies. At first, these were simply extensions of the movement to propagandize and encourage. A salary would be provided to a state superintendent or secretary, a small office would be established, and the secretary would be given the task of promoting the cause of public education by whatever means he could devise. If the secretary was energetic and dedicated, like Horace Mann or Henry Barnard, he could convert his office into a center of agitation that reached into almost every locality.

In some states, though, like New York and Pennsylvania, the post of secretary of education was at first given ex officio to whatever politician was at the moment the state's secretary of state. Its incumbent had influence, less because of any personal drive than because his official position gave him varied, if partisan, contacts in the different levels of government. In New York, too, he had the task of administering the aid that the state gave to localities. From time to time the legislature increased the fund whose income went to education, and from time to time it tightened the requirements that localities had to meet in receiving funds.

Then in 1838 the state education funds were given a symbolic boost: the New York State legislature decided to devote to education the money it received when the national government distributed the Surplus Revenue of 1837. Some other states made the same use of their shares. New funds required additional administrative staff, and also made the state educational organizations attractive to people of temperaments or political views that would originally have kept them aloof from the work. During the 1840s and 1850s these organizations became more attractive to routine politicians, though less partisan in their ideological appeal. The post of state school secretary was often given additional powers, the offices of local or county superintendent were often created, and yet the post of state secretary was made a separate one, nominally nonpartisan. As local school systems began to get more thoroughly organized, men began to come up through the systems themselves, too ambitious to be content with teaching, ready to move into administration or into school politics. The schools were becoming their own political system at the same time that they were being given a degree of independence from the day-to-day course of state politics. Many of the men who were coming up into school politics had been themselves part of the school-reform movement that had begun earlier, and were imbued with the faith and rhetoric that were important in that movement. The movement had begun as the expression of the educational needs of people who were most "up-to-date" in their responsiveness to changes in conditions around them, but who were to some extent thus responsive because they were more vulnerable to change. By the middle of the nineteenth century, that movement was becoming a distinct interest, in which informal pressure groups and teachers' associations worked with and through state departments to promote educational development.

The growing state-wide organizations came into some conflict with previously established school systems, and especially with those that had been functioning relatively well by their own standards. This meant mostly, of course, the academies, which were gradually forced to choose between becoming allies of the new organizations, either as normal schools or as high schools within the systems, and becoming more strictly "private." But it meant also the colleges, which had repeated fights with common-school spokesmen over the control of money and influence. It meant also the parochial or church-supported schools, maintained by various groups in the early part of the century, but after 1840 labeled more and more as a Roman Catholic phenomenon. And it meant also the city schools, especially in those places that had early begun reacting to the complex of pressures on education.

In Massachusetts, for example, the teachers in the Boston schools were certainly not opposed to the public-school idea; they were, after all, working within a public system that had a continuous history since the seventeenth century. And that system was not impervious to change, as had been shown by the creation of the primary schools in 1818. But it did tend to retain old practices along with any new improvements, and it fell out with Horace Mann on such issues as corporal punishment, religion in the schools, and the broader, really crucial issue of Mann's effort to assert leadership and priority in the cause of educational virtue.

In New York, the city system was more insulated from the main course of educational development, so that the clashes between state and city levels developed more gradually and less dramatically. The Public School Society had a vested position that was hard to touch, and it did take some stands that the reformers found easy to accept anyway. On religious exercises in the schools, it rejected the same kinds of Protestant orthodox or sectarian positions that people like Horace Mann opposed, but it also defended Bible reading (in the King James version) and stood out against Catholic requests for aid to church schools. But the Society had not the kind of traditional strength that toughened the actions of the Boston teachers. Its teachers and principals could, if they chose to stay in teaching, build careers only by methods similar to those used by men in the state-wide organizations, and they had no real sources of ideas or supporting ideology except the literature and the texts that were being distributed by the larger movement. When religious politics brought the collapse of the Public School Society, the ward schools that were organized to fill the gap were insecure institutions. The city system that emerged from them drew top personnel quite often from the state movement, even though the rank-and-file teachers were closer to local tradition. In New York City, therefore, the major clash between new ideas and older personnel was postponed until the 1860s. By that time the teachers had begun to pick up some of the new rhetoric. On a basic issue like corporal punishment, though, it was the administrators who called for abandoning such "correction," while many teachers defended its necessity. The daily problems of teachers often determined how such a system worked in practice, but the larger movement furnished rhetoric and official policies for city systems and country schoolmasters alike.

Much of what people tried to accomplish within the organized educational movement was, however, determinedly anti-organizational in tone. The movement advocated and obtained the establishing of normal schools, which were the first formal institutions for training schoolteachers. The methods of teaching that the normal schools inculcated in their pupils, and that men from the normal schools took to even larger numbers of teachers through local conferences and lectures, broke away from the formal rote methods of the traditional schoolmasters. The modern teacher was to treat young children gently, easing the transition from family to school. She was to realize that young children learned through their senses, and was therefore to present new ideas and facts in the most concrete way possible, only gradually leading children to the general or analytical notions behind the concrete. She was to teach children to grasp whole words, whole texts, whole ideas. She was to govern her pupils without corporal punishment wherever possible, and the fact that the teacher was now frequently a woman led people to hope that she would win children through love and mildness. Although conscientious individual teachers had for centuries advocated much of this natural regime, it was the new educational bureaucracies that claimed the credit for backing them on a large scale. Thus, in the 1820s individual teachers and textbook writers tried to import from Europe the methods of Pestalozzi, with their stress on object-teaching. But these efforts attracted only a faddish response, and the methods only acquired a kind of popularity in the 1850s when they were picked up by organizers and systems in New York.

Outside the public-school movement, parents and teachers made even more obvious efforts to retain something of the informal and familial within schools. Enterprising teachers who damned the common schools as holes of impersonality and vice were quick to label their own private, so-called select institutions as "family" schools; and occasional writers did advocate tutorial instruction in the home.

The propaganda for physical education and the very real popularity of military schools were part of the same moralistic, even antimodern reaction.

By about 1870, a standard pattern of educational organization was worked out in almost all parts of the North, and the outcome of the Civil War fixed the organizational forms of Northern culture as a guiding standard for the nation. In basic education, some local autonomy persisted, but subject to guidance and control from state-wide organizations. In higher education, pluralism and competition had won out clearly over the older sense of identification between community leadership and local colleges or professional schools. In the newer state universities, and in some yet feeble movements for reform in professional education, the oncoming generation was beginning to react against the debasing effects of competition, but the distinction persisted: basic education had developed in ways that stressed increasingly tighter, more formal organization; higher education, in ways that showed their greatest vigor in competition and pluralism. The intermediate levels of education were not clearly established as governed by one or the other of these principles. The dominant form of secondary school had been a private corporation that worked as a community-service institution. This was now obsolescent, and was being replaced by two kinds of schools: private schools that partook of the competitive style of higher education, and public high schools that extended the more organized way of the state systems.

Tighter organization on some levels and wider competition on other levels together extended the means of regular education to more and more communities, including many that had lacked regular facilities within the less systematic world of the eighteenth century. In the sense that these formal means became both more widely available and more regular, the process of economic and industrial modernization in America was clearly accomplished by a process of educational development.

But that process was only approximately like the programs of educational development that planners were later to set out for "underdeveloped" countries. Although it showed some unity of spirit at times, as in the national-university idea or in the uniform thought patterns of the common-school revival movement, it was not a unified, coherent process. Much of it emerged through interaction and competition in which few people looked to the whole pattern, and in which those who did seemed to lose out. Within the sector that achieved more thorough organization, many of the particular things that men undertook were reactive in quality, directed less at improvement and modernization than at shoring up and reasserting predevelopmental values. Within this more organized sector, reform and virtue were often measured by the warmth or personal intensity or even familial attitudes that programs were supposed to embody. Over these years, too, the press distributed larger and larger quantities of reading matter, of more varied kinds; many of these forms, such as the new children's literature, the highly organized religious periodicals, the romantic novels, and the sensational newspapers, were especially adapted to appeal to people who in earlier years might have read little but Bible and almanac. This new matter may have rested in part on wider results effected by formal education. But it and the organized lecture system that grew in the nineteenth century were means of education themselves; through them and other means, much of learning, much of any actual intellectual development in the population at large, took place outside the formal education system. This informal character of much real education, plus the loose organization of much formal education, plus the reactive, compensatory character of much that was happening within the most highly organized education, meant that American educational development during the years of modernization was no simple matter of deliberate efforts that produced corresponding increments in what people could do with their minds.

Often, the issue of whether the schools were having real effect on people's minds seemed to turn on how men felt about the schools as a bureaucratic institution. One New York official, arguing that the schools needed a good, complex administrative system like that for the canals, asserted that the "general intelligence of which we boast, the mental superiority of our people, their inventive powers, and mechanical skill, are the fruits of the schools."[1] This was partly a matter of large classes and large schools, in which pupils would feel pressed to compete more vigorously: "by comparison and emulation students become bright."[2] But emulation was also one of the favorite evils denounced by those who believed in natural, unpunitive methods. And many critics, old-fashioned in temperament or simply reacting against bureaucracy and specific abuses, doubted whether the schools were having much good effect at all. As a Cabot put it in reviewing an exposé of the schools,

> Those who see them at a distance see a good deal of show and bustle, and they are ready to conclude that the high average of intelligence and cultivation which they see, and which no doubt is highest where the schools are the best, is the direct product of the school. The opposite view is, the wonder that schools in the midst of so intelligent a people, and completely subject to their control, should be so lifeless, so little in earnest or discriminating either as to what is taught or the way in which it is taught.[3]

The only outcome of educational development that is proved by the bare facts of the process is that children were

[1] Victor M. Rice, in *Second Annual Report of the Superintendent of Public Instruction of the State of New York* (Assembly Doc. No. 65, Jan. 28, 1856), 57.

[2] Thomas McKindley, in New York State Superintendent, *Annual Report*, 12th (1866), 296.

[3] J. E. Cabot, Review of *The Daily Public School in the United States* (Philadelphia, 1866), in *North American Review*, CIII (1866), 291-302.

exposed to learning in more regular and formal ways than they had once been. Regularity and formality did not guarantee thoroughness and depth and mastery. Development happened, but did it produce any net gains in what Americans could do with their minds? The answer to this question may lie partly in what happened in the schools, but it must lie more broadly in what happened in many different aspects of people's lives.

B. The Discovery of Learning Problems: Reading, Arithmetic, Objects

Americans, and Europeans too, built school systems as one feature of their "modern" societies of the nineteenth century. The working pressure of these systems then led teachers and psychologists to invent the idea of testing intelligence. The steps in this pressure and invention were simple enough. A teacher, whether in Poughkeepsie or Paris, would be given a class to teach, composed of pupils all supposedly learning at a single grade of ability. Administrators would give the teacher a syllabus of what she was supposed to get over to the pupils during a year. After a time, administrators or citizens would enter the classroom and question the pupils to find out how much they had actually learned. On a higher level, system-wide administrators would judge the success of teaching by how many pupils were promoted from one grade to the next. They might also send into the classroom written tests on the content of syllabi. The unfortunate teacher whose pupils did not perform or move on had to answer for it. Of course, she could always talk back, insisting that the pupils she had been given were not so apt as others, and that she had done as well as anyone should expect. Some of being "not apt" was an environmental matter: pupils came from poor families, or from depressing neighborhoods, or from the hands of less competent teachers.

Naturally, though, as middle-brow thought grew more biological during the nineteenth century, the defensive teacher was likely to say that her pupils lacked the inherited qualities that made up ability to learn. There was one available way for the teacher to see any such lack of ability. If she were working in an ordinary classroom, she could observe the manner in which pupils took hold of tasks. Did certain pupils have problems with particular processes or particular subjects? If the teacher were working in an institution for handicapped children, he could observe the problems that individual children had in coping with all the tasks of life. In the case of the retarded children, many of these problems obviously had some biological base. Working in that kind of situation, the French psychologist Binet began to develop systematic schedules of tasks by which he could assign numerical grades of ability to individual children. He and others then extended these schedules to apply to "normal" school children. Thus the intelligence test.

In its origin the intelligence test was an attempt to confer order and reliability on the things teachers said about their difficulties in getting pupils to learn. Since one underlying motive was to avoid blame on teachers, these difficulties were described either as "learning problems" (less often as teaching problems) or as low I.Q. True, the clinical concern about learning problems has continued to be a more flexible drive than the number-fixing concern about I.Q. Psychologists in guidance clinics are inclined by their trade to think that pupils' abilities can be changed, and their problems alleviated. But the I.Q. test and the diagnosis of learning problems are part of a single social complex—along with the general drive of school systems to classify both pupil and teacher.

Wherever and whenever teachers talked to their employers about their problems in getting material across to pupils, they were doing the same thing that emerged after 1900 as the testing of intelligence. In the earlier America, and especially during the colonial years, this self-justifying talk was an oral process that usually left little record. The teacher who lived within a rural community that maintained its own schools hardly needed to write reports. Only when an outside agency moved in, giving financial aid but imposing some demands in exchange, did any talk about learning problems leave much of a trail. In New York, this intrusion or help took two successive forms: the work of religious mission agencies, who supported schoolteachers as well as preachers, and then the organization of a state-supported school system in the familiar modern form. One of the mission groups, the London-based Society for the Propagation of the Gospel, subsidized local teachers in America, and collected some reports from them, during the early and middle years of the eighteenth century. After a gap of sorts across the years of the American Revolution, a state educational system began to collect reports from local people, beginning in the second quarter of the nineteenth century. The things that teachers said in these reports about learning problems make up the important earlier statements that survive about the levels of intelligence that were observed, in particular children, in that part of America.

In eighteenth-century New York, schoolmasters had teaching problems, but children seemed not to have what the twentieth century would call "learning problems." Whatever blocks arose in the way of transmitting simple reading and arithmetic to children, the people who reported those blocks almost never blamed them on stupidity or dullness. That, at least, is the story in the records of one organization that supported schools in the colonies and extracted reports from its teachers on their methods and on how they were succeeding with pupils: the Society for the Propagation of the Gospel.

When S.P.G. pupils failed to learn, parents naturally blamed the teacher for incompetence, or for using a poor method, or for neglecting his duty; sometimes the master himself agreed. Daniel Denton, teaching in Oyster Bay in 1727, reported that he taught children the three Rs "as they were capable,"[4] and the word "capable" might have meant either "able because old enough" or "able because of having studied already," as well as "able because bright." But twenty inhabitants of Oyster Bay left no ambiguity four years later, when they complained that Denton failed to earn the teacher's subsidy he received from the Society, because he "does no Service for it, but Keeps a Tavern and Brewhouse and leaves us to Shift for our Selves, for a Schoolmaster." And though a Denton took care to deny the charge of negligence,[5] other teachers felt no embarrassment about confessing to various degrees of mental incompetence. To be sure, it required only pathetic self-pity, not honesty, for a Thomas Temple to report that, after he had fallen from his horse and had suffered colds, "I contracted such a Disorder in my Hearing, that tis not Easie for me to teach Small Children to Spell and Read, with that Exactness which I Could wish, which is Reason given by the people for their not Sending to my School as Usual; tho I thank God I can Still Teach Wrighting and Arithmetick and Accordingly I have Sundry Scholars to the Number of Seaven Who Attend Each Evening for instruction therein. . . ."[6] But another teacher, while admitting that his "Country People" wanted only as much writing and arithmetic for their children as would "serve the Common occasions of vulgar People," still conceded that "I could heartily wish my self better qualifyed for all those but Cheifly for writing in which

[4] Denton to Secretary of the Society for the Propagation of the Gospel, Dec. 17, 1727, S.P.G. letterbooks, A, xx, 205, from microfilm in Library of Congress.

[5] Petition of Severall of the Inhabitants at Oyster Bay against Mr. Denton, May 24, 1731, S.P.G. letterbooks, A, xxiii, 362-363. Denton to Secretary, Sept. 3, 1731, A, xxiii, 340-341.

[6] Thos. Temple to Secretary, Dec. 29, 1746, S.P.G. letterbooks, B, xiv, no. 135.

my weakness will Discover it Self but for those Children that are any thing advanced in writing my method is to procure Copies writ by the best masters and I find it answers the end very well. . . ."[7] Some men did not need to make explicit confession: Thomas Gildersleeve, who detractors said was incompetent to teach arithmetic, needed only to report that he had taken "som reeders som Righters and som sypherers," and taught them "Catechism reeding writing and a Resmatick."[8]

Teachers did not usually condemn themselves, of course. Either they insisted that they were succeeding in their efforts, or—and this is a critical point, on which they were probably quite honest—they reported that they taught well enough as much as the unambitious New Yorkers wanted their children to learn. Where one teacher observed that most ambition was limited to "Country Employments," he observed that attendance varied according to how much the people could "spare their Children from their Country business."[9] Or the same complaint about lost time was turned against a teacher, when a competitor accused him of keeping no school in the Winter: "Ye Children Cannot Improve in any thing when they have an Opportunity by a Winters Idleness to loose all they have Learn'd in ye Su̅mer Besides that many Sons of Poor Laborious Parents Cannot be Spared the whole (Some a very small part of the summer from the Assistance of their Parents in their Labours on their ffarmes. . . ."[10] Parents or competitors made such complaints repeatedly, but in no quarrel did an accused teacher adopt the particular defense that his pupils were slow or that they had even forgivable troubles in learning.

[7] Saml. Purdy to Secretary, Aug. 29, 1737, S.P.G. letterbooks, B, I, no. 20.

[8] Thomas Gildersleeve to Secretary, Dec. 1, 1729, S.P.G. letterbook, B, I, no. 47.

[9] William Forster to Secretary, May 18, 1723, S.P.G. letterbooks, A, XVII, 229. Cf. Forster to Secretary, Aug. 20, 1718, A, XIII, 382.

[10] Gerardus Clowes to Robert Jenney, Mar. 30, 1728, S.P.G. letterbooks, A, XXI, 324.

In one case an unaccused teacher did volunteer information about pupil troubles—Edward Davis, who wrote about slaves he was trying to teach: "I have with a great deal of Difficulty & pains learnt Some to Spell, Some to Read and Some to Write, as well as could be Expected, Considering their Brokeness of Speech and Age, most of them grown to mens Years, I am now preparing to Instruct them, this Winter, and hope to make this Winter a greater progress than last, they haveing Some notion of their Books now, but the last Year very few of them knew any thing."[11] That evaluation stood against another man's judgment that most Indian children, whose parents insisted that they be taught "in their own Language," proved "very apt to learn."[12]

This pattern of reactions amounts to one agreed judgment: that so long as pupils were familiar with the school process and with the language in which they were taught—so long, that is, as they did not suffer from massive "cultural deprivation"—teachers could hardly conceive of any learning blocks internal to the specific learners they were encountering. They could not, for a simple reason: between the irregular pace at which schools were conducted, and the modest subject-matter that parents expected or permitted teachers to offer, there was no extensive schoolroom transaction that served as a test of learning ability. If it makes any sense to talk about the actual or underlying ability of children in such a situation, then it is probable that few children were called on to perform anywhere near their "actual" ability. The only real test posed was the overwhelming task presented to the slaves, of learning in a language and in a social situation unfamiliar to them.

If any group of twentieth-century children were subsisting in such a diffuse, irregular context of parental expectations and "learning experiences," just how would a canny

[11] Edward Davis to Secretary, Nov. 12, 1734, S.P.G. letterbooks, A, xxv, 40-41.

[12] Will Andrews to Secretary, Sept. 7, 1713, S.P.G. letterbooks, A, viii, 185.

teacher expect them to perform on a suddenly presented standard intelligence test? Or how would a teacher expect them to perform if presented suddenly with new material to be learned—material appropriate to their real ages? He would either resign himself to their performing poorly or he would discount the whole measuring process in advance by some version of the idea that measured intelligence is a modern invention, inappropriate when applied to underdeveloped cultures.

The school is itself a kind of intelligence test, and the eventual modernization of American education meant the intensifying of actions that could produce estimates of learning ability. By the years after the Civil War, teachers and bureaucrats had worked out a clear standard of what elementary schooling was supposed to do. This standard was published in the syllabi that normal schools and education departments prepared to guide teachers. It was assumed in tests that the New York Regents set. It was used in examinations for teachers' certificates. It was soon to be used in the basic examinations given by the United States Civil Service Commission. With some variation, the expected knowledge consisted of a fairly thorough skill at spelling, an ability to perform basic arithmetical operations with large numbers, an ability to reproduce or predict the orthodox grammatical analysis of stilted English prose or poetry, and a rote knowledge of some textbook facts in geography. Along with these things, teachers expected that successful pupils would acquire other skills, notably in reading, that written tests could less easily measure.

The idea that written tests should measure capacity was in fact novel in the 1850s. School and college examinations had long been mainly oral. It is often hard to tell from the record whether a given performance was a serious examination or simply an exhibition staged to please visitors. Written tests, too, made little sense in the heterogeneous, ungraded schools that were the only kind most learners ever saw. For most people, uniform written examinations were one more feature of a new commercial, urban life. This showed in the way that the federal census took up the problem of literacy. Census-takers first asked about literacy in 1840, but only in the form of asking *how many* persons in each household could read and write, not *which individuals* could read and write. Then in 1850 census schedules provided a separate line for each individual.

As the census itself showed, the new bent for written checks on individuals did not mean that bare literacy had been uncommon. Native whites suffered really high levels of illiteracy—of the order of 40 percent—only in the South. In New York state, ordinary country populations included not much more than 5 percent who could not read and write. Even older people, who had been exposed to the schools before 1800, numbered few illiterates, although illiteracy rates in different age groups did reflect changing school conditions. Among the very old, who had attended school during or just before the Revolution, illiteracy ran somewhere around 8 percent. During or just after the Revolution, though, the level of illiteracy increased—possibly to some 12 percent of the population. According to the much later memories of one observer, the war had interfered with the quality or supply of teachers. Certainly the continuity and reliability of ordinary life suffered as much in New York as in any other province. But by early in the new century illiteracy receded, and remained stable until the 1830s, when it dropped again, to only 1 or 2 percent of the native whites coming out of the schools. That drop, which probably left few but mental defectives illiterate, may have reflected the efforts at school improvement that reformers were then mounting; or it may have resulted from the growing number of academies that were incidentally increasing the supply of schoolteachers. It may also have reflected the migration into the state of New Englanders, bringing a more thorough, no-exceptions attitude toward early schooling.[13]

For all that literacy, many school inspectors and observers of the 1850s and 1860s were reporting that children had difficulty in applying the letters and figures that they learned. They had difficulty in reading for content, in applying logic to arithmetical problems, and generally in making routine processes work as natural abilities. These failings showed in 1864 when the Regents imposed their written examinations in the subjects of arithmetic, spelling, geography, and grammar. For some decades the Regents had given an academy or high school state-aid money only for the number of its pupils who could pass examinations in the elementary-school subjects; but it had allowed secondary-school principals to conduct these examinations for their own pupils, orally, and had taken the principal's word for who passed. After the beginning of written examinations, the proportion of pupils allowed as having really completed the elementary course dropped to half the level of earlier years.[14]

The new written standards, whatever their limitations, showed that men were creating a mental role to which they might hold the performance of ordinary Americans. This standard had not existed a hundred years earlier. Now it did.

Not all growing Americans reached the standard set for

[13] On the quality of schooling just after the Revolution, see "Schools as They Were in the United States Sixty and Seventy Years Ago," *New York Teacher*, XIII (1863/64), 281-287. This observation is tentatively confirmed by a reanalysis of educational data in the United States 1850 census returns for selected towns in Dutchess County, New York, presented in the Appendix.

[14] New York Regents, *Annual Report*, 80th (1867), including James H. Hoose, "The Arithmetical Preparation Necessary to Commence the Study of Algebra," 621-628; 81st (1868), xxi-xxxiv, 557-570; 85th (1872), xvi. Walter John Gifford, *Historical Development of the New York State High School System* (Albany, 1922), ch. 5.

them then. Many did not finish elementary school. Many, both of those who finished and of those who did not, failed to progress toward the higher performance in the way that the standard expected. The particular ways in which pupils failed along this route constituted the "learning problems" that then prevailed.

During the generation up to 1870, schoolmen and observers worried about whether children were learning to read properly. What was more, they felt that this problem was governed by the whole pacing of the school system and, beyond that, by the need for Americans to keep up with the spirit of intellectual progress. Even the compiler of a cram text for teachers' certificate examinations could comment,

> Reading is a branch in which nineteen out of every twenty are deficient. Yet this is an *age* of reading, emphatically so. Notwithstanding this, we hear the testimony from every side, that "*there are but few good readers.*" How important then that we should have clear and distinct principles in Elocution, and that every person who is a candidate for a Teacher's License should be a complete master of every principle, and be able to impart the instruction in this branch to his pupils without stint.[15]

There was something universal about the complaint. Its elements dated back to early in the educational literature of America, they appeared in wide parts of the country, and they turned up in England, too. Children, men said, read without expression, in a "humdrum" or "sing-song" tone. Their manner was "unnatural" or "mechanical." Pupils rarely succeeded in reading "understandingly and effectively."[16] This complaint did not come just from the writers of propa-

[15] Isaac Stone, *The Elementary and Complete Examiner* (New York & Chicago, 1869), 19.

[16] Richard Edwards, *Analytical Fifth Reader* (Chicago, 1867), Preface.

ganda and textbooks. It came also from local supervisors who went around to district schools examining pupils and observing the methods used by teachers. Sometimes they singled out reading, or reading and a few closely related subjects, as those in which teachers and pupils did the poorest work; thus their reports, like a reference that mentions a *relative* weakness in a job applicant, were making an honest negative judgment. But if they singled out reading, they also saw its problem as something pervading the learning process. Pupils could rattle through their reading lessons, but could not talk about what they had read. "The difficulties and embarassments, experienced by pupils in the expression of their ideas, is so general and extensive, that the most earnest efforts on the part of teachers and commissioners, to induce the cultivation and use of language in the school-room, is especially desirable."[17] Naturally, the reading failure affected how children learned everything else. "Children go hurriedly through their books, grasping a few disconnected points in a rote-like manner, and when brought to a test, fail in showing any knowledge of the principles that underlie the subjects."[18]

Within the diffuse quality of the trouble, observers based their diagnoses on a simple, concrete criterion for what was good reading and what was bad. Good reading was what sounded good. It conveyed to the hearer a sense of emotional tone in the pupil and a sense of what was real in the matter covered by the exercise. All pupils had presumably learned the bare mechanics of reading; although teachers argued the merits of word methods or alphabetic methods for presenting the elements of reading, they complained little about lasting difficulty in getting the elements across

[17] Report by Commissioner for Jefferson County 3rd District, in New York State Superintendent of Public Instruction, *Annual Report*, 18th (1872), 261.

[18] Report by Commissioner for Sullivan County 2nd District, in State Superintendent, *Annual Report*, 21st (1875), 390.

by whatever method. But pupils, once they progressed to more complex matter, relied on those elements and little more. They called out the words in a selection rapidly, and articulated them plainly enough for a listener who had the same printed words to follow. But whether a pupil understood all the words he could pronounce was doubtful enough, and whether he understood whole passages and ideas was hardly doubtful. He did not. Even if he understood the intellectual content of a passage, he failed to respond to its feeling or moral value. He failed, especially, by the evangelical, nonritualistic standards often applied to oral expression. He withheld himself from the words he uttered, and left his hearers in doubt about how much of his person he gave to the meanings underlying the words.

Obviously, much depended on the viewpoint of the reporter, and those observers who were more detached from immediate American needs gave more favorable accounts. Between 1866 and 1890 several foreign visitors set down their evaluations of American schools, and at least one paid special attention to New York.

The first of these, and the most objective in his style of reporting, combining large amounts of on-the-spot description with some cautious generalizing, was the Anglican cleric James Fraser, who visited American and Canadian schools for the British School Inquiries Commission. His comment on examinations in New York City showed that he was ready to see unnatural, routine performance: "The questions and answers struck me as a little too mechanical, running along the groove of the textbooks, and hardly ever diverging even from the phraseology. They seemed, therefore, to touch the memory chiefly, the faculty which is rather too exclusively, or at least too prominently, cultivated in American schools." He believed that the American system ran not only to memorization, but to haste, superficiality, and poor taste. Yet he also observed about a New York City school: "The reading, which I heard was loud distinct, emphatic, and displayed a fair measure of intelligence."[19]

In the 1880s, Paul Passy, reporting to the French Ministry of Public Instruction described reading as the *best*-taught subject in American schools. He observed that the word method of initial reading, though perhaps less efficient than other techniques, was popular in America because it led to natural, meaningful performance when pupils came to read aloud. Then the Englishman J. G. Fitch reported in 1890 that American teaching stressed silent reading, with the pupils' comprehension tested by subsequent questions; and he recommended that English schools revise in that direction their own concentration on oral reading.[20]

Fitch, in 1890, was operating in a new setting that had its own problems. The others had said, or suggested, that Americans were not doing so poorly at oral reading as the Americans had themselves feared. His praise reflected the fact that, beginning about 1880, the long concern for meaningfulness in oral reading was being transmuted in American normal schools and school systems into a prescription that individual, silent reading for meaningful content should be the main goal of teaching. The schools of the previous generation had produced successful results beyond what most teachers had intended. Many persons coming up through the school system, responsive enough to its cues that they themselves became teachers, had picked up the drummed-in idea that meaningfulness was the criterion for oral reading. Living in a period when men were adopting the impersonal communication techniques of nationwide business, and were letting high oral expression go the way

[19] Great Britain, School Inquiries Commission, *Report . . . on the Common School System of the United States and of the Provinces of Upper and Lower Canada* (London, 1866), 83, 118*n*.

[20] Paul Passy, *L'instruction primaire aux États-unis: rapport présenté au ministre de l'instruction publique* (Paris, 1885), 55-64. J. G. Fitch, *Notes on American Schools and Training Colleges* (London & New York, 1890), 46-47.

of William Jennings Bryan, they simply accepted the trend, taking meaningfulness as the criterion for all successful reading, but adding to this criterion the idea that meaning is not a phonetic concept.

Observers had already picked up signs of improvement under way. One superintendent in Greene County, New York, reported some improvement in 1866, then withdrew his optimism the next year. A Herkimer County report of 1877 implied gains, by complaining only that a "few" teachers failed to train students to read for meaning.[21] But such optimism did not always suggest that it was reporting what everyone would agree to call improvement. An Oneida County rural superintendent reported in 1872 that the tone of schools had changed since thirty years before, when families were larger and there were fewer immigrant children.

> Hence the schools were larger then, interesting, and sometimes jolly....
>
> But when we compare the scholarship of pupils in our schools with that of thirty years ago, the result is decidedly in favor of the present. We have better scholars, and minds better disciplined, at a much younger age than formerly. We are not only living faster and moving faster, but are developing the mind, and learning faster. Yet the scholarship in our schools is by no means what it should be. This suggests the important inquiry, by what means can we elevate the character and scholarship of our schools in the rural districts?[22]

The foreigners who praised the results they saw in American schools may have been committing acts of politeness;

[21] Reports by Commissioner for Greene County 2nd District, in State Superintendent, *Annual Report*, 12th (1866), 168, and in 13th (1867), 174. Report by Commissioner for Herkimer County 1st District, in *Annual Report*, 23rd (1877), 339.

[22] Report by Commissioner for Oneida County 2nd District, State Superintendent, *Annual Report*, 18th (1872), 293.

their occasional censorious adjectives may mean more than their laudatory tone. Even so, the contradiction between observers who lamented the quality of American reading and observers who praised it does pose a problem. In part, the contradictions resulted from changes over time. Even among men looking at the same situation at the same time, different people had different notions about what had gone before and thus different notions about how things had changed.

Thus, the extent to which observers noticed the elocution movement affected how they judged other aspects of the reading problem. Increasingly by the 1860s some reading texts included instructions in elocutionary technique. The recommended techniques were sometimes formal and bizarre, running even to phonetic instructions on how to give forth with various pleasing styles of laughter. Educational reviewers were quick to ridicule the more extreme of these texts, and the sensible pointed out that most teachers simply ignored the elocutionary chapters. *Most* was not *all*, though; a New York City school official reported in 1874 that some schools, in their effort to achieve distinct articulation, were producing affectation.[23] And one observer writing in 1895 asserted that "untimely technical instruction" had replaced the sound methods of his boyhood sixty years earlier, when teachers had told him to read plainly and mind the stops, and had made him understand what he was reading. He seemed aware only of the elocutionary among the various reading movements of his own generation, and believed that it had produced a decline from an earlier high standard of oral reading.[24]

School officials' ability to change their standards for what pupils *should* learn complicates their reports as evidence for what pupils actually did learn. The sudden growth of

[23] Arthur McMullin, in New York City Board, *Annual Report*, 23rd (1874), 289.

[24] Hiram Corson, "Vocal Culture in Its Relation to Literary Culture," *Atlantic Monthly*, LXXV (1895), 810-816.

the silent-reading movement after 1880[25] suggests that teachers could shift their standards faster and further than children changed the way they behaved in class. It is then possible that error or bias had swung observers' judgments quite far from reality in earlier situations. During the middle years of the century, the school reformers and the normal schools developed a strong line on what faults prevailed in schools and on what kinds of policy-change those faults required. Their basic argument, reworked in many different details and versions, was that the schools as they existed had been primitive and unintellectual. The allegation of "mere" rote teaching was one of the standard devices within this argument. As long as normal schools and officials took the view that teachers should become skilled at eliciting natural or expressive or emotionally committed behavior from children, the people who were carrying the gospel of school reform would be disposed to see in the existing schools the mechanistic faults they thought their own movement was equipped to correct.

From about 1840 dogma and observation became too intertwined for easy disentanglement. Before that time, the local school visitors had some chance of making their own unmediated observations of how they saw pupils acting. With the founding of the *District School Journal* in 1840, and the *New York Teacher* in 1853, canned educational interpretation began to spread through the state. For many years the state legislature subsidized the distribution of these two organs.[26] Nor did state authorities rest content

[25] T.P.D. Stone, "Reading in Common Schools," in New York Regents, *Annual Report*, 83rd (1880), 529-535. John T. Prince, *Courses and Methods. A Handbook for Teachers of Primary, Grammar, and Ungraded Schools* (Boston, 1886), 1-20, 52-59. Eva D. Kellogg, ed., *Teaching Reading in Ten Cities* (Boston, 1900). Harold Boyne Lampert, *A History of the Teaching of Beginning Reading* (Chicago, 1937), 92-93.

[26] Frank Luther Mott, *A History of American Magazines, 1741-1850* (Cambridge, Mass., 1930), 491. Sheldon Emmor Davis, *Educational*

with the magazine format, which could only insinuate ideas piecemeal, in a semiofficial way. In 1842 the Superintendent of Common Schools sponsored the preparation of an official statement in book form, written in two parts—the first part general and ideological, by Alonzo Potter, professor of moral philosophy at Union College, the second part practical and pedagogical, by the Boston schoolmaster George B. Emerson. A copy of *The School and the Schoolmaster* was to be placed in each school district, in each incorporated academy, and in each county deputy superintendent's office. Potter did quote the complaining observations of one local visiting committee to support his generalization that "a wordy, superficial rote-method of teaching and learning, may be regarded as, at this time, the great and special bane of our common schools." Potter, he said himself, built his own view as a compendium of what school critics were already saying; they, presumably, were often in contact with what was actually happening. But the criticisms became an orthodoxy when a book as widely distributed as the Potter-Emerson manual included such passages as the following.

> What proportion, of those who leave these schools, or are known to have been educated at them, can read aloud from any book, which may chance to fall into their hands; and can do it so fluently, intelligently, and forcibly, as to afford both instruction and pleasure, to those who listen?
>
> . . . so soon as a child has mastered the common branches, so that he reads, both aloud and mentally, with ease and understanding, writes a good hand, and is familiar with the most important processes in arithmetic, he ought to be advanced to other studies. The great fault, at present, is, that he is advanced too soon; . . .[27]

State authorities continued to set an unofficial line for local people, only varying the line as pedagogical fashions

---

Periodicals During the Nineteenth Century, Bureau of Education, *Bulletin*, 1919, No. 28, pp. 94, 96.

[27] Potter and Emerson (New York, 1846 [1st 1842]), 182, 184, 185.

changed. At conferences of county superintendents, those attending were assigned topics for essays to present at subsequent meetings.[28] This forced the superintendents to assimilate or crib, to restate, and perhaps to internalize the published perceptions of school life that were then available. These same superintendents then wrote descriptions of what was happening in their districts, as part of their official reports to the state superintendent. Many of these reports talked about improvements that needed to be made in teaching, without advancing any arguments based on observation of pupil learning. Many or most of those that did profess to report observations reported much the same points that were being broadcast in the official or public literature. Only a few reported on pupil behavior in an idiosyncratic or authentic tone.

Probably the official view contained many elements of realistic description. Still, the machinery for homogenizing perception existed, and the broad conformities of tone in the reported observations suggest that some of that homogenizing took place.

This process was aided by the fact that some observers—those who had favorite teaching methods to advocate—chose to blame poor oral reading on the use of wrong teaching methods. Among these were the only observers who found any connection between the way very young children learned the mechanics of reading and the way older children performed in reading texts. The teacher who favored the syllabic techniques of oral spelling ("c-e-n, cen; t-u, tu, r-y, ry; century") blamed the failure to drill students in methodical, slow pronunciation.[29] To him, ideas had separable

[28] *District School Journal*, IV (1843/44), 65-66; V (1844/45), 107. On other doubtful practices in report-writing, see the description of "Professional Shuffle and Deal; or an Easy Way for Making School Reports," in "Old Wine in New Bottles," *New York Teacher*, VI (1869), 426-431.

[29] Ira Patchin to S. Young, June 1842, in *District School Journal of New York*, III (1842/43), 35.

parts just as did spellings; the pupil who hurried past one would hurry past the other. He disagreed almost diametrically with exponents of the whole-word method of teaching reading, who argued that both the alphabet method and the phonetic method of teaching initial reading encouraged the pupil to ignore the meanings in words and the ideas in passages.[30]

These were not the only people who put blame on something that happened within the teaching process, but the others focused on the ages or grades within which pupils were doing the bad oral reading. In this view the choice and pacing of textbooks was central, but the criticisms included both a warm, permissive theme and a disciplinary, demanding theme.

One of the best examples of the warm approach appeared as early as 1835 in a manual by Theodore Dwight, Jr., *The School-Master's Friend.* For initial reading he presented both the alphabet and the word methods, thus avoiding merely technical problems and reserving his intense concern for the difficulties in oral reading.

> Reading well is a much more simple thing than many pupils suppose. They should be taught to read very much as they should speak: with a natural manner in all respects.
>
> . . . Indeed a great part of the difficulty of making good readers general is the correcting of faults already acquired, or false notions which are usually derived from the example of others.
>
> Much attention, forbearance, and judgment will be necessary in the training of some children to reading. A little diffidence, apprehension or fear, fatigue, ill health, and other circumstances, affect the voices of some children very sensibly; and may lead the teacher to suppose them dull or willful. The child must be at his ease,

[30] N. Calkins, in New York City and County Board of Education, *Annual Report*, 28th (1869), 246-247.

> in body and mind, or he cannot read with advantage. The exercise is partly intellectual, partly physical, and it might be added, partly moral.

On selecting material for children to read, he stated a principle that in later years and in other hands was to lead both to the most insipid and to the most radical of texts.

> Familiar lessons should first be used in reading; and the more familiar the better. Even sentences composed by the scholars themselves, corrected if they need it by the master, may well serve for early lessons. Children should first be made to read what they understand, and something that relates to their own circumstances, and interests their feelings. They will then have the same advantages in reading which they have in conversation. They will perceive the reasonableness and application of the rules and directions given them; they will form the habit of applying them often of themselves, even perhaps in conversation, and thus will greatly lighten and expedite the master's task.[31]

Applied to the whole school course by other writers on teaching, this view merged into an argument for including new, information-bearing subjects in the studies of quite young pupils. It thus opened up the whole argument for diversifying and modernizing the subject matters taught to children. "It is not unusual for parents, on placing their daughters at school to express the wish that they may become good readers, before they proceed to other branches of education. But reason and experience pronounce it impossible for an ignorant person to read well; such an one may acquire the habit of calling words correctly, of minding stops and marks, and observing all the artificial rules, but the soul of reading will be wanting!"[32]

[31] Theodore Dwight, Jr., *School-Master's Friend* (New York, 1835), 48-49, 50.

[32] Almira H. L. Phelps, *The Female Student* (New York & Boston, 1836), 117.

The desire to give students materials they could understand did not necessarily mean a permissive or undemanding attitude. Although it could indeed carry a tolerance for fiction-reading (especially if the fictional character of a piece was pointed out to the child), a wish to introduce new subjects might also accompany a continuing disapproval of fiction as debilitating.[33] And William B. Fowle, whose *Teachers' Institute* was published in Boston in 1847 and first reprinted in New York in 1866, combined warmth and even permissiveness with a careful insistence on not making matters too easy for children. Dissatisfied with elocutionary "aids" and even with the informational selections that were supposed to stimulate the child's interest, Fowle constructed his own texts for class use, using a dialogue form that would involve pupils directly.

> I am persuaded that nothing but the incompetency of teachers has led to the preparation of various series of reading books, intended, as far as possible, to help the pupil to learn independently of the master. . . .
>
> The competent teacher needs but two rules by which to be guided in teaching his pupils to read. He must make them understand what is to be read, and then require them to read naturally. To expect a child to read what he does not understand is unreasonable, and yet nothing is more common. Until very lately, teachers were generally accustomed to pay no attention to the explanation of such pieces as are found in School Readers, and turned their attention almost entirely to the pauses and the pronunciation; important points, to be sure, but by no means the life-giving elements of good reading. . . .
>
> The child should, for a general rule, see as few things

[33] Jacob Abbott, *Rollo Learning to Read* (Philadelphia & Boston, 1845), 179-180. E. C. Wines, [On Teaching the Art of Reading in Schools] [n.p., 183–], prospectus in Harvard College Library holdings of educational pamphlets. "Value of Reading to Youth," *American Educational Monthly*, 1 (1864), 214-215.

> in school books, that he will not see in other books, as possible; for, when he leaves schools, and the helps are withdrawn, he will be the less able to go alone, the more he has trusted to such aids.

But when Fowle turned to his conception of memory-training, on which he lectured to New York school superintendents, he distinguished between *interest* and *understanding*. Memory, which he did not consider a distinct faculty, depended on the child's interest in the matter to be retained. But it was the desire of the child to gain the understandings he yet lacked that would lead him to grow without depending on artificially easy helps. Fowle argued against books written completely within a child's ability: "If I may compare great things with small, I will say that the Creator does not teach us to read in the book of nature in any such way. We are interested in every page that he has spread before us, but we understand very little of it."[34]

Far more common than Fowle's desire to challenge the child was the simple insistence that students should read only what they could understand. Both from among the normal-school spokesmen and from among old-line defenders of instruction in fundamentals came the complaint that teachers gave pupils readers too advanced for them. Since graded readers had become increasingly available in the middle years of the century, and since the number of books in each such series was increased in successive editions, teachers could keep a pupil reading through one book after another at a rapid pace, never stopping to find out whether he understood what he spoke out. Profusion of materials had the supposed advantage that it prevented students from memorizing material in the way that an infant would memorize and "read" stories that his mother had often read to him. It did less to promote depth and thoroughness of reading. It catered to the teacher who would lean on the

[34] William B. Fowle, *Teachers' Institute* (New York, 1866), 18, 24, 126.

textbook as crutch, avoiding the need to have much knowledge of subject matters himself, never questioning students in order to learn whether they understood. In time, the textbook writers themselves adjusted to this criticism—by including detailed, catechismic questions for the teacher to use. That would have deepened the dependency of the teachers, and consistent critics moved on to advocate an open-ended, topical form of recitation that could be sustained only by the pupil who comprehended what he read.

If reformers blamed the lazy teacher for haste and superficiality, they mended their fences with most teachers by blaming the ambitious parent. In many country schools, even in the 1860s, individual children read in whatever books their parents gave them to bring to the schoolhouse. While the stolid parent might give his future-dullard child worn copies of the Testament and of what little else he had himself read a generation earlier, the ambitious parent might send in with his older children some of the newly manufactured compendia of botany or moral philosophy. These selections determined the curriculum, especially if the teacher was insecure or merely politic and obliging. When book agents made graded readers available to parents who sent their children to ungraded schools, the ambitious would send in the more advanced volumes of a series. This continued the old heterogeneity of textbooks within the single classroom, and school reformers often called for statutory uniformity—which would increase the short-run textbook expenses of most parents or of the community. But even when a town or a district adopted a uniform series of readers this did not solve the problem that reformers saw. As these men described the scene, parents still brought pressure to bear on teachers to advance children as rapidly as possible from one book to the next. And when the school itself was graded, parents pressed teachers and principals to advance students as rapidly as possible from one grade to the next.

This interpretation blamed reading failure on a spirit of

excess, and only an occasional spokesman blamed some kind of deficiency. A manual issued by the Public School Society of New York in 1850 betrayed strong dissatisfaction with the speech patterns that children brought to school. During reading lessons, the teacher should insist on distinct articulation and enunciation, training the children in how to use the organs of speech for each sound. "Some of these points may be simply illustrated by directing the pupil's attention to the first attempts of an infant to speak, or to the imperfectly uttered words of a person intoxicated, or one speaking under the influence of anger. They may also be convinced of the necessity of slowness and deliberation, by detecting their own faults in the pronunciation of suitable examples given them for that purpose."[35] But the Public School Society had begun its career with intentions of uplift, and was about to collapse from its long fight against parochial schools. It seemed, by implication, to blame poor reading on the lower-class or immigrant origins of many children. By the early 1870s city authorities had labeled poor enunciation as a specific immigrant problem and were complaining that the teaching of reading beyond the elements had declined in quality, partly because of the pressure for time within a crowded curriculum, partly because of the weight of German and Irish children in the school population.[36]

For all the biases in any official or methods-conscious line, reports on learning behavior also varied widely from school to school. Some of the reported variation even made sense in terms of the normal-school line. Instruction was reported to improve in the villages and towns, which were sensitive to modernizing pressures and which sometimes hired normal-school students as teachers. It remained poor

[35] Public School Society of New York, *Manual of the System of Discipline & Instruction* (New York, 1850), 31.

[36] T. F. Harrison, in New York City and County Board of Education, *Annual Report*, 28th (1869), 214-215. See also *Annual Report*, 32nd (1873), 264-165.

in the country. But even where instruction was changing, it moved in divergent ways. The dominant direction was the official line, which was warm, diffuse, and primarily emotional. Its soft qualities did not keep it from being advocated by successful bureaucrats who were giving directions to their underlings:

> No one can read skillfully who does not appreciate the sentiment expressed in what he reads, or who does not feel for the time being as its author felt when he wrote it. He cannot read well of beauty who never saw anything beautiful, nor he of gayety, who never felt gay, nor he of sorrow who never evinced pity, nor he of wit who never enjoyed a joke.
>
> Our school classes seldom seem to feel what they undertake to read. . . .
>
> Such reading-lessons should be assigned as are calculated to interest the classes of pupils who are to learn them. If the feelings of children do not respond to the sentiments expressed in the lessons they read, it is not because their hearts are cold. Let the feelings be such as their child-nature can appreciate, and they will evince no want of sympathy with them. It is not difficult to make an application of this principle to all classes of those who are learning to read.
>
> The teacher should lose no opportunity of impressing upon his pupils the ennobling sentiments which he may find in the reading-lesson. Many occasions will present themselves to the watchful teacher of awakening in their minds a greater love for the beautiful, the true, and the good. . . .
>
> All education that tends to improve the taste and to give proper direction to the emotive nature, will be valuable preparation for the reading lesson.[37]

[37] James Pyle Wickersham, *Methods of Instruction* (Philadelphia, 1865), 224-225.

This view was compatible with the needs of a bureaucratic organizer because it put weight into the role of the individual teacher as a person, at a time when the main task of administration was that of building support for teachers who would work on their own in ungraded or barely graded schools, unhampered and unaided by daily supervision. Even Norman Calkins, who became the New York City system's expert on primary education in the 1860s, believed that reading instruction demanded a very unbureaucratic kind of teacher: "It is well for the teacher to read short sentences, and require the pupils to repeat them after her in concert, subsequently to have each pupil read the same alone. Thus it is seen that, to teach reading successfully, there must be a living teacher, and that teacher must be active in her work. Rules are of little use compared with the living example."[38]

Calkins stated for the city only one version of the normal-school line. All the leaders in the system opposed rote teaching, but they did not all oppose the use of rules to guide teachers in how to teach. It may be significant that Calkins addressed his instructions to women, who made up the overwhelming majority of the teaching staff in the primary schools (roughly, the first four grades). The grammar schools (covering approximately the second group of four grades) had a larger proportion of men teachers; and Henry Kiddle, who had responsibility for these schools within the system, picked up the observation that females, teacher and pupil alike, excelled at oral reading.

> Too much reliance is placed on the mere imitation and natural taste and appreciativeness of the pupil. On this account, from the superior refinement of taste, greater delicacy of appreciation, and finer sensibilities which they naturally possess, the girls in our schools far surpass

[38] N. A. Calkins, *Primary Object Lessons . . . a Manual for Teachers and Parents* (New York, 1861), 290.

> the boys in reading. In fact it is a rare thing to find a decidedly excellent reader among the latter. If our teachers would study reading more as a science, they would be far more successful in teaching it as an art.[39]

Beyond the question of sex differential, the Kiddle argument revealed a self-defeating tendency working within the system. Administrators were asking individuals, many of whom would never stand in front of classes for more than two or three years in their lives, to behave like natural teachers. Women might then rely on gush, but men—or so it seemed—could not. Techniques and mechanical rules were needed to help teachers who were weak at unmechanical teaching. But if men were insecure in performance because they lacked some requisite spontaneity, women were insecure in the system simply as women. And all teachers were vulnerable to the pressures of the organization itself. Here the events of the 1860s demonstrated that the pressures of system pushed many teachers toward the kind of hurried, mechanical teaching that the administrators of system professed to condemn.

Part of the pressure came from the means used to evaluate teachers. At least once a year in New York City an inspector from the city office visited each class and there examined the pupils on what they had learned. His rating of the class proficiency then became the official rating of the teacher's ability. The teacher who received an unsatisfactory rating two years in a row was supposed to leave the system. Again and again, teachers brought formal complaint against this procedure. At times they forced some adjustments, as in the degree of publicity given to the examinations or the ratings, or in whether the inspectors assigned numerical or descriptive ratings. None of this removed the continuing pressure, and the teachers forced a major hearing before the Board of Education in 1868. They complained that the examination system made no allowance for differences in the social background or motivation or

[39] New York City Board, *Annual Report*, 20th (1861), 28-29.

ability of the students they had to teach. They complained that the regulations imposed too heavy a program on pupils and teachers alike, and that the inclusion of petty reviews in the syllabus for each grade made it difficult for teachers to attend without anxiety to new material. They complained that they had to teach too many subjects. To all this, the heads of the system replied that the teachers were making most of the trouble for themselves. The regulations stipulated that a teacher was to inform the inspector how much her class had succeeded in covering, and that he was then to rate the class on how well they did on that specified material. If a teacher insisted on saying that a class had covered the whole material for a grade when they had not, she was simply yielding to pressure from parents who demanded that their children be promoted on schedule, or to pressure from principals who wanted enough children to be promoted so that each school could claim to have a highest grade among those grades formally allowed for that level of school. The principal of a primary school did not want to lose pupils to a special introductory grade at the grammar school for which the primary acted as feeder; and the principal of a grammar school wanted to have the advanced and supplementary classes that were required if he was to tell parents in his district that he prepared boys for the City College. Teachers themselves wanted to build political strength against principals or inspectors by gaining the favor of parents, and principals had their own interests in the system, distinct from the interests of both teachers and the administration. Although the regulations stated a policy of flexible promotion for individuals, and of modulated progress for classes, these allowances were little used. The set of conflicting interests worked to keep students on a path of mechanical, hurried, superficial progress. And pressure from parents or voters provided the energy to keep the whole going.[40]

[40] New York City Board, *Discussion before the Joint Committee on Studies, &c., of the Board of Education, (Appointed February 19th,*

Even the adjectives that James Fraser used to describe the intelligent reading he heard in one New York City class suggested a forced quality in what was happening: *loud, distinct, emphatic.* It was the tone of the system that seemed to determine the level and tone of what happened in the learning processes of individual pupils. On the surface, this would seem to suggest that only the city systems, or at most the graded-school organizations in the larger towns, were transmitting the kind of pressure that would produce, in large numbers of students, mechanical and superficial reading. But reformers and rural school inspectors made largely the same complaints about what children learned in the country. If there was any difference in the complaints, it was that the rural schools produced the humdrum, monotonous reading that comported with rote and tradition while the city schools produced mechanical, artificial, rule-bound reading.

With some reason, the observers tried to shift to parents some of the blame for this forced pace. Inspectors in both city and country complained that parents sent children as young as four to school, simply to get them out from under foot. Although the majority of parents probably waited until the children were five, or six, they did send enough of the very young to set off a wave of frustrated complaint from school officials in the 1860s, and they also sent older children in greater numbers during depression years when there was no profitable employment for them.[41] But since

1868,) in Reference to Modifications of the Course of Studies, &c. 1868 (New York, 1868).

[41] Hiram Orcutt, *Hints to Common School Teachers, Parents and Pupils; or Gleaning from School-Life Experience*, rev. edn. (Rutland, Vt., 1859), 111. Jacob Abbott, *Timboo and Fanny; or, The Art of Self-Instruction*, published with his *Virginia* (New York, 1855), 50-52. New York State, Superintendent of Common Schools, *Annual Report* (Albany, 1837), 5. New York Regents, *Annual Report*, 59th (1846), 74. State Superintendent, *Annual Report*, 1st (1855), 48-49; 9th (1863), 394; 10th (1864), 197-198, 217, 231-232, 258, 260, 267; 11th (1865), 197. New York City Board, *Annual Report*, 18th (1859), 65; 20th

they did not want the guilt of having neglected the children's education, they demanded that teachers produce measurable progress. Even in ungraded schools teachers used more of the reader-sets advertised by publishers, books numbered from first to fifth or sixth; these served parents as one visible standard. As the graded school became more common, parents could expect that their children would march up in regular annual sequence from one concrete situation—one teacher or classroom—to another. On the surface, this demand for labeled progress suggested pride taken in children, or at least vanity about them. To the extent that it was loving pride, it should certainly mobilize more intense learning ability in children anxious to deserve love. But the parental attitude as teachers reported it had also in it something of harshness. It carried a tone of emotional, even if not economic, exploitation. In twentieth-century psychological studies this kind of rejection turns up as a factor that encourages spatial or mechanical ability, even while it dampens verbal. Nineteenth-century culture certainly encouraged a verbal ability that ran to the compulsive and wordy. At the same time, the forcing needs of American families led children to rush through that verbalism in a mechanical way, never having the time to develop a relaxed involvement with their school words.

If the problems children met in reading stemmed from the ways parents acted in sponsoring children into the school system, the difficulties they met in arithmetic suggested less pressure than complacency about existing American abilities. Most observers agreed that teachers and pupils did better at arithmetic and other mathematical subjects than at anything else. Schools might spend too much

(1861), 50-51, 56-57. And see the attendance figures for Dutchess County in 1850, in the Appendix: they suggest that town parents, but not country parents, grew somewhat more likely to send their children (of any particular age) to school when there were many children at home.

time on arithmetic, but this only showed the secure place the subject had in popular attitudes. An inspector in northern New York explained: "A sort of ciphering mania has possession of the people and schools. Most of the people up here are New Englanders by birth, and prone to 'calculate' or 'reckon.' The calculating proclivity is a good thing, and gives assurance of economy and thrift, but with such a faculty ought to be cultivated an ability to give expression to ideas of economy and thrift, in good plain terms and grammatical language; this is neglected."[42]

Within this common ability, many observers reported a difference between male and female. For some, this was a difference among teachers, but since many teachers were recent products of the district schools, it was an indirect evaluation of how students were learning. An inspector in Sullivan County thought that he could allot praise and blame precisely: "Males are best prepared to teach grammar, arithmetic, (mental and written,) and are most deficient in spelling and reading. Females are best prepared to teach spelling, reading, and geography, and are most deficient in written arithmetic and grammar."[43] More objecttive data from New York City bore out this observation. During the early 1870s, in a fit of openness of a kind that does not always afflict school systems, the Board of Education published the examination scores of separate schools in the separate subjects. The girls' schools did uniformly better in all subjects except arithmetic. There the girls did only as well as the boys.[44] Although arbitrary selective processes might account for the generally higher level of girls'

[42] Report of Commissioner for Franklin County 1st District, in State Superintendent, *Annual Report*, 9th (1863), 214.

[43] State Superintendent, *Annual Report*, 10th (1864), 249. See also State Superintendent, *Annual Report*, 9th (1863), 395-396, 400; Josiah Clark, *The Parent's Monitor* (Boston, [1794]), 13-15; and "A Mother," *Thoughts on Domestic Education, the Result of Experience* (Boston, 1829).

[44] New York City Board, *Annual Report*, 14th (1856), 38-39; 23rd (1874), 222-225.

performance, the relative advantage of boys in the one subject is credible. Comments on the male advantage soon began to disappear, though, from reports about teacher qualifications, since the proportion of male teachers in the elementary grades was then dropping rapidly almost everywhere. Those who remained, at least in Greene County, seemed worthless: "The proportion of male to female teachers is as thirty-three to one hundred and twenty-seven; and of teaching, as fifteen to three hundred and twenty-five. A few males teach well, and but a few. The most of them are rather a damage than a benefit to their pupils."[45] But one of the more honest-sounding county superintendents was willing to concede the new female teachers more credit at routine tasks than at general culture: "The greater share of the female teachers seem to have little ambition for personal culture. . . . While they give a very good rote illustration in figures, and know well the relative geographical positions of this earth, they have no acquaintance with history or general literature—no thought beyond the frivolities of life; in short, want that thought, learning and preparation, which alone can fit them for their high trust."[46]

Such discrepancies fall into place if set into the framework that teachers used then in classifying branches of arithmetic. After pupils acquired facility in the elementary number combinations—and this, observers long assumed, was an easy task—they were to learn two kinds of problem techniques. In *mental arithmetic*, they progressed from oral practice in the elementary processes to oral solving of problems with real-life content. The main object of such work was to develop facility and spontaneity; but, because such problems could be difficult, pupils were given standard techniques for reducing problems to clarity, as by finding the price of a unit measure of the thing at issue, then work-

[45] Report by Commissioner for Greene County 2nd District, in State Superintendent, *Annual Report*, 13th (1867), 174.

[46] Report by Commissioner for Ulster County 2nd District, in State Superintendent, *Annual Report*, 10th (1864), 260.

ing from that unit measure to the desired quantity. Though such techniques were reliable enough, critics could ridicule them for ignoring intuitively obvious methods that would take less time. In *written arithmetic*, pupils had to work abstract number problems too long to be retained in the memory, and had to apply their skills to elaborate, supposedly practical commercial problems. Written arithmetic, more than mental, tended to retain the formal textbook problems and "rules" of eighteenth-century arithmetic (tare-and-trett, fellowship, and the like). Within both mental and written, the pupil might be asked not only to perform certain computations, but to explain what he had done. Reason-giving belonged more to mental arithmetic as a style. Thus a spectrum of tasks extended from the mere solving of written problems according to traditional rules, through to the giving of oral reasons why a problem in mental arithmetic had been handled in a particular way. Written arithmetic seemed to be the older discipline; mental, the more up-to-date. Mental, as introduced into America in 1821 by Warren Colburn, was concerned less with manipulating number in figures than with expressing number in words; it was, if anything could be, a nonquantitative approach to arithmetic.[47]

Observers in the schools reported, with great consistency, that teachers and pupils did well at written arithmetic, not so well at mental and giving explanations. Paradoxically, if anyone did relatively well in mental arithmetic, it was the men; and if the women did well at any kind of arithmetic, it was at the rote or written variety.[48] A relatively sophisti-

[47] [Warren Colburn], *Observations on the Method of Teaching Numbers, Proposed in the Following Sheets* (n.p., n.d.), 1-5. Roswell C. Smith, *Arithmetic on the Productive System* (Hartford, 1842). E.S.A., "The Study of Arithmetic," *New York Teacher*, 1 (1853), 176-178.

[48] Stone, *Elementary and Complete Examiner*, 69. County reports in State Superintendent, *Annual Report*, 9th (1863), 389, 400; 10th (1864), 170; 11th (1865), 198-199; 20th (1874), 332.

cated observer, Edward D. Mansfield, saw in this structuring of abilities, not so much a Yankee trait, as the defect corresponding to American virtues:

> Many respectable, and in most respects well-educated teachers, will perform any problem, and enunciate any rule upon the subject under examination, and yet be completely *nonplused* in any attempt to explain what they have done, or analyze the principles upon which it is performed. Nor is this, in my opinion, confined to any class of teachers; but it is a defect in some measure common to the majority, from the village school to the lofty university. The American mind, like that of its English ancestors, is more *deductive* than *analytical*. Nor would I have it otherwise; for it is the most useful, and, provided always there are philosophers enough in the world to do the reasoning and to make the rules, the most productive. It is a working and a thinking mind, too; but it works and thinks toward *results*, rather than *causes*.[49]

American students were slow at giving reasons for their procedures, but what educational needs did this indicate? Just as some people felt that reading would become more secure if based on strict training in spelling by pronounced syllables, so some felt that pupils in arithmetic needed a more thorough training in the tables of the basic operations. Critics like Burke A. Hinsdale in the 1870s or Francis Amasa Walker in the 1880s complained that students from the supposedly improved schools were not good enough at the basic skills. A generation earlier Jacob Abbott and one of his brothers had insisted in their Mt. Vernon text series that children needed more rote training. Abbott implied that pupils should be able to recite the multiplication table just as automatically as they did the alphabet—accurately and uninterruptedly, even in the midst of noise and distraction. Many other observers in New York made the same

[49] Mansfield, *American Education, Its Principles and Elements* (New York, 1851), 69.

point, especially when they said that students should not be allowed to go ahead to "higher" arithmetic or algebra until they had mastered elementary or mental arithmetic. They blamed those among teachers who had attended academies; there the would-be teachers picked up some smattering of algebra, which they then delighted in transmitting to the advanced pupils in one-room schools at the expense of time that they should have given to the beginners.[50] Here the spokesmen for the normal-school line agreed with those conservatives who kept harping on fundamentals and discipline. The normal schools, too, called for thoroughness, for quality of learning rather than quantity of coverage, for "not how much but how well." The occasional observer who did praise the teaching of algebra in the common schools[51] was apt to sound more up-to-date or "fast" than serious. Of course, the upper or supplementary grades of the New York City grammar schools did offer algebra, which was required for admission to the City College. But even the city school authorities thought that the drive to build college-preparatory classes had helped to encourage pressure and lock-step in the lower schools,[52] and they were still not sure

[50] B. A. Hinsdale, *Our Common Schools* (Cleveland, Ohio, 1878). Francis Amasa Walker, *Arithmetic in Primary and Grammar Schools* (Boston, 1887). Jacob and Charles E. Abbott, *The Mount Vernon Reader* (New York, 1835), 233-235; *Abbotts' Addition Columns* (New York, 1847), 70; Jacob Abbott, *The Mount Vernon Arithmetic* (New York, 1846), Title page. State Superintendent, *Annual Report*, 9th (1863), 205, 214, 356; 10th (1864), 170; 11th (1865), 161; 20th (1874), 332, 373.

[51] Report by Commissioner for Rockland County, in State Superintendent, *Annual Report*, 10th (1864), 217. H. N. Robinson, "Educational Reform," *American Journal of Education and College Review*, III (1857), 77-84, 235-240, developed the sophisticated argument that training in algebraic logic would give pupils the flexible, analytical understanding of arithmetic that they badly lacked; but this foretaste of the New Math was more than a little anachronistic.

[52] City Board, *Annual Report*, 16th (1857), 82-89; 18th (1859), 44-53; 20th (1861), 42-43, 51; 24th (1865), 29-31; *Discussion before the Joint Committee on Studies* (New York, 1868), 114, 132-136.

whether the City College (called the Free Academy until 1866), was an American-style college or a European-style *lycée.*

But drill in the elementary number combinations was not the only way out, even for that majority who felt that American students were weakest in mental arithmetic. Rather than imprinting the combinations on memory, the teacher might plant them as part of the natural thought-processes of the child. This was what Warren Colburn was trying to do when he imported and adapted concrete Pestalozzian techniques in an American text, and what other textbook-writers were attempting when they presented material in such a way that pupils could study number combinations "in the same manner as they practise reading lessons in the common language."[53] Curriculum reformers of the 1870s sought it when they imported the Grube method, in which the teacher trained pupils to make oral analysis of each whole number in succession, learning all the summations and multiplications that produced one number before they progressed to the next number.[54]

The stated reason for these naturalistic reforms was bound up in views of what American abilities had been in the past. The standard view was that American pupils in some earlier period like the beginning of the century had learned only a rote knowledge of arithmetic-by-the-rules, that they had perhaps developed considerable mechanical facility but had understood little, and that they had been vulnerable to any change in the kinds of problems that teachers or life presented.[55] All this the new methods were now trying to transform into a thinking child's approach

53 Charles Davies, *First Lessons in Arithmetic, Combining the Oral Method, with the Method of Teaching the Combinations of Figures by Sight* (New York, 1849), iv.

54 Louis Soldan, *Grube's Method. Two Essays on Elementary Instruction in Arithmetic* (Chicago, 1878). John Swett, *Methods of Teaching* (New York, 1880), 141-149.

55 See, for example, David P. Page, *Advancement in the Means and Methods of Instruction* (Boston, 1844), 17-25.

to number. But there was another view, which showed part of its character in the idea that Yankees or farm people had made a specialty of arithmetic, giving that study its strong position in the existing country schools. This rural aptitude lingered as a contrast to the mechanical habits that resulted from parental pressure.[56] William A. Alcott agreed that men observed correctly the rote evils of the 1840s, but he saw an earlier golden age of natural, thoughtful skill.

> Instead of teaching a child how to use his thinking powers, our ordinary courses teach him how to get along *without* using them. The old fashioned method which prevails among our farmers—or which did prevail half a century ago—of "reckoning in their heads," as it was called, is greatly preferable to the method of our schools—that of doing every thing by figures, and of having *no mind about it.* Our fathers were the true mental arithmeticians after all; and not our young disciples of Colburn. We are deceived by names. The name of Mental Arithmetic, when applied to that which is only an *apology* for thinking, will not answer the purpose.
>
> Whenever the processes of our schools, . . . shall come to fit the young for that head-work which their fathers aimed at, and in which they partially succeeded, then will they be worth something to us. But before this can happen, there must be a great deal more of sensible arithmetic taught among us. By sensible arithmetic, I mean the addition, subtraction, multiplication, &c, of fingers, corn, beans, apples, blocks, and other sensible or tangible objects.[57]

Through these lamentations and descriptions there seeped up what was at worst a mythical explanation of the capacities men and children showed for quantitative skill. This skill had arisen out of the needs of rural life; on that

[56] Charles Northend, *Obstacles to the Greater Success of Common Schools* (Boston, 1844), 15-18, 21-26.

[57] *District School Journal of New York*, v (1844-45), 239.

level it had been natural and reliable. But, at some more recent time, parents had begun to press themselves and their children away from too much reliance on the farm and its ways. While much of the older natural skill persisted, it began to decay into mere routine tradition even as pressure overlaid it with a formal, rule-bound mechanism.

Whether the implied explanation was valid or not, the description of American ability seemed unanimous, and it was confirmed by some of those foreign observers who seemed to complicate the picture of reading ability. Fitch in 1890 made the same kind of favorable report that he did on reading: because of the general use of the Grube method, American pupils escaped depending on mechanical application of rules; though perhaps less accurate than English pupils, they seemed to understand better the reasons for what they did. But Fitch seems to have described what he was shown of the very best teaching. Passy, five years earlier, had seen the analogy between the Grube method and the wide American use of the word method for initial reading instruction; he reported that American pupils did well enough in early lessons in which teachers used the Grube method, but that older students were too bound to mechanical rules and wooden business practicality.[58]

As with reading, some fault lay in the spirit of the system. Teachers and pupils alike, even when they attended to explaining a process, were said to mistake describing *how* they did certain things for showing *why* they so acted. And teachers, who themselves understood that textbook rules were misleadingly rigid, nevertheless failed to get that idea across to students. Some hope lay in the possibility that teachers failed as much in conveying rigidity as they did in conveying thoughtfulness. One school superintendent in Kansas City reported a classroom visitation in which the teacher objected to the visitor's asking children questions about fractions, which they had not studied, only to discov-

[58] Fitch, *Notes on American Schools*, 52-55. Passy, *L'instruction primaire aux États-unis*, 85-90.

er that the children offered intuitively correct answers without prompting.[59] "Natural" development, absorption of the logic of the subject, and exposure to the quantitative tasks of the American environment might be carrying the children further than official ideas expected.

But there was a historical flaw. During the long generations when schooling had puttered along in the localism of eighteenth-century practice, closeness to the people had not brought out natural teaching, but had simply permitted rote instruction to persist. When supposedly natural Pestalozzian techniques were imported into America early in the nineteenth century they at first made little impression beyond the visions and fads of the more precious reformers. Adding apples before adding abstract numbers, or symbolizing A by Apple instead of Adam, did not change much. On a high level, academic psychology might make much of perception as the first of the faculties to develop; on a lower level, phrenology might popularize the same idea. Educational theorists might translate these ideas into a conception of the order in which the faculties should be trained, beginning with the senses and perception. But few teachers did anything more with this idea than adopt the whole-word method as a "natural" way to introduce reading to children.

Then, in the 1850s, social workers and school administrators grew sharply more conscious that slum children were a mental as well as a moral problem. Street arabs knew little of the natural or crafted objects that other children saw in ordinary farmers' and clerks' households, yet they had so little verbal culture that men who wanted to preach at them needed to adopt an especially graphic, concrete style. Whether in New York City or Oswego, even administrators who accepted without qualm the new gospel of bureaucracy felt also that children entering the system had to be eased in through a period of object-teaching that would

[59] J. M. Greenwood, *Principles of Education Practically Applied* (New York, 1887), 158.

seem home-like and that would establish a concrete vocabulary common to teacher and pupils.[60]

Object-teaching was now taken up more or less independently by both public and parochial schools, and by both large-city and small-city systems. But because naturalistic reform was difficult in a large system like that of New York City, it was Edward A. Sheldon in Oswego who established his city's system and its normal school as the regional center for diffusing this new subject.[61] Even so, when the subject and its methods aroused controversy in the 1860s the critics concentrated their fire on bureaucratic, mechanical features that the system was displaying in practice. Just as expressive reading became elocution, just as mental arithmetic ran into formulas to be memorized, so object-teaching could degenerate into giving children long strings of abstruse descriptive terms with which to demonstrate

[60] New York City Board, *Annual Report*, 13th (1855), 19; 16th (1857), 28-30; 20th (1861), 90-91. Brooklyn City Superintendent, *Annual Report*, 2nd (1857), 21-25. State Superintendent, *Annual Report*, 8th (1862), 67-73. "The Object-System of Teaching in an Industrial School," Children's Aid Society, *Annual Report*, 11th (1884), 44-47. James Pyle Wickersham, *Methods of Instruction* (Philadelphia, 1865), 109-122, 151-160. Richard Edwards and J. Russell Webb, *Analytical First Reader* (New York, 1866), iii. Charles Loring Brace, *Short Sermons to News Boys* (New York, 1866), v. William N. Hailmann, *Outline of a System of Object-Teaching* (New York, 1867). William Wells, "The Infusion of Pestalozzi," *Christian Advocate*, XLIV (1869), 321. Alfred Holbrook, *School Management* (New York & Chicago, 1872), Preface and 255. *Teaching: Its Theory and Practice. A Course of Notes by the Brothers of the Christian Schools* (Westchester, N.Y., 1884).

[61] Edward Austin Sheldon, *Autobiography* (New York, 1911). Ned Herland Dearborn, *The Oswego Movement in American Education* (New York, 1925). S. S. Greene, Report of Committee of the National Teachers' Association, 1865, "Object Teaching; Its General Principles, and the Oswego System," in Henry Barnard, *Pestalozzi and His Educational System* (Syracuse, N.Y., 1881), 443-468. E. A. Sheldon, "Object Teaching," in *ibid.*, 469-478. Sheldon, comp., *Lessons on Objects* (New York, 1863). Sheldon, *A Manual of Elementary Instruction*, 6th edn. (New York, 1869), Preface and 146, 153.

their knowledge of common objects. The "graminivorous" horse and the "membranaceous" wing of a lady-bird were typical horror cases in the criticism, to which Sheldon simply replied that those were abuses, not the real thing. The most pointed attack came from a leader in the handling of mentally defective children—an area from which would later come Alfred Binet's pioneer work in measuring degrees of intelligence. Dr. H. B. Wilbur, superintendent of the State Asylum for Idiots at Syracuse, denounced the verbalism that he said the Oswego system imposed under the guise of naturalness, and it was only with difficulty that he could be persuaded to sign a compromise report that the National Education Association issued on the system in 1865.[62]

Beyond these terms the dispute did not go at the time, and much of its detail only reappeared in different form two decades later, in the child-study movement that was stimulated by G. Stanley Hall's inquiries into whether children were familiar with objects in the natural world. In the 1860s the positions of Sheldon and Wilbur were paradoxical. Both accepted the idea that children entering school needed to have a natural knowledge of things on which the teacher should build before proceeding to formal work on words. Sheldon was dealing with relatively normal children; he adopted object-teaching in order to meet the needs of children learning on schedule in the primary grades. Yet this method could be used in a spirit of distrust toward spontaneous knowledge. Wilbur, dealing with children whose existing knowledge was most certainly unreliable, showed himself the more willing to take the child out-

[62] H. B. Wilbur, "Object System of Instruction as pursued in the Schools of Oswego," in Barnard, *Pestalozzi and His Educational System*, 479-498. "The Education of Idiots," *New York Teacher*, VI (1869), 169-176. "Object-Teaching According to the Oswego Method," *ibid.*, VI (1869), 443-446. But compare the apparent change of editorial view represented by the excerpt from N. A. Calkins, *New Primary Object Lessons*, in *ibid.*, VII (1870), 324-327.

look as he found it. As a practical matter, each man considered most important the kinds of learning at which his own charges could best perform. But that did not settle the question: what was, or should be, the relation between the natural perception of objects and the culturally given use of symbols in the children with whom these teachers worked? Did deliberate attention to objects provide a basis on which minds could grow to abstract thinking, or did it simply provide a plateau in which children could find only formal rules and no growth?[63]

The controversy over object-teaching overlapped with the controversy over the effects of environment or heredity on mentality, which was emerging as Americans took up phrenological and then Darwinian notions;[64] and the irresolute character of the object-teaching controversy showed also in the way Americans have misinterpreted the one great contribution to educational research that came out of New York in that period. In 1874 the Prison Association of New York sent Richard Dugdale to study conditions in county jails. His given task was much like that with which Tocqueville visited America in the 1830s; what he produced, while hardly so elegant or so extensive as *Democracy in America*, had the same quality of mediating between local particulars and human universals. He found in one county a family of

[63] Note the caution expressed in Edward Brooks, *The Course of Study in Arithmetic for the Public Schools in Philadelphia* (Philadelphia, 1898), 12: "A child soon learns to think independently of objects, and it is a mistake to fetter the mind with things when it is ready for abstract thought."

[64] Jacob Abbott, *The Mount Vernon Arithmetic. Part II. Vulgar and Decimal Fractions* (New York, 1847), vii, expresses the indifference to hereditary distinctions of ability that was common among people thinking about small or ungraded schools. The opposing phrenological view is stated in O. S. Fowler, *Hereditary Descent: Its Laws and Facts Applied to Human Improvement* (New York, 1848), and John Hecker, *Scientific Basis of Education Demonstrated by an Analysis of the Temperaments and of Phrenological Facts* (New York, 1868), iii-viii, 126.

deviates and defectives who had contributed heavily to the institutional population, and he traced their forebears back to the Revolutionary period. His methodical citation of cases, his systematic summation of results in charts, and even such a device as his care in preserving the anonymity of persons and places, gave a modern cast to his efforts. He set himself the specific task of judging whether heredity or experience contributed most to produce deficiency. Because of his scientific tone, because of his obvious pessimism about the prospects for remedying defect in individuals, and because of the growing genetic outlook of his generation, people came to assume that he blamed imbecility and crime on physical inheritance, and they came to lump his book, *The Jukes*, with much bluntly hereditarian work. But that is not what Dugdale actually said. Though he did not rule out an important genetic effect, he concluded from the balance of his findings that crime and deficiency grew out of cumulated evil family conditions, which exerted compulsive effect on even the strong and able within a family.[65] His conclusions were transparent, but not to many readers.

Another similar case of social-service reporting in New York provides a key to why people misinterpreted Dugdale, and through that to a little of why they could not resolve difficulties within the problem of words versus things. From as early as 1823, philanthropists in New York City worked to block the spread of vagrancy and crime among children. In 1824 they opened the House of Refuge, to shelter and rehabilitate these newly labeled "juvenile delinquents." In order to collect funds their organizations issued reports that

[65] Richard L. Dugdale, *The Jukes*, 3rd edn. (New York, 1877). Edward Morse Shepard, *The Work of a Social Teacher, Being a Memorial of Richard L. Dugdale* (New York, 1884). Dugdale's report was part of a more general suspicion that rural areas of New York were perpetuating the cultural torpor of earlier generations. See the comments on country schools in State Superintendent, *Annual Report*, 21st (1875), 358; 24th (1878), 338-343; 26th (1880), 30-34.

assembled pathetic case histories of children led astray into lives of homeless vice. Beginning in the 1830s, and especially by the 1850s, these cases embodied a specific social diagnosis: immigrant families, unable to adjust to American life, brought and produced the great bulk of the children who became delinquents. Virtually without exception the children described had foreign parents. At a time when observers were noting the natural cleverness of unschooled slum children,[66] this pattern of cases supported a quite specific program. Philanthropists, at least Protestant philanthropists, wanted to use the House of Refuge as a way-station for funneling children to rural homes, homes that were usually Protestant and often located somewhere to the west. That program was served if they could describe the delinquent child as a sharp threat, but a threat somehow external to native American society. The only difficulty was that this presentation was dishonest. In the private records of the House of Refuge, a large part, but by no means all, of the systematically kept case histories were indeed those of Irish or German children. Although immigrant children were committed out of proportion to their numbers in the population, there was a large population of native Protestant delinquents whom the published reports no longer de-

[66] New York City Board, *Annual Report*, 17th (1858), 70-73; 19th (1860), 19. Micaiah Hill and C. F. Cornwallis, *Two Prize Essays on Juvenile Delinquency* (London, 1853), 9-10. [J. H. Allen], Review of Mary Carpenter, *Reformatory Schools* (London, 1851) and *Juvenile Delinquents* (London, 1853), in *North American Review*, LXXIX (1854), 415. E. H. Chapin, *Humanity in the City* (New York, 1854), 196-197. Samuel B. Halliday, *The Lost and Found; or Life among the Poor* (New York, 1859), 143. Edwin Wright, *Juvenile Criminals, and a Plan for Saving Them* (Boston, 1865), 12-13. Charles Loring Brace, *Short Sermons to News Boys* (New York, 1866), 33. Charles Dawson Shanley, "The Small Arabs of New York," *Atlantic*, XXIII (1869), 279-286. But compare the less lively opinion in School Committee Report, Dec. 4, 1863, and Principal's Report, June 7, 1867, in House of Refuge Board of Managers' Reports 1857-1880, House of Refuge Collection, Syracuse University.

scribed.[67] Donors preferred not to know that the problem of delinquency worked among their own kind of people, just as the readers of Dugdale refused the nongenetic, nonracial core of his argument. They could not unite to the image of a problem a detailed and honest analysis.

The social metaphor of race, the very concrete-looking family trees scattered through Dugdale's report, the specific objects presented for description in Sheldon's syllabi—all these offered a solid-seeming introduction to new understandings, but threatened also to simplify the thought beneath their surfaces. This weakness helps to explain a gap in the abilities that Americans displayed while moving from the lower-pressure life of the eighteenth century into the disillusioning demands of the nineteenth. Observer after observer insisted that skill at calculating was part of a traditional "ciphering mania." Other observers, almost as numerous, reported, or professed to remember, that the schools of earlier generations had not really taught much arithmetic. Massachusetts schools, for example, were not re-

[67] Histories, Volumes 1-32 (1824-1871), House of Refuge Collection, Syracuse University. Society for the Prevention of Pauperism in the City of New York, *Report of a Committee . . . on the Expediency of Erecting an Institution for the Reformation of Juvenile Delinquents* (New York, 1824). Society for the Reformation of Juvenile Delinquents in the City of New York, *Annual Report*, 1st (1825), 3-5; 10th (1835), 17-20; 13th (1838), 7; 14th (1839), 36; 25th (1850), 14-15, 28; 27th (1852), 23. Society for the Reformation of Juvenile Delinquents, *Examination of Subjects Who Are in the House of Refuge in the City of New-York* (Albany, 1825). Children's Aid Society, *Annual Report*, 1st (1854), 3-4, 23. Bradford Kinney Peirce, *A Half Century with Juvenile Delinquents; or, the New York House of Refuge and Its Times* (New York, 1869). William P. Letchworth, *Report on Dependent and Delinquent Children* (Boston, 1877), 5-19. C. L. Brace, "What Is the Best Method for the Care of Poor and Vicious Children?" *Journal of Social Science*, XI (1880), 93-103. Emma Brace, ed., *The Life of Charles Loring Brace, Chiefly Told in His Own Letters* (New York, 1894), 156-161. Francis Emmet Lane, *American Charities and the Child of the Immigrant* (Washington, 1932).

quired to offer arithmetic until 1789.[68] But observers also complained that the quantitative and the verbal abilities of earlier generations had depended much on rote processes and memory, even while they feared that Americans were losing the vocabulary of concrete and visual imagery that had been part of rural life. The learning of concrete imagery was supposedly relevant to American life, but attempts to make that learning explicit met little general response until after the middle of the nineteenth century. In all this, the puzzling elements are the lack of response to object-teaching and the inadequacy of earlier schooling to have produced the reckoning abilities of American men.

On these points, one of the forlorn early efforts at object-teaching provides some incidental but unifying comments. In 1827 Dr. John M. Keagy produced a little volume, *The Pestalozzian Primer, or, First Steps in Teaching Children the Art of Reading and Thinking*. The curriculum implicit in his text was hardly radical. Though Keagy provided lists of questions with which a teacher might stimulate children to think about the characteristics of familiar objects, he did not suggest using actual objects in instruction, and he suggested no real innovations over conventional methods of teaching reading. But he thought he was doing more, and gave reasons for his supposed departures. He ventured

[68] Warren Colburn, "On the Teaching of Arithmetic," American Institute of Instruction, *Lectures*, 1830, pp. 280-281. "Schools as They Were in the United States Sixty and Seventy Years Ago," *New York Teacher*, XIII (1863/64), 282. State Superintendent, *Annual Report*, 20th (1874), 284. "The Old School-House and the New; or, Fifty Years Ago and To-Day," *American Educational Monthly*, VIII (1871), 480. James M. Greenwood and Artemas Martin, *Notes on the History of American Text-Books on Arithmetic* (Washington, 1899-1900). Clifton Johnson, *Old-Time Schools and School-Books* (New York, 1904), 301. Walter Scott Monroe, *Development of Arithmetic as a School Subject* (Washington, 1917). Henry Lester Smith and Merrill Thomas Eaton, *An Analysis of Arithmetic Text-books* (Bloomington, Ind., 1942-1943).

> the position, *that we think in pictures and scenes.* . . . To exemplify the correctness of our views with regard to the influence of ocular perception and location in arresting attention and securing mental retention, we need only refer to the art of *Mnemonics*; an art whose sole dependence is upon the visible imagery and symbols which it calls to its assistance.
>
> . . . .
>
> Following out these views in a course of practical education, we ought to make *all nature a tablet of Mnemonic symbols*, with which we might *naturally* associate appropriate ideas. All the scenic ideas thus located would form a world of experimental facts to supply us with funds in our generalization of principles; or in other words, in the construction of our system of science.[69]

The very priggishness of his tone suggests that he was describing a mental strategy that was already common enough among Americans on a half-conscious basis. This strategy, similar to the "eidetic imagery" that later psychologists would use in explaining the freakish calculating abilities of some otherwise ordinary minds, may have been sufficiently well embedded in popular thought that people did not need to adopt curricula that made it explicit.

Even before Keagy produced his hint that both memory and systematic sciences might flourish in the individual whose life grounded him in the visual world, Americans were confronted with an arithmetical child prodigy who was clearly being forced by his family, but whose skills no family pressure seemed to explain. Zerah Colburn said himself later that he had learned the multiplication table by overhearing it, before he could read either words or the ordinary notation of figures. Soon enough his father began displaying him on the platform, forcing him on tours to the neglect of his real education. Just as when Frederick Doug-

[69] John M. Keagy, *The Pestalozzian Primer* (Harrisburg, Pa., 1827), 6, 7.

lass' early knowledge of family lore surprised the people around him in the slave quarters of a Maryland plantation, elders encouraged the able young one to think of his own ability as something miraculous. But if natural heredity provides no satisfactory explanation for such ability, neither does supernatural providence. Douglass, the young slave, had probably been listening to his elders telling stories before they realized that the still inarticulate infant could attend to things. Colburn, the young Yankee, had been absorbing the routines of calculating from what his relatives did aloud around the fireside—and before literacy had provided pencil-and-paper algorithms that could block him from developing flexible ways to work numbers in his head.

From Colburn's case to the general problem of Yankee ciphering ability is something of a leap, yet the very extreme character of his performance suggests much about what may have been going on. A society of isolated farm households, not consciously equipped to promote special abilities in its young, still could provide the kind of close family groups in which the infant could secure his own membership by absorbing ideas and skills from what the elders around him said. If this natural environment also provided the child with strategies that would help the working of some critical intermediate ability, then the general popular ability might be focused into precocity. For the *procedures* of arithmetic, it is not at all clear just what such strategies involved; certainly Colburn himself gave no satisfactory account. But for the *memory* required in any precocity, the literature on prodigies suggests that visual or spatial imagery was the most likely basis for the necessary strategy.[70]

[70] William A. Alcott, one of the writers who expatiated on Yankee calculating ability, used interchangeably the expressions, to "estimate" sums and to "reckon" sums. See his *Young Man's Guide*, 40th edn. (Boston, 1849), 214-215. Was it only accidental that he implied that popular ability involved some kind of non-precise shortcut?

This problem of the bizarrely talented calculator (or chess player)

As between verbal and numerical abilities, it is hard to say which was stronger in earlier American thinking, without entering into qualifications about what *kind* of verbal, or what *kind* of numerical, ability is involved. But among verbal, numerical, and spatial abilities, it seems possible that Americans were relatively weak at the first two, but strong in the third—and in those aspects of verbal and numerical thought to which spatial imagery might provide a shortcut. On one level this spatial strategy meant a willingness to think in terms of surface and appearance; on another it meant a willingness to make the most out of the familiar, secure scene of American rural life, which could be used as an ideal comparison scene in any assimilating of words to be remembered or foreigners to be naturalized. Relying on spatial imagery was one part of assimilating phenomena, appearance, surfaces, without stopping to analyze or challenge—without, that is, pausing to undermine the vivid, organizing, imprinting effect of the image. This literalness about images, even when the perception of them has been conditioned by social ideas, is often a mark of the chess or number wizard; but it is also a mark of the bigot. In the use of natural, familiar, dogmatic images to promote action and problem-solving, Americans have displayed a naive strategy that may run as a common theme through both their social reflexes and their Yankee abilities.

Of course, there were people who thought that mental problems could be internal to Americans, not just a wicked

---

has long been used as a test in discussions of the nature of intelligence. See especially the account of "Alfred Binet's Approach" in Joan Wynn Reeves, *Thinking about Thinking* (New York, 1965), ch. 7. Binet expected to find eidetic imagery more important than it turned out to be, but he did find some examples, and he found his wizards relying on strategic conceptions that ignored conventional notation for their problems. On Colburn, see *A Memoir of Zerah Colburn; Written by Himself. Containing an Account of the First Discovery of His Remarkable Powers* (Springfield, Mass., 1833), 15, 180, 182-83.

immigrant import. These were sometimes the same people, such as H. B. Wilbur, who harbored romantic doubts about the pressures that schools and other institutions transmitted to children.

Beyond the specifics of reading or arithmetic or any other subject, many reformers complained that the operation of the school system itself frustrated effects that it might have gained. Mary Mann agreed in principle with the idea common in the mouths of reform-sounding administrators who hired women teachers at low wages—that women might bring into the schools the true maternal spirit that would keep alive natural motivation. But when she looked at actual schools she saw "hard, knotty women" who transmitted the discomfort and routine of prescribed lessons. Alfred Holbrook said that teachers admitted that they would themselves have been restive under the methods of discipline they imposed on pupils. He declared against "this line of hereditary descent, in which each successive teacher becomes more pernicious than his predecessor." And he declared that object-teaching, supposed to foster continuity between nature and learning, worked in the large city systems as a mere "safety-valve" or as had bread and circuses in despotic Rome.[71] The mixture of systematic environment and naturalistic teaching had a manipulative quality, seeming rather to keep children in consenting relation to the system than to give as much of instruction as the children's own development would allow.

The extent to which the learning problems of children could depend on the attitudes and time-perspective of adults was indicated by a running dispute over whether instruction, when taking up the basic elements of motivation and technique, should handle them simultaneously or in sequence. The less anxious could accept the idea of working back and forth between interest and discipline through-

[71] Mary Mann and Elizabeth P. Peabody, *The Moral Culture of Infancy, and Kindergarten Guide*, 2nd edn. (New York, 1869), 105-107. Holbrook, *School Management*, 179-180, 244-247.

out the school years. This free and opportunistic temperament, which was to become identified with Parker and Dewey, did appear in some persons during the middle years of the century, but it was not the dominant tone. Even a clear-headed pedagogue like Edward Olney, writing on arithmetic for Henry Kiddle's *Cyclopædia of Education*, stated both views in a kind of uneasy and unresolved conjunction. He could in one context tell teachers that they should address themselves to different modes of thought at the same time:

> There are two distinct and strongly marked general aims in arithmetical study: (1) To master the rationale of the processes, and (2) To acquire facility and accuracy in the performance of these operations. The means which secure one of these are not necessarily adapted to secure the other. . . . But . . . there are . . . two general purposes—the theoretical and the practical—which must run parallel through all good teaching in arithmetic, . . .

But this joining of theory and practice did not keep him from endorsing also the concept of a sequence of learning stages, beginning with observation and ending in adult reason, stages to which the teacher should conform his methods and by which he should stratify his expectations of pupils:

> There are *three* stages of mental development which should be carefully kept in view in all elementary teaching: (1) *The earliest stage*, in which the faculties chiefly exercised are observation, or perception, and memory, and in which the pupil is not competent to formulate thought, or to derive benefit from abstract, formal statement of principles, definitions, or processes; (2) *An intermediate stage*, in which the reasoning faculties (abstraction, judgement, etc.) are coming into prominence, and in which the pupil needs to be shown the truth, so that he may have a clear perception of it, before he is pre-

> sented with a formal, abstract statement, the work, however, not being concluded until he can state the truth (definition, principle, proposition, or rule) intelligently, in good language, and in general (abstract) terms; (3) *An ultimate stage*, or that in which the mental powers are so matured and trained, that the pupil is competent to receive truth from the general, abstract, or formal statement of it.[72]

Although these two conceptions could be reconciled by allowing the intermediate, mixed stage to cover a long span of years, some advisers on teaching injected abrupt closure into what might have been the long flexible phase. One, who did believe that the teacher could lead children from a mechanical to a genuinely intellectual style of *reading*, advised that the teacher in arithmetic, once he had gotten the child to understand the logic of a particular kind of problem, should then require the child to memorize the exact words with which to explain the process, and accept no other form in recitation. The same reflex appeared in *How to Teach*, a manual that Henry Kiddle, Norman Calkins, and T. F. Harrison wrote as a generalization of their official instructions to New York City teachers. They urged leading the child from a merely concrete to a really "conceptive" style. But while they thundered against rote, they called for leading the child by induction to precise, accurate definitions, then having the child commit those definitions to memory.[73] It is easy to see why the New York City methods looked to a less anxious teacher like a scheme for enticing the child, by warmth and perception-catching objects, into a system of mechanism and routine. And the New York primary schools were so beset by large classes and pressure that

[72] Henry Kiddle and Alexander J. Schem, *The Cyclopædia of Education* (New York, 1877), 43-44, 45.

[73] E. V. DeGraff, *The School-Room Guide*, 2nd edn. (Syracuse, N.Y., 1879), 43-46, 225-226. Henry Kiddle and others, *How to Teach* (New York, 1874), 18-19.

there is great doubt how much warmth even penetrated the official use of object-teaching as an introductory device.

Greater consistency and warmth almost certainly marked the object-teaching done by Oswego teachers but there were rigidities there too. Both critics and defenders of the system saw in it a way to bridge the gap between family and school. Once the gap was closed, or once object-training had made up for the worst cognitive inadequacies of home background, then the city-type graded school could take over. Old-fashioned teachers, who admitted to imposing initial authority and initial precision in the tables of arithmetic, and initial precision in syllabic pronunciation and spelling, had some reason to feel that their conception of instructional stages permitted greater freedom of style in the later stages of schooling.

Interlaced with the concern over parallel versus sequential teaching ran the quantitative-verbal tension and the things-before-words dispute. The terms of these two dichotomies came close to cancelling each other out. In the quantitative-verbal pair, the verbal member carried the advantage of closeness to nature. Verbal ability was defined as facility, spontaneity, emotiveness. In the things-words pair, the verbal member carried the opprobrium of artifice. Henry Kiddle might call for reducing elocution to rules (that is, quasi-quantitative procedures) so that males could teach expressive reading; but Mary Putnam Jacobi, wanting to improve the capacity of women to study medicine, condemned the merely wordy, linguistic education that disqualified girls from thinking about real phenomena.[74] And Charles Davies, who produced a widely successful series of arithmetic textbooks by adapting and revising his product to conform to each new pedagogic fashion, fell into confusion when he tried to assimilate number instruction to linguistic consciousness, apparently for the benefit of teachers who shied away from number.

[74] Mary Putnam Jacobi, *Physiological Notes on Primary Education and the Study of Language* (New York, 1889).

> Having presented the combinations of numbers by the common language, we next teach them by means of figures: that is, we so train the mind that it shall, by the aid of the eye alone, catch instantly the idea which any combination of figures is designed to express. We thus present the combinations of figures purely through the arithmetical symbols, so that the pupil is not obliged to pause at every step and translate his conceptions into common language, and then re-translate them into the language of arithmetic....
>
> This is all to be done by *the simple process of reading;* and the method consists,
>
> 1st. In teaching the arithmetical alphabet, and
>
> 2dly. In teaching the combinations of the alphabet, which become the exponents, or signs, of ideas.
>
> After this is done, the pupils of a class should be taught to read together, all the combinations, in the same manner as they practise reading lessons in the common language.[75]

First Professor Davies offers quantitative thinking. Then he takes it away. Then he offers it again. Or does he? The point is not that the Davies formulation, or the Kiddle formulation, or the Mary Jacobi formulation, was typical of how teachers confronted children. There were many teachers—even teachers writing normal-school texts—who saw the problems of instructional style in an unorganized, conventional way, who saw reading tasks as one problem, arithmetic tasks as another problem, geography tasks as another, and disciplinary tasks as yet another, each to be handled in whatever way worked. But when teachers in that generation did try to think systematically, they displayed frequent anxiety, and sometimes outright confusion, about relating properly the three areas that were reality-perception, quantitative thought, and verbal thought.

[75] Davies, *First Lessons*, iii-iv. For a bitter comment on Davies as a textbook-producer, see [Joseph Ray], *An Exposure of the Falsehoods of "Justice"* [Cincinnati, 1854].

The anxiety that teachers felt about cognitive strategy overlapped with a hardly concealed anxiety about the defining of male and female roles in the society, and that in turn with anxiety about how to control sexual behavior. Though this diffuse uncertainty and fear was logically grounded in family problems, it produced many symptoms within talk about intellectual training. It rested on the contradiction between traditional moral guide-lines and the desire for intensity between teacher and child. The traditional view rejected both leadership for women and promiscuous social life for children, as was stated plainly in two rules in a Rochester teachers' magazine. The first point was peremptory enough: "Never bring forward young ladies, or girls, to make a display of themselves, or of their learning, before an assembly of spectators. This rule is according to nature, reason, and the Bible." But wouldn't a female teacher's class be an "assembly of spectators," however childish? And the second rule was of a piece with the first: "Pupils should never be allowed to mix in company with each other, without the presence, supervision and control of a parent, or a duly authorized teacher, or a trusty regulator. This rule is essential to prevent the vitiating tendencies of schools, now reckoned to be one of the greatest dangers of this free republican nation."[76] Much of this social fear led to a simple solution—private or "select" schools, where the children of the respectable would not be contaminated by mixing with the progeny of the low. The managers of such schools were explicit in *not* taking for granted that their pupils would come from proper families. Notably in the 1860s school after school advertised that it would not take pupils who had vicious habits, or who had not been subjected to proper restraint at home.[77]

[76] "Notes on Teaching," *Monthly Educator*, 1 (1847/48), 83.

[77] *Catalogue of the Officers and Students of Friends' New York Yearly Meeting Boarding School. Incorporated under the Name of Friends' Academy, at Union Spring, N.Y. For the Year Ending 9th Month, 14th, 1866* (Auburn, 1866), 16. *Mount Pleasant Academy, a*

Part of the problem was that people could not make up their minds to believe that children were capable of a spontaneous sensuality that they had not learned from others. True, a headmaster-clergyman with Calvinist leanings could argue,

> The amount of evil in most schools is over-rated and mis-stated. The character of the evil is often not even understood. Where domestics are employed, and where any companions are allowed to associate with children, they will be exposed to as much evil at home as at school, not infrequently to more and greater evil. To isolate children so perfectly as to cut them off from all contact with evil is not practicable, nor is it desirable; but if children are shut up, a kind of prisoners, within rooms and yards, separate from all playmates, they will yet corrupt themselves. This may not be in the ways and with the words of school-boys, but in ways and with words equally bad. We cannot bring a clean thing from an unclean; children *in puris naturalibus*, under the most favorable of domestic circumstances, if yet suffered to be together a few hours every day, will demonstrate the truth of David's words, who confesses that "he was shapen in iniquity."

But the same man would still insist that keeping children out of school would be preferable to sending them to a morally bad school: "Nay, solitary wickedness and idleness are not so bad as the associate and combined."[78]

Select Boarding School for Boys, at Sing Sing, Westchester County, New York. Maj. W. W. Benjamin, Superintendent (New York, 1865), 23-24. Adelphi Academy, *Annual Circular*, 7th (1869), 17.

[78] Baynard R. Hall, *Teaching, a Science: The Teacher an Artist* (New York, 1848), 163-164, 169. Hall stated, carefully, a concern about schools that recurs in the prurient pseudo-scientific literature of phrenology; see the often-reprinted Orson S. Fowler, *Amativeness, or Evils and Remedies of Excessive and Perverted Sexuality*, 14th edn. (New York, 1852), 13. See also Alcott, *Young Man's Guide*, 306-354, and Abraham Jacobi, "Masturbation and 'Hysteria' in Young Children" (1875), *Works* (New York, 1909), II, 403-438.

Teachers' language sometimes showed that they felt a contrast, not between solitary vice and social, but between solitary preoccupation and a satisfactory pupil-teacher relation. Children at the innocent age might not present the problem: "It has, doubtless, been observed by most persons, that it is not unfrequently the case that a child six or eight years of age reads better—more distinctly, more naturally, and more understandingly, and therefore more entertainingly to others—than it ever does after. . . . It has not yet learned to read aloud to others, while indulging in silent reverie on more interesting matters of its own, perhaps better adapted, choice." But once the child had begun to withdraw his absorption, the teacher would have to court him: "In speaking and in reading aloud, as in giving, there are always two parties, and each has a positive duty to perform. . . . Let the complaint be, in every case, that you can not get the sense, you do not understand, you do not enjoy the reading, giving in every case the specific cause for your complaint, and suggesting the remedy for the evil; and when you lose the sense, or think that the pupil does not understand, let him read it over again, and repeatedly do so till you are mutually satisfied."[79] Simply enough, teachers wanted to harness to instruction the impulses and social spirit of children; but the moral standards of the age did not always permit them to express this object in a direct, matter-of-fact way.

As commentators took a more positive attitude toward womanly, maternal roles in teaching, they sometimes combined insight with a willingness to use both group pressure and female influence in order to divert childhood energies from indulgence into learning. While some teachers feared even object-teaching as a form of sensationalism that would encourage dangerous emotions,[80] a writer like Mary Mann

[79] B., "Learning to Read," *New York Teacher*, v (1855/56), 259, 263.

[80] "The Artificial Production of Stupidity in Schools," *American Educational Monthly*, x (1873), 445-451.

had sufficient confidence in purity and repression that she could let herself recommend a strong emotional tone for the classroom. A thumb-sucking boy she would deal with by tying his hands behind his back, and by enlisting the class to sympathize with him in his efforts at self-control. She hardly wanted emotional or intellectual privacy for children:

> As the germ of the maternal sentiment is in all women, relations may be established between teacher and child that may take the place of the natural one, so far as to answer all the purposes required. Such a relation is the only foundation upon which a true education can go on. It leaves no room for division of interests between child and teacher, which division alone has the power forever to destroy all the best benefits of the communication of mind, and is generally, indeed, an effectual barrier against any *communication* at all. Such a relation as I would have does away with every feeling of reserve that might check the full and free expression of thought and feeling. . . . When my little scholars call me "mother," which they often do from inadvertence, I feel most that I am in the true relation to them.

But she did not feel that women teachers could act in this way so long as they were directed by school committees composed of any but other women; until then, such trust in "their own instincts about the children" would be simply a "stolen liberty."[81]

During renewed controversy between public-school spokesmen and their critics, in the 1860s and 1870s, the role of female teachers emerged as one point of contention—the critics censuring reliance on females, the spokesmen defending both that reliance and the bureaucratic context within which it progressed.[82] This disagreement set into

[81] Mary Mann and Elizabeth P. Peabody, *Moral Culture of Infancy* (1869), 107, 116-117, 123-124.

[82] Burke A. Hinsdale, *Our Common Schools* (Cleveland, 1878),

opposite camps the elements of a concern that had worked within some minds as ambivalence and uncertainty. Even a woman who feared the influence of "precocious" delinquent boys on society could also blame slip-shod learning on the "effeminate, ease and pleasure-loving age."[83] And a man who insisted that female teachers should be directed by a "strong-minded, clear-headed, thoroughly educated, male principal" could also show himself complacent about the blandishments that female teachers would use: "Their manners are more pleasing to the young; and (what must not be overlooked) they excel in personal attractions, which are eminently ancillary to the acquisition of a moral power over the youthful mind; and which we must acknowledge are ever potential in their influence upon the most unimpressible of our sex."[84] The schools themselves communicated anxiety about sexual behavior, and even more confusion or uncertainty about the male and female roles that observers then, and psychologists since then, have been convinced have real effects on the cognitive behavior of children. And this communication of learning problems to pupils was connected with the bureaucratic administrative problems of schools.

Something of the interaction between organizational style, sexual problems, and attitudes toward learning was displayed in the affairs of Adelphi Academy, in Brooklyn, over the years from 1863 to 1876. As first organized in 1863, the Academy was very much the select school, disclaiming corporal punishment yet spelling out its intention to enroll no pupil guilty of obscenity, profanity, or "a habit of vice." It strove also for the flexibility of the old-fashioned acad-

---

21-43. Andrew J. Rickoff, *Past and Present of Our Common School Education* (Cleveland, 1877), 79-87.

[83] Mary B. Tenny, "Essay on Thoroughness in Teaching," *New York Teacher*, II (1853/54), 231-233.

[84] A. C. Paige, in Schenectady Board of Education, *Annual Report*, 1st (1856), 50.

emy, omitting any mention of its pupils' ages in its announcement, and describing how its examinations would be frequent, informal, and helpful. It grew rapidly, especially in the elementary grades, and soon announced plans to begin object-teaching. In 1876 the school began a new building, with none other than the greatest local celebrity to give the cornerstone address: the Reverend Henry Ward Beecher. He praised the school for reviving the virtues of the old district school (in contrast to the new city schools), he praised it for emphasizing physical training (which was taught by T. J. Ellinwood, the stenographer who reported Beecher's sermons for the press), and he praised it for educating boys and girls together (which it had just begun to do that year).

But this regime of the informal and physical, protected by strict moral rules, was not to last. Though the school was not incorporated, not subject to the Regents' regulations, it could only suffer from the fact that the Regents' written examinations were beginning to establish a prestigious standard. And the larger world of business and colleges provided a context whose standards were also hard to escape. In 1869 a committee of local men, including the textbook publisher Alfred S. Barnes, bought the school, incorporated it under the Regents, and brought in a new principal from Yale. Ellinwood stayed on for a while to teach "Vocal Culture and Phonography"; but the school's bulletins began to describe its examination requirements in stricter terms, its moral requirements in less explicit terms (asking simply "unblemished moral character"). Over 1874 one of the school's old friends suffered social reverses, when Theodore Tilton named the Reverend Mr. Beecher in an adultery case. By 1876 most of the old faculty had left, including Ellinwood, and the school seemed to have come through a cycle of modernization. It did retain some of its old emphases, such as coeducation, which was supposed to make "boys more manly and girls more ladylike"; but it based these modern, home-like virtues on the security of a place in the larger educational bureaucracy.[85] From patronage by Beecher the celebrity to patronage by Barnes the information tycoon—this was the transition that was only just beginning to disinfect the uncertainties that men felt about the emotional problems of learning.

Behind all the uncertainties of observation and reporting, behind too the preconceived notions that served instead of reporting, the pattern of observation indicated what kinds of learning problems children were actually experiencing.

The most serious problem, taking many forms, was an inability to accept learned ideas and techniques as having much to do with ongoing real life. This was clearest in reading, where lack of expression in oral performance indicated children's refusal to adopt even the fiction of assimilating material to their own personalities. From the viewpoint of their own real interests, or even of how an outside observer would define reality, they might have had every reason to reject much of the matter that teachers gave them. And though rote instruction in subjects like geography may have induced the most absurd examples of failure at assimilating, that failure worked at an emotional level that indicated more than mere pedagogical neglect. Whether in the verbal or the quantitative sphere, children seemed amply impressed with the importance of getting at symbolic knowledge and manipulation, yet less able to cut loose and act or work with that knowledge. They might be developing ideas on their own, no matter whether out of some innate developmental schedule or out of response to the larger environment, but these self-developed ideas had little way to feed back into the formal learning process. The young mind was competently empirical in one sense: it could absorb the automatic responses and rule-of-thumb techniques by which

[85] Adelphi Academy, *Annual Circular*, 2nd (1864), 10-13, 15-20; 4th (1866), 13, 24; 5th (1867), 5, 12-14, 33-39; 7th (1869), 3, 17; *Annual Catalogue*, 1872, pp. 12, 17, 19-21, 32, 35; 1876, pp. 14-16.

it became a productive member of society. But it was not empirical in the higher, active sense: it could not set up an interchange between ideas, needs, and external reality.

A second problem, the tension over male and female cognitive roles, discouraged subtle development in either verbal or quantitative ability. The society was adopting the assumption that verbal and numerical abilities were sex-typed —an arguable idea at best—even while it was communicating uncertainty about what things male or female could do best within school organizations. In part, this uncertainty was realistic: the real difficulty in any simple sex-typing is that practical problem-solving requires interplay between verbal and quantitative, global and analytic styles of thought. When children accepted a rigid or anxious sex-typing of abilities, routine numerical tasks and the more mechanical among linguistic skills (such as spelling and parsing) might cause little trouble. Anything involving connected discourse would cause trouble. The schools were in fact turning out the nation of readers that observers described, but when failures occurred in this process they were apt to be failures at dealing with any but the most literal, unprobing concepts.

Third, there appeared some signs of strained overcompensating for these very problems. Pupil inability to give verbal explanations of problems in arithmetic led teachers to dish out explanations for students to memorize. Pupil inability to respond naturally to verbal material led teachers to accept the quackery of the elocution movement. The seeming inability of pupils to associate real-life meanings with words led to the precisionism of some object-teaching. These strains added some reinforcement to the very artificialities they were intended to relieve.

Finally, students tried to learn too quickly in the early stages. This took several forms, some of them apparently at odds with each other. In some cases, it meant study of only the bare fundamentals and the ignoring of all refinements and diversions. In other cases, it meant rushing on to prestige subjects like algebra or philosophy without adequate attention to arithmetic or general reading. But in the first situation the fundamentals were not being given enough accompanying matter to join them to the whole mind; and in the second, haste showed itself in the raw. In either form, haste facilitated the embracing of the central problem, which was an inability to mobilize some working relation between the processes taught by the school and the perceptions or intuitions taught by reality. The "high pressure" of new school systems helped to force haste and had to be contained by hermetic bonds that strengthened the barrier between school and reality.

Over the years from 1750 to 1870, the learning behavior of pupils gained in pace, and probably in some kind of efficiency. But that gain exposed gaps between skill and reality and between precision and intuition. Genuine progress seemed threatened by disjunction.

There remained the strong possibility that Americans were thinking in ways less rigid than observation of schools suggested. This possibility rested partly on the attitudes that children brought to the school in the first place, yet partly also on the success that practical men scored in building a culture outside any schools.

These topics—the early socialization of children and the working out of the end-products of education—may also fill in obvious gaps in the evidence about how learning problems changed after 1750. A fair amount of evidence shows how teachers saw change in pupil behavior during the middle of the nineteenth century. Only wisps of evidence and later memory or tradition say anything about the middle of the eighteenth century. Though evidence on colonial child-raising and styles of thought is also meager, compared to that on similar topics for the later period, the colonial scraps should multiply, not simply add to, each other. Child-raising practices may not automatically determine later learning problems, any more than schooling determines the nature of cultural products. But infants, pupils, and adult workers were part of the same changing culture. If that culture was moving on coherent lines, then infancy and maturity may give a fix on childhood.

THREE

PARENTS' NOTIONS AND CHILDREN'S MINDS

AMERICANS, until about 1750, and many of them long after that, professed a standard for child-raising that had all the surface traits of the good strong paternalistic family of nostalgia and tradition. But the fears that some men stated and the criticisms that other men leveled against that standard reveal now that that kind of family life had a layered, ambivalent, unstable quality. Order seemed always in danger of running out into indulgence and torpor. About 1750, following the prescriptions of English reformers, Americans began to revise their standard, converting the model from that of the strongly governed family to that of the family whose children governed themselves with the aid of consciences implanted during early infancy.

The two standards were not completely different. They shared a conviction, at first undisturbed, that the father had the right to rule, by whatever means recommended. No one supporting either view thought that parents should indulge children, and all writers warned against spoiling children or letting them grow up to be self-willed. At the same time, all concerned tried to keep some balance. Just as they urged that a husband should observe the spirit of love in exercising authority over his wife, so they warned against any unnecessary harshness or passion in the governing of children. They warned parents against selfishness and condemned any parents who indulged themselves by neglecting the training of children. And whether men concerned themselves with religious training or more general character training, they insisted on the importance of early education, beginning as soon as the infant could receive any impressions at all. In this broad area of agreement, they were stating the attitudes that have seemed mere common sense during much of the history of Western society, and they were stating some attitudes that have continued as unofficial common sense during all the shifts in family life during the twentieth century.

This broad agreement may be unimportant, however much it may distinguish Western culture from other cultures. In the same way, there may not be much final importance in whether all families followed out all the specified child-raising techniques—either those recommended to them or those ascribed to them. As some psychologists have pointed out, the specific techniques have less effect on children than does the spirit in which they are applied. The standard Western child-raising practices can have one meaning in one atmosphere, another in a different atmosphere. And the best clue to the family atmosphere—to its administrative climate—may be the kind of criticism and innovation that men are willing to undertake within so stable an institution.

One of the fullest, most influential statements of the older way was set forth by Richard Baxter, that seventeenth-century Anglican evangelical whose industry in writing has made him an inescapable source on Puritan social standards. Baxter's conception of that way was implied in the two different definitions that he gave to the family, in his *Christian Directory*. First he gave a descriptive definition, saying that the complete family consisted of four parts: a father, a mother, a son, and a servant. If not an extended family in any anthropological sense, it was at least a household, not a mere nuclear family. But Baxter chose also, in the scholastic manner common among Puritans, to define the essence of the family. This essence required only two parts: "pars imperans, et pars subsida."[1] The exercise of government, not affection or child-raising, was what made a family. Ac-

[1] Richard Baxter, *A Christian Directory* (London, 1825), III, 50. First published 1673.

tually, he distinguished little between government and education: when setting out the motives that should induce a man to look to the government of his household he included the argument according to political stability, which was to turn up later as a major part of much American argument for attention to education. "Well-governed families tend to make a happy state and commonwealth; a good education is the first and greatest work to make good magistrates and good subjects, because it tends to make good men."[2] Within this kind of family, governing well was, however, an end in itself, or at least a means to more of itself as the continuing end and standard. This government for the sake of more government was certainly true of the stern side of parental technique:

> "Train them up in exact obedience to yourselves, and break them of their own wills." To that end, suffer them not to carry themselves unreverently or contemptuously towards you; but to keep their distance. For too much familiarity breedeth contempt, and emboldeneth to disobedience. The common course of parents is to please their children so long, by letting them have what they crave, and what they will, till their wills are so used to be fulfilled, that they cannot endure to have them denied, and so can endure no government, because they endure no crossing of their wills.[3]

But parents should accompany this strictness with much love, in order to keep children from distrusting the parents, from concealing their childish actions, or from fleeing to other society—and in order that the children accept occasional severity as in their own interest. The central idea in all this was not the anti-spoiling logic, which was a staple in many kinds of child-raising advice, nor the desire to break the child's will, which was to persist even within later humanitarian standards, but the simple assumption that

[2] *Ibid.*, III, 101.

[3] *Ibid.*, III, 177.

government and severity were continuing processes. When Baxter warned the parent to correct his children discriminately and dispassionately, when he said that the parent should quote appropriate Scripture and adjust the nature of the correction to the temper of the child, he was in the first place assuming that correction should be administered as a standard thing in the treatment of children old enough to understand Scripture.[4] And "correction," in the vocabulary of the period, usually meant whipping.

The continuing atmosphere of government was also the central feature of many treatises on the family that appeared in America during the early part of the eighteenth century. Benjamin Wadsworth of Boston and Harvard described *The Well-ordered Family* as one in which parents should govern and correct children, and children should bear chastisement patiently.[5] In New York, a short-lived magazine of 1755, *The Instructor*, revealed the same basic assumptions even while it described the abuse of government by that father-surrogate, the teacher:

> Soon after the Infant is weaned, and the Nurse dismissed, the little Creature is put into the Hands of a Tutor, or Schoolmaster; who endeavors to harden his tender Skin, with the Rod and the Ferula. And now the young Brain must be ploughed and harrowed, to prepare it for receiving the Rudiments of Grammar; which, if the Head be not capable of retaining, the Hands and Back must smart for it. This Discipline may indeed be tolerated, provided it is only exercised to the Child's Advantage: for, as Valetudinarians take disagreeable Medicines to improve their Constitution; untoward Youngsters may submit to Correction, when they know that every Lash, and every Knock is a Token of Love: tho' many a Boy may say with the Poet: "*A foce de m'aimer tu me rends miserable.*" But

[4] *Ibid.*, III, 90-96, 178, 187-189.

[5] Benjamin Wadsworth, *The Well-ordered Family*, 2nd edn. (Boston, 1719), 55-56, 94.

> Masters usually dispense Correction according to the innate Acid of their own Tempers; and retaliate upon the Backs of others, those Stripes they received when School-Boys themselves.[6]

The setting here is first the family, then largely the school, but the sequence of atmospheres at various stages in the child's life is approximately the same that was assumed by Baxter: relative mildness in infancy, then recurring correction for many years after that. Baxter, to be sure, censured the early mildness, but he and some Americans who followed him still assumed the same long swings in the cycle of family discipline. This rhythm was assumed whenever preachers urged on parents the duty of "family government."[7] It was assumed in repeated American reprintings of Daniel Defoe's *The Family-Instructor*, until near the end of the eighteenth century: Defoe followed the Baxter line, insisting that parents exercise authority even after their children were grown.[8]

The weakness in this older concept of family was the point that Baxter criticized: the frequency with which parents neglected early education, postponing discipline until children were accustomed to acting without it. This is also the point at which John Locke and others applied revisions. The older family did not live as any neat collection of ruling part and subordinate parts, in the way that Baxter formulated its essence. Actual families did not consist only of father and son. They included also mother and servants,

[6] "A Sketch of Human Life," *The Instructor*, April 17, 1755, p. 25.

[7] Josiah Smith, *The Young Man Warn'd: or Solomon's Counsel to His Son. A Discourse Delivered at Cainhoy, in the Province of South-Carolina* (Boston, 1730), 19, 20, 28. Society of Friends, *Advice and Caution from Our Monthly Meeting at Philadelphia, Held the 25th Day of the Sixth Month, 1732, Concerning Children and Slaves* [Philadelphia, 1732], 7. *The Poor Orphans Legacy* (Philadelphia, 1734), 37. John Barnard, *A Call to Parents, and Children* (Boston, 1737), 20, 26, 32-33.

[8] [Daniel Defoe], *The Family-Instructor* (Philadelphia, 1792), esp. Part III.

and these intervened between father and child. Sometimes they were in fact stronger-willed than the Baxter theory allowed. Especially during the early years of a child's life, they could surround the child with an atmosphere of maternal indulgence *and* continuing correction. The strains that this tension imposed have been described by Edmund Morgan in his accounts of colonial American families, whether the Puritan families of the seventeenth century or the Virginia families of the eighteenth. These strains added acute tenderness to the motives that led some parents to send growing children into other men's households to be educated, whether as apprentices or as gentlemen students. Only someone other than the natural parents could apply the required severity without flinching and recoiling toward the old indulgence.[9]

In America, as also in Britain to some extent, sending children outside the household did not always mean putting them into other, possibly well-governed families. Increasingly, it meant letting adolescents go out into the world on their own. Without continuing correction, what emotional supports would sustain such children? And how could the family itself be relieved of the tension between civilized paternal authority and archaic maternal indulgence? On these questions, the physician and philosopher John Locke provided answers that became available to people after about 1700.

His larger intentions did not differ much from Baxter's. He was working out a secular, rural equivalent to the other's latter-day Puritanism. Where the preacher urged ways to preserve the spiritual welfare of people who were caught up in the insecurities and ambitions of seventeenth-century England, the political physician urged ways to preserve the gentry from temptations toward urban display or social ambition. Their common attitude, preservative rather than ex-

[9] Edmund S. Morgan, *The Puritan Family* (Boston, 1944) and *Virginians at Home* (Williamsburg, Va., 1952).

ploitative, was proper in any thoughtful, temperate intellectual of their period.

Locke told gentlemen fathers to raise their children in the same natural, tough, unconstricted way that (so Locke thought) honest farmers and substantial yeomen raised theirs. They should give plain, unstimulating food, rough and loose clothing, much time in the open air. They should inure children to all kinds of weather, taking only the barest precautions against exposure. As children grew older, fathers should adjust the details of education in order to fit children for lives of simplicity and attention to business. They should avoid pedantic methods of teaching the learned languages. They should value travel as a part of education—but not by susceptible adolescents, who might only be corrupted.[10] The social aim of his advice was conservative.

Not so the emotional aim. This was reactionary—that is, aimed at preserving traditional values through specially defensive, antitraditional means. In the same passage in which he described the "gentleman's son" as "white paper, or wax" whom the father could mold in any way he wished, he also exhorted fathers to "be so irregularly bold, that they dare venture to consult their own reason, in the education of their children, rather than wholly to rely upon old custom."[11] Before everything else, "old custom" meant letting mothers and nurses ruin the early training of children. Locke's famous *tabula rasa* or white paper had a psychological, developmental meaning. However much Locke the philosopher may have assumed that the human mind began life with no content, no innate ideas, Locke the physician did not think this about the real infant just starting life in the real nursery. In his specific instructions on handling infants, he did not use the *tabula rasa* image, but described infants as "flexible waters" whose courses could be directed

[10] John Locke, *Some Thoughts Concerning Education*, in *Works* (London, 1823), IX, paragraphs 4, 9, 10, 163-168, 212-214.

[11] *Ibid.*, paragraph 216.

in any way the father wished.[12] Locke's desire to preserve the child's flexibility and pliability showed in his advice against putting tight clothing on children. That constriction against growth he blamed on women, who "destroy their young ones by senseless fondness, and too much embracing." It was, especially, "fond mothers and foolish servants" who plied very young children with too much food, including too much meat at a time when Locke thought children should best abstain from "flesh" altogether.[13] Parents, especially mothers, were apt to indulge their own appetites by indulging the appetites of children, using them as mere toys.

But the essence of virtue, as Locke saw it, was the ability to follow reason in denying one's own desires and appetites. This was not natural. The mind had rather to be "made obedient to discipline, and pliant to reason, when at first it was most tender, most easy to be bowed."[14] To do this the father should make a practice of denying the child liberty, of denying it anything that it particularly wished to have. Absolute consistency in this course would then permit the parent to avoid severity in later years. In this Locke was deliberately reversing the sequence of indulgence first and continuing authority afterward,[15] which was assumed in the life of the older, much-governed family. To parents he advised: "Fear and awe ought to give you the first power over their minds, and love and friendship in riper years to hold it; for the time must come, when they will be past the rod and correction: and then, if the love of you make them not obedient and dutiful; if the love of virtue and reputation keep them not in laudable courses; I ask, what hold will you have upon them, to turn them to it?" And once pliability was obtained parents should avoid overt correction. "For I am very apt to think, that great severity of punishment does but very little good; nay, great harm in education: and I believe it will be found, that caeteris paribus, those chil-

[12] *Ibid.*, paragraph 1.

[13] *Ibid.*, paragraphs 11, 13.

[14] *Ibid.*, paragraphs 33-35.

[15] *Ibid.*, paragraphs 40, 78.

dren who have been most chastised, seldom make the best men." Pliability was to be induced "before children have memories to retain the beginnings of it," so that it would seem natural and not block the spontaneity with which children could take the air and looseness that Locke would then allow them.[16]

After such treatment children would pass through the later stages of education able to receive instruction, undisturbed by the pressure within them of innate irrational appetites and passions: "God has stamped certain characters upon men's minds, which, like their shapes, may perhaps be a little mended; but can hardly be totally altered and transformed into the contrary."[17] But if the later teacher or parent insisted on applying punishment, such interfering passions might become again active. "It is impossible children should learn any thing, whilst their thoughts are possessed and disturbed with any passion, especially fear, which makes the strongest impression on their yet tender and weak spirits. Keep the mind in an easy calm temper, when you would have it receive your instructions, or any increase of knowledge. It is as impossible to draw fair and regular characters on a trembling mind, as on a shaking paper."[18]

Now Locke was not quite consistent about whether he thought the infant mind capable of genuine tremblings and passion. In some contexts he said plainly that the infant had, at the outset, desires and appetites that had to be checked by fear. In another context he asked: during "the first seven years, what vices can a child be guilty of, but lying, or some ill-natured tricks?" These the father should not forbid until the child actually became guilty. Blandness was all. The father should "show wonder and amazement at any such action as hath a vicious tendency, when it is first taken notice of in a child. For example, when he is first found in a lie, or any ill-natured trick, the first remedy should be, to talk to him of it as a strange monstrous matter, that it could not be

[16] *Ibid.*, paragraphs 42-44.
[17] *Ibid.*, paragraph 66.
[18] *Ibid.*, paragraph 167.

imagined he would have done: and to shame him out of it." And again: "If vicious inclinations were watched from the beginning, and the first irregularities which they caused corrected by those gentler ways, we should seldom have to do with more than one disorder at once; which would be easily set right without any stir or noise, and not require so harsh a discipline as beating. Thus, one by one, as they appeared, they might all be weeded out, without any signs or memory that ever they had been done there."[19] The key to Locke's inconsistency lies in his very blandness. In psychoanalytic terms, he was recommending that a regime of strict, continuing family authority be replaced by a regime of "repression"—by the imposition of a single, all-at-once authority on the very young infant, such that the wishes and values of the father would be taken into the infant, and erected into conscience or "super-ego," and such that any violation of those values would become simply unthinkable. The *tabula rasa* was the outcome of repression, not a pure primitive state. And a parent or teacher is best qualified to inculcate unthinkability if he accepts it himself. He may not accept it literally, on the intellectual level. He may, like Locke, know that the infant has demanding appetites and passions that would interfere with any well-ordered household. But he may also, like Locke, manage to tell himself that the only vices of which a small child is capable are rather formal, self-protective ones—lies and tricks.

Certain cautions are necessary. Locke was articulating a major innovation in family structure, the change from the regime of continuing correction to what was to become the classic Victorian regime, relying on early repression as a technique for developing independent, self-sufficient individuals. But the innovation that he articulated was neither drastic nor quickly achieved. In the first place, repression of some kind—that is, the imposing of socially necessary discipline at an age and personality level where it

[19] *Ibid.*, paragraphs 84-85.

can never be reached by the maturing or conscious memory —is surely inevitable in any family. What Locke was proposing was that parents, particularly fathers, become aware of repression, relying on it as a uniquely effective and productive technique. Not a drastic change, but perhaps enough to make any difference between the "traditional" family and the "achieving" family.

In the second place, bachelor Locke's innovation could make a difference in society only as it was taken up by wider groups in Britain and, eventually, America. His ideas had less general importance than did how they were used. On this the story is clear. In the years around 1750 Locke's ideas became the core of new child-raising techniques that were recommended to all classes in Britain. Some suggestion of these changes appeared soon in America, and they were imported quite extensively during the following generation. American child-raising advice, after the middle of the eighteenth century, was a gradually joined conflict between Locke's ideas and the traditional family. Americans, though, put Locke to polite uses rather at variance from his own country-gentry ideals.

Some distortion of Locke's aims was implicit even in the reasons why his ideas spread within Britain in the middle years of the century. The urban, artificial, self-indulgent life that he disliked continued to attract people in eighteenth-century England, and it became an offense to the tender humanitarian consciences that many Britons were developing in the same years. The treatment of children by both poor and rich became a cause of guilt in those people who took on themselves the burden of feeling guilt. The infant death rate was high, and it seemed to be growing worse. In the respectable classes, anxious to live fashionably, mothers seemed to pay less personal attention to their children than they once had. They did not breast-feed the children themselves, but subjected the infants to impersonal dry-feeding or put them out to wet-nurses, who might be diseased and were certainly irresponsible. As in later generations, fathers ambitious to display their wives and their wealth may have encouraged such treatment of children. Although a crude, callous indulgence in fashion at the expense of children may have been rare, there must have been enough people torn between older simplicity and newer fashion to furnish an audience for the appeals to guilt in humanitarian literature. And those humanitarians who were more objective or less sentimental had enough to worry about in the mistreatment of children by the poor. Whether or not illegitimacy was actually increasing, the growth of London and of an ill-organized city life made the worst aspects of illegitimacy more visible. Unwanted children, whether bastards or not, were abandoned in jails, in workhouses, abandoned even on public dumps. More forthrightly, mothers killed children. More subtly and less forthrightly, mothers and nurses neglected children and allowed them to die.

In one attempt to cope with the mistreatment of infants, humanitarians established the London Foundling Hospital in 1741. They planned to take in abandoned children, treat them properly in their early years, then apprentice them in decent situations when they became old enough to make themselves useful. The task of devising and supervising ways to handle the infants fell to William Cadogan, the hospital physician. Certain requirements were imposed by the purpose of the institution. The methods had to be suited to the handling of large numbers of infants by a much smaller ratio of adults than was available even in overcrowded families. Sanitation had to be preserved, if only by the standards of the period. Children had to learn to take care of themselves, and they had to become independent enough to become apprentices at a fairly early age, under fairly impersonal conditions. The methods that Cadogan adopted were obvious: accustom children to plain food; wean them early and firmly; insist on cleanliness; forget such dependency-inducing devices as swaddling, the cradle, and leading-strings.[20] Produce, in short, the compulsive and therefore self-sufficient personality.

Cadogan then combined these techniques for saving underprivileged children with Locke's techniques for saving privileged children, and produced a short essay on child-raising that he published as applying to all kinds of families. The Foundling Hospital would not only prevent infanticide, but would save even more children "by introducing a more reasonable and more natural method of nursing." He took the animus of his plan from Locke: the nursery had been left too much under the control of women, who thought it their province but who followed the "custom of their Great grandmothers, who were taught by the Physicians of their unenlightened days." Mothers and nurses had spoiled children by feeding them candy and other rich food "till they foul their blood, choak their vessels, pall the appetite, and ruin every faculty of their bodies; [and] by cockering and indulging them, to the utter perversion of their naturally good temper, till they become quite froward and indocile." The father, not the mother, should regulate the handling of children, making it natural, plain, and regular. Cadogan made his object of training for early independence clear when he advised against using baby talk: "I think they cannot be made reasonable creatures too soon."[21]

The Cadogan line was taken up, repeated, and elaborated by other men of his generation. Their books went through many editions in Britain and were reprinted in America. Thus the balance and tone of child-raising literature shifted after 1750 from a relatively unstrenuous acceptance of infants to a demand for early, rigid training in bodily control

[20] Ernest Caulfield, *The Infant Welfare Movement in the Eighteenth Century* (New York, 1931), esp. pp. 92-93, 97-98, 107. Morwenna and John Rendle-Short, *The Father of Child Care: Life of William Cadogan (1711-1797)* (Bristol, 1966).

[21] William Cadogan, *An Essay upon Nursing and the Management of Children, from Their Birth to Three Years of Age*, 10th ed. (London: reprinted Boston, 1772), 3-6, 8-9, 11, 49 and *passim*.

and the essentials of independence.[22] By the end of the eighteenth century, the rare physician who favored cradles and later weaning was complaining that moderns were following the Locke-Cadogan lines.[23]

Elements of this line were stated by Americans who may have taken it directly from Locke, without any intervening dependence on the foundling-care movement or on fashionable English guilt. Americans also turned Locke's social attitude on its head, in the few instances when they bothered to make explicit statements about the child-raising needs of their own society. Often, they repeated in a provincially dependent way the ideas or the books they imported from England; that provincial dependence gave the clue to their own way of adapting Locke and Cadogan. For all the preacherly attacks on vanity, Americans did not enjoy quite the extent of luxury that seemed to weigh on the native British conscience. Where luxury in England depended partly on a mobile servant class that crowded into cities, America suffered from a chronic labor shortage. Where English philanthropy sought to find suitable apprenticeships for neglected children, Americans were more likely to see children as a supply from which to fill out the ranks of labor.

Some Americans, such as the Massachusetts pastor John Mellen, tried to adapt Locke to the traditional family attitudes. Mellen, preaching in 1756 on the occasion of a natural epidemic in his neighborhood (in contrast to the

[22] Alice Ryerson, "Medical Advice on Child Rearing, 1550-1900," Harvard Ed.D. diss. 1960. Hugh Smith, *Letters to Married Ladies, to Which is Added, a Letter on Corsets, and Copious Notes by an American Physician*, 3rd edn. (New York, 1832 [1st English ed. 1772], i-xix, 145, 148-150, 266, 270-271, and esp. 91, where on toilet-training Smith adopts the same evasive blandness that Locke took toward infant discipline generally. James Nelson, *An Essay on the Government of Children* (London, 1793), 8, 139, 160-163.

[23] H. W. Tyler, M.D., translator, in Scévole de Sainte-Marthe, *Pædotrophia, or, The Art of Nursing and Rearing Children* (London, 1797), 54*n*-55*n*, 82*n*, 95*n*-98*n*.

man-made slaughter that alarmed Englishmen), took disaster as a warning that people would return to the old faith and the old virtues. The old virtues included the well-governed family: . . . "let the divine Correction towards *you*, teach you proper Discipline towards your Children. When your Children make themselves vile, neglect not to restrain them: Give not the Reigns too much into their Hands, nor suffer Sin upon them. Let Family Order, Worship and Government, be observed. . . . Be slow to Wrath, and loth to punish: But yet when the Necessity calls for it, with-hold not the Rod."[24] But he also made a moralistic, somewhat sentimental adaptation of Locke's argument for early attention to children: "The Heart of a Child is in some Respects like clean Paper, on which you may write what Characters you please. But it is apt soon to become blur'd and defac'd by Vice and Folly."[25]

Locke had advised the father to see that his son learned a trade and became apt for business. This was quite of a piece with the religious idea of using diligence to prevent vice, but Mellen saw in this tactic also a way to close a gap between the American family and the American labor market. He had to insist on work as a child-raising technique

> because I think this Means of early Vertue is too generally neglected amongst us: and Children are allow'd to grow up to an Age and Stature for Business, much too long, oftentimes, before they are put to it. . . .
>
> I pity the unhappy Children, of those indigent Parents, who have neither Business, or Subsistence at Home, but yet are fondly detain'd there, lest they should be put to proper Work and Service in better Families.[26]

This attitude was not confined to New England, but turned up in other areas when moralistic or diligence-mind-

[24] John Mellen, *A Discourse Containing a Serious Address to Persons of Several Ages and Characters* (Boston, 1757), 29.

[25] *Ibid.*, 26.

[26] *Ibid.*, 26*n*-27*n*.

ed men took offense at the self-satisfied condition of the poor American family. In 1762 an anonymous writer addressed "to the inhabitants of New-Jersey" a pamphlet, *The Countryman's Lamentation, on the Neglect of a Proper Education of Children*, which he cast in the form of an allegorical trial of parents guilty of cruelty to their children. The accused insisted that they loved their children, wanted to have them at home as comforts and as parts of their own lives, and saw no reason to let children be taken away. But the accusers answered that true love for children would put future welfare first. By staying at home children grew into the same easy sloth that had kept their parents poor. The parents lacked any spirit of industry, economy, or improvement. They could give their children none of the motives or habits that would put them on the way to improvement. Parents who did raise their children to industry, religion, and learning had the right to keep their children, but it was better that children be taken from the idle poor and put under householders who would raise them properly.[27]

Where English moralists saw the neglect of children as a special fault of the luxurious rich or the dependent poor, Americans saw it as a fault of the independent poor or, even more to the point, of the typical, comfortable, but unassuming family. One commentator who argued from the typical family to a Lockean prescription was Ahimaaz Harker, a callow self-styled "candidate for the ministry" who presented himself to the public by writing a handbook on conduct and family life for the "young people" of New York, New Jersey and Pennsylvania. Although his pretentious language showed that he depended somewhat on pious and fashionable ideas about how to raise children, he insisted that he described conditions that one might observe in most of the families of the area. And he described the parents and children of these families as bound in a diffuse emotionalistic

[27] *The Countryman's Lamentation, on the Neglect of a Proper Education of Children; with an Address to the Inhabitants of New-Jersey* (Princeton, 1762).

relation that precluded the development of proper social and intellectual abilities in the children. For the existing ways, both father and mother were responsible.

> How seldom do we observe the affectionate Embraces of a Father, or the endearing Caresses of an indulgent Mother, accompanied with Instructions becoming their passionate Fondness? But on the contrary, with a lavish profusion of fulsome Circumlocutions; such as tend in no respect, either to improve the Understanding, or regulate the Affections. And yet those helpless Lambs of their own Bowels must be in subordinate Thraldom to those Monsters of Neglect; looking to them for Direction and Support, till they arrive to Years of legal Independency, when their Morals have become vitiated by copying parental Precedents.[28]

Much as in the diagnoses by Locke and Cadogan, the other side of indulgence was a continuing regime of coercion and conflict. The language in which Harker described this regime was concrete, not altogether bookish in tone, and may have resulted from some honest observation of the American scene. He described how a child developed when parents neglected to make the proper impressions at a very early age:

> Soon it was able to throw its Clothes into the Fire; now the Parent begins in a hurry to slap and bluster about, by which Time, the Devil had been so forehanded in his Cunning, that he had taught the Child to cry immoderately when denied any Play-thing, tho' it should be a Gold Watch; it would use foul Expressions, call its Mother a Bitch, or the like; then she falls to exclaiming against the Servants or Prentices for their Vicious Dis-

[28] Ahimaaz Harker, *A Companion for the Young People of North America. Particularly Recommended to Those within the Provinces of New-York, New-Jersey, and Pennsylvania* (New York, 1767), 2.

> course, that corrupts the Child. Thus it is full of Mischief and Wickedness, before the good natured Soul of a Parent thinks it capable of dicerning or receiving the least Check. By which Time, the Child might have known the Letters of the Alphabet, as well as the Chairs and other Utensils about the House; could have sounded B as distinct as Bitch, or D as well as Devil. Might be delighted in looking at Cuts and Pictures, as well as playing with the Properties of other Children, which frequently makes Clamour, and reiterates Mischief. But here many are grossly mistaken, which arises from too much Fondness and Affection, wrongly indulged.[29]

This fondness then worked to deprive children of the opportunity to model themselves on their parents. Once children had passed the cuddly stage, and were becoming difficult to handle, parents assumed toward their own children "supercilious Airs" that they assumed toward no one else. Where they would "discourse as familiarly with a neighboring Child, tho' neither so old or sensible as their own, as with a Companion or Stranger," they now avoided intelligent exchange with their own children and yet were ashamed that the children behaved like "rustick Swains" when they went into society. The honeymoon of baby-petting was over, and mutual boredom became a part of the rural torpor. "Many are the Evenings which are loitered away in a sluggish Inactivity, for want of, or rather neglect of Employment; while Children are exercising their Petulance among each other, which, perhaps is the only Thing that disturbs the Slumbers of their Parents." Although Harker followed Locke in many things, as in advising parents to let children eat freely, according to the timing of natural appetite, he certainly did not believe in letting children grow according to the natural, hardy pattern supposedly found among the children of yeomen and farmers.

[29] *Ibid.*, 120.

Rather, the father should use the long free country evenings to teach his son "an easy Carriage and polite Address."[30] Nor should he have his son wear simple, rough clothing, such as homespun, as was suggested by some writers who talked up "natural" ways of raising children. The child who was raised in country clothes would turn into a self-conscious snob when he got his first proper suit. Rather, the father should quite early give his son a full suit of clothes, should instruct the son in forms of address until those forms become natural, and should admit his son to the table after supper, to participate in the healths that were proposed in beer and cider when neighbors came to visit.[31]

This same emphasis on politeness was put by John Witherspoon, who came from Scotland to be president of the College of New Jersey in 1768, the year after Harker's handbook was published. In 1775 he brought out his own child-raising advice, the *Letters on Education* that were often reprinted in succeeding decades.

In part a predictable attack on pampering and a defense of religious education, these followed the Lockean line in many specifics. The child's health, for example, should be preserved by "cleanliness, liberty, and free air." It should play at large, not be "handled and carried about by women." Just as did Locke, he combined this belief in freedom for children with a conviction that parents should early establish absolute authority. This strategy he contrasted both to the older way of continued "savage and barbarous" severity, and to the newer way of mere liberty and "persuasion" by "every soft and gentle method."[32] The failure to establish authority could be found among all classes. It was obvious among the poor: "Among the lower ranks of peo-

[30] *Ibid.*, 121-126. [31] *Ibid.*, 130-133.

[32] John Witherspoon, *A Series of Letters on Education* (New York, 1797), 13, 25-27. One comment suggested that Witherspoon's firm piece was not so popular as it should have been in the South: Samuel K. Jennings, *The Married Lady's Companion; or, Poor Man's Friend* (Richmond [1804]), 133.

ple, who are under no restraint from decency, you may sometimes see a father or mother running out into the street after a child who is fled from them, with looks of fury and words of execration; and they are often stupid enough to imagine that neighbors or passengers will approve them in this conduct, though in fact it fills every beholder with horror."[33] In families of higher rank, the same pattern took the form of bickering in front of company, or even worse. "There are some families, not contemptible either in station or character, in which the parents are literally and properly obedient to their children, are forced to do things against their will, and chidden if they discover the least backwardness to comply. If you know none such, I am sure I do."[34] Though he admitted that Americans would "perhaps smile" at his recommendation, he said that the parent could establish his authority by working carefully between the time the child was eight or nine months old and the time he was twelve or fourteen months. Like Locke, he insisted that the father was the proper person to establish this authority, and like Locke he made much of putting this authority beyond the reach of later memory. But he also argued that the mother or nurse was the wrong person to establish authority because she was "obliged in many cases to do things displeasing to the child, as in dressing, washing, &c. which spoil the operation."[35] Now it is not true in any obvious, unambiguous way that children dislike procedures that are one form of physical attention; it seems more likely that Witherspoon felt an identity between the father as child-raising agent, the selection of an early age at which to impose authority, *and also* the erasing of memory or thought about the period when bodily processes were handled in a messy, undisciplined way.

In this same mood, Witherspoon the clergyman endorsed the value of politeness as a goal in education. Though piety was desirable in people of all ranks, there was an alliance

[33] Witherspoon, 29-30. [34] *Ibid.*, 38. [35] *Ibid.*, 30-34.

between worldly politeness and religious piety. At least in mixed company, one did not have to fear profane or obscene language as much from the worldly man as from the clown or from the "rough, unpolished, country gentleman."[36] Partly out of evangelical rigidity, partly out of fear of rustic provincialism, men in America were directing the new child-raising ideas less toward the goal of "natural" life than toward social improvement and toward proper city life as the ideal.

As Americans entered the latter part of the eighteenth century, they followed two different patterns of effort and advice about child-raising. On the one hand, some tried to maintain the old ideal of well-ordered family government, with conscious authority as the lifelong pattern of relation between parent and child. Their efforts to maintain this ideal were not too successful, and the maternal indulgence that had always been a latent feature of the well-ordered family was coming to the fore as the regime of liberty and persuasion that fitted the temper of the revolutionary generation. There was no essential difference between the well-ordered family and the libertarian family: the liberty was simply an unfolding of possibilities that had always been partly realized even within order. On the other hand, there was something genuinely new and different about the kind of family that a Locke or a Cadogan or a Witherspoon wanted to create. Perceiving that a basic feature of the well-ordered family was its actual failure to achieve the authority it claimed, these men addressed themselves to the crucial problem of technique, and recommended that mere continuing authority be replaced by clearcut repression, making the father the actual governor of the family, not simply the appellate judge to whom all disputes were ultimately referred. The well-governed family had been patriarchal, but it had not been rigid or, in the technical sense, repressive. It had not been the classic Victorian family. That Victorian family ideal, stern and humanitarian at

[36] *Ibid.*, 61-62.

the same time, was an innovation designed to remedy defects and decays in the older pattern. It was derived partly from Locke, and it was adopted in popular child-raising advice from the middle of the eighteenth century on. In America, these ideas were identified with improvement, warring against rustic backwardness in the cause of intellectual, moral, and economic development. The central feature of eighteenth-century attitudes on child-raising was precisely the conflict between the new repressive improvement and an older patriarchalism that was forever decaying toward ill-ordered laxity.

People of the Civil War generation held child-raising attitudes at least as various as did people of a century earlier. Their different views were each widely distributed, and each complex. The views differed in how much weight they gave to authority or nurture within the ideal parental attitude, and in the weight they gave to the roles of father and mother within child-raising. These differences, in turn, ran at angles to a difference over how much thought parents should take for the future performances of their children. Parents confronted no one accepted prescription about how they would behave, but rather a set of overlapping prescriptions reflecting the different historical experiences or the different degrees of prosperity through which families had passed.

By that time the Lockean ideas had spread through the literature on the physical handling of young children, and had become orthodox.[37] Arrival at consensus on these matters was like the acceptance of urban middle-class morality in public literature. Tone and style and the pace or dynamic of the transaction between parents and children, were, however, a vital part of what men communicated by specific child-rearing practices. Even people who stood for firm, uncompromising techniques could reveal more complex un-

[37] Alice Ryerson, "Medical Advice."

derlying attitudes if they kept talking enough, and these attitudes could determine what the techniques "really" meant.

Fortunately for investigation, the one American who stood above all others for the uncompromising early training of children talked a great deal. This was Jacob Abbott, who was both Spock and Seuss to the generation between 1830 and 1860, and who remained the figure against whom people contended in trying to establish new attitudes. Abbott began his career as a New England theological student who took to teaching more readily than to preaching. He soon opened his own girls' school in Boston, and he began writing on educational topics. He became the principal writer of children's books for the house of Harper, and moved to New York. He did operate another school in New York after he moved there; but this effort was overshadowed by his writing. With the Little Rollo books, the Jasper books, the Little Learner books, the Marco Paul books, and dozens of others, he kept busy into the 1870s, establishing himself as the glut on the market in decent books for children.[38]

Abbott also wrote for teachers and parents, telling them how to handle children. He shifted his emphases somewhat with mood or immediate purpose, but never his two themes: first, that parents should at the outset secure "*unlimited, unqualified entire submission* to their authority"; and, second, that parents or teachers should then adopt gentle, even democratic methods.[39] Which of these themes stood out the

[38] Carl J. Weber, *A Bibliography of Jacob Abbott* (Waterville, Maine, 1948), 7-27. And see the reference to the "platitudes of Abbott and others of less ability" in a review of Richard Edwards and T. Russell Webb, *The Analytical Series of School Readers*, in *American Educational Monthly*, IV (1867), 410.

[39] Abbott, *Early Piety* (New York, 1834), 12. Abbott, *The Duties of Parents* (Boston, 1834), 16. Abbott, *The Way to Do Good* (Boston, 1836), ch. 9. Abbott, *The Teacher: or, Moral Influences Employed in the Instruction and Government of the Young* (Boston, 1836). Abbott, *The Rollo Code of Morals* (Boston, 1841). Abbott, *Gentle Measures in the Management and Training of the Young; or, The*

clearer to members of Abbott's generation is not clear. The two were logically joined; although some later observers who had lived through the Abbott torrent (some of his books remained in print until as late as 1913) reacted against him as old-fashioned, the gentleness might have seemed the more striking to people in mid-century. He overflowed with devices and expedients for managing children without coercion, culminating in devices he used in school: student committees, rules adopted by student resolution, and student essays on moral topics, including even the subject of "bad management by teachers." To Abbott gentleness and consent were aspects of discipline, not of freedom. He insisted that parliamentary forms in the classroom were only forms, and that the teacher should keep his authority always in ready reserve. In a lecture in which he described these forms, speaking to a New England audience in 1831, he concluded:

> There must be in the generation which is to come upon the stage, a greater portion of social virtue than will come spontaneously, or the dangers which even now threaten our country will thicken into deeper and deeper gloom. To be mild and gentle in spirit, kind and conciliatory in temper and conduct, and submissive to proper authority, are not the natural characteristics of Americans. The stern unbending spirit of freedom which prevails in this land is with difficulty retained in union with the gentler and more peaceful virtues of social life. We must then earnestly exert ourselves to sustain the latter, or else this extended government over our immensely varied country will soon become a very unstable equilibrium of the fierce elements of whirlwind and storm.[40]

Principles on Which a Firm Parental Authority May be Established (New York, 1871). A possible immediate source for his two basic points was John Angell James, *The Family Monitor, or, A Help to Domestic Happiness*, 1st American edn. (Boston & New York, 1829).

[40] Abbott, *A Lecture on Moral Education, Delivered in Boston, before the American Institute of Instruction* (Boston, 1831), 21.

Whether it was South Carolina or Jackson he was attacking —or both—he left little room for any calculus by which gentleness or affection might lead to independence and energy.

In his thinking, authority insured both affection and harmony in the home. Where others might advise the parent to build up bonds of affection, assuming that these would become internalized as conscience, he assumed that parental authority would quite early plant conscience where it could be subjected to symbolic manipulation.[41] When he discussed parents' duties toward the school, his first concern (reasonable in itself, and shared by many other teachers) was that parents not take the side of pupils against the teacher. Beyond that, parents should send children to school already well trained.

From that prior good training he did not demand that the children get warmth, or security, or intellectual advantages, or nicety of sensory stimulation. He feared rather lest "irregularity, insubordination and passion reign at home," and he juxtaposed what children would learn from such a home and what they would learn from being allowed to run with "bad company": "What folly, to think that a boy can play with profane, impure, passionate boys which herd in the streets, six days in the week, and have the stains all wiped away by being compelled to learn his Sunday-school lesson on the seventh, or that children who make the kitchen or the nursery scenes of riot and noise, from the age of three to eight years, will be prepared for anything in after life, but to carry the spirit of insubordination and riot wherever they may go." Abbott believed that intellectual instruction could always be counted on to succeed, somehow or other, but that moral education was difficult and chancy. His system for moral training smacked more of the gymnasium than of the playing-field. Parents should introduce the child to temptations that he was strong enough to overcome, then

[41] Abbott, *Parental Duties in the Promotion of Early Piety* (London, 1836), 19-20.

gradually increase the severity until the child could overcome great ones. In this, gentleness consisted in not giving the child too great increments in temptation, lest he acquire practice in doing wrong. And when Abbott followed his remarks on riot in the kitchen or nursery by saying, "No; children should be *taught* most certainly,—but they must also be *taken care of*,"[42] he was already using the phrase "take care of" in the sardonic tone of later slang.

He was himself far from consistent in attitude. In one of his early books, *The Way to Do Good*, he went to both extremes at once: that of willingness to reach out to children's motives, and that of horror at what children will do on their own to satisfy their needs. He listed the motives that parents and teachers could tap: the desire to exercise one's faculties or powers, beginning with the senses and going on to the active powers as they developed; the desire to learn, and to learn not just what might seem new to the adult, but anything real about the world; affection for those who gave children sympathetic aid in these desires; and a disposition to imitate those they loved. Influence over children could be gained through satisfying their natural curiosity and arousing their affections. Parents often paid too little attention to this, and their intercourse with children was only the necessary intercourse of command and obedience. But Abbott recoiled quickly from taking this tactical advice in any strategic sense. Distinguishing between proper sympathy and any attempt to win children through "improper indulgence," he moved on to one of the most extreme of all warnings on the selection of children's associates:

> . . . keep children as much as possible by themselves,—away from evil influences,—separate,—alone. Keep them from bad company, is very common advice. We may go much farther, and almost say, keep them from *company*, good or bad. . . .

[42] Abbott, *The Duties of Parents, in Regard to the Schools Where Their Children are Instructed* (Boston, 1834), 14, 16. Compare his *Lecture on Moral Education*, 10.

> In fact, all history and experience shows, and it is rather a dark sign in respect to poor human nature, that the mutual influence of man upon man, is an influence of deterioriation and corruption. Where men congregate in masses, there depravity thrives, and they can keep near to innocence only by being remote from one another . . . and how often has the mother found that either one of two troublesome children, seem subdued and softened and dutiful, when the other is away. It seems as if human nature can be safe only in a state of segregation; in a mass, it runs at once to corruption and ruin.
>
> So far then, as promiscuous intercommunication among the children of a town or neighborhood is impeded, so far, within proper limits and restrictions, will the moral welfare of the whole be advanced.[43]

This is not conventional horror of the city, but neo-Calvinism deduced from an assumption about small-group dynamics.

In his major career of writing books for children themselves, Abbott finally revealed something of the motivation underlying his contradictory attitudes. In much, he did implement that early strategy of appeal to children's interests. Some of his storybooks were merely edifying. Some carried explicit morals, such as: don't be troublesome; don't complain about accepting correction; don't think it unmanly to play with, and help, sisters or younger children. During the 1850s, when his own sons (Lyman and the others) were growing up, he wrote several books for children about the process of child-raising. In *Prank, or the Philosophy of Tricks and Mischief* (1855), he professed to write for those boys who did wrong more through thoughtlessness or ignorance than through deliberate action. He had his hero pull a series of capers that hurt others, requiring eventual apology and reform; but Abbott was clearly engaged by high spirits as such, he did not condemn capers that were inno-

[43] *Way to Do Good*, 291, 293-294, 297-298.

cent and not thoughtless, and he enjoyed writing about even the wilder and more destructive acts. Then in 1857 he produced two books on the technique and spirit of discipline. He justified his introducing self-consciousness into the child's side of the child-raising process on the grounds that such awareness would help older brothers and sisters take care of younger.

In *Jasper; or, The Spoiled Child Recovered*, Abbott presented a situation in which he confused the theme of maternal versus paternal influence with the related theme of city versus country influence, then disentangled the confusion in the outcome that he presented. Two persons contend for influence over Jasper: his mother, a well-meaning but weak girl from western Massachusetts who has married a New York City banker named Bleeker, and her father Mr. Grant. Mr. Bleeker appears on the scene only once: called home from the bank by a report that Jasper has had an accident, he makes the trip uptown even though he realizes that Jasper is only feigning, he stays at home just long enough to shed a little dandified good sense on the disorder, and then he goes back to the office. City life means the absence of father, and Jasper has two possible lives. He can stay in the city and be raised indulgently by a woman, or he can go to his grandfather's place in the country and be raised firmly by a man. Abbott sets up the differences between these two as differences between two schools of thought. Mrs. Bleeker argues for governing the child by reason, as soon as he can speak, and her father counters that the child has no reason—

> that is, none that you can place the least reliance upon for the government of his conduct. A child for the first ten years of his life is all impulse, appetite, and passion. His judgment and his reasoning powers are in embryo. You can't rely upon them at all. It is his mother's reason that is to govern, and not his. It is indeed for that very purpose that God and nature gave him a mother. You may

> depend upon it, that unless you govern him by *authority*, he will not be governed at all, and I am quite sure you will *not* govern him by authority, and so I think it very highly probable that you will not govern him at all. You will spoil him. You will be able to get along somehow or other for six or eight years, and then he will become so entirely uncontrollable that you can not have him in the house, and you will have to send him to me.

The boy does become uncontrollable and Mrs. Bleeker does send him away—but at first to a boarding-school, not to the old homestead. Jasper soon runs away from school, and catches a train headed back for the city. Naturally, his grandfather just happens to be on the train. Mr. Grant reprimands the boy for his wickedness, judiciously praises him for the courage he showed within the act of running away, and takes him back to New York only long enough to arrange for transferring him to the country. There Mr. Grant avoids treating the boy as a child, talks to him in "manly" terms, but insists on obedience. The old problem persists, of course ("His excellences are his own, and faults are his mother's"), and Jasper disobeys. Mr. Grant has the hired man bind Jasper with straps, gag him with a handkerchief, and put him aside until he is willing to obey. The boy is quite won over by this treatment, and there follows a grand reconciliation. In time the grandfather takes the boy back to town for a visit, where he shows the boy's behavior off to the mother, like Petruchio displaying Kate. And the mother lets the boy continue living with his grandfather. "Whether it was the country air that had had a soothing and softening effect on his disposition, or whether he had simply outgrown his childish faults by growing older, she never could positively determine. She rather thought it was the country air."[44]

In the outcome, then, Abbott saw the idea of a difference between city and country as a superficial, weak-minded generalization. Different kinds of life in city and country

[44] Abbott, *Jasper* (New York, 1857), 27-28, 91, 160.

might of course entail more important differences in family structure, in male or female governance, and in disciplinary strategy. But it was in these that the mechanism of influence really operated.

This is the official line that Abbott took with older children. Even in *Jasper*, the important thing may have been less the set of doctrines than the dramatic structure of flight, conflict, and reconciliation in which the feeling-tone of the book came to a head. To this structure he kept returning, that same year, when he wrote *The Little Learner, Learning about Right and Wrong, or Entertaining and Instructive Lessons for Young Children in Respect to Their Duty*.

The Little Learner was intended for children so young that Mother would read the stories and show the pictures to them, but that did not keep Abbott from insisting on something like the same self-consciousness that he sought to inculcate in older children who had nursery responsibilities. Mother was instructed to accompany each story with a talk about its subject, and to read only a little at a time, so that the story would be a "*lesson* rather than a mere means of amusement." He himself saw for the stories a test-like use that gave rather more credit to mothers than he always conceded: "The reading should also be made a means not only of instructing the child, but of informing the mother what are the thoughts and ideas which prevail in its mind in regard to the subjects brought to view in the book. To obtain in this way an exact and precise knowledge of the actual condition of the child's mind in respect to its moral and intellectual perceptions will give a mother very great assistance in her efforts to cultivate his thinking and reasoning power, and to form his character."

In "The Cups and Saucers," the story-book mother has her daughter play with a delightful toy tea set, precisely in order to increase the difficulty of the choice the girl would face when given a command. At the conclusion of the story, the real-life mother is supposed to be reading to *her* child:

"Children have to be taught to obey, just as they have to be taught to read or to sew, and I think this was an excellent way to teach Minnie." But in the animal stories that he scattered through the book, each usually depicting a child acting out an authority role toward a helpless beast, Abbott began to let out feelings less proper, priggish, and secure. On one picture of a girl riding a disobedient pony, he commented, "I advise the girl to whip him until she *makes* him obey. He ought to be willing to obey of his own accord, and if he is not willing to obey he ought to be made to obey." And if children chose to ignore that remark, they could attend to "The Two Little Bears":

> Great bears, roaming through the woods, are sometimes very ferocious; but little bears, if they are caught when they are young, are very gentle, and they play about together like two kittens. . . .
>
> The reason they shoot great bears is because they do mischief. They kill the sheep. Besides, they trample down the corn-fields in order to get the corn and carry it off.
>
> If children do mischief, they have to be punished. If animals do mischief, they have to be shot.

To the plight of a rabbit caught in a box trap, he compared the tensions of children obliged to stay indoors. And when the rabbit escapes from the trap as a boy was reaching into it, Abbott expressed pleasure for the rabbit but sorrow for the boy. "There is no harm in trying to catch rabbits that are playing about the yard except that it makes them wild; and if a boy wishes to make his rabbits tame, and is trying to tame them, do you think it would be right for his sister to run after them and try to catch them, so as to make them wild? No, indeed!" The same principle applied to larger, more important animals:

> Deer are very wild, but if men catch them, and put them in a field where they can have plenty of grass to eat,

> and treat them kindly, they become tame. They will come and eat grass out of your hand.
>
> But if you do not treat them well—if you do not give them enough to eat, and if, instead, you drive them about and frighten them, then they become more wild than ever, and they will get away and go back to the woods if they possibly can.[45]

Abbott was afraid. He was afraid that children would get out of control and slip away, that they would succumb to a spirit somewhat like depravity, but far less leaden and reprehensible in quality. Despite all his repressive sternness, the behavior he described in nursery rioters, neighborhood loafers, and even plain spoiled brats suggested less the violence of bear than the scurrying of rabbits and deer. The great defender of paternal influence, he betrayed a vulnerability, a fear that social fluidity and American liberty could rob the patriarch of those gentler parental rewards about which he preferred not to speak too openly.[46]

Abbott was enormously successful in his writings, offering what many people of his generation wanted to hear, whether or not they acted upon his prescriptions. Both his thinking and much of his success were paralleled in the career of Gardiner Spring, pastor of the Brick Presbyterian Church in New York. Spring's rhetorical task was the adapting of rural Calvinism to a successful, sentimental urban audience, combining an uncomplicated fidelity to orthodoxy with a warm, personal approach to pastoral visiting and counseling. When he discussed child-raising, he advised parents to implant early the "*habit of subordination*,"

[45] Abbott, *The Little Learner* (New York, 1857), x, 12, 16-19, 87, 96, 175-176.

[46] Compare [Erastus Hopkins], *The Family a Religious Institution; or Heaven Its Model* (Troy, N.Y., 1840), 116-117, warning fathers to "guard against that ascetic influence of their avocations, by which they too often forfeit their appropriate share of ardent, filial affection."

in order to avoid much need for later punishing. To handle the child successfully, the parent had to recognize that he was a "depraved being." But Spring betrayed also an Abbott-like touchiness when he warned children that, after the death of their parents, "You will be ashamed, and humbled, that you ever questioned the purity of their motives in their conduct toward *you*." He recognized the same difficulty in reconciling authority and familiarity between parents and children. As a partial solution, he recommended using familiarity as one means of control. Parents should not leave the tasks of education to servants or even to that recent invention, the Sunday School. They should govern the child's selection of associates, and should make the family "a little world within itself," even though "absolute exclusion from the world" was "undesirable." And they should use confidence as bond:

> Every lawful expedient should be adopted to secure the affections of our children; to induce them to choose our society, enter into conversation with us without embarrassment, and trust us with their own private affairs....
>
> The most critical period of human life is between fifteen and twenty years of age. And it is at this period especially, when young persons begin to extend their acquaintance with the world, that parents will find it inexpressibly advantageous to have preserved the cords of domestic endearment so bright and strong, that they can easily draw an affectionate child away from snares, and bind him to his natal bower.

The parent should use mostly kind measures, and no corporal punishment after the child was fourteen or fifteen.[47]

[47] Gardiner Spring, *Hints to Parents: a Sermon on the Religious Education of Children* (New York, 1833), 4, 9-10, 22, 27, 58. Compare the Rev. H. W. Bulkely (of Balston, N.Y.), *A Word to Parents; or*

Spring furnishes a clue both to the way people throughout the Anglo-American world shared ideas on child-raising, and to the way that a partial sharing could unite individuals who disagreed on such basic matters as the relative influence of mother and father. He, an American, was one of the authors commended by an Englishwoman, Mrs. J. Bakewell, in her *Mother's Practical Guide in the Early Training of Her Children.* Her book, in turn, was reprinted in New York in 1843 by the Methodist Book Concern, with the tacit approval of New York Methodist leaders. On only one point did their editor see fit to add a disagreeing note to Mrs. Bakewell's text, which minus that element became a codification for mothers of the common elements of precept.

Her work met one of the first requirements for a tract: it looked with fear on the present low state of behavior. She bewailed how little attention parents gave to moral education during the first four or five years of a child's life. But she bypassed theological dogmas by mixing contradictory ideas together. First attacking optimism about education, she picked up an easy appeal to evangelical pessimism, then turned back with relief to a fresh and hopeful concept of nurture:

> We are not to be told in this enlightened age that the human mind is like a sheet of white paper, ready to receive any impression that we may wish to make upon it. No; for we find, by experience, that it may more properly be compared to a plot of ground, in which weeds will spring up the more abundantly the less good seed we sow in it. Cultivate it as carefully and as diligently as we may, weeds *will* spring up; but if we gently remove them as soon as they appear, they will be prevented from taking

---

The Obligations and Limitations of Parental Authority (Philadelphia: Presbyterian Board of Education, 1858), 23, 37.

deep root, and from injuring those valuable and tender plants which it is our highest ambition to rear.[48]

She did try to face honestly the dilemmas confronting her generation. She knew the main point that defenders of true virtue expected—that parents should train a child early to obey completely, as a matter of habit. Parents should be firm and consistent in requiring obedience. But though she demanded obedience, she warned,

> Great care must however be taken not to weaken the child's affection for you, while you cultivate this essential virtue. . . .
>
> Parents who have properly cultivated the love of their children will have an amazing power over them by the exercise of sympathy and expressions of commendation: they value the praise of those they love, and will exert all their energies to obtain it. . . .
>
> By thus training your child to habits of rational and cheerful obedience, you are in no danger of weakening that *moral energy* so essential to success in life. Many parents greatly err in this respect. Some break the will by severity; others enervate and subdue it by persuasive kindness; forgetting that without energy and decision of character the most virtuous habits may easily be destroyed and the best resolutions rendered abortive. A young person without power to direct his own will is, so soon as released from parental control, left to the dominion of his desires and affections, or more frequently, feels himself governed for good or evil by the first powerful mind with which he may associate. How important is it, then, that this principle of self-government, this moral energy on which so much aftergood depends, he carefully nurtured in early youth![49]

[48] Mrs. J. Bakewell, *Mother's Practical Guide in the Early Training of Her Children* (New York, 1843), 14-15.

[49] *Ibid.*, 133, 135-136, 159.

Here was a language about "energy" that would have made sense in a society where an athletic gentry furnished the model for aspiring persons. It would also have made sense in the word-patterns that American high Federalists had once used, with their touchiness to defend either personal honor or the "energy" of executive branches in government. But Mrs. Bakewell was outlining a way for parents to set their children loose in a turbulent world, and these precepts carried a message to American Methodists, members of a sect whose virtues were introducing them to the bewildering process of social mobility. For children leaving home, obedience would not suffice. Neither would a naked independence, which might succumb to insinuations from parent surrogates—or which might, in strong individuals, become itself a source of evil. Instead, assuming that the child's feelings toward his parents were a major source of energy in him, she recommended that parents build conscience or superego by fixing into his personality a sense of affectionate dependence.

Certain details in this solution bothered Mrs. Bakewell. She feared that mothers, seeing to the affection side of the affection-obedience union, would become indulgent, that they would spoon out praise indiscriminately. This would be dangerous in a world where children could expect praise from nobody except loving parents, where the only comfort they could long expect was the right to evaluate, approvingly, the "success" of their own conduct. Parents, therefore, should be stingy with praise to children, and should "early accustom them to do with as small a portion of it as may enable them to make the needful exertions." Continuing to keep her precepts in neat balance, she acknowledged that some people would doubt that children under five could benefit from moral training. That small children could not really practice the virtues, she admitted; that they could develop the "seeds" or emotional basis of the virtues, she insisted.

From one of her reasons for not expecting full responsibility from children, she began on the line of thought that her New York editor refused to follow to its conclusion. She said that it would be difficult to give moral education to a child who had had too little intellectual education to understand it. From the indicated need for early intellect she moved to the question of how to encourage it. At one point she argued against any attempt to force development, accepting the view that precocity would drain vitality from the body. But what she defined as forcing was giving children too much to do at once, not starting them early. Three or three-and-a-half was the right age for a child to begin learning to read, even if only for a few minutes a day. Such an early start was possible for infants whose parents raised them in an atmosphere of precise, varied, modulated stimulation.

Here Mrs. Bakewell transcended her didactic tone. Instead of lecturing parents on providing advantages, she attacked the complacency of middle-class parents who could not see the reality of the advantages they did provide.

> Those who are accustomed to see only tolerably well-trained children without observing minutely the various means by which their powers of body and of mind are cultivated, will think it scarcely possible that a child who freely uses his limbs can suffer much injury from not having his sense and his mind exercised; but could they be brought into immediate contact with the neglected children of the poor, especially where infant schools have not exerted their highly beneficial influence, they would be convinced of the necessity of properly training both the mind and the senses. I once undertook the task of teaching a boy of six years old, who had run wild on a farm near to my residence. I was much struck with the difficulty he had in properly using his senses, especially on small objects placed near to him. . . . Unless I spoke very slowly and distinctly, and but a few easy words at once,

> he did not seem to hear, because he was not accustomed to listen, except to loud tones. He did not know the names of the different parts of his body, and it was some months before he could be taught the difference between his right and left hand. Yet he turned out to be a sharp boy, when his sense and his mind had been properly educated.[50]

From this position she pushed straight through to the egalitarian conclusion. For generations, writers on child-rearing had warned against letting children associate with servants in any way. Writers would continue to spout the warning for years more. With the simplest argument here—that servants as they existed were often immoral, dangerous influences—she did not disagree. She simply blamed this danger on the failure of poor parents to give their own children the proper early training, which in this scheme of analysis was mainly intellectual training. She endorsed what was then the talked-of armory of devices for early education—object-teaching and infant schools—and recommended infant schools for all, whether of lower or middle ranks, whose parents could not afford governesses.

And it was to this point that Mrs. Bakewell's American editor added the one important footnote he inserted in her book: "Daily infant schools are of doubtful utility, except for such children as have neither home nor mother."[51] The spokesman for American virtue could follow her careful balancing between obedience and affection. He made no complaint when she asked parents to suppress their indulgent impulses in order to make sure that the essence of parental affection and control would go with children through life. But when she doubted the mother's ability to manage, when she suggested sending children outside the home, as one way to head off the influence of servants, the American spokesman refused to follow. Proletarianized servants were less common in America, and so were proletarianized moth-

[50] *Ibid.*, 80-81.

[51] *Ibid.*, 113*n.*

ers. To Americans, even in the years when school organization was growing, nurture still meant something less institutional, more personal and maternal.

That his view made great appeal, particularly to people on the social level of the Methodists, became clear in the child-rearing advice given by phrenologists. These men, somewhat like the Lombrosos and Sheldons of later years, gave an apparently serious and certainly complex form to contemporary popular notions about the relation between bodily structure and human character. And they did more. They took over the terms and even the concepts of the "faculty psychology" and popularized them by attaching them to objective form: the bumps-and-skull charts for which phrenologists became a joke to quick-witted men on all social levels. In popularizing their ideas, though, they talked and wrote about much else besides the details of analyzing heads. They discussed anything about the life of the mind that would touch the concerns of ordinary people. They did much, for instance, giving of vocational advice, thus appealing to any people anxious to preserve a stable self-image against the shifting patterns of economic change. And they discussed family life and sex with a frankness—often prurience—that make them indicators of what was stirring within popular anxiety. Most important, they stayed in business, selling their works in edition after edition, for a long generation through the middle years of the century. Somewhat more proper men, like the editors of the Methodist *Christian Advocate*,[52] were apt to discount the mere jargon and system of phrenology, but admitted that the phrenologists purveyed good along with their eccentricities.

Their child-rearing advices took up all that was warm in the American footnote to Mrs. Bakewell, yet also put into

[52] Reviews in *Christian Advocate*, Jan. 14 and July 29, 1869. On the appeals offered by phrenology generally see John Davies, *Phrenology: Fad and Science* (New Haven, 1955), Orson S. Fowler, *Practical Phrenology* (New York, 1849), and Nelson Sizer, *Thoughts of Domestic Life* (New York, 1850).

sexual terms the logic she used about the sources of moral energy. Their explicit advice was simple, and only occasionally rigorous. Be responsible in marriage, marrying neither too early nor for money. Avoid improper attitudes in the pregnant woman, since they might harm the fetus. Let children eat as appetite dictates. Rely on mother-love. Have the mother see to the intellectual development of her children. Govern by persuasion, not force. Encourage aggressiveness in timid children. Force children to be independent in small things. But do not provoke the acting-out of aggression. Do not shelter children from all evil. But do educate children at home, away from vulgar contamination in school, until age fourteen or fifteen.[53]

Even in this series of precepts, the tone vacillated between affection and anxiety. Some of this range reflected the pace of social feeling. Phrenologists accepted both the opportunity of the age and the sense of responsibility that opportunity imposed on the individual. Consistency rarely bothered them when they were offering appeals to men caught in an inconsistent society. The New York phrenologist O. S. Fowler would one moment lament that few men, in the rush toward material progress, bothered to worry about intellectual or moral improvement. Then the next moment he would say that "applicants for phrenological examinations" were expressing precisely such higher aspirations by "daily and earnestly inquiring—'How can I REMEDY my defect? By what MEANS can I increase my deficient organs and diminish or regulate those that are too large?'" The

[53] Fowler, *Self-Culture and Perfection of Character, Including the Management of Youth* (New York, 1868 [copyright 1847; 1st ed. 1842]). Fowler, *Maternity, or the Bearing and Nursing of Children, Including Female Education and Beauty* (New York, 1869) [copyright 1848]). Fowler, *Sexual Science*; . . . (Philadelphia, 1870), 846-860. Fowler, *Private Lectures on Perfect Men, Women and Children in Happy Families*; . . . (New York, 1880), 156-171. Nelson Sizer, *How to Teach According to Temperament and Mental Development; or, Phrenology in the Schoolroom and the Family* (New York, 1876). Sizer, *Forty Years in Phrenology* (New York, 1882).

organs to which Fowler referred were of course those outlined by the bumps on the head, but a diffuse, easily displaced tone of personal anxiety showed in the next question Fowler ascribed to his customers: "Parents, in particular, are inquiring with deep solicitude—'How can I make my children better? ['] That new and most powerful mental stimulant furnished by our republican institutions, has waked up a mighty hungering and thirsting, especially in parents and the young, after moral excellence."[54]

Even in a scheme of emotional eschatology, Fowler expressed both a sense of optimistic trust toward the young, and a determination to impose on them radically new demands for moral improvement. He began with a long view of the past, in which man progressed with increasing speed through the dominance of successive organs (organ, of course, in the phrenological sense). Man

> commenced his career under the dominion of the organs located in the back and lower portion of the head—the social. For three thousand years he cared and lived mainly for offspring and sodomy; . . . But the power of these passions . . . finally yielded its sway to Combativeness and Destructiveness, the organs of which are located higher up and farther forward than the social. War succeeded love, first uniting with it in chivalry, and the world has run mad, almost down to our own times, after martial glory. . . .
>
> Alimentiveness—still farther forward—united with war, and Bacchus revelled with Venus and Mars. But within the last three centuries a new divinity—a god of gold and goods—has become a joint partner with sensuality, war, and feasting, and is now fast usurping universal dominion. . . . But within the last fifty years, Constructiveness—located still farther forward and upward—has ascended the throne, and is now ruling man in conjunc-

[54] *Self-Culture*, iv-v.

> tion with Acquisitiveness, of which modern mechanical inventions, manufacturers, and the like, furnish examples.

The difficulty with this scheme of things was that Constructiveness figured as the "last of the propensities." Beyond it lay Intellectuality, which was no mere instinct—and which had a much less clear place in the phrenological scheme than did the concrete impulses. This did not mean that man would falter in improvement. "Backward this progressive principle will never let him go. His next step will dethrone propensity, and give dominion to the higher faculties."[55] Fowler, speaking for a generation that was supposedly bringing animal man to the brink, left to the younger generation the task of jumping past the edge.

This view accepted what was common enough in the moral speculations of faculty psychologists then and was to persist when the faculty psychology was transformed into the depth psychologies of later years: the assumption that the relation between any two faculties or segments of the personality would be one of antagonism or alliance, and that a shifting sequence of such conflicts or alliances was a principal means of psychic growth. For the short run, in which growth was not at issue, the phrenologists could talk conventionally about some hierarchy among the faculties, with the higher having ultimate dominance over the passions. Typically, though, they played down this psychic pecking order, or said at most that the higher faculties should prevent the abnormal or perverted expression of the lower. Harmony of the faculties—often the comfort of gross creature harmony—was the point. "Happy he whose conscience APPROVES what his appetite craves, and thereby sweetens his rich repast—whose love of family and of money each redouble the energy and augment the happiness of the other; . . ." Harmony would, too, give "increased POWER . . . to all the faculties."[56]

[55] *Ibid.*, 24-25, 27.

[56] *Ibid.*, 37, 38.

It was in this relation between an indulgent harmony and emotional strength that the phrenological literature carried the Bakewell calculus to its extreme conclusion. In the phrenological literature, strength of any faculty was good if, of course, rightly used. This included the faculty of "amativeness," and some of the literature sounded like a pep talk against impotence. Within the family, Fowler said, personal relations should be "sexuo-parental" or "sexuo-fraternal." Mothers should not be afraid of a demonstrativeness that some persons might think impure; this would instill proper strong sexual feelings that the child could then display toward others in later life. And if the mode of maternal affections was thus extreme, so was the means by which to reconcile the divergent demands of affection and discipline. The parent should govern by persuasion, or should tell the child that any punishment was not what the parent wanted to do. Anxiety was the principal control on parents' use of means: if children died young, parents would feel guilty for having punished them; and if parents could not govern by love they should take this as a sign that their own faculties were weak. But anxiety would also be the means by which parents could control children without leaving marks. What began as a conventional recommendation for "Arraying the Moral Faculties Against the Animal" acquired real meaning from its tone. This conflict was "incomparably the most severe PUNISHMENT which can be inflicted. The mental anguish consequent on contention among the faculties, has already been pointed out. When this conflict occurs between the moral and the animal, not anguish merely, but AGONY is the necessary product. This horror of horrors is NATURE's punishment, and constitutionally calculated to restrain propensity and develop morality, whereas artificial punishment inflames the passions but blunts the moral feelings."[57]

Here, then, was another type among the child-rearing attitudes that appealed to Americans in the middle of the

[57] *Ibid.*, 310.

nineteenth century. Its focus was the mother, and the use of her affection as a way of binding the child to right behavior. It also sought to produce such qualities of behavior as energy and independence, which the twentieth century does not usually associate with the mother's predominance. The paradox here was only superficial. Because of the very intensity of her influence, the mother could lead children to internalize more completely any standards given them, could thus make more painful and energizing any conflicts that the child (or, later, adult) might feel between immediate needs and persisting conscience. People of this view recognized an attendant danger—that the mother might deal out so much indulgence that the child could never achieve independence—but they were willing to risk this. Knowing that geographical and social mobility would break soon enough the closeness of the family, they chose even to exploit the sexualizing of child-raising, in order to make more effective the independent, self-judging, self-propelling character of later behavior.[58] Abbott and his kind argued for the father's early authority as a way to create independence, but recoiled toward a more arbitrary, old-fashioned kind of authority when they sensed that independence might take children away from the home, where their company was pleasurable. Fowler and his kind put a mother-oriented pleasurable companionship first but argued that it would promote a more effective energy and independence.

The Abbott view and the Fowler view define two apparent extremes among the child-raising attitudes of the period. Because the two views shared much it was easy for the eclectic to work out compromise positions. Both favored a

[58] Louisa Hoare, *Hints for the Improvement of Early Education, and Nursery Discipline*, 1st American edn. (New York, 1820). Lydia Huntley Sigourney, *Letters to Mothers*, 2nd edn. (New York, 1839). Mary Mann and Elizabeth P. Peabody, *The Moral Culture of Infancy*, 184-185. [Helen Hunt Jackson], *Bits of Talk about Home Matters* (Boston, 1874), 39-49, 76-82. Mrs. A. G. Whittelsay, ed., *The Mother's Magazine* (New York, 1833-1867), *passim.*

natural regime for children, from breast-feeding for the infant up through loose clothing for the active pre-adolescent. Both proposed strategies for keeping corporal punishment to a minimum, though both were also willing to use rigor of some kind. They differed on whether the father or mother should be the central figure in the family. They differed in their sense of timing, with one for concentrating impact on earliest infancy, the other for a more persistent intrusiveness. And they therefore differed in the way they related to the historical perspective. From the tradition of the well-ordered family, one retained the stress on the father's authority and the other retained the demand for continuity of control and relationship. Those who favored the maternal strategy sometimes betrayed an aggressive or intrusive attitude toward the child ego, like that of the old well-governed family. Lydia Maria Child, for example, spoke for a continuing didactic verbal interchange between mother and child, and a flexible approach to goals such as early weaning. She opposed corporal punishment but in home medicine favored the heroic remedies that were associated with country rigor: to promote bladder regularity, the mother should if necessary give cantharides.[59]

Probably each of the two strategies was attempted by some parents, but it is unlikely that the extreme strategies often worked reliably. Observers did say that children were being given less discipline than formerly.[60] They had said that earlier, too. This might mean that, generation after generation, discipline was becoming milder; and it is likely that discipline was milder in nineteenth-century America

[59] Lydia Maria Child, *The Mother's Book* (Boston & Baltimore, 1831); 6th edn. (New York, 1849); and Child, *The Family Nurse; or Companion of the Frugal Housewife* (Boston, 1837), 74. Contrast the opposition to dosing of the newborn, in the generally antitraditional manual by Dr. G. Ackerley, *On the Management of Children in Sickness and in Health*, 2nd edn. (New York, 1836), 45.

[60] Norman Blowers, in New York State Superintendent of Public Instruction, *Annual Report*, 15th (1869), 249-250.

than it had been in sixteenth-century Europe. More likely, the persistent observation that discipline was growing milder meant that, in each generation of the nineteenth century, parents were trying to use one of the shame-oriented techniques children were not supposed to remember, but that they were failing in this heroic task. As former children they remembered discipline; as adults they perceived the efforts to minimize discipline.

Beyond this observation about weaker discipline, the complaints that teachers and moralists made against parents indicate that most people still lived in the undeveloped, solidaristic way of the eighteenth century, making just so much adjustment to the newer economy as would serve their own interests. Families in isolated areas, and the poor everywhere, were still likely to nurture children's minds in an unstimulating torpor.[61]

On one level, inspectors complained that even families in unprogressive communities would support schools if they could use them as places to send bothersome children. Most parents made no continuing effort to keep young children away from "corrupt association" with other children of the community. Even the frequent warnings about the dangers of bad company may have meant less or other than they seemed to say. Much of this stated the danger as one of the horrors of city life. Especially as the century wore on, "the streets" were the source of a diffuse evil for children. But Isaac Ferris, a New York clergyman who gave businessmen advice in the Jacob Abbott vein on how to govern their families, doubted that urban temptation was a valid argument for sending children to boarding school:

> Some men use glowing terms in depicting the disadvantages of raising boys in a city; and one would suppose the city-bred boy must of necessity be ruined. But it is

[61] William P. Page, *Common Schools* (Geneseo, 1838), 20-21. A.E.S., "Educational Aspects of Ulster County," *New York Teacher*, II (1853-54), 14-15.

> mere talk—a cover, in many cases, for a fashion which the parental heart should shrink from. The truth is, there are evil influences everywhere; . . . How much of the practice spoken of may be set down to mere selfish desire to get rid of care and to secure more interrupted opportunity for the slavery to money-making, we do not say. . . .
>
> Again, say some, it is not good to have children grow up in so much society as we have, and amid such distractions. The simple reply is, have less.[62]

Some of the polemics in favor of educating children at home bore out Ferris' suspicions. Writers who harangued about the danger of exposing children to outsiders or servants made exceptions for the "select" school. Even when such argument was imported from England, carrying country-house assumptions,[63] it entered a society where its most likely audience was the commercial and professional classes of the growing towns. For these, the argument that a mother should leave no child-care to servants was less apt to make her assume the whole task herself than to let her accept the allowed help from a select school—or any school. And so the complaints of the reformers ran—that parents who were engaged in business or society indulged themselves by paying too little attention to their children, to whom they showed indulgence in turn, as the least strenuous course.

Sometimes a complaint described a complex family culture in which neglect and indulgence were combined. The physician and teacher William A. Alcott condemned the utilitarian attitudes toward children that prevailed throughout America, both city and country. He urged par-

[62] Isaac Ferris, "Men of Business: Their Home Responsibilities," 52-55 (separate pagination), in James W. Alexander and others, *The Man of Business, Considered in His Various Relations* (New York, 1857).

[63] Isaac Taylor, *Home Education*, 1st American from 2nd London edn. (New York, 1838), Preface and 2-3. Lydia Huntley Sigourney, *Letters to Mothers* (New York, 1839), 108-120, 140.

ents to attend to the physical welfare of their children, to take part naturally in children's activities, to allow them the natural outlets of laughing and crying, and to let boys and girls mix naturally.

> All our family arrangements tend to repress amusement. Everything is contrived to facilitate business—especially the business or employments of adults. The child is hardly regarded as a human being,—certainly not as a *perfect* being. He is considered as a mere fragment; or to change the figure, as a plant too young to be of any real service to mankind, because too young to bear any of its appropriate fruits. . . .
>
> The arrangements of the infant school, also, seem designed for the same purpose—to repress as much as possible the infantile desire for amusement. . . .
>
> I might speak of other schools and places of resort for children, and proceed to show how all our arrangements appear to be the offspring of a species of utilitarianism which rejects every sport whose value cannot be estimated in dollars and cents.

Alcott anticipated the obvious interpretation that liking for the outdoors was a nostalgia for the receding rural past. He made it clear that the farm was not remote enough for him to sentimentalize it, and he doubted that country people were even any healthier than city people.

> Their active sports and employments in the open air give them a stronger appetite than any other class of people; and the indulgence of this appetite, not only with articles which are heating or indigestible in their nature, but with an unreasonable quantity even of those which are considered highly proper, is almost in an exact proportion. And it is hence scarcely possible for the causes of disease and premature death to be more operative in factories and in cities than in farm houses and the country. Indeed it may be questioned whether the abuses of the ANIMAL part of

> man—more common in some of their forms in country than in city—though they may be less conspicuous, are not more certainly and even more immediately destructive than those abuses which, in city life, and bustle, and competition, affect more the MORAL nature.

While adults indulged their animal selves, the child was treated like a domestic animal, allowed scarcely "any free juvenile conversation at the table or fireside. Here the child must sit as a blank cypher, to ruminate on the past, or to receive half formed and passive impressions from the present."[64] Not only did parents continue the regime of torpor that observers had lamented in the previous century; they also continued the specific child-raising practice of the pre-modern regime. Quoting William Cadogan at length, Alcott insisted that the English physician's warnings against leading-strings, swaddling, and overfeeding were still relevant to the United States of the 1830s: a band for the infant abdomen was acceptable to Alcott, but two-thirds of American nurses, he said, erred in thinking that the band should be tight.[65]

In Alcott's view, the underlying standards of family behavior had changed little in any moves from country to city. Country children were least troublesome and most serviceable if allowed to subsist within the household, presumably picking up whatever impressions and scraps of animal indulgence might fall their way. Moved to the town, they were put into more specialized "schools and places of resort," absorbed thereby into a different pace of life. Suppressed in natural childhood amusements in either place,

[64] William A. Alcott, *The Young Mother, or Management of Children in Regard to Health*, 17th stereotype edn. (Boston, 1849 [1st 1836]), 28, 245-248. Compare this belief that young couples should stay in a parental household, not move hurriedly to the frontier: Alcott, *The Young Husband* (Boston & New York, 1839), 57, 61-67, 68*n*-69*n*.

[65] Alcott, *The Young Mother*, 47-51, 145*n*, 145-151, 216, 220, 222-226.

they could look for compensation to later self-indulgence in improper or excessive adult appetites. Ignored by adults who were long alienated from spontaneity, children would learn alienation and indulgence as their own adult cultural standards. The nature to which Alcott looked was something new, defined along the line of children's interests versus adults' interests, not something old that was defined in any terms of rural past versus urban present.

Thirty years later than Alcott, the academy teacher Hiram Orcutt articulated a similar feeling, within a framework of apparently conventional ideas about the family. Orcutt had taught in schools across northern New England and upstate New York during this generation. He upheld the Jacob Abbott line on discipline, and he managed to combine a general support of the common-school system with a barrage of insinuations that parents would provide their children with more competent, moral, patriotic, and Bible-oriented teaching in an academy. Thus he warned that children were in danger from corrupt associations everywhere, city or country, and in danger even at home. Evil parents could be a source of danger. "The corrupt society of the school and neighborhood increases the peril in such cases, and makes more sure the destruction that awaits these unfortunate children." Although he defined the mind as "an *activity*" rather than "a receptacle," and advocated modern, natural methods of teaching, he saw activity and energy as traits to be nurtured by "mental discipline" in the solid liberal studies. Continuing the conventional mental-discipline line, he argued that professional training should begin late, after liberal education, and not be imposed as chunks of bare knowledge on the minds of youths. But all this reflected on the family. He decried the "deluded" parents who forced their children into the professions, and saw the right kind of school as a way to train children for individual choice, releasing them from the cycle of familial and vocational forcing. "When we consider the exclusiveness of family-life, the clannish tendency of all business-connections, the violent prejudices that influence individual members of homes, churches, and professional cliques, we can realize the importance of that generous discipline of manhood and womanhood which alone can fit our children for American citizenship." And yet Orcutt also feared the effects of moving children from the warmth of family into the "cold and lifeless formality" of society and "community."[66]

Between the family as described by Alcott and the family as described by Orcutt, there was an important difference. One saw the embracing, using tendency of the family as relatively inactive and stolid; the other saw it as active and sponsoring, even while clannish and possessive. By the time Orcutt wrote, men who were sensitive to changing ideas as well as changing realities were ready to conclude that family life had actually been transformed in that generation, from the stolid to the sponsoring posture. Samuel Osgood, minister at the Church of the Messiah in New York, applying the terms that Henry Maine had just introduced for legal history, argued that the American family had changed too much from a regime of *status* to one of *contract* and choice.[67] Of course, such commentators were themselves often new to the city, and their grand observations may have reflected little except change of setting.

The existing family, as criticized by the reformers, worked as a natural interest group. At the ages when children had to stay at home, doing little, it included the children without separating them much from other family activities. But it began quite early to force them out from the crowded household into the school. Through successive years, it continued pressure on the child to move through

[66] Hiram Orcutt, *Home and School Training* (Boston, 1892 [1st edn., 1874]), 97, 219, 254-255, 260-261, 291-292, and biographical supplement. He used "community," not to suggest a warm past, but to designate an impersonal present.

[67] Samuel Osgood, *The Hearth-Stone: Thoughts Upon Home-Life in Our Cities*, 1st edn., 1853, rev. edn. (New York, 1876), 321-337. Osgood, *American Boys and Girls. Two Essays from the Recently Published Volume, "American Leaves"* (New York, 1867).

the educational and vocational course, toward independence from the immediate household. At the same time, it showed them indulgence, encouraging them to assert impulse in various directions and to see the family as a unit within which to expect gratification. The pattern encouraged children toward formal independence, and certainly toward independence as to locale. It probably did less to encourage real freedom or initiative, since it established the indulgent, bounded small group as the social model to which the growing individual would revert in any new situation.

Countering all this, the conscientious spokesmen for a better family life asked a more deliberate way of handling children. Whether they emphasized the father's role or the mother's, some of the import was the same; and one writer managed the obvious synthesis, "A happy combination for children is there in an uncompromising father and an all-hoping mother."[68] The parent, whether by imposing or by giving, was to provide order to the child. The mother, for example, was to take the time and the energy and the self-discipline to provide a sense of warmth with firmness, and of predictability without indulgence. Though the child was certainly to be trained to those habits of cleanliness and neatness that would make for independence within the household, the repeated demand that warmth be shown him suggested a realistic desire to ease the child over the abrupt, major disciplines of his early years. The combination of order and warmth was to foster reliable, autonomous decision-making by the child in later years. The family was to be a means for transmitting personal integrity, not a conspiracy for mutual indulgence and exploitation.

In the way it treated children, the American family of 1850-1870 lived in tension between two ways of reacting to the modern world. One was the way of exploitation. The

[68] Catharine Sedgwick, *Home*, as quoted in *District School Journal of New York*, II (1841-42), 8.

other was the way of earnestness and endeavor. The way of exploitation was not merely old-fashioned, nor yet a behavior only of those farmers or city workers who needed to have child laborers within the family. It was available to middle-class families, too, as long as new resources promised rapid expansion of what a family had been able to enjoy. For the America of the Gilded Age, the nouveau bourgeois was as real as the nouveau riche. A kind of child-using familism had been a major part of life for almost all earlier Americans, and this attitude slipped easily from viewing the child as a resource—a worker in the household economy—to viewing him as its representative in enjoyment. This shift had long been part of a family's rise toward substance in the world, and it was now, in years of national economic expansion, a natural way for families to react to the economic tone of the period. The mere shift from the child as resource to the child as representative was not a real change in the underlying structure of society. It was rather a mechanical adjustment by the family to changed circumstances. The barely nubile girl, hustled to saunter along the paths of a fashionable watering-place, would have been dull not to feel exploited.

But exploitation had never been the only available pattern, even in parts of the country from which moralists expected the worst. When Philip Fithian went south in 1773 to work as tutor in the Carter family of Virginia, he was agreeably surprised to find that the family demanded standards of order, propriety, and accomplishment even while participating in a surrounding plantation life that was racier than Fithian quite liked.[69] Whether in this version, or in the form of those evangelical families who encouraged early piety in children, or in the form of families who encouraged a prudent, independently acquisitive attitude among children, there was available a kind of parental attitude that, whether authoritarian or nurturing in tone,

[69] *Journal & Letters of Philip Vicker Fithian, 1773-1774*, ed. H. D. Farish (Williamsburg, Va., 1943).

sought to adjust both authority and nurture to the consequences for what children would do in the future. The mere existence of such an attitude, which parents would transmit by unspoken feelings as well as by conscious techniques, already tended to bias some of American child-raising toward a pattern more dynamic and productive than the common rural stolidity. The question of what was the dominant "line" on child-raising in the Civil War generation is, like most such questions, one about the relative emphasis given to various attitudes. Two points characterize that generation. First, the exploitative attitude may have continued to be that of most parents, since the desire to get some enjoyment or good out of children could always undermine any resolution to discipline the child for the sake of its future. One form of that undermining was the rapid growth of the sense-oriented, mother-oriented school of thought at the expense of the Lockean, even within attempts to make children independent. Second, almost all spokesmen expressed a conflict over the relative roles of the mother and the father. This conflict meant the introduction of anxiety into what was communicated to children, and it kept open a serious fault in the prescription of firmness and consistency that was central to the attempts at implanting conscience and independence.

Anxiety had at least three components. One was the tensions associated with the limitation of family size, at a time when contraceptive techniques were commonly known but considered morally suspect, and were in any case not yet quite reliable. The production of children whose quality would represent the family entailed limiting the number of children produced, and this might mean the postponement of marriage or the cramping of sexual activity within marriage. Guilt or discomfort about this process could spill over into a second anxiety, about infantile sex-play or infantile self-handling habits generally, and this component of anxiety did find increasing expression in late nineteenth-century pediatric literature. For one thing, infantile sexual activity was obviously analogous to some of the cruder and more disturbing forms of contraception, such as *coitus interruptus*.[70] And a third component of anxiety centered on the allocation of conventional or socially defined roles between the sexes. In some twentieth-century psychological studies, analysis of parents' attitudes has shown that these three components tend to cluster so that those parents who convey anxiety about one to their children tend also to convey anxiety about the others.[71] These attitudes probably went together in 1870, and it was typical of the period that it evaded the implied difficulties by the simple device of sentimentalizing the family in general and the mother in particular. By the 1860s and 1870s, medical advice was putting less stress on promoting independence in children, and those who bothered to notice Jacob Abbott's earlier views at all were apt to dismiss as old-fashioned his concern for the father's strict authority. Sentimentality seemed the only comfortable attitude available to middle-class families who risked the anxieties involved in producing fewer but better children. Sentimentality provided mothers with no clear statement of *how* they could avoid overindulgence and promote independence. Then, just before 1890, the pediatrician L. Emmett Holt began applying to child-care the concepts of asepsis and scheduling. Infants should not only be weaned and house-broken and subjected to discipline quite early in life; they should be put on strict feeding schedules, should never be picked up when they cried, and should be handled and kissed as little as possible. Austere but unpanicky techniques should instill habits to control sexual behavior. These procedures would presumably neutralize or confine the pattern of anxieties within middle-class families.

[70] The logic of the connection between contraception and sexual anxiety in the nineteenth century is explored by Oscar Handlin, "The Horror," in his *Race and Nationality in American Life* (Boston, 1957), 149-156.

[71] Robert R. Sears, Eleanor Marcoby, and Harry Levin, *Patterns of Child Rearing* (Evanston, Ill., 1957), ch. 6.

And it was only in that same generation, about the turn of the century, that the application of aseptic techniques to contraception made it less necessary to postpone marriage and sex. Within the handling of middle-class children, sentimentality became simply a surface tone that colored attempts to build a bureaucratic, aseptic style of child-care. There thus appeared a new version of the Lockean repressive family, but with the mother now the main antiseptic agent.[72] Just as the actual diffusion of Locke's ideas had depended first on their applicability to the needs of the London Foundling Hospital in the 1740s, so the later diffusion of neo-Lockean ideas depended first on their usefulness at the New York Babies' Hospital of which Holt was the first attending physician. But where earlier the urban, organizational bent of Cadogan's work had seemed irrelevant to American conditions, now the impulse to base child-care on organizational practice arose within the American city.

Back in the middle of the eighteenth century, Americans (at least as far as they had left any record of their own distinct ideas on child-raising) had been moving into a period of tension between the ideal of the well-ordered family and that of the repressive family. The latter ideal seemed to appeal particularly to men who wanted to combat the provincialism and the stolidity of intellect that they felt were American weaknesses. The kind of actual practice that these few reformers assumed to prevail was in fact what would naturally follow from an unsuccessful, unstrenuous effort by parents to follow some vague notion of the ideal of the well-ordered family.

[72] L. Emmett Holt, M.D., "The Feeding of Older Infants and Young Children," *Babyhood*, III (1886/87), 122-128. Walter L. Carr, M.D., "Early Regularity in Diet and Sleep," *ibid.*, III, 334-336. L. Emmett Holt, "How Infants Should be Nursed and Fed," *ibid.*, IV (1887/88), 331-333, 359-363. Susan H. Hinkley, "The Spirit of the Age in Education," *ibid.*, XI (1894/95), 268-271, 299-302. L. Emmett Holt, *The Care and Feeding of Children*, 1st edn. (New York, 1895), 21, 36-43, 50-57, 64-66; 3rd edn. (New York, 1904), 131.

By the years after the Civil War, the focus of explicit child-raising ideas had shifted toward a tension between the now orthodox repressive ideal and a new, maternalized version of the well-ordered family. But beneath this explicit tension there worked an underlying conflict between, on the one hand, the whole set of planful, future-oriented structures and, on the other, an actual practice that moralists and reformers felt was marked by indulgence or exploitation of children.

Real change did transpire between 1750 and 1870, change both in what observers assumed was the actual practice and in the method that they recommended to cope with this practice. The simplest way to characterize this complex is to concentrate on what men assumed about actual practice: this shifted from a regime of laxness and stolidity to a regime of indulgence and parental conflict. Laxness and indulgence amount to much the same thing, and overt child-raising practices probably changed little either among isolated farm families or among the city poor. But if middle-class, socially mobile families were as responsive to moral and medical advice then as they have been in the twentieth century, then those families probably made certain concrete changes in practice and certain equally real but less tangible changes in attitude. They probably did impose earlier and more abrupt disciplines on feeding and elimination (and possibly on infant sexual behavior), retaining much of this even during the Civil War generation when the maternally oriented literature was saying less about the need to encourage independence. They probably also reduced the amount of physical and arbitrary punishment, trying instead whatever emotional or manipulative techniques might work. The changes in *attitude* probably followed the curve of the shifting stands on the relative roles of mother and father—from a fairly easy acceptance of the old combination of overt paternal authority with covert maternal influence, through a period of anxiety to shore up the father's authority, into a period when families accepted the larger overt maternal role that was inevitable in city families, but when they also fell back on sentimentality as one way to gloss over uncertainties about whether that role could be effective.

Levels of discipline and indulgence may also have fluctuated considerably in the short term, according to whether economic conditions favored the existing household as an economic unit, or favored migration and the seeking of outside opportunity. Persisting concern about how long children should live at home indicated that this matter was long open to variation, and families are known to have made such adjustments in some communities as early as the seventeenth century.[73] Such short-term fluctuation may well have had considerable impact on children, as it almost certainly has in the twentieth century, but it is hardly accessible to historical investigation. Really short-term change, within the span of a single generation or less, is inaccessible unless we make mechanical assumptions about the relations between family life, population fluctuations, and economic fluctuations. Intermediate-term change, extending somewhat beyond a single generation, is accessible if we use evidence about the kinds of anxiety that were getting an audience at particular times. And for longer-term change, running to a century or more, we have evidence about changes in attitude.

But how can we apply any evidence about changing attitudes and practices to the question of changing intelligence? One way is to mine the psychological literature for hints on how family life affects children's minds. Research workers have in fact amassed a variety of such relationships, forming a consistent pattern. Converted into rules of

[73] Philip J. Greven, Jr., "Family Structure in Seventeenth-Century Andover, Massachusetts," *William and Mary Quarterly*, 3 ser., XXIII (1966), 234-256. And see the treatment of cyclical changes in family and status behavior, by P.M.G. Harris, "The Social Origins of American Leaders: The Demographic Foundations," in *Perspectives in American History*, III (1969).

thumb, these findings suggest far more than they can possibly prove. These simplified "rules" range from the obvious to the precise:

—that arbitrary, rejecting attitudes or behavior from parents limits the development of symbolic thought, and encourages the development of spatial and visual intelligence.
—that maternal warmth and nurture foster especially the development of verbal intelligence.
—that paternal involvement in child-rearing fosters quantitative and analytic thought.[74]
—that the combination of nurture before about age five with relative independence after that age is optimal for the development of intelligence in boys.
—that the combination of continuing nurture through childhood, with a warm relation to the father, is optimal for the development of intelligence in girls.[75]
—that inattentive, neglectful attitudes in parents discourage the development of intelligence.
—that overanxiety in parents and anxiety in children dampen intelligence in the children.

[74] Eleanor E. Maccoby and Lucy Rau, *Differential Cognitive Abilities* (Stanford, 1962). Elizabeth Bing, "Effect of Child-Rearing Practices on the Development of Differential Cognitive Abilites," *Child Development*, XXXIV (1963), 631-648.

[75] Marjorie P. Honzik, "Environmental Correlates of Mental Growth: Prediction from the Family Environment at 21 Months," *ibid.*, XXXVIII (1967), 337-364. Nancy Bayley and Earl S. Schaefer, "Correlations of Maternal and Child Behavior with the Development of Mental Abilities," Society for Research in Child Development, *Monographs*, XXIX (1964), No. 6. Norman L. Corah, "Differentiation in Children and Their Parents," *Journal of Personality*, XXXIII (1965), 300-308. John R. Hurley, "Parental Acceptance-Rejection and Children's Intelligence," *Merrill-Palmer Quarterly of Behavior and Development*, XI (1965), 19-30. Nancy Bayley, "Research in Child Development: a Longitudinal Perspective," *ibid.*, XI, 183-208.

—that firm but not arbitrary discipline fosters creative intelligence.[76]
—that anxiety and pressure for performance foster academic achievement more than intelligence, and intelligence more than creativity.
—that anxiety about sex roles dampens both analytic ability and creativity.

The inferences that follow are precarious and tentative but straightforward. They are confined as nearly as possible to the syllogistic form: such-and-such were the attitudes and practices; such-and-such attitudes and practices have certain effects; therefore these effects characterized the population. The specific syllogisms are hardly strict or literal, and they may well suffer some contamination from the material that is presented in chapter two on learning problems or in chapter four on cultural products. The aim, however, has been to form the conclusions of the three chapters independently. If the conclusions agree, fine; if not quite, which will be the case, then the exercise of reconciling them may refine the whole picture.

Early in the eighteenth century, the balance of influences from father and mother, in the moderate form of the well-ordered family, fostered anxiety-free mental development in both boys and girls; but the family applied low pressure for achievement, so that the effect of balance in parental roles was not fully realized. Furthermore, the education of women was sufficiently skimpy in all things, and that of men sufficiently skimpy in things quantitative, that the allocation of quantitative and verbal roles between the sexes was probably not so clear as it was later to become. The meager education of women had some dampening effect on intelligence

[76] Stanley Coopersmith, *The Antecedents of Self-Esteem* (San Francisco & London, 1967). Diana Baumrind and Allen E. Black, "Socialization Practices Associated with Dimensions of Competence in Preschool Boys and Girls," *Child Development*, XXXVIII (1967), 291-327.

in women, and through them in all children. Though the rigor of discipline was beginning to moderate, this very fact meant that it was less consistent, more arbitrary, and therefore sometimes rejecting in its effect on mental development. The whole situation fostered a condition of only partly realized potential, without strong anxieties that would prevent development when outside stimulation intervened, but with some drag on the transition from spatial to verbal ability.

This continued to be the pattern for rural and working-class families for many generations, with the one major change that for them, as for the whole society, what had been partly an intellectual subordination of females in all kinds of thought was transformed into a more clear verbal specialization for females as against quantitative for males.

Among the socially mobile and middle classes, substantial change began in the latter part of the eighteenth century. Partly as a political phenomenon—the domestic side of the drive to emulate Britain—pressure for independent behavior increased, and with it the pressure to realize intellectual potential. But this pressure relied on an increased disciplinary role for the father in *early* childhood, a strategy that may have been fine when it worked but that was probably as difficult of real success as it was absolutistic in tone. To the extent that it succeeded, it fostered a full trajectory of development toward analytic thought. To the extent that it failed, it intensified the arbitrary atmosphere that had already encouraged some concentration on spatial ability. During this process, which extended through roughly the first generation of the nineteenth century, the male continued to have the responsibility for bearing the verbal culture as well as the quantitative, even while the wider education of women was beginning to bring out the special female role in the verbal culture. This encouraged verbal ability to grow in the whole population, but with the domestic expression of that ability still lagging behind the public: in ordinary terms, it fostered the combination of public loquacity and dinner-table silence that was to be observed in Americans late into the nineteenth century.[77] Over this whole period two things brought gradual increase in anxiety about sex roles: the fact that some slight shift was actually taking place in the male-female balance, and the fact that people were consciously attempting a sharper disciplinary role for the father but not consistently achieving it. This anxiety was still moderate, though, partly because the shift of the American population into cities had not yet gone far enough to make any real difference to the obvious functional relation between male and female roles in the average, still rural household. Among the American families who did pick up improvement-minded cues in this period, the outcome in mental development was: to realize some general potential that would otherwise have sagged, to force a somewhat compulsive verbal expression, and to impose a kind of alternative between the analytic ability that would be fostered in the best of circumstances and the spatial ability that would develop in the frequent cases when analytic influences misfired.

Because the effort to intensify the father's early authority was associated with efforts to refine or develop American society, it was part of the system of changes in which many families adopted urban ways. As cities grew, uncertainty grew about the allotment of work roles, mental roles, and family-management roles between male and female. This increased the problems of those who saw the father's early authority as essential to development within the family, and their anxiety about sex roles increased sharply by about the 1830s. At the same time, more and more people within the middle classes accepted the changed roles of women, seeking to make those roles central in family-development strategy. The conflict between these two strategies, rein-

[77] "Learning to Speak," *Wood's*, XIV (1847), 101-102. "Speaking and Reading," *American Educational Monthly*, IV (1867), 114-117. Frances Anne Butler, *Journal of a Residence in America* (Paris, 1835), 142*n*-143*n*, 172*n*.

forced by the strains of family limitation and adjustment to city life, brought a sharp increase in the sexual anxiety that middle-class families conveyed to children during the generation after the 1830s. The family was increasingly preoccupied with decisions about sex roles and sexual behavior even while the increasingly sentimental public culture threw up a barrier of silence against these matters. Growth in the maternal role almost certainly fostered an increase in verbal abilities, and thus a break upward for many individuals whose development would otherwise have been fixated at the spatial level; but the attendant anxiety discouraged both verbal and quantitative from achieving much penetration. The conflict between paternal and maternal influences set a barrier at the crucial stage of male mental development, at about five years, and discouraged quantitative ability generally. At the same time families were putting increasing, intense pressure on children for formal mental achievement. This pattern of pressures, which continued after the Civil War, was exceedingly unstable, carrying a potential for emotional disturbance in those families who tried to transmit all the influences involved. In fact, many sought to avoid extreme pressure. Some middle-class families took a cue from the vagueness in the prevailing sentimentality, and simply tried to respond in moderation to each of these pressures, not worrying about consistency, and thus achieving a kind of syrupy, pragmatic equivalent of the less self-conscious family style that prevailed in rural and working-class families. But this was obviously an inelegant, evasive solution, and it was due to be superseded when anyone could work out a pattern of family life that gave the mother an unsentimental, reliable technique by which she could impose the kind of training in early independence that had been a speciality of the father-oriented discipline.

It was the Holtian combination of asepsis and rigid scheduling that provided a synthesis between the Lockean and the maternal conceptions of family life. It was widely followed, even by parents who accepted reluctantly the coldness and emotional sacrifices it required, and it almost certainly had consequences for mental development. By intensifying repression, even while effective contraception was making sexual expression easier, it served to contain overt sexual anxiety, including that about sex-typed cognitive roles. Though much conscious anxiety might persist, there was less reason for the kind of massive mental confusion that had been encouraged by middle-class family problems a generation or so earlier. Thus far, creativity and analytic ability were encouraged. But the severe restrictions on handling children, or on responding spontaneously to their needs, meant that discipline grew both less arbitrary in pace and more rejecting in tone, even among those families who made only a half-hearted attempt to apply the new line. The whole pattern did help to bring a halt to the compulsive verbalism of the mid-nineteenth century, but its combination of developmental pressure with rejecting tone worked to reaffirm the paradox that had appeared earlier in American thinking—between a strong pressure for analytic performance and a tendency to fixate on spatial ability. The early discipline that was imposed did not, however, reverse the long-term trend toward declining rigor within family discipline as a whole, and the net effect was to foster a new acceleration in mental development for the middle classes even while directing that development toward a precarious mixture of cognitive styles. For all its emotional pains, the Holtian line was probably more easily and more effectively applied than any of the earlier developmental strategies proposed for the family. It therefore probably did more to differentiate those families who adopted it from the rest of the population, and thus more to create a genuine mental difference between social classes.

The pattern of child-raising attitudes strengthens some parts of the picture suggested by teachers' observations, and forces revisions in other parts.

Whatever teachers or moralists observed in children was no simple phenomenon, but rather the surface appearance of a whole network of social problems, choices, and strategies. Take the matter of the independent, "republican" manner that foreign observers noted in American children in the eighteenth century. Although moralists often lamented outright impertinence in children, they saw social advantages and attractive personal qualities in the independence of young men setting out for themselves. The complexity of John Witherspoon's position is fully to the point. He arrived in America as an imported Calvinist intellectual shortly before the Revolution. He lent his own authority to sentiment supporting the father's role within the family. At the same time, he took an enthusiastic part in the movement for political independence. The problem of family attitudes had the same structure as the problem of "deference" in politics. Over wide areas, the society was one of small independent farmers each having the right to vote and each free from direct economic pressure by the wealthy. In many communities these "independent" farmers gave easy acknowledgment to leadership exercised by the wealthy and the established, but they also expected some "deference" from those of their own families who were not (or not yet) independent. The logic of the situation entailed less a straight-out tension between authoritative fathers and republican children than a natural continuum and interchange of roles.

Even though the material on colonial parents is hardly better than the material on colonial pupils, it does support the same sense of a slack, uncompulsive situation, in which men believed authority was normal but failed to make the most of it. Even the larger eighteenth-century families were not maintaining order and prestige against a tight, traditional social system. Much of the drive for "achievement" that had been working in European culture for some time was satisfied by the relative ease with which householders in America could pick up enough material goods to support families that were large by European standards. Outside the South, large families reached their size mostly by natural reproduction, not by including servants who had to be directed by patriarchal authority. (And even in the South, natural reproduction of slaves was coming to be important, in contrast to the more artificial systems for recruiting servants in Europe.) Though the prosperity of the colonials would contribute to their motives for asserting independence from European society, it then kept the American mind from having to develop any real driven quality. The typically American trait in Benjamin Franklin was less his business drive than the casual, even serene manner that he preserved during his rise in the world. Whatever the Puritan mind may have been like earlier, and whatever complexities of mind may have been involved in the religious emotionalism of the early eighteenth century, the domestic temper of Americans simply did not support any great straining after mental efficiency.

The moderately complex structure of parental attitudes in the colonial years suggest, then, that a similar complexity may have marked the slackness teachers noted in pupils' attitudes toward learning. Slackness in schools went along with docility in the household. Since sons did not feel that the father's authority threatened their independence in any long run, they could easily absorb skills from him without putting up any of the emotional barriers that later observers might read as a deficit in intelligence. The traditional calculating ability of Yankee men makes little sense in terms of school patterns alone. It makes perfectly good sense within the republican deference that sons gave to their fathers.

Another complex structure ran through the growth of differences between male and female abilities. In terms of historical labels, this growth was part of the Romantic Movement. If a nationality had rights because it was "different," so might females. Such labels do miss, though, the uncertainty that churned through nineteenth-century American attitudes about male-female relations. Many people gave explicit recognition to the positive authority of mothers, quite beyond what earlier generations would have conceded. Others insisted just as strongly that maternal influence was one of the depraving aspects of modern city life. Aside from trite statements that a child needed the influence of both parents, no one made any real effort to resolve these contradictory attitudes. Perhaps the generation from the 1840s to the 1870s was "too busy" to think through these matters. But there was more involved. The same generation was worrying out loud about abortion and divorce, even while it would not talk about its increasing efforts to limit family size. The same generation was worrying about the dangers of large city schools where children of different ages, or different social classes, or even different sexes might contaminate each other. The same generation was beginning to worry about how parents could prevent masturbation by small children. The same generation was trying to persuade itself of the utter sexual innocence of children. In all this anxiety, the idea that males and females had different *kinds* of ability served as one more way to draw a line between behaviors or feelings that should not mix.

This very complex of uncertainty forces a revision in what teachers' observations indicated about intelligence. The "pressure" that teachers and outsiders alike saw in nineteenth-century schools did not result from any plain pattern of parental authority. If some people were still willing to use the father's authority as a springboard for the young man seeking independence, others were just as willing to use the mother's strength to make the family a cushioning shelter from the pressures of city commerce. If these two attitudes met, it was in the evasions that they assumed, not in any positive notions. The sentimental conception of home as haven did assume that the pressures in the outside world were real and continuing. This attitude could accept schoolroom demands in the same way that it accepted pressure on young stock-exchange clerks. Neither the father-oriented nor the mother-oriented approach to children included much willingness to stop, take time, and look honestly at what was really going on inside children's minds. Together, economic impatience and sexual evasion led many different kinds of people to accept by default the pressures working through school systems. Some few may actually have believed that the pressures would promote the economic advancement of children moving out into the world. Many, though, obviously disliked the pace even while they accepted the system. What looked like pressure had in it a large element of the compulsive: default and indecision concealed by movement, routine, and busy-work.

The competing parental attitudes of the Civil War generation suggest a dynamic inner mechanism for the strain between verbal and quantitative aptitudes, or between male and female mentalities, that runs through the school talk of the period. The compartmentalization between the sexes was a real part of the emotional preoccupations extending into an ongoing folk controversy over the relative roles that mothers and fathers should take in raising children. The uncertainty about authority that had marked colonial life had been supplanted by an uncertainty, even an anxiety, about sexual expression and sexual style. The same shift had marked people's political concerns. Whether or not Americans have been peculiarly vulnerable to fear of political conspiracy, they have certainly had their political anxieties from generation to generation. But those anxieties have not always focused on the same objects. Where fearful colonials worried about danger from conspiracies to impose executive or legislative tyranny, Americans of a century later worried more about conspiracies to insinuate change into the moral or religious style of the nation's life. As a scare-figure, the royal customs agent gave way to the schoolteaching nun. Underneath all the unfolding religious and ethnic variety of nineteenth-century society, the most fundamental American pluralism was simply a dualism, between workplace and home, between westward migration and cityward migration, between male and female spheres, between calculation and speech. With profound ambiguity about which role was analogous to which sex, the same dualism extended to that between preacher and priest, Protestant and Catholic.

The shift from uncertainty about authority to uncertainty about sex roles did not mean that earlier generations had not known anxiety about the psychological influence of women, or that the newly acute anxiety would persist without any effort at resolution. As a matter of fact, later generations did move on to child-raising formulas that did seem to make the mother's role more predictable and reliable, or at least more scheduled and sanitary. The rigid styles of child-raising that were recommended to mothers after about 1890 were very much of a piece with the routine tasks that were being found for women in business organizations at the same time. In general, where one period had experienced a shift into preoccupation with problems of moral or sexual style, a later generation became more worried about problems of organization, scale, and bureaucracy, especially in economic organizations. Within this larger and more up-to-date worry, that about sexual and moral styles became a secondary theme, working within people's minds to be sure, but not salient again until the latter part of the twentieth century.

But one early female role that was designed to make woman's influence regular and safe within an organized system was precisely that of the teacher within increasingly complex school bureaucracies, right at the middle of the nineteenth century; this early appearance of the bureaucratized woman raises serious questions about the relative place of school and family in any chain of influences that led to particular levels or styles of popular intelligence. These questions do not touch in any formal way the technique of using schools and learning behavior as *surface-level* measures of intelligence while treating parental attitudes as an *indirect* measure based on the assumption that such attitudes do affect children's abilities. They *do* touch the off-hand sequence that one might erroneously read into this situation. It is all too easy to assume that the whole argument is a matter of the way intelligence results from the life experiences of a typical individual in chronological order of his life, with parental guidance determining the mental equipment children take to school, schools then giving direction and discipline to the abilities students take into higher education, and the higher education of experts then determining the cultural products that display the whole workings of social intelligence. Antebellum schools, though, began making bureaucratic adjustments to female influence long before the people who scribbled about family life got around to any similar reworking of their ideas. Only in the bizarre but popular field of phrenology did some hint of later changes appear. Some phrenologists did support an emotionally intense maternalism within the family, and all phrenologists accepted a schematic, departmentalized conception of human abilities. The rapid adjustment of schools both to bureaucracy and to a new definition of sex roles seems to undercut the long-standing complaint that schools can never produce any real changes either in social structure or in pupils' attitudes. The solution to this difficulty lies in the fact that the *problem* of sex roles was in fact becoming clear for the family long before it became an issue in the schools. Locke gave one semiphilosophical definition to the distrust of maternal influence as early as the late seventeenth century. Although his definition did not evoke much popular response at that time, it did begin to strike home only a century later in America, during the time after the Revolution when patterns of migration were beginning to unbalance the ratio between male and female population in different places, and when urbanization was just beginning to introduce unfamiliar strains into the differences between work roles of men and women. There was a surplus of spinsters in many Eastern communities, well before school districts began replacing men with women teachers. When a moralist like Jacob Abbott complained that indulgent city mothers were endangering the father's authority within the family, he did not seem to be taking cues from adjustments that were already beginning in the schools.

The very ease with which schools responded to anxiety about sex roles indicates—just that. It *indicates*. Really profound changes had been taking place in the ways population was distributed and in the kinds of tasks people performed. Family life did respond to these shifts by taking up new ways for men and women to behave and by taking up new demands for pace and precision in the habits young people would bring to new work roles. But families made these adjustments very gradually indeed, even sluggishly. Controversy between spokesmen for the influence of fathers and spokesmen for the influence of mothers expressed a sense of dilemma that kept family life from moving very far away from its eighteenth-century pragmatic tone. Precisely because schools were less vital to people, society could displace onto the school system needs that were acute but nearly insoluble within the family. There were, of course, good practical reasons why administrators hired low-paid women and set them to implementing routine tasks. But there was something almost too quick about the way society snapped up this change in the schools, as if it met needs that were insistent and difficult outside the school setting. Families were changing, as was indicated by the steady decline in the size of urban families. Families also had trouble talking about the way they were changing, as was indicated by taboos against the most delicate discussion of birth control. In this situation, the more responsive changes taking place within schools provided both a measure of what was the mental state of learners and a sensitive, unstable indicator of effects that deeper problems might be having on that same mental state.

These considerations point quite beyond the realms of family and school. Family attitudes are presumably an *input* into the growth of mental states. Whatever the effects of school, behavior observed in the classroom may at least be used as an indication of ability. But only if something is different in the mental set of people *after* they leave school can any particular effect be attributed to the schools. The cultural behavior of adults, or their behavior as audience, is a general measure of that mental set. But at this point the whole causal argument turns circular again. The culture in which adults participate includes, above all, those overlapping bodies of action called "technology" and "the media." And changes in technology, including the media, are among those basic changes in economic process that pose difficulties for family life to solve. In the late twentieth century, technological innovations have made possible both the child's television program and the oral contraceptive. But children's television grew up partly because families could use a major new preoccupying instrument with which to organize the young, and oral contraception was adapted from pharmacology into commercial drug sales to meet demands for female initiative and religious reconciliation. Much earlier, did the urban jobs that opened up the split between female and male roles "result from" technology (such as the steam engine), or did the importation of machine techniques from England "result from" the pervasive underemployment and slack morale within the eighteenth-century family?

Again, it is unrealistic to talk about any simple development from family life through intelligence and education to expression in the wider culture. The network is so much a whole that family attitudes, school behavior, and the public culture are each simply another facet of the thing that is the intelligence of the people. The significance of any one element in the array can be evaluated only in terms of how it fits in with the others.

At this point, then, the process of triangulation on the mental landscape may benefit from a set of probes into the sector of the public culture.

FOUR

THE DISPLAY OF INTELLIGENCE

THE FEW PEOPLE who went through the whole course of education that was available at any time faced a pointed test. Having passed the successive narrowings of opportunity from the nursery to professional apprenticeship or schooling, they were then to produce words or objects or choices that would serve needs of the whole society. They delivered sermons, they treated illnesses or the ill, they argued cases in court and wrote briefs or delivered judicial decisions, they designed ships or buildings or bridges or roads. The same men who did these things also wrote a major part of the general literature written by Americans for Americans. Even aside from this general literature, what these men did was symptomatic of the quality of the whole educational system, and in three ways.

First, the elementary schools and the work-places or intermediate schools had to have given these men the skills and knowledge they needed in order to take up professional training at all. For some professionals, such as the cruder kinds of revival preacher, these preliminary skills might amount to no more than an illiterate wallowing in the traditional verbal culture; but preliminaries there had to be, and the character of early learning determined how large and how precise an effect later professional training could produce. The exceptional genius might rise quite above the educational "pyramid," but the average professional man hardly could.

Second, if there were any general turns of thought determined by the nursery and the lower schools, they showed in the recorded work of professional men, just as they also showed in the larger body of work these men did without leaving any record, and just as they showed in the speech and jottings of the whole population. The habit, for example, of solving new problems by classifying them under some already codified rule or pattern can be taught quite early in the learning cycle of a particular culture, and it can operate through the fine words and elaborate information of the professional worker, just as much as it can in the simple calculations of the farmer at market.

Third, most professional products depended to some extent on whether people at large could appreciate them. These products had to be heard or paid for or enforced by people who were not professionally trained. With some kinds of product, this relation was of course remote, as it was with a legal brief that was supposed to appeal to the judge in a technical case, or with an industrial structure whose complexities few men could either see or understand. But with other kinds the relation was intimate. Some kinds of legal decision or courtroom oration received immediate popular attention. Sermons given to general congregations had to appeal to ordinary people if they were to succeed at all, and any differences in the kinds of sermon directed to different audiences—to revival gathering or to stable congregation, to adherents of one denomination or to those of another—reflected the range of taste and education in the whole population. In the case of real emotional interchange between speaker and audience, the sermon was hardly even the work of the professional man acting alone; it was produced by people and practitioner together.

This difference between levels of audience contact follows somewhat the same lines as another difference, that between the kinds of thinking appropriate to different kinds of professional product. Some kinds gave greatest scope to verbal thinking that would seize reality in wholes, and in the same wholes that were obviously available in the surrounding culture. The popular sermon and the courtroom harangue were of this type. Other kinds gave scope to quantitative or analytical talent. The medical research report or the engineer's structural design could be of this type—although either could also be carried out by methods largely intuitive, visual, or descriptive. Seen as the difference between verbal and quantitative thought, or between intuitive and analytic, this difference corresponds to those between kinds of learning problem that nineteenth-century observers saw in the schools. It corresponds also to dimensions that twentieth-century students have used as one first step in analyzing the varieties of intelligence.

Actually, anything in the culture gave expression to intelligence. Mental energy went into the selection of political candidates, or the invention of household gadgets, or the writing of philosophical treatises. For the sake of focus, though, this chapter treats in some detail the changes that took place between 1750 and 1870 in two extreme kinds of professional product: the sermon and the design of load-bearing structures. In broad ways, both of these developed in the same way as did learning problems in schools. They developed a tone of compression and hurry that alarmed men who worried about the thoroughness of what was being accomplished. And they evolved toward simpler, clearer, more accessible forms. In this change the verbal culture seemed to take the lead. In 1750 complex scholastic sermons were already giving way to discourses elegant yet simple that were supposed to convey meaning in some intellectually respectable form to men of all levels of taste and capacity. Only later, and as American transportation problems became severe, did designers begin to propose and then execute daring, simple structures to convey loads across wide spans of water or gulch. Older forms of preaching and building continued, of course, and provided a point of view from which men could question the quality of the work that preachers and builders were turning out.

About 1870 Americans discovered that their accomplishments in these areas were being challenged in wide and shocking ways. Their merchant marine, after the clipper-ship splendors of the 1850s, found itself suddenly crowded out by the commercial and technical advantages of the British. On their railroads, bridges that the public had trusted failed under the impact of larger trains, with great loss of life. And the man whom almost everyone acknowledged to be the prince of the American pulpit, Henry Ward Beecher, slipped into a sexual scandal that for more than accidental reasons called into question a whole style that bound preacher and public. For both preaching and building, criticism and new thoughts became then unavoidable, however difficult.

In both areas, criticism may turn less on complexity of skill or elaborateness of knowledge than it does on the quality or integrity of isolated intellectual acts. To a culture that was moving toward simplicity as a standard, this kind of criticism is more appropriate than any demand that either practitioner or audience should have had great resources of information. Assessment of the separate intellectual act is also more appropriate to a culture in which educational reformers kept insisting that they wanted to teach children how to think, not what to think, and that they wanted to provide a training that would enable all men to participate in the essentials of the culture. This kind of criticism asks about the preacher: when he took up with his congregation a difficult subject such as original sin or the nature of church membership or commercial ethics, how did he deal with the intellectual or moral embarrassments it presented? Plainly and intelligently, or evasively and superficially? Such criticism asks about the builder: when he took up a new project did he deal with all the real difficulties or did he hide them behind formula and tradition? It asks about all people: was the American mind, whatever its gains in formal schooling, capable of facing and handling real intellectual difficulties within the problems it took up?

This competence entailed more than any mental good intentions. It involved specific sermons, specific ships, specific bridges. The way a person dealt with one of these products led him through mental actions that might move in analogy with family and school experience. If these analogies are to sharpen evaluation, rhetoric and structure can be approached only through many specific examples. The casual inquirer may, if he wishes, accept as demonstrated the interactions that emerge from these specifics. The critical inquirer will insist that each meeting between public culture and private experience remains arguable, even now, because it was then alive, precarious.

A. A Case in the Verbal: Colonial Preaching

For all American provincialism, colonial preaching moved within a pattern of styles and standards that had its main locus in England. Styles had changed considerably over the previous century and a half, and Americans perpetuated or adopted virtually all the forms that had been introduced. In the early seventeenth century, two high intellectual preaching styles enjoyed favor in England. On the one hand, the elaborate analogies, word-play, and imagery of the medieval scholastic sermon had, under the influence of literary styles from southern Europe, developed into the so-called metaphysical style, in which the preacher exploited the multiple meanings within any strenuously interpreted image in order to convey the paradoxical, emotionally rich quality of serious religion. This style, exemplified by Bishop Lancelot Andrewes and carried to a high level of personal quality by John Donne, was favored among one part of the Jacobean court and aristocratic society. On the other hand, the Puritan intellectuals had developed, partly out of the rationalistic vein within medieval scholasticism, a kind of didactic, highly analytic sermon. Urging plain speech instead of lush imagery or self-indulgent conceits, they produced discourses in which the intellectual skeleton was naked, highly articulated, and unavoidable. Their style was the origin of the "fifthlys" and "sixthlys" that are legendary in reminiscences of old-time American sermons. It was not, however, this complexity that marked such sermons as intellectually strenuous. Puritan hearers were expected to remember and ponder Puritan sermons. At least as originally intended, the multiple divisions were a device to aid the understanding and memory of the ordinary hearer.

Not all British sermons achieved either of these heights—the metaphoric or the analytic. Some remained simple exhortations to the people, illustrated by whatever detail the preacher's story-telling ability might command. Some remained bluff homilies to the gentry. Some remained straightforward discourses by church hierarchs and administrators who lacked the time or temperament for word-play. These types were supported by Charles II himself, after the Restoration. Somewhat out of touch with the detailed intellectual styles of Great Britain, he had been exposed to recent French court preaching, oratorical but plain and evangelical. He now gave church preferment to men who preached in a tasteful but plain style, such as John Tillotson, and the adaptable Tillotson survived the Glorious Revolution to become Archbishop of Canterbury. The Tillotson style also survived, and it was this that Anglican missionaries and spokesmen like Samuel Johnson were introducing into America during the middle years of the eighteenth century. This genteel version of the plain style won many Puritans, too, such as those who became an important segment of the Royal Society. Aside from any specific patronage and organizational influences, this manner was the appropriate stylistic expression for the slightly tired social accommodation that was worked out in Britain between the middle of the seventeenth century and the middle of the eighteenth.[1]

Yet the best of American colonial sermons were often

[1] Charles H. E. Smyth, *The Art of Preaching. A Practical Survey of Preaching in the Church of England, 1747-1939* (London, 1939). William Fraser Mitchell, *English Pulpit Oratory, from Andrewes to Tillotson; a Study of Its Literary Aspects* (New York, 1962). J. W. Blench, *Preaching in England in the Late Fifteenth and Sixteenth Centuries: a Study of English Sermons 1450-c.1600* (Oxford, 1964).

produced in country towns, away from the centers of polite culture. This did not mean that the great preacher was an intellectual exiled to the country, where he then talked above the comprehension of his hearers. A Jonathan Edwards could win impressive successes with some of his congregation in Northampton, whatever difficulties he may have had with the alien minds of Stockbridge.

In the New York area,[2] this kind of relation of preacher with hearers was enjoyed and sustained by Jonathan Dickinson, who until his death in 1747 was pastor at a Yankee settlement in New Jersey. Those of Dickinson's sermons of the 1730s and 1740s that have survived in published form dealt with problems wider than those of his parish, but their form and style assumed an understanding between him and his immediate audience. He might be speaking to combat the influence of extreme revivalist activity throughout the Middle Atlantic area, and he might polish his discourses when they came to be published; but he spoke in the first place to the pace of local thinking.

When Dickinson preached his *Call to the Weary & Heavy Laden to Come Unto Christ for Rest* in 1739, he began in a way that was common in exegetical sermons, by breaking into separate phrases his text (Matthew xi.28: "Come unto me, all ye that labor and are heavy laden, and I will give you rest"). "All" he took as a point on which he could expound the universality of sinfulness; "labor," the workings of the soul under a growing sense of sin; "heavy laden," the condition of the soul under conviction of sin and danger of hell. To the converted Christian he offered the consolations of the gospel, but he warned against accepting the consolations in a spirit of carnal security. He described duties to which the careful convert should attend. Especially should the convert guard against any divisions within

[2] For this section on colonial preaching I selected all entries through 1761 in Evans's *Bibliography* for sermons either printed or delivered in New York or New Jersey, and read all of those available on microcard.

the Christian community, resisting the attacks that those who pretended to spiritual security might make against Christians, whom they slandered as hypocrites. This last, just before a peroration appealing for conversion, was of course the tactical point of the sermon. Having established his own title to evangelical piety, he could then attack as presumptuous, even carnal in their sense of assurance, those preachers who denounced more cautious ministers as "unconverted." And he did more than establish a title to piety. He stated it in a way that both assumed and re-enforced a bond between him and the hearers whom revivalists were trying to entice away. He assumed throughout that those hearers understood the terms and concepts that made up the Calvinist description of the process of conviction and conversion. But he used those ideas within a running account of the emotional trials that the individual soul experienced in its struggles between sin and consolation. The general tone of his discourse was available to hearers who lacked technical knowledge, and offered even a context that suggested meanings for the difficult terms. By stating in emotionally impelling terms much that he and hearers shared from a common world of discourse, he prepared those hearers to be persuaded of his immediate thesis.[3]

In part, this achievement of a structure of shared discourse resulted from Dickinson's own intellectual versatility. Although *A Call to the Weary & Heavy Laden* was typical of his sermons, he achieved the same intellectual resonance in other ways, when others were appropriate. Preaching for the funeral of a neighboring minister's wife,

[3] Jonathan Dickinson, *A Call to the Weary & Heavy Laden to Come unto Christ for Rest. A Sermon Preached at Connecticut Farms in Elizabeth-Town, New Jersey, Dec. 23, 1739* (New York, 1740). Compare Dickinson's similar *The Witness of the Spirit. A Sermon Preached at Newark in New-Jersey, May 7th, 1740. . . . On Occasion of a Wonderful Progress of Converting Grace in Those Parts* (Boston, 1740), and also *The Nature and Necessity of Regeneration, . . . Preached at Newark, in New-Jersey, Jan. 19, 1742-3* (New York, 1743).

he built the larger part of his discourse on the stern orthodox theme that God's deliberate Providence was revealed even in the loss of near and dear relatives, but he supported that theme with a—for him—unusually thick fabric of proof-texts: Bible verses that helped to cumulate intensity through the central doctrinal argument, then provided a point of apparently extra-human authority on which consolation could rest in a brief concluding section. Again, in preaching against the formal liturgy of the Anglican church, he used, not a style of polemical biblicism, but a mild, discursive essay form, rather like that then fashionable for sermons in the Church of England.[4] Whatever the variations, though, his underlying practice was to find an intellectual pattern and terms that preacher and hearers could share, to offer enough of discourse according to that pattern and those terms in order to cement a sense of intellectual identity, and then finally to offer as an extension of that world his concluding idea, which his hearers might otherwise have hesitated to accept.

This assumption that intellectual sharing was possible, was also used by other preachers of the period, though not all displayed Dickinson's virtuosity. Ebenezer Pemberton, minister of the Presbyterian Church in New York City, relied on agreement in the elements of Biblical culture and Calvinist doctrine, much as did Dickinson. But where a Dickinson made his somewhat paradoxical concluding section grow out of and extend the agreement that he had already elicited, a Pemberton simply stuck a topical conclusion on the end of a conventional exegesis that met his hearers' expectations of what a preacher might say. Thus in 1746, on the occasion of the defeat of the Young Pretender in Scotland, he gave a formal discourse in which he outlined

[4] Jonathan Dickinson, *A Sermon Preached at the Funeral of Mrs. Ruth Pierson, Wife of the Reverend Mr. John Pierson, Minister of the Gospel at Woodbridge, in New Jersey* (New York, 1733). Dickinson, *The Vanity of Human Institutions in the Worship of God, A Sermon Preached at Newark, June 2, 1736* (New York, 1736).

many kinds of wordly blessing or salvation in which Christians could agree to praise God as the real agent—and then finished this with a burst of anti-popery and British patriotism, in which he made no serious attempt to adjust evangelical themes to fashionable verbal styles and fashionable social appeals.[5] The difficulty of this task showed in structural devices he adopted. Often, following the new fashion that called for sermons to approximate the essay form, he would limit to two the number of main divisions that he announced for his discourse. But in one case he blundered immediately by announcing as these two divisions (1) the evidences and (2) the improvements that he would offer for the main point, which was the doctrine of a future judgment. He thus evaded any responsibility for offering a logical opening or analysis of his subject, and used the reasonable but mechanical distinction between argument and application as a substitute for explanation.

Or, in another case, after beginning with a somewhat more adequate two-fold division, he then proceeded to divide his second division and his application into six and four numbered subdivisions, respectively. He was uncertain whether to operate in the Calvinist or in the Addisonian mode, and tended to slip back into the older. At the same time, his responsiveness to fashion or to downright worldliness cut him off from the intellectual subtleties of the Calvinist tradition, and made his judgments superficial to the point of evasion and dishonesty. On problems where analogy could mix social ideas into theological, he tended to be more royalist than the Deity, but in a way that brought God within the Hanoverian horizon. He argued that the gospel must have been spread by the agency of the Holy Spirit, because this spread was "beyond the power of second Causes." But, where any well-trained Puritan would have shown considerable skepticism about the psychological "second causes" that could lead worldly individuals to take up an

[5] Ebenezer Pemberton, *A Sermon Delivered at the Presbyterian Church in New-York, July 31, 1746* (New York, 1746).

apparently unpopular gospel, Pemberton assumed flatly that the Jews and Romans would have been put off by the strangeness of the gospel, by persecutions, and by "*the Meanness and Simplicity of the Instruments, that were employed in this Blessed Work.*" Assigning in another context reasons why Christ rather than the Father would be the judge at the Last Judgment, he assimilated these reasons to the public-relations considerations in the appointment of, say, a colonial governor: the selection of Christ "may convince us with what kindness, condescension and equity, this great transaction will be managed, and assures us that he will condemn only those, who have obstinately despis'd his Goodness, and defeated the endearing methods of his Grace." Even more: "This appointment is design'd to *increase the visible pomp and splendour of the future judgment.*" Despite all this, he continued to conclude his sermons with little evangelical appeals to his hearers to seek a saving knowledge of Christ.[6]

Other preachers who relied on some possibility of intellectual sharing with their congregations included Samuel Buell on Long Island, Chauncey Graham in Dutchess County, and David Bostwick in New York City. All, like Dickinson and Pemberton, were Presbyterians. They spoke for a theological tradition that sought intellectual consent as a major part of Christian faith, and they spoke as men working in situations that realized much of the Presbyterian-Congregational ideal of the relation between minister and people. In general, each was pastor over his one congregation for most of a lifetime career. Each had the opportunity not only to presume on the tradition but to offer his congre-

[6] Ebenezer Pemberton, *Sermons on Several Subjects. Preach'd at the Presbyterian Church in the City of New-York* (Boston, 1738). The quotations are from pp. 2, 5, 38, 40. For a similar attempt to straddle the polite style and the logical style, though from a different doctrinal point of view, see William Tennent, Jr., *God's Sovereignty, No Objection to the Sinner's Striving. A Sermon, Preached at New-York on the 20th of January, 1765* (New York, 1765).

gation a continued, even repetitious, instruction that would re-create and re-enforce the tradition. One besetting temptation into which such preachers often fell was that of text-chopping: taking isolated words and phrases out of the Bible, then using some plausible inference in order to erect on each some conventional point of doctrine. But the ideal toward which they tended, the ideal that has become the basis for idyllic accounts of theological literacy among the American colonial populace, was the accomplishment that John Pierson described in his funeral sermon for Dickinson:

> He had uncommonly clear Views of the Scripture System of Gospel Doctrine, and glorious Scheme and Design of divine Revelation; had a Body of Divinity treasured up in his Mind, and was very careful to hold fast the Form of sound Words in the present dark Day, in which many corrupt Opinions, and Soul destroying Errors, do so much prevail and abound in the Protestant World, and even in this Land; And he shewed a warm Zeal in the Cause of Truth: He was very communicative of his Knowledge to others, and peculiarly happy and skilful in imparting his Thoughts: His Stile and Diction was correct, masculine, and nervous [i.e., strong-nerved]: He had a remarkable Capacity to treat of Things with a comprehensive Succinctness, and perspicuous Brevity, and to confirm Truths by irrefragable Arguments, and set them in a clear and advantageous Light.[7]

The variant manners that turned up in the work of the Dickinson-Pemberton group—essay-writing, word-chopping, the stringing together of proof-texts—were only slight reflections of the varieties in larger style and accomplishment that other ministers in the area displayed. The other styles reflected kinds of intellectual life quite different from

[7] John Pierson, *The Faithful Minister: A Funeral Sermon, Preached at Elizabeth-Town, October 9, 1747. Occasioned by the Death of the Reverend Mr. Jonathan Dickinson* (New York, 1748), p. 20.

any idyllic community of discourse, although the failure to achieve such community did not necessarily reflect any lack of ability in the preacher.

Among the revivalist preachers whom Dickinson resisted, one from the New York area has left some published sermons, all from 1735. Gilbert Tennent, who was minister to a church in New Brunswick but preached also in New York, was no ordinary mouthing ranter. His father, William Tennent, had established the "Log College" at Neshaminy, Pennsylvania, where he worked to train preachers who would be evangelical, yet strong in the Calvinist intellectual tradition. The younger Tennent demonstrated in his own work one way to combine traditional sermon form with emotional appeal. Taking such topics as *The Necessity of Religious Violence in Order to Obtain Durable Happiness*, he made his revivalist intent clear. At the same time, he professed not to understand why other ministers objected to his preaching. By religious "violence," after all, he meant simply diligence and intensity. When he preached in New York on *The Danger of Forgetting God*, he made a point of publishing the sermon, as the best reply to clamors that men had raised against it. The burden of the sermon was in fact orthodox, however evangelical: men should take thought for their conditions, lest it become too late and God in anger punish them. Conventional sermon technique had long called for dividing the preacher's thesis into numbered points (firstly, secondly, thirdly, and so forth), and Tennent observed this convention by providing two divisions within his main proposition, and six subdivisions. As the more analytic preachers did, he then provided sub-points within each of the subdivisions. But here began the difference. Where the conventional analyzing preacher would have presented sub-points that divided the main idea into logically separate aspects, so that he could treat each distinctly, Tennent simply made each sub-point a concrete illustration accompanied by a few sentences of exhortation to the one main point. Thus, under the general idea that "the Wicked shall be turned into Hell, and all the Nations that forget God," he gave five numbered types of those who forget God: secure sinners, delaying sinners, profane sinners, sensualists, and hypocrites.[8] Delaying sinners, for example, he described as those "who studiously avoid the thoughts of God's Justice, and thereby stab their Souls, and strangle their gasping Consciences! [And he apostrophized them:] O ye Murderers! Ye are the *Forgetters of God*, whose doleful Doom (so continuing) is to be *torn to Pieces*." Then Tennent moved to the next point without any further development. These illustrations and little exhortations built cumulatively and insistently toward the one point. While using far more formal classification and sub-classification than did most preachers, Tennent directed this technique toward hitting his listeners with a mounting series of particulars, repetitious yet gripping. Intellectual quality and persuasiveness he achieved less by logic or analysis than through fertility of image and gorgeousness of texture.

The technique of dazzling the ear with particulars was common enough in that generation, even though Tennent excelled in his single-minded drive to make impact on the feelings. Pemberton's weakness for breaking a text into separate words, then preaching what amounted to a little sermon on each one, was a version of the same technique. Other ministers fell into this same trap, especially when they took a single adjective as text, then divided it by stringing out a series of synonyms or aspects. Thus the Pierson funeral sermon on Jonathan Dickinson, although its con-

[8] Gilbert Tennent, *The Danger of Forgetting God, Describ'd. . . . Preach'd at New York, March, 1735* (New York, 1735), esp. pp. 14-15. See also Tennent, *The Necessity of Religious Violence in Order to Obtain Durable Happiness. . . . Preached at Perth-Amboy, June 29, 1735* (New York, [1735]), and Tennent, *The Espousals or a Passionate Perswasive to a Marriage with the Lamb of God, . . . Preach'd at N. Brunswyck, June the 22nd, 1735* (New York, [1735]).

cluding eulogy gave a useful description of Dickinson's intellectual style, consisted in its main section of nothing more than a series of separate little pieces on each of several ways in which a minister could be described as "faithful." In this he adapted a technique that ministers often used for ordination sermons—the running together of paragraphs on the traits desirable in a man. Although the congregations at ordination sermons were always of somewhat higher intellectual caliber than the average, including at least as many neighboring ministers as were necessary for the ceremony, and although the frequent publication of ordination sermons in the colonial period indicated that men thought of them as dealing seriously with the status of the professional religious intellectual, these sermons were in fact among the dullest, most routine productions of the colonial pulpit.

The bible-verse sermon and the prophecy sermon were more sustained efforts to dazzle through repetitious wordplay. On those hearers who were trained in the Bible, a preacher could score impact by larding a single sermon with scores of fat proof-texts, sometimes alternating and illustrating virtually every sentence of his own with a sentence of Scripture. The minister who was more learned in Biblical history and exegesis could extend this form into a disquisition on the prophecies, not only performing the safe task of showing how the obscure and poetic phrases in the Hebrew Scriptures prefigured the coming of Christ, but even offering his own interpretation of what the prophecies and the apocalypse said about the modern age and millennium. The elder Aaron Burr, president of the College of New Jersey, indulged himself in displaying his erudition in such set-pieces—taking full advantage of a ministerial audience in 1756 by setting out an elaborate millennial scheme to the Synod of New York, or introducting a well-attended funeral sermon (sure to be well-attended because its subject was the governor of New Jersey, Jonathan Belcher) with a finely crabbed exegesis of a passage from the book of Daniel.[9] The same form that a Tennent used for hammering in an evangelical point could also be used for the social display of personal erudition. The point was not that Burr could not preach a plain gospel appeal, but that he chose to distinguish between the plain and the elevated. Where a Dickinson sought to bring different kinds of hearers into an intellectual unity, a Burr kept his aims separate. As his eulogist said, "His Diction was expressive, and his Stile neat and flowing; his Language was well suited to the Business of a Christian Orator: When he thought proper, and Occasion required, it was either plain or polished; for he could speak freely with such Simplicity as a Child might understand, or with Elegance that would please the politest Ear."[10]

In certain situations the technique of impressiveness through detail could even diverge toward its apparent opposite, the smooth and genteel essay. Theodorus Frelinghuysen, pastor of the Dutch Reformed church in Albany, displayed this transition in two political sermons of the 1750s. In one, a sermon on the occasion of an Indian treaty, he betrayed his literary tastes by including within a conventional jeremiad a long quotation from Berkeley's prophetic poem that culminated in "westward the course of empire takes its way." More out of his own resources, he sought similar effect when he preached to New England soldiers camped near Albany on *War and Rumors of War, Heavens Decree over the World*. Although he began with a straightforward exposition of his text from Matthew, he converted this quickly into a display piece. Along with many Latin phrases and verse quotations, he presented allusions to Bib-

[9] Aaron Burr, *A Sermon Preached before the Synod of New-York, Convened at Newark, in New-Jersey, September 30, 1756* (New York, 1756. Burr, *A Servant of God Dismissed from Labour to Rest. A Funeral Sermon, Preached at the Interment of His Late Excellency Jonathan Belcher* (New York, 1757).

[10] Caleb Smith, *Diligence in the Work of God, and, Activity during Life. A Sermon Occasioned by the Much-lamented Death of the Reverend Mr. Aaron Burr* (New York, 1758), p. 26.

lical war passages, making much of euphonious, rarely remembered Hebrew names. All this language for the sake of language he directed toward exhorting the soldiers to courage.[11] Personal display seemed quite compatible with social purpose and with an audience that was probably much less preoccupied with piety than New Englanders were usually supposed to be.

There was available another kind of polite excellence, that represented by the Anglican minister Samuel Johnson, who became the first president of King's College. Except when engaged in rancorous pamphlet controversy, Johnson achieved a simple formality like that of the good secular prose of the period. He found his style especially appropriate to preaching the virtues of the Prayer Book: praising this prescribed service for its easy formality that yet avoided personal idiosyncrasy, he could illustrate in his own manner the very qualities he recommended. He argued also, however, that orderly prayer was more important than any preaching: both his manner and his ideological stand put him outside the American preaching tradition, which was still mainly Calvinist or evangelical.[12]

The difficulty was not that men of taste in the American pulpit did not appreciate simplicity, and even elegant simplicity, but that most of them included in their rhetorical goals a variety of emotional and psychological aims that no mere balance and order could serve. These goals were very much part of the New England tradition, which was influential among English-speaking Calvinists throughout the New York area, and it was stated clearly by Samuel Buell, pastor at Easthampton, in the New-Englandish section of

[11] Theodorus Frelinghuysen, *A Sermon Preached on Occasion of the Late Treaty Held in Albany* (New York, 1754). Frelinghuysen, *War and Rumors of War, Heavens [sic] Decree over the World. A Sermon, Preached in the Camp of the New-England Forces* (New York, 1755).

[12] Samuel Johnson, *A Sermon on the Beauty of Holiness in the Worship of the Church of England* (New York, 1761).

Long Island. In one ordination sermon he did advise the new pastor in terms that united the goal of classic simplicity to the goals of instruction and shared discourse:

> Cast your publick Discourses into the most regular and becoming Scheme; observe a steady Strain of Thought, good Connection, and natural Transitions through the Whole of them; while you make Use of Art to conceal Art, and endeavour to avoid antiquated, multiferious Divisions, and the dry Exactness of metaphysical Accuracy of Distinctions: Labour also to avoid meer loose Harangue, and a confus'd Huddle of Words, shuffl'd together in a wild and incoherent Manner. Let so much of distinct Method be observable to your Auditory, (at least to the Judicious) as that they may be able to commit to the Memory, the main Branches of your Discourse, or the leading Point in View; least nothing be fix'd in the Mind for after-Improvement, and the Sermon be lost as soon as heard: Good Order hath Power and Beauty in it. Let your Stile and Diction be correct, masculine, nervous and striking; . . . Dress not up divine and glorious Truths, in a coarse and contemptible Garb; nor give them such Polish and Ornament, as does not conduce to their Usefulness: . . . your Stile must be so far crucified as to be level to the Capacities of the Unlearned and Unskilful: . . .[13]

In this much Buell presented a standard of simplicity and communication that would appeal to the genteel Anglican, even while he reproved gentility for not devoting its talents to wider circles of men. But he had not only the Johnsons to cope with; he had also the Burrs and Frelinghuysens and Tennents, men whose word-play would seem vulgarly individualistic to a Johnson. So Buell commented, in another ordination sermon:

[13] Samuel Buell, *Christ the Grand Subject of Gospel-Preaching; . . . A Sermon Preach'd at Brook-Haven, October 23, 1754. At the Ordination of Mr. Benjamin Tallmadge* (New York, 1755), 24.

'Tis true indeed, Men have their various Gifts, Talents, and Turns of Mind; 'tis natural to some Men to communicate their Thoughts in a correct, masculine, nervous, striking and charming Stile and Diction; as truly natural, it appears beautiful. Some such there are, who from the spiritual Frame of their Hearts, are zealous, lively and practical Preachers, and excel in making the most warm Applications and earnest Addresses to the hearts and Consciences of them that hear. Their Delivery and Gestures are natural, grave and decent, Action is lively and significant, void of Affectation; their Sermons are evidently calculated, not to gratify Men's Curiosity with pleasing Speculations, but to pierce their Hearts with pungent Convictions; not to please their Fances, but to awaken their Consciences, and to convert and save their Souls. . . . If we would act the Orator, the Minister, or the Christian, we must endeavour to know and to cultivate the peculiar Turn of our own Mind, and not indulge a vain Affectation, nor Attempt a forced Imitation of any Man. It will appear unnatural and disagreeable to a judicious Hearer, when it becomes too evident, that the Preacher who has not a natural spontaneous flow of ready and elegant Expressions, has labour'd hard to polish his little Composition, by the constant Glitter of shining Phrases, by arranging his Words, beautifying his Language, rounding his Periods, so as really to stiffen his Discourse: . . . . While loose and general Harangues are now grown so fashionable in Pulpits, that the true Spirit of evangelical Preaching may not be lost, let young Preachers learn true Oratory from *Jesus Christ*, and seek copious Measures of his gracious, spiritual Presence with them. That Preacher has hit upon the true Master-Key of sacred Eloquence, and obtain'd the best Part of a Pulpit Orator, who is Master of a good Discourse, and is skilful in applying of it, in its full weight[,] home upon the Consciences of Men, who knows how to lay open the human Heart, and trace it's Windings, it's Disguises and Corruptions, and how to

> draw Voice and Passion from the Heart, so that every one shall hear, see, and recognize himself, and stand acquitted or condemn'd in his own Breast, according as he deserves one or the other: But no Man is like to do *this* to Purpose, unless the Lord is with him, and speaks by him.[14]

In other words, the kind of reality which it was the part of intellectual honesty for a preacher to face was emotional reality, but this reality could be faced savingly, or even just safely, only in terms of authoritative Christian language and doctrine. The preacher was in duty bound to face emotional realities, but neither he nor his hearers could easily bear to face those realities, except under cover of some metaphor. For most preachers, this metaphoric cover was mainly some version of Calvinist doctrine with its account of the soul's career.

Buell himself, in one of his published sermons prepared for something other than an ordination, dealt with a peculiarly difficult problem in emotional realism: that of a pious woman, for whose funeral he was preaching, who had kept her emotions so in reserve that she had seemed obnoxious to people around her. As he described Mrs. Catherine Davis, she sounded in fact as if she disliked those people toward whom she did her Christian duty, and was glad enough when death came to take her from them. This problem Buell sought to cope with in three ways. First, he spent most of the funeral sermon on an exposition, plain and rather coldly intellectual, of the beatific vision that departed saints enjoyed. This was the conventional answer. Second, he quoted the language in which Mrs. Davis described her willingness to die; this expressed an erotic, mystical tone toward Jesus Christ, and thus began to lay open some of the

[14] Samuel Buell, *The Excellence and Importance of the Saving Knowledge of the Lord Jesus Christ in the Gospel-Preacher, . . . a Sermon, at the Ordination of Mr. Samson Occum, a Missionary among the Indians* (New York, 1761), 35-36.

emotional fires within orthodox piety. Third, he presented three questions whereby the uncertainly pious might test whether they were really converted. If they had the choice, would they prefer being converted now or being converted a quarter-hour before death? If they had the choice, would they prefer to live in perpetual happiness on earth or to go to heaven? And did they really believe that knowledge of God brings "substantial Happiness"?[15] These questions were in the same vein as that "willingness to be damned for the greater glory of God," which Samuel Hopkins was soon to begin emphasizing in his own American reworking of the Calvinist tradition. Buell, when he did quote secular literature in his sermons, was apt to take extracts from the early romantic yet pious poetry of men like Edward Young. His impulse to deal with emotional realities was strong and obvious.[16] By formulating tests of piety that were absolutistic in their unworldly tone, he was achieving a point of view within which formal doctrine and erotic mysticism automatically constituted an "honest" translation of those emotional realities into the only available language. This was a peculiar accomplishment, but a real one, and it did take into account more of human life than either a Johnson or a Burr could encompass.

The interplay between rational discourse and mysticism that Buell achieved he may have derived in part from the man who came over to Long Island to preach for Buell's installation at Easthampton back in 1746: Jonathan Edwards. At that time, when there were still alive some of the same tensions between revivalists and settled pastors to which Jonathan Dickinson had addressed himself in New Jersey in 1739, Edwards also sought to preach some recon-

[15] Samuel Buell, *The Happiness of the Blessed in Heaven; or the Saint with Christ in Glory. A Sermon Occasioned, by the Decease of Mrs. Catharine Davis, . . . April 11, 1759* (New York, 1760), 18-27.

[16] Samuel Buell, *The Divine Agency Acknowledged in the Death of Our Dearest Friends. A Sermon Occasioned by the Decease of Mrs. Esther Darbe* (New York, 1757), ii, 27.

ciliation between piety and order. But he used a very different technique. Instead of Dickinson's method of using, teaching, and re-enforcing an accepted body of doctrine, Edwards began by assuming that his hearers were familiar with the Biblical imagery that various ministers applied to the relation between pastor and people. The more conventional had described this relation as a close, intimate, and permanent bond, like marriage. The revivalists who attacked an unconverted ministry had, on the other hand, compared the minister to the messenger who was sent to woo Rebecca for Isaac: he was only a proxy, subject to displacement, and the real marital relation was that between people and Christ. Edwards used both images. The minister was husband to his people, so that they owed him loving duty and respect; he was also proxy for Christ, and should never presume on his office. Making free use of the easy contradictions possible within amorous language, Edwards managed to merge the prudent, wordly ideals of the genteel pastor with the demanding unworldliness of the itinerant revivalist. With his kindness, seriousness, and grace, he also managed to achieve one of the most beautiful of eighteenth-century sermons.[17]

But here was the range of sermon discourse that New Yorkers knew: some sermons that assumed and conveyed a real community of intellectual discourse; all too many that were the slack, degenerate, text-chopping versions of these achievements in community discourse; still others that appealed to the populace through reiterations of vivid imagery; others yet that entertained people with samples of the preacher's erudition, Biblical or other; a few that reacted away from this rank individualism, presenting instead a chaste simplicity in which sophistication took care not to puff itself up; and, finally, a metaphoric, somewhat mystical

[17] Jonathan Edwards, *The Church's Marriage to Her Sons, and to Her God: A Sermon Preached at the Instalment of the Rev. Mr. Samuel Buel* [*sic*] *as Pastor of the Church and Congregation at East-Hampton on Long-Island, September 19, 1746* (Boston, 1746).

style of sermon that at its best combined the virtues of simplicity, imagery, and intellectual community. Did all this imply any identifiable intellectual level achieved by preachers or people?

One unifying clue to the American situation is provided by a complaint that Tillotsonians made in England. The common people, they said, did not appreciate simplicity. Far from accepting the man who gave them food for their understandings, they delighted in bombast and even in the lacing of sermons with Latin quotations that they could not pretend to understand.[18] But if the extravagant word-play of some Jacobean preaching had popular potential, why could not the analytic play of Puritan preaching—whether or not the people understood the content that analysis framed? And once popular appeal was being built, why not combine the two styles? This is just what Gilbert Tennent did in his repetitiously lush revival preaching.

There were thus three qualities of preaching common in America. First, there was one style that often took its elements from patterns quite old, as from the antiquated complexities of early seventeenth-century English preaching. This style, which used the shreds of older complexity within a continuing tissue of bombast, seemed to be the most popular style, but in America "popular" extended through a large part of society. Encampments of soldiers and synods of Presbyterian ministers provided audiences for their own variants on revival oratory. Second, though, some preachers sought or achieved a relation with their peoples in which they built ideas that assumed understanding and thought. This preaching was usually rationalistic in tone, but occasionally revealed a vein of metaphorical, metaphysical feeling. Third, there was the Tillotsonian essay, which in England was fairly common as a form of real preaching, but which in America was still a new kind of anti-preaching. Although the Anglican priests who imported it made some efforts to appeal to ordinary people over the heads of a

[18] Smyth, *Art of Preaching*, 120-121 and *n.*

stubborn Presbyterian gentry, they were really setting up congregations for people who aspired to urbane gentility. This style was perhaps less important in the examples produced by the few ministers who were committed to it outright than it was as a pervasive influence from general eighteenth-century literature, working into the verbal manners of men in all groups.

This last style was the one that was to become the vehicle of rational, scientific thought. It had its companion and analogue in the plain language that the Royal Society had recommended as standard for scientific reports and discussion. The future, as far as intellectual development was concerned, lay not in training people to accept greater and greater degrees of intellectual complexity, but in training them to seek insight through simple, objective language. This kind of developmental modernization was certainly available in America in 1750, but it had to contend with the broad popularity of a language that drew many of its elements from older traditions. Much of American thinking was—as school reformers were later to say—directed more to words than to ideas, more to images than to objects. In this the American popular taste may have regressed to a level more nearly "medieval" than the level to be found in Britain in the same period.

Real quality depended on the maintenance of those situations in which preachers could build their people up to a sharing of intellectual discourse. Within such a sharing, the preacher could ease up on the formal divisions and other verbal cues that the older analytical Puritan preaching had used as a frame for intelligibility. Without sacrificing meaning, he could relax into that plainer plain style that later English Puritanism shared with evangelicals generally and with the new science. Relying on its sharings, he could even work up a modest form of the metaphoric language that was most helpful in dealing with psychological reality.

Intellectual community was possible in colonial America, and it was sometimes achieved at a fairly high level. But it was vulnerable to anything that might divide populations into separate social groups, each seeking its own proper verbal style. And it was unsilently mocked by the possibility that some of the people who participated in the community might be understanding its terms as mere rhetorical sound. There was intellectual reality in the twin threat that the orthodox saw from complacency and enthusiasm: both gentility and regression drew men away from a community of discourse that they sometimes achieved.

B. A Case in the Spatial: Shipbuilding

Henry Adams, whose own interest in the religious mind ran more to symbolism than to preaching, nevertheless believed that he could discern important facts about American "popular intelligence" of the generations when his family had made its first impact on the nation. Writing about a people who had endured Jeffersonianism and the War of 1812, he chose to evaluate them by asking what level of mental activity they had displayed. For all his misgivings, he concluded that that level was high, though he took as his main criterion an accomplishment that had been achieved by the seafaring rather than the plantation sections, therefore more by Adams neighbors than by Jefferson neighbors. The fast smuggling ships and privateers that Americans had begun to build even before the Revolution, and that had reached their highest state during the Napoleonic wars, displayed a problem-solving and productive capacity to all the world. Shipbuilding proved the American mind.[19]

The elements of Adams' observation were factual enough. Britons and Europeans had long noted the peculiar features and then the peculiar virtues of some American vessels. During the years when Americans were becoming defensively assertive, the quality of ships became a conventional

[19] Henry Adams, *History of the United States of America during the Administration of James Madison* (New York, 1930), Book IX, pp. 227-241.

item in claims for national accomplishment (illustration 1). But Adams was not conventional or insensitive when he took shipbuilding as a useful test of intellect.

Although the task of shipbuilding depended always on a kind of intuitive experience, it included some problems that could be stated in straightforward, rationalistic terms. Most of the objectives were simple: speed, capacity for cargo or guns, stability for safety and comfort, economy of construction. Speed, lesser problems aside, was to be achieved by making vessels longer and lighter. Capacity was to be increased by making vessels larger, or by making hulls more full and boxlike in shape. Stability was to be achieved by making hulls relatively deep and straight-walled (this was not the only way, but it was the way that stood most in contrast to the conventional hulls of the seventeenth and eighteenth centuries, which were typically too round-bottomed and round-sided). Economy was to be achieved by using lighter materials, relative to their strength, and by reducing to a minimum any unnecessary elements in the structure. The relations between these factors sometimes created contradictions. Of four factors—speed, stability, capacity, and economy—it was generally possible to achieve any three only at the expense of the fourth.[20] The builder

[20] The analysis here is a much simplified version of that in Howard I. Chapelle, *The Search for Speed under Sail 1700-1855* (New York, 1967), on which I have heavily depended. Especially have I left out the question of weatherliness—the ability of a vessel to sail to windward—which would involve additional complexities without modifying the basic points. That the considerations discussed here were all familiar to eighteenth-century and nineteenth-century builders, even if in terms sometimes different from those of present-day naval architecture, is shown by works like: Frederick Henry de Chapman, *A Treatise on Ship-Building, with Explanations and Demonstrations Respecting the Architectura Navalis Mercatoria*, tr. James Inman (Cambridge, 1820); John Fincham, *An Outline of Ship Building* (London, 1852); John W. Griffiths, *The Ship-Builder's Manual, and Nautical Referee*, 2nd edn. (New York, 1856); William Hutchinson, *A Treatise on Naval Architecture*, 4th edn. (Liverpool, 1794); Mungo Murray, *A Treatise on Ship-Building and Navigation* (London, 1754);

had to weigh his various needs and tastes against each other.

On some matters, uncertainty long prevailed. Although the gross strength of a hull could be increased by increasing the size of its beams and planks, a vessel had to be supported through constantly shifting forces in the water. The pitching, rolling, and twisting of a hull would subject it to stresses in a total pattern that was impossible to calculate. Until at least the middle of the nineteenth century, a similar confusion attended any detailed handling of hydrodynamic problems and hull shape. Among builders' rules of thumb, those that were to prove valid in the long run amounted to little more than a general preference in favor of smooth or "fair" lines, and a growing preference in favor of sharp or fine lines. The desirable characteristics were: length, lightness, fullness of hull volume, sharpness of keel shape, and strength. The first four of these five posed fairly definite problems. Length and lightness were inconsistent with strength, and fullness of hull was inconsistent with sharpness of keel. Quite often the choice among these features would be determined by the purposes for which a vessel was designed, but the scope for choice meant that there could grow up design conventions that were influenced by the social or intellectual climate.

Quite early, American ship design began moving toward simple, seemingly rationalistic styles. Builders of the early eighteenth century had hardly departed from the English or Dutch models that they or their fathers had known. The hull and rigging types that they used had been familiar elsewhere, though perhaps not always in quite the same combinations. The early colonial vessels had been small, seaworthy by the trusting standards of the seventeenth century, but still of a size more generally adapted to coastal or

---

Lauchlan McKay, *The Practical Ship-Builder* (New York, 1839); and Norman S. Russell, "On American River Steamers," Institution of Naval Architects, *Transactions*, II (1861), 109.

short voyages. Neither did colonials build vessels specifically for naval use, which would have imposed the weight-carrying problems of gunnery and the inspectorial standards of admiralty officials. They adopted the framing and construction that were appropriate to small vessels, and sometimes used light woods, such as cedar, which were more available in the New World. As long as vessel size remained small, none of this except perhaps the light timber was visible as innovation. Then, over the eighteenth century, Americans began building larger craft. Construction methods remained light during the middle of the century, perhaps because of a shortage of skilled labor, certainly not because of any scarcity of timber. Perhaps Americans simply found that they could get by with light construction, even while they were advancing to vessel sizes that in European practice would have required larger timbers. This in itself tended to make medium-sized American vessels faster than comparable British models.[21]

Beyond this, other elements of a distinct achievement were available, many of them in Europe. One was the practice of making a hull not flat-bottomed and full-bilged but with considerable deadrise—that is, with the hull angling sharply up from the keel to where it curved into the sides (illustration 2). Another was a bow that raked sharply back to the lowest part of the keel; because such a vessel would be longer on the water line when it heeled to one side, it would be correspondingly fast as it went to windward. Another was a reduction in the complexity of sails and rigging, which permitted relatively small crews in times of international competition for the seafaring labor supply, and smaller crews relative to capacity and speed (illustration 3). And there was also developing a "French manner" of construction that put care into details of joining and finish; this, which at least became familiar to Americans during the

[21] Chapelle, *The Baltimore Clipper* (Salem, Mass., 1930). Charles G. Davis, *Ships of the Past* (Salem, Mass., 1929), 80.

American Revolution, favored less weight relative to strength, and less frictional drag from the surface of the hull.[22]

The type of American vessel that first attracted favorable attention abroad was one that combined most of these features with the light construction that had already developed (illustration 4). Depending on where it was built, or when, or for what particular purposes, it was known variously as "Virginia-built" or the "Baltimore clipper," common through and after the War of 1812. Given the special character of smuggling, privateering, and other trades that needed speed and maneuverability more than cargo capacity, and given the prior availability of all the elements of the form, the style resulted partly from routine adaptation to conditions.

As the lightly built, sharp-keeled American vessels emerged, they embodied certain details of design procedure that, though common enough in Europe, became characteristic of American practice and even of the relation between design products and the public on the western side of the Atlantic. Much as with the variation that preachers began working into sermons styles, these shifts revealed both the essentially international character of intellectual change and the real differences among nations. Constructers in the United States Navy worked in ways not radically different from those common in the Royal Navy, but official Navy practice was not central to American developments.

An early minor development that became common enough to arouse remark in British observers was the use of unequal frame-spacing in hulls. Traditionally, a builder had erected the riblike members called frames at equal distances along the keel. The frames, to which most of the other planking and beams were attached, had to bear the shifting stresses placed on the hull, and there had to be

[22] A. Thevenard, *Mémoires relatifs à la marine* (Paris, An VIII [1800]), 477-496. John Knowles and David Steel, *The Elements and Practice of Naval Architecture* (London, 1822), 177 & *n.*

as many frames, at close enough spaces, as were needed to take these stresses. But the probable stresses were not equally spaced, being likely to be much greater amidships than in either end of the hull. From the point of view of economy, it was sensible to put frames farther apart in the ends, even though there were no methods available for calculating how far apart was safe. When Americans did sometimes use unequal spacing, in the latter years of the eighteenth century, British opinion condemned as unsafe this attempt to achieve the benefits of a close figuring that could not really be performed.[23]

A second characteristic development involved American skills directly, and not simply through a bias toward a particular design form. The Baltimore-clipper form had appeared to English thought as a special case of American superiority during the early part of the nineteenth century, at first because of the concrete observations that were enforced by the encounters of the Napoleonic wars and the War of 1812, somewhat later by a maritime competition in which British ships sometimes did poorly.[24] The style was perceived in the form of completed ships in use, as a finished product; but it came along at about the same time that a "new" process of ship design appeared in both America and Europe. This process, the use of lift or section models, was sometimes considered a particularly American

[23] *Ibid.*, 181. Chapelle, *Search for Speed*, 209. Griffiths, *Ship-Builder's Manual*, II, 20.

[24] Actually, British commentators made their grudging comparisons to French or other European ships at least as often as they did to American; but the references to American ships were part of a consistent pattern during the 1820s and 1830s. "Report of the Lords' Committee on Trade with the East Indies and China," *Parliamentary Papers*, 1821, VII, 16-17, 62-63, 68. Knowles and Steel, *Elements and Practice of Naval Architecture*, 136. William Morgan and Augustin Creuze, *Papers on Naval Architecture and Other Subjects Connected with Naval Science* (London, 1826/32), I, 1-8, 45-48, 218-224. "Report from the Select Committee on Manufactures, Commerce, and Shipping," *Parliamentary Papers*, 1833, VI, 59, 230, 236, 362-363, 415.

manner of operating. It raises subtle questions, both about what was peculiarly American, and about whether there was any underlying connection between the appearance of the Baltimore-clipper form and the appearance of the lift-model process.

The lift model and the section model are varieties of the same device for reducing the dependence of the shipbuilder on complex drafting techniques (illustration 5). The builder carves his design for a hull in a block of wood, which he has prepared by joining together a number of thin layers of wood, typically held together with dowels or screws. The layers may be arranged to run parallel to the water line, producing a "water-line model" or "lift model"; or they may be arranged to produce vertical elements corresponding to the frames, producing a "sectional model." Once the hull form is satisfactory to the builder, he can separate the layers and use the outlines of each one in taking off the lines for the full-scale members of the ship.[25] But the whole meaning of this device depended on the way that design and building processes evolved from the late seventeenth century to the early nineteenth. This evolution, in turn, was related to developments in how the general population was learning elementary skills.

During the seventeenth and early eighteenth centuries, top-level English shipbuilders, like their counterparts in other countries, took the detailed draft on paper as the nor-

[25] Charles Kirtland Stillman, "The Development of the Builders' Half-Hull Model in America," Marine Historical Association, Mystic, Connecticut, *Publications*, vol. I, no. 7 (1933), 108-111. Isaac Blackburn, *The Theory and Science of Naval Architecture, Familiarly Explained and Intimately Blended with the Art* (Plymouth, 1836), 101-103. W. J. Macquorn Rankine, ed., *Shipbuilding, Theoretical and Practical* (London, 1866), 100-101, 124. George W. Rogers, *The Shipwright's Own Book: Being a Key to Most of the Different Kinds of Lines Made Use of by Ship Builders; Illustrated by Seventeen Copper Plate Engravings of Drafts and Models, Carefully Arranged and Explained in So Plain and Correct a Manner, as to Be Understood by the Most Ordinary Capacity* (Pittsburgh, 1845), 39-54 and plates VII-IX.

mal way to design a hull. From that draft the full-scale lines could be taken. But there were two difficulties. Middling shipyard workers did not always have the elementary arithmetical abilities needed in this drafting and enlarging. And the actual process of producing plans from which full-scale lines could be "faired"—that is, projected without the bulges or depressions that would obviously cause turbulence—was difficult at best. When builders then produced instruction manuals, they made a point of including a great deal of quite elementary material on arithmetic and geometry for the draftsman, and they described their procedures as rules to be followed by rote. They presented only certain standard hull forms, presumably those for which fair lines had already been worked out in practice, and they gave the most minute instructions for producing only those forms, or others that could be scaled proportionately from them. Since they gave little hint that it was even conceivable to design, deliberately, a new hull form to satisfy new needs, they seemed to be allowing for only that kind of progress that could seep up within a stable tradition.[26]

Of course, practice was more flexible than the manuals. Builders tended to keep secret any new, adaptive tricks that they discovered for their trade. And the most important trick was not any process that one could specify or describe, but the visual skill that a good builder derived from intuition or experience. Partly because he worked within a range of hull forms that changed only slowly, he could work from

[26] Charles Romme, *L'art de la marine* (La Rochelle, 1787), 178-206. William Hutchinson, *A Treatise Founded upon Philosophical and Rational Principles, towards Establishing Fixed Rules, for the Proportional Dimensions in Length, Breadth and Depth of Merchant's Ships in General; and Also the Management of Them to the Greatest Advantage, by Practical Seamanship* (Liverpool, 1791), especially plate f.p. 21. Knowles and Steel, *Elements and Practice of Naval Architecture*, 242-286. Anthony Deane, Doctrine of Naval Architecture and Table of Dimensions, Materials, Furniture and Expense Appertaining Thereto (1675; photostat in National Maritime Museum, Greenwich, from Pepsyian Library Mss.), 21.

inadequate drawings or specifications, going from little more than a knowledge of how large a vessel he wanted to giving his workmen specific directions on the sizes of frames and other parts. This skill and the reliance on rote could substitute for each other. The English naval architect John Scott Russell, whose achievements depended heavily on brilliant drafting, recognized this interaction as late as 1861:

> Nothing, . . . will dispense with what is, after all, the most important part of the builder's craft,—the carrying about the shape in his head as well as in the mould; and there are skilled craftsmen who can do it without a single mould, merely with their foot-rule: there are many men, who, looking at a plan, and taking a few dimensions, can carry away the shape in their heads, and cut it out accurately in wood, and fit it precisely to its place and purpose, without intermediate moulds or patterns of any kind. These are the men who have become so famous for working by the eye merely,—or as it is called, by "rule of thumb;" but such men must always be the exception, and for general use it is essential to know how to do all this by rule.[27]

During the eighteenth century, builders may have derived some indirect help from the solid ship models that they had already begun to make for show or for record. But they also developed more specific devices, such as the technique called "whole-moulding." In whole-moulding, the largest vertical section of a hull—that is, the one located approximately amidships—was designed first, and the other frames were then formed simply by making them gradually, proportionately smaller toward stem or stern, but keeping

[27] John Scott Russell, *The Modern System of Naval Architecture* (London, 1865), I, 308. Compare John Fincham, "Dimensions, and Calculated Elements, of Some of the Vessels of the Royal Yacht Club, with a Few Remarks on Their Construction," Morgan and Creuze, *Papers*, I, 210.

them all the same shape. This was a fairly simple-minded process, and was eventually considered useful only for long-boats. For more sophisticated hulls, builders devised other geometrical processes, based on "segments of circles" or the "parabolic curve"—devices that provided definite ways to decide the shapes of intermediate hull lines from a few basic lines. These procedures had the disadvantage, of course, that the resulting lines might or might not have any real relation to what made a ship sail well. Although proposals for such crankish procedures became common in the latter part of the eighteenth century, no one of them seems to have much challenged the reliance on rote and visual intuition.[28]

Out in the provinces, though, builders below the top level managed things somewhat differently. In Scotland and in the smaller yards of England, Denmark, and Sweden, builders were using models during the generations when the big national yards were struggling to maintain quality and precision in drafting.[29] It was not that the provincial builders did not rely on visual intuition. But where the ideal master shipbuilder was one who could carry the exact image of his hull and its parts in his head, some provincial builders used the model as a way to make this image concrete and manipulable. Where revising an image in the head might threaten to make it diffuse and unreliable, revision by whittling made each new adaptation instantly available for exact concep-

[28] *Marine Architecture: or, the Ship-Builder's Assistant: . . . the Whole Illustrated with Schemes or Draughts, to Render it Intelligible to All Capacities* (London, 1748), 6-22. Mungo Murray, *A Treatise on Ship-Building and Naval Architecture* (London, 1754). Marmaduke Stalkartt, *Naval Architecture* (London, 1781), I, 1-2 and *passim.* William Sutherland, *The Ship-Builder's Assistant; or, Marine Architecture*, rev. edn. (London, 1784), 55-64 and plates. Knowles and Steel, *Elements and Practice of Naval Architecture*, 75, 369. "On Mechanical Methods of Designing Ships' Bodies," in Morgan and Creuze, *Papers*, II, 1-22.

[29] Olfa Hasslöf, "Wrecks, Archives and Living Tradition: Topical Problems in Marine-Historical Research," *Mariner's Mirror*, XLIX (1963), 162-177.

tualization or use. And though the evidence on eighteenth-century American practice is sketchy—to say the least—the New England yards were part of a community of provincial shipyards that followed similar practice throughout the Atlantic world. Although lift models seem not to have been known then in the middle and Chesapeake provinces, they soon formed one part of the continuity of small-yard shipbuilding practices from Europe to America.

As long as high-level shipbuilding was a fairly stable, traditionalistic undertaking, kept stable partly by the inertia of naval bureaucracies, shipbuilding practice was divided into two kinds of tradition: the "high" tradition of the navies and the larger centers, and the somewhat "folkish" tradition of the provinces. This stable division was upset by the intensifying naval competition that came to a head during the Napoleonic wars. Competing governments needed more ships, faster ships, larger ships. Even after peace came in 1815, it fostered a generation of commercial expansion in which private builders continued the drive to increase their achievements. In Britain, the expansion of construction outran the supply of carefully trained shipyard draftsmen, and builders became anxious about maintaining standards. In America, expansion brought the rise of some shipbuilding centers, such as New York, that had been relatively quiet during the Revolutionary years. During the first half of the nineteenth century, New York builders imported some shipwrights from the areas to the northeast of them, and they also adopted the lift model as a technique in design and loft work. In effect, the lift model meant that builders did not need to force a large number of workers to acquire difficult drafting skills in a hurry: "We can most of us whittle better than we can draw."[30] When designers in Navy yards continued to rely solely on drafts, they met the criticism that men in workshops several miles away from the drafting

[30] Norman S. Russell, "On American River Steamers," Institution of Naval Architects, *Transactions*, II (1861), 109.

rooms simply did not have the knowledge to work from something as theoretical as drawings.[31]

This adoption of the lift model in major shipyards was not peculiar to New York. It spread down the Atlantic coast, and may even have spread "back" to small yards that had not used it before.[32] Major builders in Europe also adopted it, although without giving up drafts. Where some builders relied heavily on the model as a nearly exclusive design technique, others used it as an intermediate stage between rough drafts and final drafts, in order to clarify the more difficult stages in drafting. During the rest of the century both the draft and the model were available techniques for builders on many levels, though the development of sophisticated naval engineering after the middle of the century meant that builders needed much less to look on the model as a compulsive, urgent device.

By the 1830s Americans saw the model as a peculiar technique that they had developed apart from the traditional ways of Europe. This image of themselves as the unique craftsmen in concrete materials was not strictly accurate, but it did summarize what was special in the American way of taking hold of design problems. The Americans were the great case in the nineteenth century of a people who had just moved through the transition from provincialism to national importance. In this rapid development or modernization they transferred many features of provincial life into the center of public thought. This was one case of the way

[31] Knowles and Steel, *Elements and Practice of Naval Architecture* (London, 1822), v. Leonard H. Boole, *The Shipwright's Handbook and Draughtsman's Guide* (Milwaukee, 1858), 7-8, 12, 15, 34. John McLeod Murphy, *American Ships and Ship-Builders* (New York, 1860), 10-13. John W. Nystrom, *On Technological Education and Shipbuilding, for Naval and Marine Engineers* (Philadelphia, 1865), 23-24, 30-31, 48-49, 55, 97-98, 101-103.

[32] That the direction of transmission was not always from provincial to sophisticated yards is indicated by the following models in the collection of the United States National Museum: 311,188; 311,520; 311,522; 312,331; 315,714; 318,029.

men can combine sophisticated with folkish techniques to achieve new designs and new flexibility. Americans took the lead in the shipbuilding phase of this process, and they gave the concrete, folkish side of design, embodied in the model, much greater prominence than it was accorded in the major design centers of Europe.

The same thing had been happening in the development of the Baltimore clipper and its imitation in Europe. All the particular elements in the form had been known in Europe. They were combined in light, weatherly vessels that proved useful as privateers during the same competitive years that saw the weakening and dilution of traditional design techniques. The increasing size of these vessels, and their frequent success in competition with naval ships, meant that a form initially most important in provincial trades was being absorbed into the repertory of traditionally sophisticated design. The development of America from province to nation was a political event. But it carried with it an emerging test: how far could the economies and simplicities, the concrete devices and short-cuts of provincial thought be elevated into service within sophisticated thought? In one sense, the lift model was an attempt to adapt the intuitive, secretive methods of small yards and traditional apprenticeship to the growing demands of a large shipping industry. It became less satisfactory in the 1840s and 1850s, as ship size increased even more, as shipyards became less personal in organization, and as pressure began to grow for using iron or steel in place of wood. But plentiful timber gave American yards a cost advantage in wood; they held back from metal construction, even at the risk of obsolescence, and a real gap opened between American and British styles of construction.[33]

[33] Chapelle, *The National Water Craft Collection* (Washington, 1960), 8-12. Basil Greenhill, *The Merchant Schooners* (London, 1951), I, 30-35. John W. Griffiths, *The Progressive Ship Builder* (New York, 1875), I, 66. W. Salisbury, "Navy Board Models," *Mariner's Mirror*, LI (1965), 70-72. Lauchlan McKay, *The Practical Ship-Builder* (New York, 1839), 13-17, 19.

Unequal frame-spacing and the lift model involved a common underlying mental turn: a preference for spatial rather than analytical representation of problems, but an ability to achieve desired qualities in a design—qualities such as economy or reproducibility—through working on the concrete form as separated into smaller parallel elements. In terms of types of intelligence, this amounted to a shift from quantitative to spatial emphasis, which was on the face of it regressive. While practical shipyard and sailing men in both Britain and America furnished an audience for simplifications of mathematics in these years, this simplification took somewhat different forms in the two countries. In England, the significant simplifier was Mungo Murray, who in 1754 presented a compend of theory that could be used by builders whose own skills had advanced no further than common arithmetic; he still assumed reliance on plans, and he bridged the gap between arithmetic and complexity by urging the slide rule. His work was reprinted and imported into America, where one Richard Burroughs took it as the basis for further simplification in 1807. Burroughs dropped even the slide rule, presenting a little handbook on navigation in which the key feature was "a new method of working trigonometry by memory." He insisted that no subject so important should be accessible only through weighty books "since not only safety in the art of navigation, but the happiness and welfare of a nation are promoted by a diffusion of mental light. In fine, those who bring down philosophy from its towering heights to a level with common capacity, by stripping off the mask of mystery, perform an office little less useful than the first discoverer."[34]

In the same way, for the American physician and publicist Benjamin Rush, light was the medium for ultimate ac-

[34] Richard Burroughs, *A Treatise on Trigonometry & Navigation, Containing an Explanation of Their Principles and Tables, and a New Method of Working Trigonometry by Memory* (Middlebury, 1807), ix. Mungo Murray, *A Treatise on Ship-Building and Navigation* (London, 1754).

cess to knowlege: where he felt that ordinary virtue and language would be instilled by "vocal music," "eloquence," and "the ear," he discovered real "genius" for discovering truth in the man whose "imagination surveyed all nature at a glance, and, like a camera obscura, seemed to produce in his mind a picture of the whole visible creation."[35] It was this use of the eye as the instrument of instantaneous thought that figured in one of the earliest accounts of the lift model, published in the *Encyclopedia Americana* in 1831 and reprinted in pamphlet form in England three years later:

> Our American builders have a different mode, very easy and satisfactory. They begin by making a wooden model of the proposed construction, the thing itself in miniature. Here the length, breadth, bulk, all the dimensions, and most minute inflections of the whole, are seen at a single glance; the eye of the architect considers and reconsiders the adaptation of his model to the proposed object, dwells minutely on every part, and is thus able to correct the faults of his future ship, at the mere expense of a few chips, and while yet in embryo.[36]

Visual intuition, whether it transcended the verbalism of tradition or bypassed the need for quantitative skill, facilitated the emergence of simple, clean-lined styles within a new culture. Even when the elements of design were all old, as in shipbuilding, the break in cognitive styles fostered recombination within simplicity.

This break meant also that the skill Americans had in shipbuilding was becoming a more public, social phenomenon. Aside from the people who bought and worked

[35] Benjamin Rush, *Essays, Literary, Moral, and Philosophical*, 2nd edn. (Philadelphia, 1806), 13-16, 31, 47, 317, 362.

[36] *The Sea-Service: or, Popular Sketches of Ship-Building, Navigation, and Naval Warfare; from the Earliest Period to the Present Time* (London, 1834), 28.

American ships, there were two significant audiences for the builders' product. One was the European consumer of American ships, notably the English navy, which captured American vessels from time to time and prepared from them the detailed drafts that American builders did without.[37] The other was the American public itself, which had early been widely involved in shipping investment, and which in the early part of the nineteenth century retained or was developing a vicarious fascination with ships. It was probably not a completely new development that the New York shipbuilder J. W. Griffiths indicated when he wrote: "So deeply interested are the population of the commercial cities of the Western World, that all classes of society must see for themselves the latest specimen of marine architecture; not only the merchant hurries down to the wharf to learn the tidings of her success, but the man of furrowed cheek, who has frittered away his life in talk, as well as the complacent youth, who would remonstrate at the indignity of being supposed capable of earning his own bread."[38] The less sophisticated Pennsylvania builder George W. Rogers displayed much the same sensitivity to a wider audience when he published a handbook on drafts and models in 1845. Complaining that the men who understood the theory of shipbuilding usually tried hard not to teach it to others, he proceeded to his "explanation with the certainty of doing that which will be acceptable to a large portion of the community."[39]

Griffiths, like Rogers, was displeased by any lingering elements of secrecy or guild-like behavior among American builders. These builders of mid-century tried to present what they knew about ship design and construction in practical, systematic texts; and Griffiths published his *Nautical Magazine* as an open forum for controversy about design.

[37] Chapelle, *Search for Speed*, 39, 147, 209.

[38] Griffiths, *Ship-Builder's Manual*, 85.

[39] Rogers, *Shipwright's Own Book*, iv, vi.

Griffiths and Lauchlan McKay also set themselves to attack the influence that federal tonnage-measurement regulations exercised on design. These regulations, they insisted, encouraged shipowners to demand vessels that would save money on port duties, rather than vessels that were safe and efficient. They believed that the best American vessels were those, such as slavers and privateers, that had been built without reference to any rules for measuring and taxing tonnage, and they argued that free public competition among builders would make the industry progressive. In 1864 the tonnage regulations were in fact made more realistic, but by then other influences were undercutting the vigor of the industry.[40]

In the meantime, the popular reaction to shipbuilding as a visibly exciting, competitive enterprise marked both a continuity of the mental habits involved in the earlier public for preaching, and an eventual blurring of these habits. The emphasis on separable parallel elements was much of a piece with the way preachers had traditionally handled material that was supposed to be reproducible in the memories of the congregation. But just as memory could be fostered also by the graphic and the vivid, so the use of parallel elements and the reliance on the visually concrete became identified in this aspect of American design practice. Some preachers, such as Tennent or Burr, had tended to make the relation between parallel elements imagistic rather than logical. This either reflected or encouraged a potential for passivity and consumption-orientation in their auditors. It was also the relation that in the early nineteenth century was developing between the shipbuilder, who used concrete practice as a way to develop technological detail, and the public, who took the visual as a mode of immediate

[40] John W. Griffiths, *Treatise on Marine and Naval Architecture, or Theory and Practice Blended in Ship Building* (London, 1856), 26, 47-48. Griffiths, *Progressive Ship Builder*, I, 11. Lauchlan McKay, *Practical Ship-Builder*, 85-86.

response. The public was real, and shared in some sense in the builder's accomplishments; but the sharing was passive rather than technical.

After about 1818 the design ideas that had made the Baltimore clipper distinctive achieved their final proof as an autonomous style: they helped to create a line of trade, in contrast to the usual sequence in which ship forms were contrived to suite the available trades. It had been normal for ships, even those carrying passengers, to sail whenever they assembled cargoes sufficient to make a voyage pay. But now there was available a well-publicized ship style that put little emphasis on ample cargo and more on speed, dispatch, and the carrying of people. That form was now repeated literally in the ships that served exactly those functions, especially the pilot ships and the illegal slavers. The form was adapted with minor modifications when New York entrepreneurs decided to offer a scheduled sailing service, leaving the port on stated days with cargo if possible but without cargo if necessary. To take the possible cargo, hulls were made somewhat boxier than had been usual with the earlier clippers; but to attain the speed and stability needed to make service reliable, deadrise was kept fairly sharp.

From 1832 to 1847 this American style received its maximum recognition: adoption as the official design standard of the British Navy. Sir William Symonds, succeeding to the post of surveyor that had long been held by Sir Robert Seppings, insisted that the Royal Navy stop relying on specialist shipbuilders who never went to sea, and instead let working ship captains (of whom he was one) develop the skills to implement what they had learned from experience. His rivals insisted that he had been unable either to draw designs or to make calculations for ships at the time he took his new office. But in what they labeled his "Intuitive School of Shipbuilding" he argued the practical stability of the V-shaped hull with sharp deadrise—a form that made sense at a time when the Navy had few heavy engagements to fight but many lighter far-flung tasks, including the tracking down of American-built slavers.[41]

Within the British merchant service, however, and during the 1840s in American merchant-shipbuilding, this classically logical American style aroused dissatisfaction. Cargo capacity was still important, notably in the increasing cotton trade, and much of the American fleet was engaged in coastal waters and sometimes in shallow inlets. Large flat-bottomed ships were built for the New York–New Orleans cotton trade, and they turned out to be almost as fast for their length as were the sharp-bottomed packet ships (illustration 6). This discovery set off a doctrinal quarrel among builders, between those who favored deadrise and those who now insisted that flat bottoms did not prevent speed. Like many doctrinal controversies, this one served partly to cover up uncertainties on either side.

John W. Griffiths, for example, helped to lead builders away from the American style—in which he had done significant work—and in the process found himself in a bizarre intellectual trap. The *Rainbow*, which he designed in 1844, carried the packet-ship style about as far as it went in a ship of its size, 165 feet; after that, he, the Webbs, and the McKays led in the development of the long, flat-bottomed cargo-carriers that came to be known as clipper ships. Though noted for their sharp lines, the clipper ships were essentially a reversion to the style of large-ship design that had prevailed just before 1815; as Howard I. Chapelle has

[41] W. Henwood, "A Method of Connecting the Frame Timbers of Ships; Together with a Mode of Forming Decks," in Morgan and Creuze, *Papers*, II, 23-49. *An Apology for English Ship-Builders; Shewing that It Is Not Necessary the Country Should Look to the Navy for Naval Architects* (London, 1833), 12, 35 & *n*. *Facts versus Fiction; or, Sir Wm. Symonds' Principles of Naval Architecture Vindicated by a Compilation of Official and Other Documents* (London, 1845). *Review of the Course Pursued by the Shipbuilding Department of the Admiralty between the Years 1832 and 1847* (Plymouth, 1847), 29 & *n*, 31, 33.

demonstrated, they were not especially faster for their size than were the Baltimore clippers or the packet ships. When builders who favored high deadrise resisted this development, they had good reason within their own outlook. And when William H. Webb insisted that he built sharp-bottomed ships only for perverse owners who demanded them, he oversimplified his own practice. Like many other builders, he adapted hull forms to the trade for which a ship was intended; and the amount of deadrise he used continued to vary even after he began to build many ships in the extreme clipper style. In their rhetoric, American builders of the 1850s claimed to be executing new, radical principles, and tended to point up only one principle at a time. From their chaste privateers, which had been economical in both concept and material, Americans were moving back toward the complexity, traditionalism, and informed practicality of earlier British ships—and of the United States Navy. But with the mental habits they had acquired, they insisted on considering the clipper ships much more single-minded in design than they actually were.[42]

Typical also of this single-mindedness was the lesser use to which Americans put one important technique that they had themselves elaborated early in the century. Ships, to be fast, needed to be long, whatever the means of propulsion. When Fulton began his steam experiments on the Hudson, he found that engine weight and vibration put an unacceptable strain on the relatively long hulls that he used. To provide the longitudinal strength that would permit speed, he added bracing members, as in a diagonal or triangular bracing arrangement that he used on the *Raritan* of 1808

[42] Robert G. Albion, *Square-Riggers on Schedule: the New York Sailing Packets to England, France, and the Cotton Ports* (Princeton, 1938), 77-98. Chapelle, *The History of the American Sailing Navy* (New York, 1949), 238, 405-407. Chapelle, *National Water Craft Collection*, 27-28, 34-36. Basil Greenhill, *The Merchant Schooners* (London, 1951), I, 11. William H. Webb, *Plans of Wooden Vessels . . . Built . . . in the City of New York (1840-1869)*, I, plans for *Gazelle, Swordfish, Flying Dutchman*, and *Fanny*.

(illustration 7). Such systems became usual, and on American river boats were visible as open structures above the long flat deck. As ocean-going ships increased in size, they too met problems of longitudinal strength, even where no engines were involved. British builders commonly introduced strengthening struts or braces, and Sir Robert Seppings transformed this device into a genuinely new way of constructing hulls. Instead of using frames set at right angles to the keel, he used a complex system of intersecting diagonal frames, giving the basic structure of the hull a lattice-like pattern (illustration 8). His methods required far more technical control and far more tolerance for novelty than were acceptable in the ordinary shipyard that relied on a traditional transmission of skills. In America, similar strengthening was needed, but it was typically done in a more superficial, tacked-on way (illustrations 9 and 10). Clipper ships especially, since they derived their speed more from size than from any new subtleties of design, often needed extra strengthening if their hulls were to be secure. Builders like Donald McKay and William H. Webb applied lattice-like structures to the inside of a hull, typically in the form of a set of members bolted to an otherwise conventional light arrangement of frames.[43] Ameri-

[43] Thomas Gordon, *Principles of Naval Architecture* (London, 1784), 53-55, 73. John Walters, *Explanation of Certain Improvements in Naval Architecture* (London, 1815). Sir Robert Seppings, *New Principle of Constructing Ships of War* (London, 1817). Seppings, *On a New Principle of Constructing Ships in the Mercantile Navy* (London, 1820). "On the New Principle of Constructing His Majesty's Ships of War," in *Essays and Gleanings on Naval Architecture and Nautical Economy* (London, 1826), 51, 55. Sir Westcott Abell, *The Shipwright's Trade* (Cambridge, Eng., 1948), 74, 95, 176. Chapelle, *History of the American Sailing Navy*, 365. Chapelle, *National Water Craft Collection*, 28. Chapelle, *Search for Speed*, 206-207, 269-271, 412. John Fincham, *An Outline of Ship Building*, 3rd edn., (London, 1852). Griffiths, *Ship-Builder's Manual*, 2nd edn. (New York, 1856), 1, 66, 148-149. Griffiths, *Treatise on Marine and Naval Architecture*, plate 22. Norman S. Russell, "On American River Steamers," 111. D. L. Dennis, "The Deficiencies of Wooden Shipbuilding," *Mar-*

cans, even when they took up technical problems for which solutions had to be complex, tended to the stripped and the simple.

And the contradiction between complex practice and single-minded principle showed in the rhetoric of the endlessly rhetorical Griffiths. From a lecture on shipbuilding in 1844, through magazine publishing ventures, to his *Progressive Ship Builder* in the early 1870s, he kept using a romantic conception of cultural change in an effort to unite the popular and technical publics for ship literature. Like many writers of the period, he addressed himself often to the conflict between theory and practice. But where the conventional rhetoric called for a judicious balance of the two modes, Griffiths kept fluctuating between an emotional insistence on one and an emotional insistence on the other. In a single work he could adopt all views. He began with standard language in favor of theory as liberalizing: "It is mortifying to witness in the shipwright the mere mechanic. It is, indeed, humiliating, to see the most prominent intellectual art in the catalogue, reduced to a mere drudgery." But he went on to praise American reliance on "common sense" and "practice." And finally he praised one design for proving *both* the case for common sense *and* the importance of experiments that did not rely on "prejudice."[44] He was groping toward a notion of how verified theory grows in relation to concrete fact, but the rhetoric he found comfortable was an alternate denial of either theory or practice.

Griffiths reached his most complex understanding early in the 1850s, when he dealt with the contradictory demands of length, breadth, and massiveness, and accepted the

---

iner's Mirror, XLVIII (1962), 221; L (1964), 62-63. John Robinson and George Francis Dow, *The Sailing Ships of New England, 1607-1907* (Salem, 1922-1928), II, 26-27. John Scott Russell, *The Modern System of Naval Architecture*, I (London, 1865), 339-344. William H. Webb, *Plans for Wooden Vessels*, II, *passim*. John Fincham, *History of Naval Architecture* (London, 1851), plate 26.

[44] Griffiths, *Treatise on Marine and Naval Architecture*, 26, 195-196.

growing use of iron as a way to resolve these demands in a compact material. This analysis he retained into the 1870s, using it to explain some of the reasons why British shipbuilding had replaced American in the ocean trades. Though he did not ignore the matter of British cost advantage in iron, he argued more strongly that the British had manipulated design in order to appeal to the American mind and the American purse. Over twenty years the British, in building iron ships, had discovered that breadth increased the dangers of torsion on a hull. They therefore went to narrower ships, but in order to keep up capacity they made ships longer, which threatened longitudinal strength. These longer ships they justified to "the credulous go-ahead proclivities of the American people" on grounds of speed. Even though the longer British ships suffered some striking losses at sea, Americans imitated the design when they tried to build iron ships in competition with the British. Griffiths, to this knot of difficulties, responded with a massive intellectual funk. In his work of the 1850s he had shown some flexibility in appreciating the quite different styles of the square-rigger, the yacht, and the coastal vessel, as they had developed under various hands. In the 1870s he insisted that the "nautical phase" in the development of the American mind had culminated in the shallow-draft centerboard vessels that were used in the lake and coastal trades. His stand here was essentially a caricature of the principles that had been carried out in the development of the flat-bottomed clipper ships; in it, he demonstrated his own version of the weakness for single-principle design that had plagued American building since early in the century.

He demonstrated a similar weakness in the way that he attacked, cogently but at bottom fallaciously, the old reliance on models in ship design. He recognized how models had contributed to the expansion of American talent. He noted that as size increased, and as both style and materials changed rapidly, safety would be improved by more and

1. The Use of History: 1856 Picture, American, of 1812 Vessels.

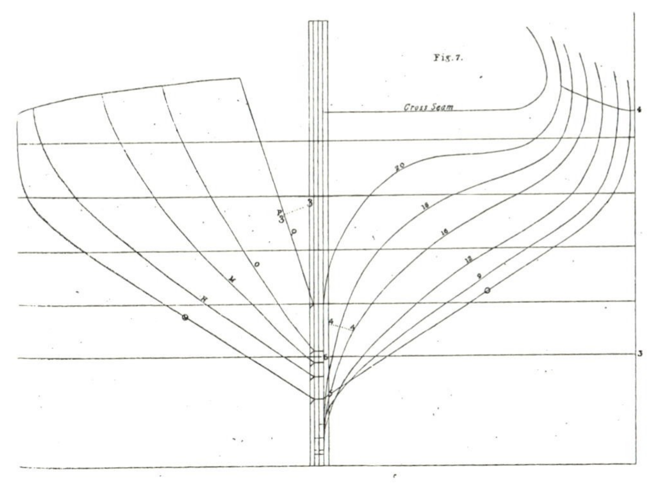

2. Hull Design, Showing Extreme Deadrise Common in Baltimore Clippers and Pilot Boats.

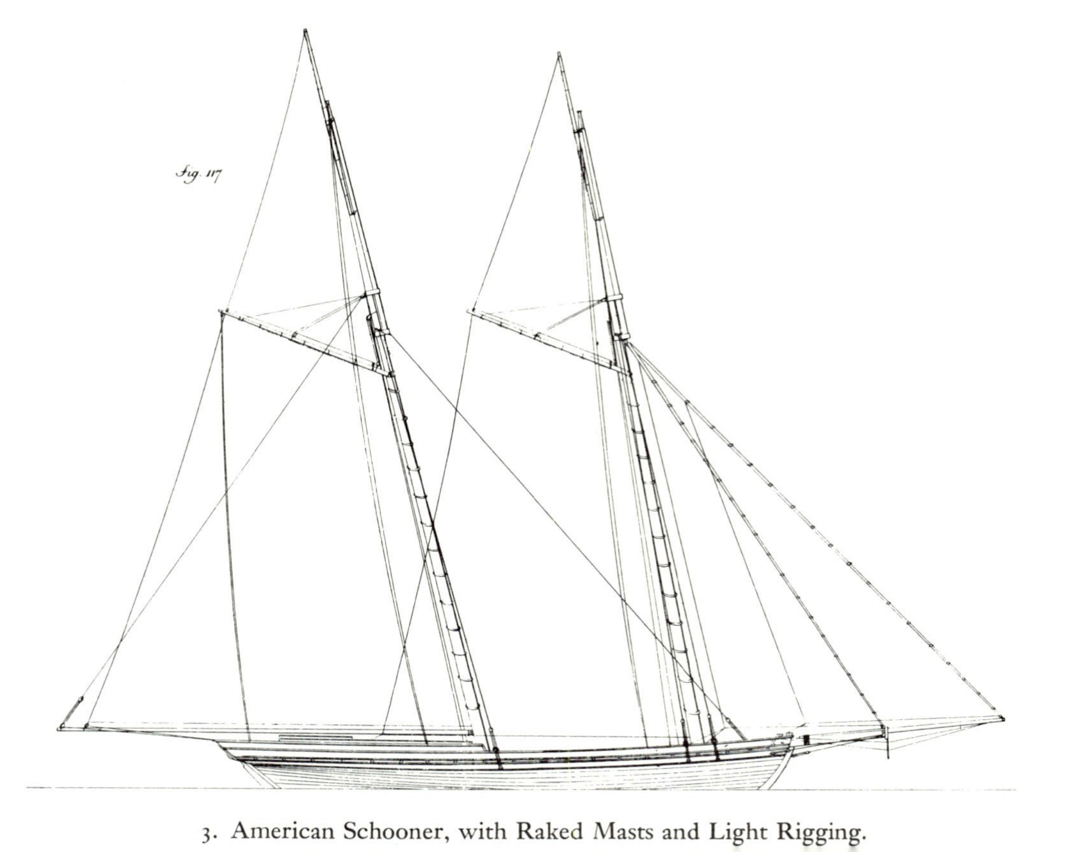

3. American Schooner, with Raked Masts and Light Rigging.

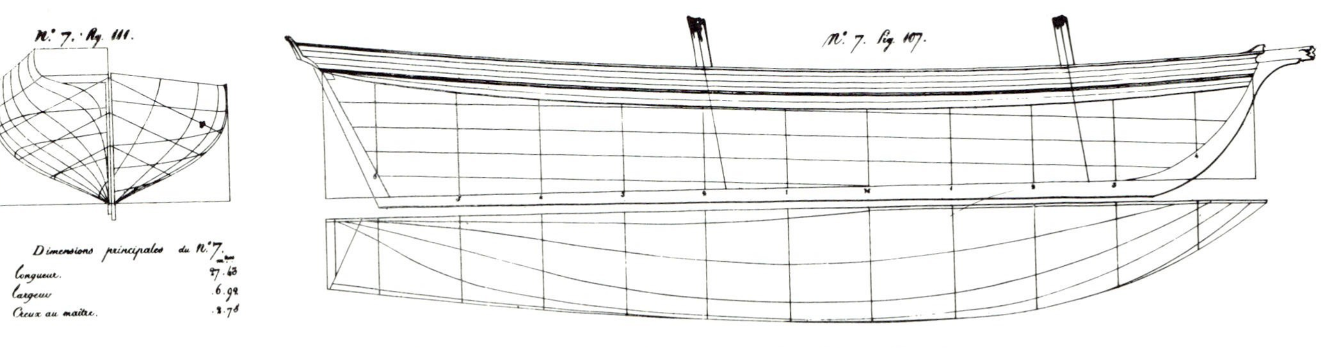

4. American Schooner, Hull Lines, Showing Sharp Deadrise.

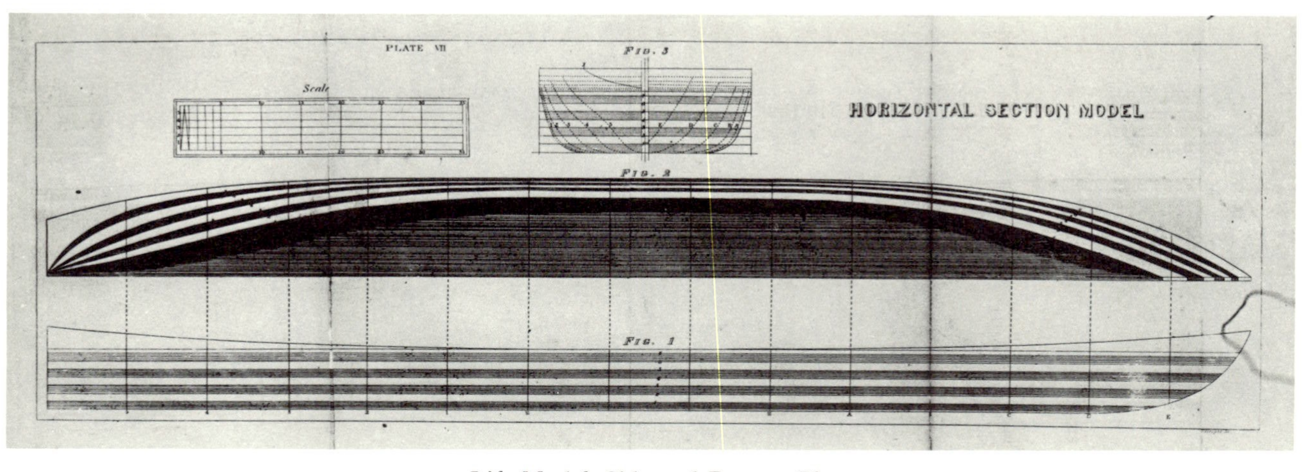

5. Lift Model, Side and Bottom Plans.

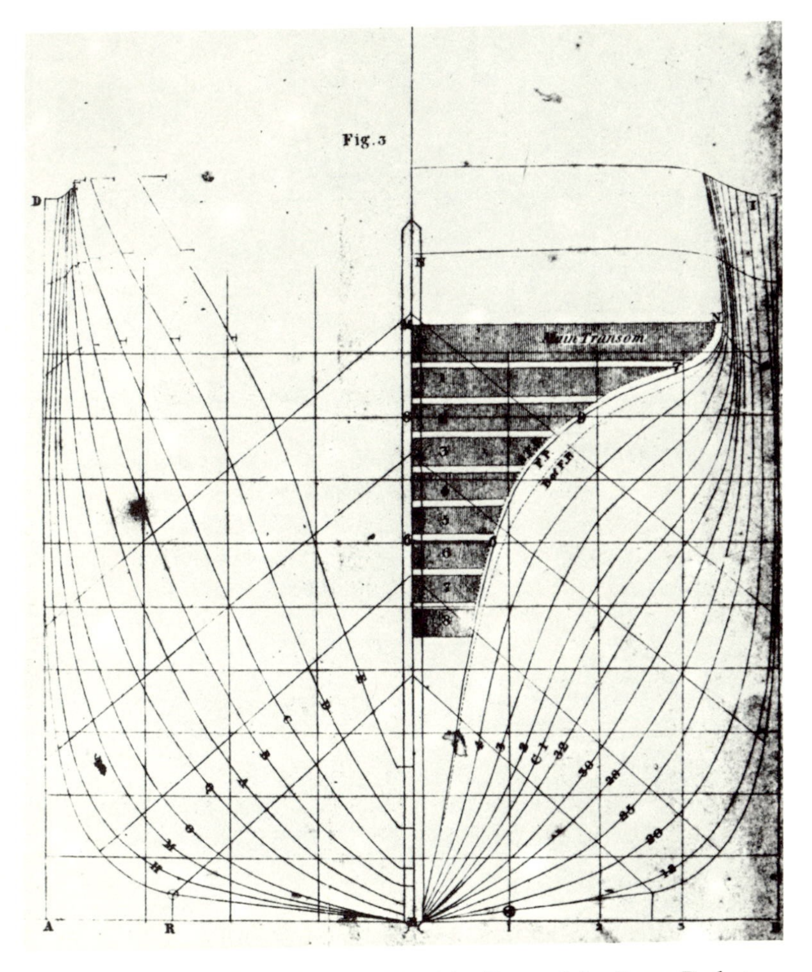

6. Hull Design, Showing Low Deadrise Favored by Later Packet and Clipper Builders.

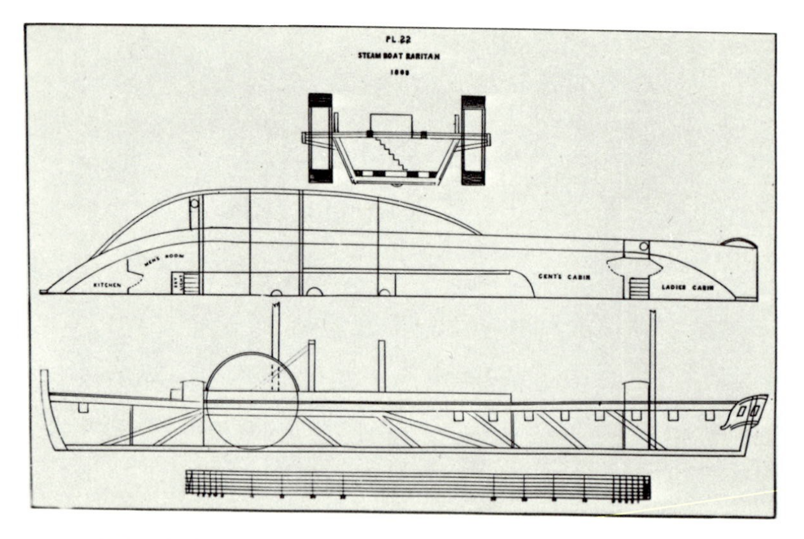

7. Fulton's *Raritan*, Showing Simple Truss-Type Longitudinal Strengthening Members (1808).

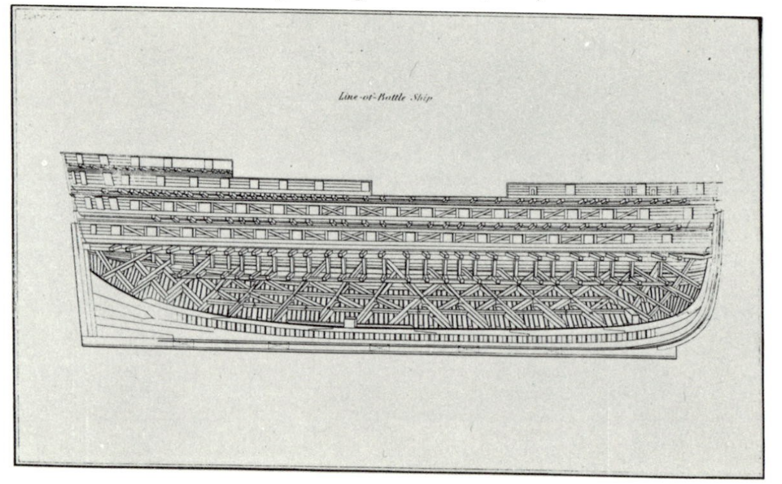

8. The Seppings Trussed Frame, Showing Amalgamation of Diagonal Members into Basic Hull Design.

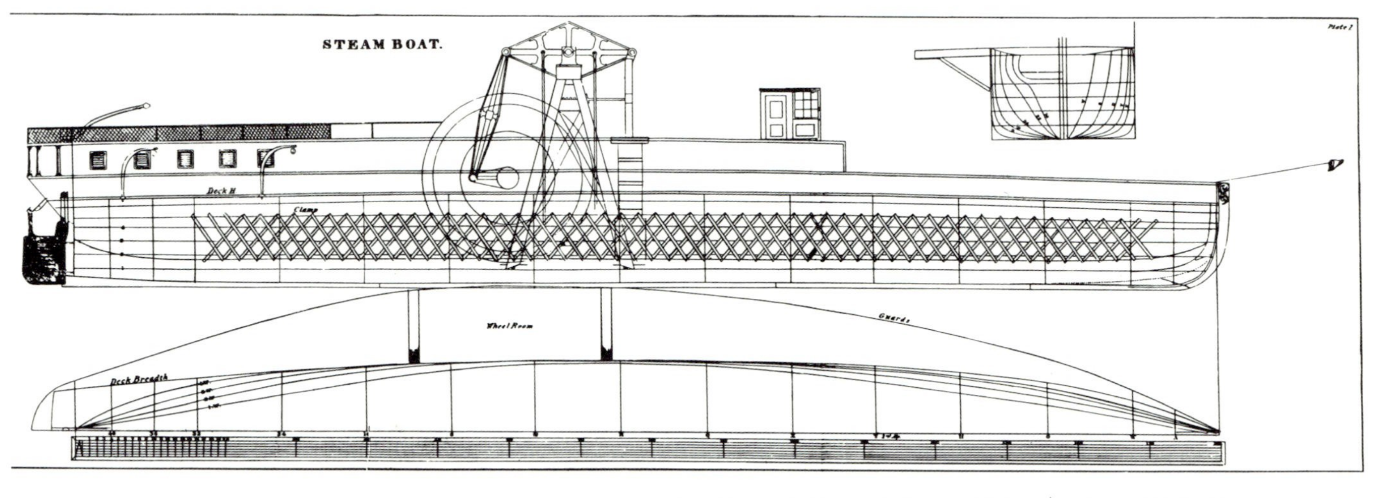

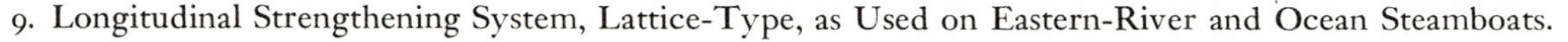

9. Longitudinal Strengthening System, Lattice-Type, as Used on Eastern-River and Ocean Steamboats.

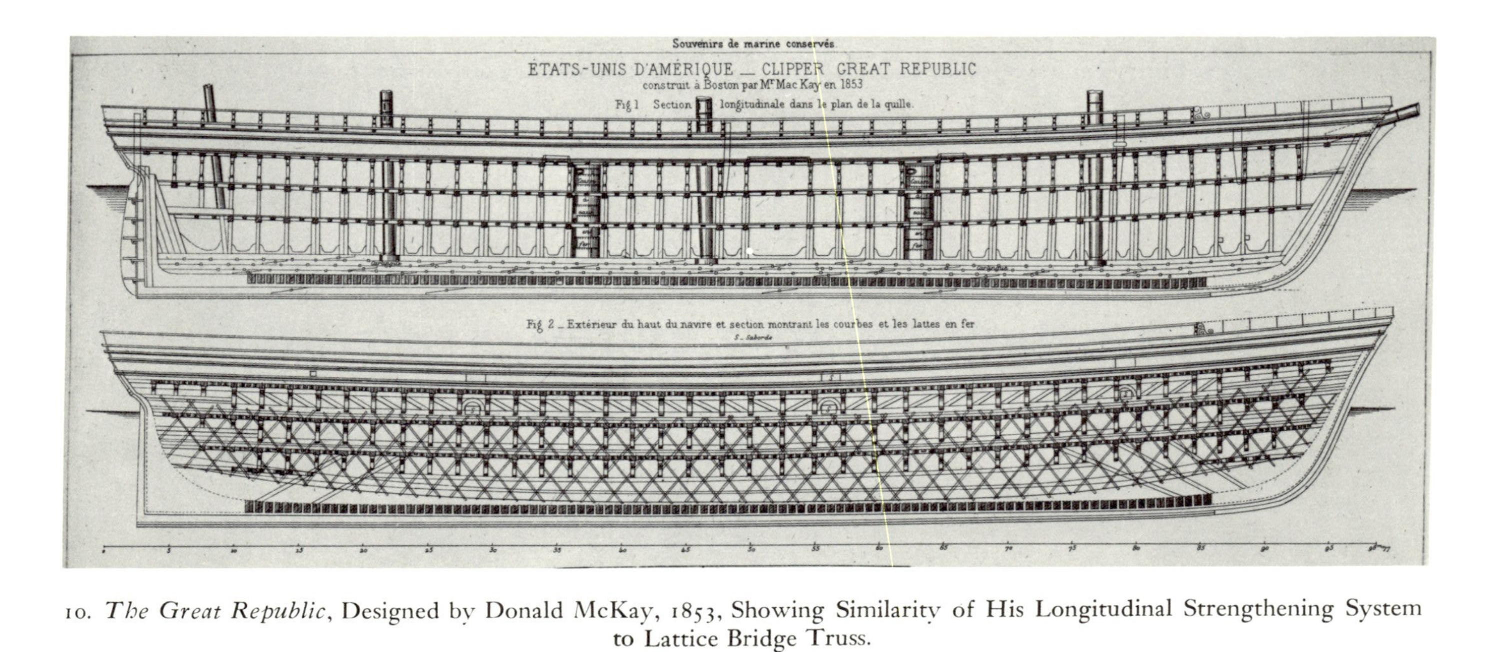

10. *The Great Republic*, Designed by Donald McKay, 1853, Showing Similarity of His Longitudinal Strengthening System to Lattice Bridge Truss.

11. Aftermath of the Royal Yacht Squadron Cup Race, 1851.

READING R. R.

ARCHED TRUSS BRIDGE.

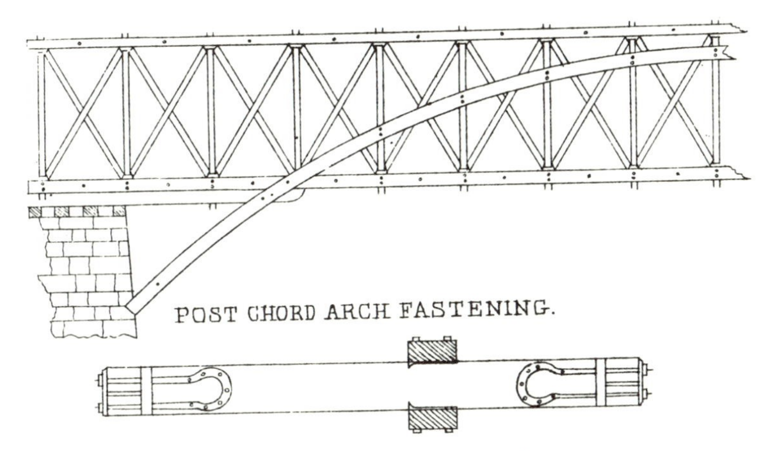

12. The Combined Arch-Truss Form.

Member.	Strain.	Composition.	Sectional area.	Strain per sq. inch.
I	66872	2 angles 3×3×½", 1 web plate 10×½"	8.62 net.	7758
II	95164	2 " 3×3×½", 1 " " 10×½", 1 bottom plate 10×½"	12.21 "	7794
III	113168	Same as panel *II*	12.21 "	9268
IV	118312	2 angles 3×3×½", 1 web plate 10×½", 1 bottom plate 10×½", 1 bottom plate 6½×⅜"	13.95 "	8481

Trusses, 5′ 6″ apart center to center. No iron floor system. Ties rest directly on top chords. Built, 1872.

TROY AND SCHENECTADY BRANCH—ERIE CANAL BRIDGE, WEST TROY.

One span, single track, through, riveted lattice bridge. Length for computation, 106′ 0″. Height, 19′ 0″. Twelve panels of 8′ 10″ each.

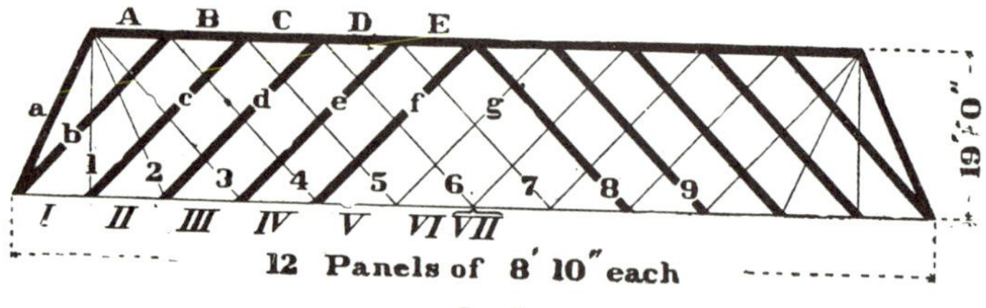

Loads.

Dead load = 1,060 pounds per foot.
Moving load = 3,000 pounds per foot.

Member.	Strain.	Composition.	Sectional area.	Strain per sq. inch.
a	88992	2 angles 3½×3½×½", 2 web plates 12×½", 1 cover plate 18×½"	27.72	3210
b	24324	2 angles 3½×3½×½"	6.72	3635
c	19741	2 " 3 ×3 ×⅜"	4.35	4538
d	15158	2 " 3 ×3 ×⅜"	4.35	3485
e	10575	2 " 3 ×3 ×⅜"	4.35	2431
f	5992	2 " 3 ×3 ×⅜"	4.35	1377
g	2907	Same as tension bar No. 7	3.82	Nominal.
1	31374	Two 5" channels	5.37 net.	5842
2	29664	" 4" "	3.28 "	9044
3	30405	" 4" "	3.28 "	9268
4	24324	" 4" "	3.28 "	7416
5	19741	" 3" "	3.11 "	6348

13. Stress Calculations for Lattice Bridges, from

Member.	Strain.	Composition.	Sectional area.	Strain per sq. inch.
6	15158	Two 3" channels	3.11 net.	4876
7	10575	" 3" "	3.11 "	3400
8	5992	Same as compression bar f	3.64 "	1646
9	2907	" " " " e	3.64 "	Nominal.
A	69870	2 angles 3½×3½×½", 2 web plates 12×⅜", 1 top plate 24×¼"	21.72	3217
B	102750	Same as panel A	21.72	4731
C	127410	2 angles 3½×3½×½", 2 web plates 12×⅜", 1 top plate 24×½"	27.72	4596
D	143850	Same as panel C	27.72	5190
E	152070	" " " C	27.72	5486
I	53430	2 angles 3½×3½×½", 2 web plates 12×⅜"	12.47 net.	4285
II	65760	Same as panel *I*	13.08 "	5027
III	86310	" " " *I*	12.44 "	6938
IV	110970	2 angles 3½×3½×½", 2 web plates 12×⅜", 1 bottom plate 24×¼"	17.64 "	6291
V	127410	Same as panel *IV*	17.64 "	7223
VI	135630	" " " *IV*	17.64 "	7689
VII	143850	2 angles 3½×3½×½", 2 web plates 12×⅜", 1 bottom plate 24×⅜"	22.51 "	6346

Trusses, 15′ 8″ apart center to center. Floor consists of 9″ I beams, 87 lbs. per yard, placed underneath the lower chords and riveted thereto by eight 1″ rivets at each end of each beam passing through the top flange of the beam and the horizontal leg of chord angles. There are four such beams in each panel, spaced 2′ 2½″ apart center to center. On top of these beams are placed two 6×6×$\frac{7}{16}$″ angles, ten feet apart, which in turn support the rails and cross-ties, the latter being 8×10″ in size and spaced 5½″ apart in the clear. Built, 1868.

NOTE.— *The moving load of 3,000 lbs. per foot used in the above computations is that given in the railroad company's strain sheet and is retained because it was found to give slightly greater results than the wheel loads of any engines and cars which actually cross the bridge.*

TROY AND SCHENECTADY BRANCH — BRIDGE OVER COHOES TURNPIKE, WEST TROY.

One span, single track, through, riveted lattice bridge. Length for computation, 76′ 0″. Height, 9′ 0″. One panel 7′ 6″ long, six panels each 9′ 6″ long and one panel 11′ 6″ long.

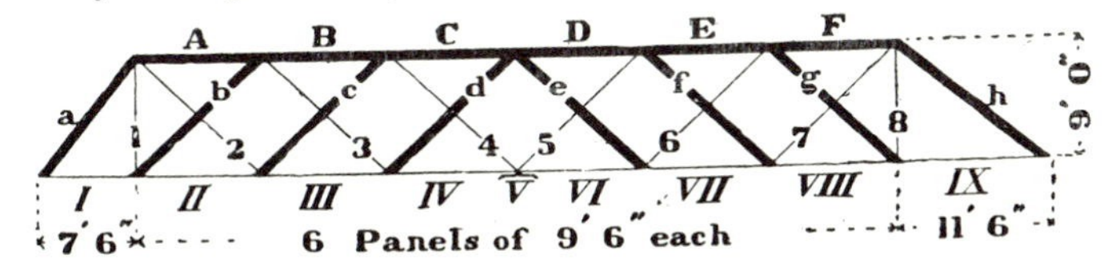

New York Investigation of 1891.

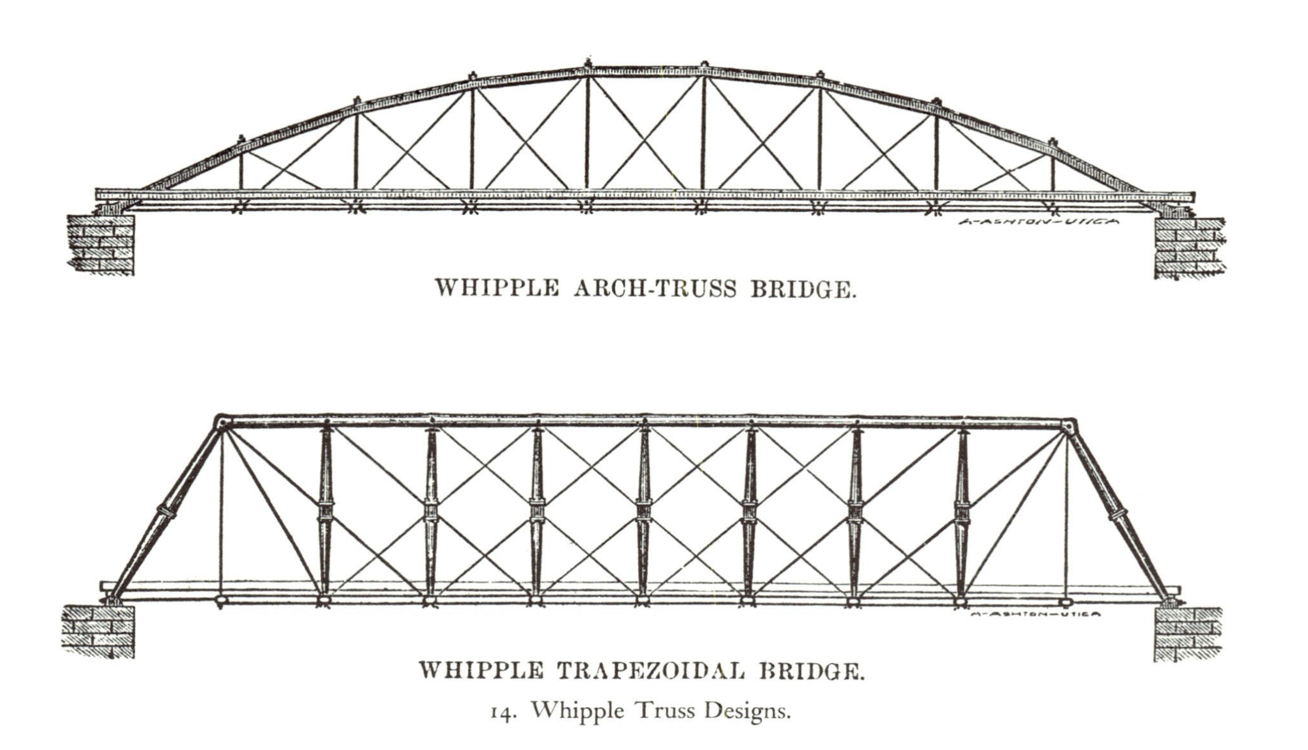

14. Whipple Truss Designs.

INDIAN RIVER BRIDGE, NEAR THERESA.

One span, single track, through, Whipple truss bridge. Length for computation, 103′ 4″. Height, center to center of chords, 20′ 0″. Eight panels of 12′ 11″ each.

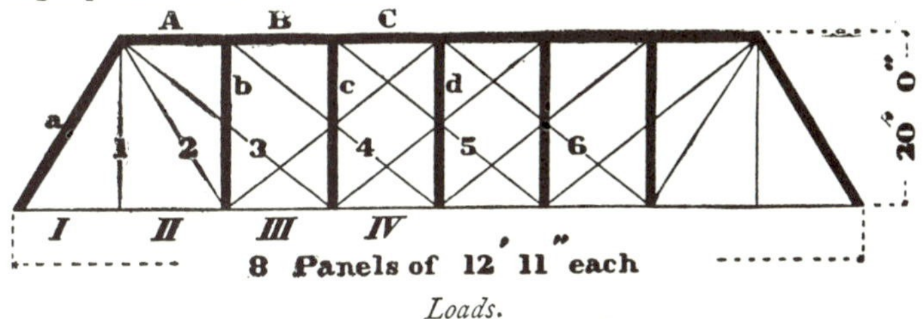

Loads.

Dead load = 900 pounds per foot.

Moving load = U. and B. R. standard locomotive followed by train of 25-ton cars.

Member.	Strain.	Composition.	Sectional area.	Strain per sq. inch.
a	94903	4 segment Phœnix column	15.00	6327
b	14701	4 " " "	7.00	2100
c	9277	4 " " "	7.00	1325
d	2183	4 " " "	7.00	Nominal.
1	24719	2 bars 2 ×¾″	3.00	8240
2	42223	2 " 2½×⅞″	4.38	9640
3	43627	2 " 2½×⅞″	4.38	9961
4	23963	2 " 2 ×¾″	3.00	7988
5	15422	2 rods 1⅛″ diameter	1.99	7750
6	3558	2 " ⅞″ "	1.20	2965
A	88228	4 segment Phœnix column	11.00	8021
B	100832	4 " " "	12.50	8007
C	100832	4 " " "	12.50	8007
I	51439	2 bars 3×15-16″	5.63	9137
II	51439	2 " 3×15-16″	5.63	9137
III	63020	2 " 3×1 5-16″	7.88	8000
IV	88228	4 " 3×15-16″	11.25	7842

Trusses 16′ 4″ apart center to center. Each floor beam consists of two 15″ I beams, 150 lbs. per yd. Stringers two, spaced 8′ 6″ apart center to center, resting on top of floor beams. Each stringer consists of a web plate $18\frac{1}{2}\times\frac{3}{8}''$, top flange two angles $4\times3\times\frac{7}{16}''$, and bottom flange two angles $4\times3\times\frac{3}{8}''$.

(*See report beyond.*)

(In this bridge the stringers originally consisted of two 9′ I beams, 84 lbs. per yard, spaced 5′ 0″ apart center to center. The Board having recommended that the floor beams and stringers be strengthened, the latter were replaced by new ones of the size noted above, spaced 8′ 6″ apart, thus relieving the floor beams.)

15. Stress Calculations for Whipple Truss, from New York Investigation of 1891.

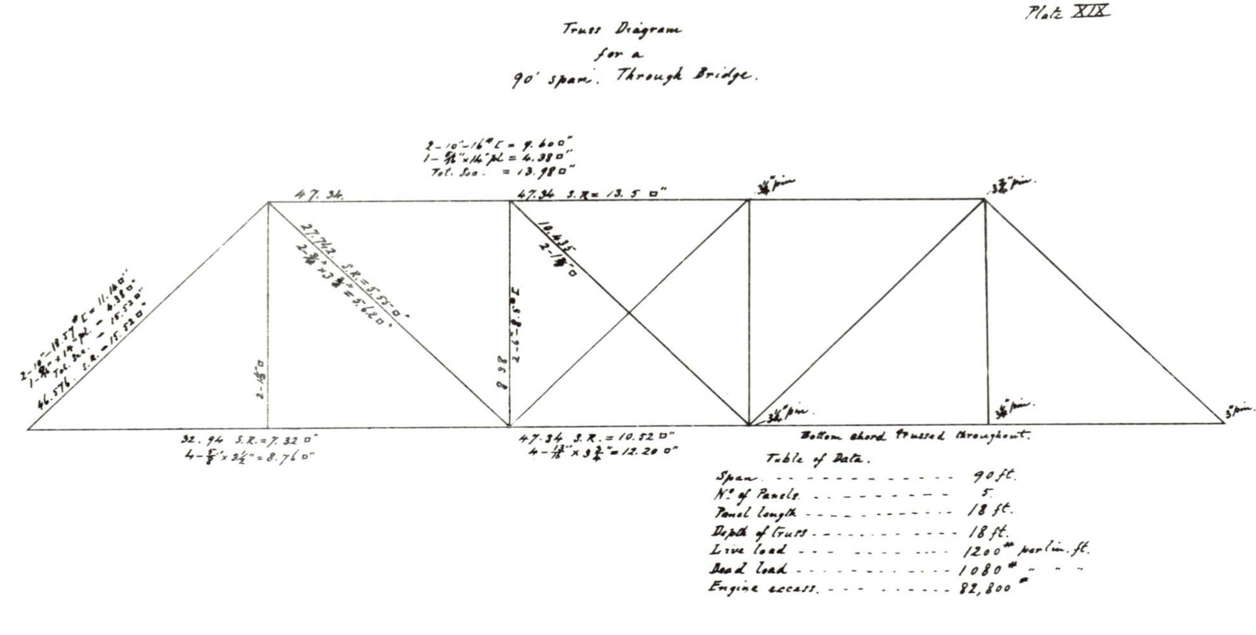

16. Stress Calculations for Bridge in the American Style, Proposed for Japanese Railroads.

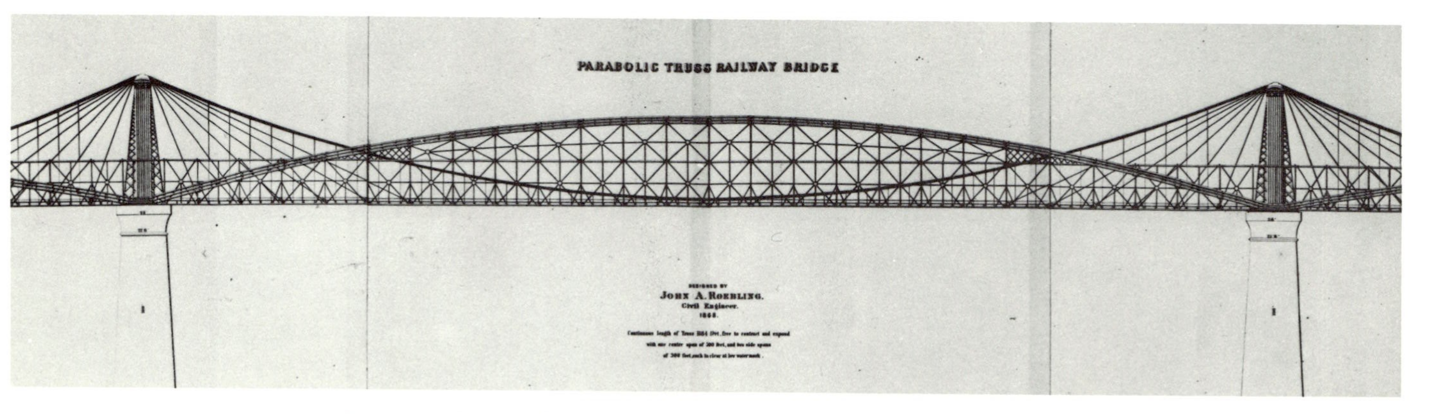

17. Roebling's Proposal to Combine the Suspension and Truss Principles.

18. Henry Ward Beecher and the Beecher Pulpit.

more extensive calculation of the engineering problems involved. Calculation demanded advance plans, not just models that did not facilitate consideration of the interior or the fabric. He presented his own drafting techniques as a key to the analysis of ship problems—then in the detail of his argument explained those techniques only as ways of taking off exact lines for shipyard calculation.[45] Such a transition from models to a greater use of drafts did not dissipate the usual builder's commitment to visual intuition. As one of them noted in 1851, "In making a Model, or Drawing a plan for a vessel, it matters not what Scale be taken or used, but the smaller the best, as the Eye will the more readily scan the entire work; and the small irregularities can be repaired much sooner than the larger ones."[46]

Americans, like others, sometimes denounced the statements of theorists as irrelevant to practice, less to be relied on than the eye and touch of the practical builder. But professedly "practical" men like Lauchlan McKay also drew up statements of the general principles or rules that should govern construction, in which they accepted as relevant certain among the hydrodynamic theories then available. What characterized these statements by American builders was less a lack of theory than a lack of any principled understanding of how to balance off the indications of different theories. This tendency to garble the best of understandings persisted through the whole middle part of the century. It appeared as late as 1873 in a textbook that Theodore D. Wilson drew up for use at Annapolis: in critical places, he simply lifted articles out of British journals, by

[45] Griffiths, *Progressive Ship Builder*, 66-90, 120-124, 158-159.

[46] Ship Wrights Guide (1851), in William R. Hanscom Letter Copybook, G. W. Blunt White Library, Mystic, Connecticut. It is unclear whether this guide was originally composed by Hanscom or by Samuel Moore Pook. See Pook, *A Method of Comparing the Lines and Draughting Vessels, Propelled by Sail or Steam* (New York, 1866).

men as extreme and dogmatic as John Scott Russell, without attempting to form any systematic relation between one dogma and another.[47] In constructing ships for general purposes American builders were just as likely as any others to blend various principles along with customary practice into fairly conservative products. The later packets and the clipper ships were of this conservative type, evolving more in size than anything else. But where the purposes for which a vessel was intended were special, designers could concentrate on some single, presumably appropriate, principle without real inhibition from a coherent system of understandings.

In the large, the popular mind seems at first to have been more impressed with the growing scale of the packets and clippers. But the cost and supply problems of American builders made this grand accomplishment vulnerable. As Griffiths noted in 1853, Americans were building larger and larger ships out of wood, in which they had a competitive advantage; but the requirement of greater hull strength with increased length was posing problems of limit. Even if enough wood were available, the cross-sections of interior beams needed to increase out of proportion to length, and this ran against the need for cargo capacity. It was also becoming more and more difficult to get large enough timbers, so that builders had to compound beams out of smaller pieces. The obvious course was to move over to partial or total metal construction, but in this the British had then an almost unchallengeable competitive advantage. Even early in the 1850s, American prestige and sensitivity were threatened.

[47] Richard W. Meade, *A Treatise on Naval Architecture and Ship-Building . . . Compiled from Various Standard Authorities* (Philadelphia, 1869). Theodore D. Wilson, *An Outline of Ship Building, Theoretical and Practical* (New York, 1873). These two textbooks are much the same in form and in many of their inclusions; but the Meade is an honest compilation, while the Wilson fluctuates between coy honesty and blunt plagiarism.

Ability that is exercised in successful practice hardly needs a specially devised audience to prove itself. Ability that is being threatened by larger developments may need to separate itself off, and seek out some means of being tested as formal intelligence. American pleasure sailing had begun to take organized form, as in the New York Yacht Club of 1844; British yachting, much older, presented an obvious challenge. Commercial shipbuilders did not treat this activity as a diversion, but paid it the tribute of fascination. The critical figure was George Steers, who had been trained in a family of builders during the packet years, then became himself active in building schooners and some larger vessels after 1840. It was Steers who designed the yacht *America* on lines evolved directly out of the slavers and pilot boats. After the *America* took the Royal Yacht Squadron's Cup at Cowes in 1851 (illustration 11) American commercial builders like Griffiths clung to it as a demonstration of prowess, even when they were increasingly unable to demonstrate success through profitable building contracts.[48] "Pure" intelligence was being precipitated out by real-life pressures.

This precipitation was paralleled by certain features in other parts of American thought. As was argued in Horace Bushnell's comments on the "play" theme, in 1848,[49] and in John Dewey's much more elaborate discussion later, the exercise of pure intelligence required playfulness in addition to work—so that the testing of intelligence was a playful relation between performer and observer. This was be-

[48] Griffiths, *Ship-Builder's Manual*, I, 66, 97-99, 117-118, 149; II, 20. Griffiths, *Treatise on Marine and Naval Architecture*, 195-196. Chapelle, *History of American Sailing Ships*, 304-305, 314. Chapelle, *National Water Craft Collection*, 34-36. Roland F. Coffin, *The America's Cup* (New York, 1885), 5-8. Webb, *Plans of Wooden Vessels*, I, under Yacht *Dream*. Henry Cleaver Chapman, *The Laws of Dynamics Applied to Yacht Building; Explained in Letters Addressed to the Yacht Builders of Great Britain* (Liverpool, 1851), iii-iv, 21-24.

[49] Horace Bushnell, *Work and Play; or Literary Varieties* (New York, 1864), 9-42.

ing demonstrated in the success of the *America.* But if Dewey's ideas are relevant here, so are Veblen's. The success was a demonstration of "prowess," in the sense that Veblen was to use in explaining aristocratic leisure activity, and its partial descent from the privateers is appropriate.

C. A Case in the Verbal: the Preaching of 1870

The social forms that supported quality in colonial preaching were controversial at the time, and turned out to be fragile. During the last part of the eighteenth century and the early part of the nineteenth, real intellectual community collapsed. Feelings against central authority, partly reinforced by the Revolution, worked on the local level to undermine the attention and support that people gave to pastors. Groups alienated from older religious ideas and leaders fell away from church life or set up competing denominations. In the New York area, the entry of Methodist organization in 1768 and the renewal of Methodist activity after the Revolution gave form and leadership to much of this stirring. The Methodist system, which provided tight hierarchical control over itinerant preachers, was a strong way of reaching unsatisfied, migratory populations. But it was inherently unsuited to sustaining any kind of complex discourse, and it was in its early years actually hostile or indifferent to education for preachers. The years around the turn of the century saw the beginning of camp meetings that drew men away from settled pastors. The camp meetings were not a mere frontier outburst; they and the other revivals also attracted people in long-settled parts of the eastern seaboard.[50] Nor were they only rural. Revivals

[50] See the following complaints, referring to Long Island, the Maryland Eastern Shore, the Hudson Valley, and New Jersey, in the Bishop Hobart Papers, Church Historical Society, Austin, Texas: John C. Rudd to John Henry Hobart, Sept. 3, 1806; Joseph Jackson to Hobart, Sept. 22, 1806; James Bill to Hobart, July 16, 1812; J. C. Rudd to Hobart, Jan. 25, 1820.

brought large gains to Methodist congregations in New York City during the first decade of the century.[51]

From quite early in this splintering, a counter-movement grew. Few of the evangelical groups took an unambiguous stand against intellectual training. When pressed, they would argue that education was of course a good thing, but that piety and not education was the essential quality in a preacher. Some individuals within these denominations were more friendly than others to the cause of intellectual quality. These individuals gained influence over the years as their followers settled down, made some money, found respectable places in their communities, and began to share in the growing educational life of the new century. Where many of these people might have found themselves marked for work in the less dignifying jobs in the growing cities, the appearance of immigrant labor permitted them to escape the more easily from that trap. Since much of the new labor turned out to be Roman Catholic, the desire of the evangelicals to distinguish themselves gave them additional reason to look to the intellectual supports for their position.

During the same years, those denominations with longer intellectual tradition began to pay more particular attention to ways of training ministers. In some cases the secular tone of older schools and colleges drove them to seek their own institutions. In other cases the pressure to compete for influence against other denominations, be they churchly or evangelical, led them to create schools and colleges as weapons of domestic mission work. Competition tended to pull each group into the same measures adopted by any large or aggressive part of the others, so that by the middle of the nineteenth century the differences in intellectual institutions from one denomination to another were differences of circumstance and temperament, not of basic com-

[51] Amory Stevens Bucke, ed., *The History of American Methodism* (New York & Nashville, 1964), I, 174-175, 405-409. Henry Wade Barclay, *History of Methodist Missions*, Part One: *Early American Methodism, 1769-1844*, I (New York, 1949), 130.

mitment. Virtually every group organized local secondary schools to keep a lien on potential leaders among adolescents. Virtually every group was making some effort to support colleges. Virtually every group maintained seminaries and encouraged ministerial candidates to study in seminary or some other proper school. And virtually every denomination sponsored some agency to recruit, subsidize, and educate young men for the ministry. Ministers were certainly getting more formal education of some sort than they often had at the beginning of the century. Congregations, too, were more extensively schooled, because they had been caught up in the common-school revival, or because they were people who had moved to the cities, where schools were better, or simply because they had been exposed to the increasing availability of information through lectures, newspapers, libraries, and magazines. Ministers complained that they were forced to work harder on sermons because modern congregations demanded more.[52]

The situation, then, by the years after the Civil War, was one of apparent institutional recovery from the earlier collapse of a sometimes achieved community of religious discourse. The new institutions were committed to maintaining and improving intellectual life within the churches, and they were part of a society thoroughly "modern." But what kind of intellectual life—specifically, what kind of preaching—did these churches and institutions support?[53]

[52] John Wayland, *Causes of the Prevalent Failures in Pulpit Eloquence* (Boston, 1840). Hugh Smith, *Theory and Regulation of Public Sentiment* (New York, 1842), 46. William Adams, "Politics and the Pulpit," *American Presbyterian Review*, n.s. I (1863), 134-135. "Records of a Christian College," *Christian Advocate*, XLIV (1869), 236. S. Fitch, "Ministerial Demand," *ibid.*, XLV (1870), 338. "The Sermon Not an Oration," *ibid.*, XLV (1869), 60. "Clerical Study of the Natural Sciences," *ibid.*, XLV (1870), 124. H. H. Fairall, "Our Theological Schools," *Methodist*, XI (1870), 393.

[53] The sermons discussed in this section I selected informally, by pulling from the shelves of the library of the Harvard Divinity School all the sermon collections I could find that included New York items

New York in 1870 meant, first of all, Henry Ward Beecher. To the Pilgrim Church in Brooklyn, vast crowds flocked to hear Beecher. Although he did not operate as near the intellectual peak of his society as had Jonathan Dickinson in 1740, many people were willing to accept him as if he did. Other preachers who worked in the same style that he did took him as their sanction and leader. Those who stood aside and complained about the preaching standard of the age often took Beecher as their example.[54] Although his intellectual and social status was closer to that of, say, Ebenezer Pemberton in colonial New York, it is with him rather than with anyone more austere that discussion must begin. In 1871, furthermore, one of his parishioners endowed a lectureship in preaching for the divinity students at Yale. Named the Lyman Beecher Lectures after Henry Ward Beecher's father, they were eventually to be given by a different man every year, each to be chosen from some evangelical denomination for his success in the practical work in the ministry, each to give the students more of practical advice than they might otherwise get in the academic seminary program. For the first three years, though, the lecturer was always the same: Henry Ward Beecher.[55] The volumes that resulted then gave an additional and wider intellectual respectability to his preaching.

But the preaching itself was the main thing. It was fairly

---

close to 1870. Among these I concentrated on fifty that seemed representative. This meant that I accepted up to a point the opinions implied in collections like *The American Pulpit of the Day* (London, 1875) about who were the important preachers, but that I made an additional effort to include some sermons preached by evangelists and some sermons reported verbatim by stenographers.

[54] Samuel Graves, *Baptist Quarterly*, II (1868), 294. "The Modern Pulpit," *American Quarterly Church Review*, XXIII (1871), 9. Thomas Nichols, "Preaching to the Conscience," *Presbyterian Quarterly and Princeton Review*, n.s. IV (1875), 24-27, makes an especially strong statement without actually naming Beecher.

[55] Edgar DeWitt Jones, *The Royalty of the Pulpit* (New York, 1951), xxiii, xxvi, 3-10.

consistent in style. Beecher usually began a sermon with a conventional exposition of some scriptural text. If the text demanded that he give instruction about the historical circumstances surrounding it, he could do this in a clear, reasonably accurate way. More often, though, he sought some way to apply the text to everyday personal feelings, even if this application took some wrenching. Thus he took the text for his New Year's sermon in 1870 from the Old Testament description of Samuel's setting up the memorial stone that he named "Eben-ezer": "Hitherto hath the Lord helped us." Beecher gave an elaborate picture of the occasion for this action, condescending only a little toward the primitive quality of life among the Israelites. He then compared the circumstances of American life to those of conflict among the Israelites, as if he were about to enter on a topical discussion of civil strife, but then quickly insisted that the real conflicts of life are inward, and that the major events of the inward life deserve to be memorialized. Here he set out on the kind of main exposition that was characteristic of his work. He chatted on through item after item, recommending different ways of memorializing: notebooks of important dates tagged with scripture texts; significant objects and pictures around the house; memorial windows in churches. "If such a course of noting God's dealing with us, if such a course of setting up memorials by way of recognising the hand of God in the shaping of our lives, be established and followed out, by-and-by we shall come to a habitual sense of God's presence with us." This rather domestic application of Israelite primitivism led him finally to the occasion of the New Year, and thus to a direct address to the congregation on the subject of himself: he thanked them for the compliments they had paid to his sermons during the past year, and asked their prayers for him during the coming year. A brief conclusion then tagged this to the need for gratitude and remembrance to God.[56] Beecher had

[56] *The Sermons of Henry Ward Beecher, in Plymouth Church, Brooklyn. From Verbatim Reports by T. J. Ellinwood.* "Plymouth

started with a fairly intelligent application of a text, then had relaxed into a series of rambling notations and anecdotes, wandering over a point-by-point searching path until he homed in on a point that contained the driving force behind his apparently spontaneous rhetoric: something involving himself, his own experience or feelings, and his relation to his hearers.

Beecher did not always feed his audience with such explicit cues to how they should feel about himself, but he did consistently develop a sermon through a series of anecdotes climaxing in a personal anecdote or revelation that could have been serving *him* as a subsurface cue to each of the less personal anecdotes in the preceding development. Some of the inward structure of this pattern Beecher indicated in an impromptu weeknight talk, "The Death of Little Children." This was not a formal sermon, but a talk interspersed with questions from the audience. Still, Beecher went through the same process of rambling around and up to a point of personal experience, in this case the loss of his own child. It had long been common in religious discourse to ask God to bless bereavements to the spiritual growth of the bereaved; callous though this may sound to later men, the plea had at least had a stern, self-mortifying intent. Beecher, though, found a more professional use for the occasion of his own loss: "Those sad hours were to me a kind of ordination, as in laying-on of hands. They have been blessed to me so, that I think no happiness from that child, had it lived, could have equalled the good to me and to others through me, from its early death."[57]

Few men exploited their personalities and private lives so explicitly as did Beecher, but the salient fact of much post-Civil War preaching was its dependency on personality and personal experience. The revivalist Dwight L.

Pulpit," *Third Series: September, 1869-March, 1870* (New York, 1872), 263-276, with quotation at 273.

[57] Henry Ward Beecher, "The Death of Little Children. A Lecture-Room Talk," *Methodist*, Jan. 4, 1873.

Moody, though he talked more about interviews with sinners than about mere domestic sentiment, sustained his extemporaneous discourse with personal anecdote. He began each sermon by announcing a simple topic largely independent of his nominal text; often it was a general trait, such as "Faith" or "Courage and Enthusiasm" or "Love and Sympathy." He then set out on a string of narrative anecdotes, following one on the other in a free-association order, with no particular development, and concluded the whole by stating the initial theme within a brief call to conversion. The anecdotes were usually pertinent to the stated theme, but they had also, and always, a latent subject matter: the conversion and revival process itself. About half were first-person accounts from his own earlier work. His sermons had not the centripetal structure that Beecher's did, since he used personal anecdote both less inhibitedly and less intimately, neither postponing the personal to the end of discourse nor putting it into acute focus. He could, though, fall into self-revelation. Referring to a recent English tour, he said, "The last time I heard Dr. Arnold speak—he died soon afterward—he used a homely illustration." Arnold described how to teach a calf to drink: put fingers into the calf's mouth, then thrust the calf's head into a pail of milk, then pull the fingers out. "So," said Arnold in Moody's report, "you must get the people to love you, and then turn them over to Christ." The pace and formal structure of Moody's preaching did not differ much from that of Gilbert Tennent's revival preaching in the previous century, but the central strategy had changed: where Tennent had scored impact by iterating images that touched on a garbled popular memory of more learned sermon material, Moody iterated stories about the revival process, a large proportion of which afforded what later fan magazines might call "exciting glimpses" into the life of the celebrity revivalist.[58]

[58] Dwight L. Moody, *Glad Tidings. Comprising Sermons and Prayer-Meeting Talks. Delivered at the N. Y. Hippodrome* (New York, 1876), *passim*, quotation p. 56.

The Beecher-Moody strategy was not the only one that preachers used at that time. Other men, less sensationally popular, rarely intruded self except on such occasions as the inaugural discourse of a pastorate, when it was usual for a man to say something about his general intentions and his need for the prayers and sympathy of the congregation. Often, rather, they talked about conventional religious problems. Sometimes, in a manner that the next generation would extend, deepen, and label as the "Social Gospel," they talked about problems of economic class and social reform that offered little opening for details of personality. For such sermons the evaluative criterion is not simply, Did these men face up to the implications of the problems they raised? but also, Did they use rhetorically honest language in exploring their problems?

Among the more conventional, consider Joseph T. Duryea, pastor of the Classon Avenue Presbyterian Church in Brooklyn. Taking as his text the sentence, "God is a spirit," he could produce a perfectly neat textbook specimen of what a polite sermon should be. He began by stating a little problem, the impossibility of defining God. He then set up a distinction between spirit (which he called "the vital, intelligent, voluntary principle") and matter. He then developed three inferences, carefully observing three as the classic limit between helpful enumeration and multifarious pedantry: first, that God is invisible; second, that spirit has never assumed a definite, invariable form; and third, that spirit has however assumed a variety of forms, beginning with the angels of the Old Testament and culminating in Christ. These various forms he described in a devotional tone. Then he concluded with a paragraph of exhortation to worship God in spirit and in truth.[59] Though this was orthodox enough, nothing could have been more polite or more insipid. He made no urgent appeals. He raised no difficult psychological issues. He did not even attempt to trans-

[59] Joseph T. Duryea, "The Spirituality of God," *The American Pulpit of the Day* (London, 1875), 70-80.

late into common or acceptable language any of the difficulties in the meaning of "spirit," much less push through to any possible solution of those difficulties.

Few preachers were so insipid as this, but many who tried to do anything more within the formal sermon structure ended up in a combination of pragmatic fideism and anecdotal escapism. This difficulty was illustrated by a sermon that George H. Hepworth delivered at the Church of the Disciples on Madison Avenue. His text was daringly familiar—"The Lord is my shepherd"—and the problem he drew from it was plausibly important: that belief in Providence is necessary to religious faith, but that "what we want in these latter times is a reasonable theory concerning Providence." But, instead of exploring what "Providence" might actually mean in the thought-patterns of the people he addressed, he simply presented, clearly enough, two standard theories from which to choose: the deistic theory that God had created the world and left it to act by itself, and the theistic that God was continuing to act. On the first, he revealed his standard of judgment: "I hate that theory. It is extant throughout the community. It is to-day exerting a baleful influence upon religion and religious institutions, and it is false because it is baleful. That is the everlasting logic of events; whatever leads you to a higher life through the best standard of measurement you can discover, is likely to be true; whatsoever hurts you is false; whatsoever lifts you to enthusiasm, makes you more favoured as father, friend, business man, is likely to be true; what chills, makes you cold, careless, and selfish, is likely to be false."

On the theistic theory, he offered only a series of assertions that there is in fact a Providence, capping these with two images: one, of the tapestry that makes no sense on its wrong side but reveals a coherent pattern on its right side; the other, of the Swiss chamois-hunter. This last was a story whose dousing impact was reserved as a surprise ending. The hunter fell into a crevasse or ravine, couldn't get out up the sides, but found a stream that he followed until it flowed through a hole in the ground. Seeing that he had no other course, he threw himself into the icy water, was swallowed in wet tumult for a time, then suddenly was cast up into a sunny, happy valley. The sermon ended abruptly, with only one line following this story: "If we have faith enough, all will come right at last. God be thanked for that."[60] This was bathos disguised as drama. The evil did not lie in the shocking sensory quality of the picture. Such in itself had been practiced with both effect and integrity by Jonathan Edwards in his picture of the soul as a loathsome spider held over a burning fire. But Edwards had used shock to present his hearers with a difficulty that they in complacency might otherwise have avoided. Hepworth used shock to get both himself and his hearers out of a difficult intellectual problem. And he presented even that shock in the form of a pseudo-travel story, providing at the end of his sermon an easy transition back into the worlds of bourgeois vacation and vicarious enjoyment.

On the borderline between the conventional and the social, consider Charles S. Robinson, pastor of the Presbyterian Memorial Church on Madison Avenue in New York. He arrived as minister announcing that he intended to preach simply the "full, true gospel," and he noted that his new congregation knew enough about him to realize that he was not going to preach any disorganizing social doctrines. And he operated thus, delivering evangelical ideas in an orderly, developed form that would appeal to a respectable, well-to-do congregation. A typical sermon took as its text a verse from Psalm 85: "Mercy and truth are met together; righteousness and peace have kissed each other." He began, presumably illustrating the true availability of mercy, by retelling the story of the boat that ran out of fresh water while in the equatorial region of the Atlantic: it met another boat, asked for water, and was told to drop buckets on the spot—that is, into the fresh water flowing out from the mouth of the Amazon. From there he moved

[60] George H. Hepworth, "The Providence of God," *ibid.*, 23-33.

into a long central section on three merciful promises contained in Old Testament prophecy: promises of the Redeemer, of the Holy Spirit, and of the Church. On each he set out a few of the standard proof-texts and arguments used to show that the coming of Christ was prophesied in the Hebrew Scriptures, but he kept each subsection short enough and simple enough that he did not fall into the kind of prophecy-crabbing that would have been displayed by a Burr or Frelinghuysen in the previous century. From there he then moved into another set piece, ascribed to "Arabian allegory" and much longer than his opening anecdote, on the debate in Heaven between the attributes of God, over whether man should be created: the stern attributes such as Prudence, Truth, and Justice advise against it, until Mercy pleads for the idea and converts the others to her side—to which Robinson added a little picture of the attributes kissing and making up after their argument, much as in terms of his text.[61] And that was the sermon. It was grossly sentimental. It showed no compunction about using woodenly borrowed illustrations. It also showed not even passing sensitivity to the intellectual difficulties in interpreting Old Testament prophecy, difficulties that had long existed in some form and had in that generation been made unavoidable by the popularization of historical criticism of the Bible.

In that sermon on the "full, true gospel," Robinson showed himself able to consume time with the inflated capsule story, time that might honestly have gone to a plain dealing with the issues he raised. In another, on the text "The rich and poor meet together," he was trapped by his biases into making technical rhetorical error. The whole piece was a smooth deploring of class conflict. In most of it, Robinson used an easy topical vocabulary, and avoided any obvious imbalance in his remarks about the two classes.

[61] Charles S. Robinson, *The Memorial Pulpit.—Vol.* 1 (New York, 1873), 29-40.

One of his comments on the text itself was typical of his thought:

> The word *meet* does not mean encounter or fight. Nor does the text teach that rich and poor are all mixed up with each other; nor that they ought to associate more closely, or cherish more familiar intercourse. Nor does the verse assert that they are alike in gifts, or culture, or manners; nor that they meet in capacities, or in conditions, or even in responsibilities.
>
> What the text does teach is this: that outside of all these particulars just enumerated, the rich and poor have one common ground on which they are equal. They share alike in the need of God's mercy, and in the supply of it. That is to say, the point of contact is religious, and is found in the gospel of Jesus Christ. I choose to put the entire truth into one distinct proposition; namely, this;—
>
> There is no property-qualification whatsoever for citizenship in the kingdom of God.

But having committed himself to the idea of equality before God, he then said in his peroration: "Oh, we are just alike before God! The rich are not worse, the poor are not better. The poor are not perfect; the rich can improve."[62] Perhaps, as some writers on the theory of preaching said, defects in moral or spiritual seriousness could lead to defects in rhetoric.

Not all the tentative, somewhat new preaching on social issues fell into the same kind of trap as Robinson's. Some used literary tastefulness as one way to diffuse the impact of conscience. Some even combined theological learning with real earnestness.

Henry Codman Potter, who came from Boston to be rector of Grace Church in 1868, brought with him a politic but vigorous conscience. He preached in favor of both Sabbath-observance and the liturgy of the Prayer Book. He gave

[62] *Ibid.*, 15-26, quotations at 23, 26.

consistent, public support to the movement for abolishing from Episcopalian churches the system of rented pews, but he assumed the role of cautionary leader in that movement, advising against any steps that would violate either sensibilities or the existing property rights in pews. He sometimes used sharp language to express smug savagery, as in calling it "impertinence" for immigrants to seek a freer observance of the Sabbath.[63] But he also made effective use of sharpness in supporting the cause of free pews, as on one occasion when he too used the text, "The rich and poor meet together." Having made the obvious ethical application of this text at the outset, he made the bulk of his sermon a political tract built around a Tocquevillean comparison of English and American society, the one hierarchical but fostering a degree of personal egalitarianism, the other fostering anxiety over status and thus an increasing willingness to purchase the elements of status. While it may have been cheap irony for him to point out how New England Puritans and, more recently, New York Methodists had been active in backing the pew system, it was also the clever political rhetoric to use toward an Episcopalian audience.[64]

The limits of Potter's preaching showed rather in a number of social-problem sermons that he delivered over the course of the 1870s. He usually showed himself well informed, whether about the problems of institutionalism in the raising of children, about the house-opening and house-closing habits of his leisured parishioners, or about Horace Bushnell's theological analogy between play and regeneration. But he preached each sermon in a pattern of relaxation from vigor into propriety. After beginning a sermon on "amusements" with Bushnell's modern idea that the ultimate regenerated state is one of playfulness, he then

[63] Henry C. Potter, *The Liturgy, and Its Uses* (St. Johnsland [N.Y.], 1871). Potter, *A Plea for the American Sunday* (New York, 1878). George Hodges, *Henry Codman Potter* (New York, 1915), 68.

[64] Potter, *A Sermon Preached at the Consecration of Grace Chapel, New York, . . . September 25th, 1876* (New York, [ca. 1876]).

simply turned this point on itself by declaring that the New York of the 1870s was in no need of further emancipation from a repressive attitude toward play. He explained, in neat but not overcomplicated divisions, what was the proper nature of play. First, it had its sequential place in a well-ordered life: it came *after* work. Second, it had three traits: it was genuine (thus balls were questionable); it was innocent (thus immodest plays should be boycotted by heroic families); and it was moderate (thus the current sports revival was in danger of excess, spilling over into gambling and professionalism). Concluding, he presented as a criterion the proper goal for amusements: "a character sanctified by the life and sunshine of the Holy Spirit."[65] The difficulty was not just that Potter's specific moral recommendations rose little above the level of the etiquette manual. It was that, after confronting in Bushnell's mysticism a serious *religious* idea, he fled from it into the world of the clergyman who was never sure where he belonged when the ladies left the gentlemen to their after-dinner brandy.

Perhaps it was not surprising that when Potter preached on "our debtors" in 1873, soon after the panic of that year, he said less about economic problems than he did about the evils of emotional aggressiveness and of the "grasping Israelite." Or that when preaching on "the impotence of money," he described Simon of Samaria as "a child of Israel, of that race which has always been a buyer when it could not be a seller, and which in one generation bought a brother's birthright for a mess of pottage, even as in another it sold its Saviour for thirty pieces of silver."[66]

It is tempting to label Potter's approach as typical simply of his denomination. But his approach differed from that of the Presbyterian Robinson only in his Tillotsonian smoothness and his relative indifference to textual exposition.

[65] Potter, *Sermons of the City* (New York, 1881), esp. 142-161, 267-279, 280-293.

[66] *Ibid.*, 176-189, 237.

Within his own communion, E. A. Washburn of Calvary Church, New York, accepted the same challenges that Potter funked. Washburn used a technique both more evangelical and more traditional than Potter's. When he wanted to preach on social problems, he gave textual sermons on the Ten Commandments. Where a Henry Ward Beecher could display a picturesque knowledge of the detail of Hebrew life, Washburn showed that he had read thoughtfully in the historical criticism that his own century had produced, and he adopted a mildly relativistic tone toward the meaning of the Commandments. He was, of course, not exempt from the biases of his own society: he spoke condescendingly about Judaism as the older, more primitive way, and he did oppose the excesses of the "continental" Sabbath. But he was not ethnocentric in a physically racial sense, and he took care to present the Sanhedrin and Caiaphas as types of nineteenth-century American institutions and leaders. The central, developmental section of one typical sermon was an iteration of specific violations against the Ten Commandments being committed in New York, from which he omitted only the kind of personal detail that would identify or insinuate. Where Potter took the Panic of 1873 as an occasion for preaching on emotional aggressiveness, Washburn illustrated the commandment against theft by giving a catalogue of specific business frauds, including the collapse of a poorly built factory structure in which many workmen were victims. This was not profound radicalism, only an early version of middle-class muckraking; but it was at least plain-spoken. Washburn reinforced the main rhetorical lesson himself in his sermon on false witness, when he attacked resort to cant and unfair argument in preaching: they were more dangerous to the gospel than was any modern criticism.[67]

What made Washburn superior to Robinson and Potter was, however, neither his modern learning nor his social

[67] E. A. Washburn, *The Social Law of God*, 2nd edn. (New York, 1875), esp. 164, 176-179.

bluntness. It was a quality of consistency and follow-through in thought that can be examined more easily in someone of less obvious intellectual equipment. In one comparable sermon, Emory J. Haynes, minister of the Hanson Place Methodist Episcopal Church in Brooklyn, used no set pieces, no allusions to fashionable theory, virtually no material except obvious scripture and daily observation, yet achieved an intellectual structure somewhat more honest than did either Robinson or Potter. By using two familiar but divergent texts he faced a difficulty similar to that implied in Potter's name-dropping allusion to the Bushnell play theory. The formal text for the sermon came from the Beatitudes: "Blessed are the pure in heart." And he began with a wordy, flowery exposition of this text that pointed up the differences between worldly and spiritual notions of blessedness. But then he introduced his contrasting text: "Every creature of God is good." Although he did not take from this the extreme libertarian idea that would have undercut any ordinary notion of what is "pure," he did take from it the idea of natural purity or grace: that there is a reasonable use for every object or process, and that there exist people who do react spontaneously to "every creature" around them—spontaneously but without forced or ulterior motive. The blessing of this natural purity, which some men enjoy without any particular theological consciousness, he contrasted to the inward trials of men who are spiritually insecure and must be on guard against weaknesses. He piled up illustrations of this insecurity, culminating in a litany-like iteration of ways that the impure may avoid overt sin yet be plagued by loss of self-respect:

> There are those who, in thought, creep to the utmost verge of commercial honesty, and sketch upon paper the very figures of dishonest gains; then look, and think, and look again with hesitancy. Aye, tear it up, sir, and say, "I'll be true." *But you have lost your self-respect; you are not the soul of honour.* There are those who buy ques-

> tionable illustrated papers at the ferry news-stand, and turn them over furtively, and blushingly say, *when they have seen the last picture*, "Why, I must not carry that home! Why did I buy it?" Aye, throw it away, sir, throw it away; but *you have lost your self-respect*; *you are not the soul of chastity*.

And so on, through other sins. He concluded with a description of the simple, pure, unenvious man, and a brief last paragraph exhorting his hearers to prayer that would win the desired purity.[68] In a way, this was all unfair sentimentality, exploiting the self-pitying notion that the self is beset by complexities that never afflict others. But he did face up to the fact that one common turn of emotional consciousness presented a difficulty to Christian casuistry, and he presented it mainly *as a difficulty*, offering little relief except a formal gospel tag.

Men like Haynes were dealing with issues to which new psychological thought might become especially relevant. Sometimes, in other men, this emerging relevance showed in the fact that the very failures to achieve it had a bald, unfeeling tone. In the evangelical Episcopalian Stephen H. Tyng, Jr., who had many of the same virtues and defects as Henry Codman Potter or Charles S. Robinson, the tone of complacency showed when he tried to describe the "true believer," the man who is visibly a saint:

> . . . in one way they who are in Christ Jesus are esteemed of men as separate. There is a large class of men in this community who are counted out in every time of iniquity. When the tongue of man becomes vulgar, the believers in Christ, whose presence and influence are known by their testimony and their example, are instantly separated from the mass of ungodly. There are certain things that will never be said in the presence of a true Christian man. He who stands firmly in Christ, pronounced for Christ,

[68] Emory J. Haynes, "Blessed Are the Pure in Heart," *The American Pulpit of the Day* (London, 1875), 46-54.

> is marked off by the world as not of their company, and not to be entertained in their frivolity and sin.[69]

Now Tyng did preach on that one subject which was both traditional and an appropriate one for psychological elaboration—namely, the stages of conversion. In his own analysis he took the sense of estrangement from God as the first of these stages. A psychological approach would have sought to describe this estrangement in terms of feelings or mechanisms common in the human personality, feelings that might be recognizable to hearers of all kinds. Tyng, however:

> Now you will admit that this is not a common experience among men. You do not see many shadowed faces on the street; you do not know many lives darkened with doubt and fear; you do not read many records which are blackened with this awful pressure of alienation from God. A single look at men will refute any allegation that they are conscious of estrangement, of themselves and by themselves. . . . Under the ministry of the Gospel a man commences to see that this fact is asserted. He does not realize it, but he hears it preached. . . . Now, all conversions begin here; and no power but that which is divine can make a man realize that great truth.[70]

This is indeed more Calvinistic in tone than would be true of most Episcopalian preachers or even most evangelical preachers of any denomination in the late nineteenth century. It is also probably accurate enough in its perception of the superficially optimistic tone of American daily life. But it uses biblicism in a way that erects a barrier between preaching and psychological thought.

The quality that a Haynes achieved in a moderate way, and that a Tyng approached but failed to achieve, was

[69] Stephen H. Tyng, Jr., "Christian Salutation," *The American Pulpit of the Day* (London, 1875), 381.

[70] Tyng, "God's Glory in the Soul," *ibid.*, 404-405.

achieved elaborately and explicitly by the man who was the true prince of the pulpit in the New York area: William G. T. Shedd. Shedd's career and status illustrate, though, one of the difficulties in using the sermon form as a measure of general intellect in the late nineteenth century. Social specialization had already progressed so far that the best work in any field was apt to be oriented to some restricted audience. Shedd was specializing as early as the 1850s, when he was professor of sacred rhetoric at the Auburn Theological Seminary (Presbyterian) in upstate New York. From there he was called to the same post at Union Theological Seminary in New York. His leadership was official, and he expressed it in treatises for students.

As some of his sermons show, his leadership was also well deserved. Whether or not these sermons were delivered to student congregations, they were general in aim. Though they may have been prepared for a special audience, Shedd's sermons provided answers to a concern that cropped up in the preaching of many men who did serve regular congregations—for the psychological relevance and sophistication of the gospel. Much of this continued the old tradition of the preacher as public physician to souls. Some of it represented the mere spill into preaching of notions borrowed from the current arguments of mental philosophy, borrowed with little more thoughtfulness than Potter showed in taking up Bushnell's ideas about play and regeneration.[71]

Shedd prefaced the published version of his *Sermons to the Natural Man* with a statement that made explicit connection between the old cure of souls and the newer preoccupations:

[71] Tentative and somewhat commonplace examples of this psychologism can be found in: Charles F. Deems, *Dr. Deems' Sermons . . . from October 16th, 1870, to November 19th, 1871* (New York, 1873), 7-13, 29-31; and S. H. Platt, "Victory over the World," *Methodist*, XI (1870), 418.

> The purpose is psychological. I would if possible, anatomize the natural heart. It is in vain to offer the gospel unless the law has been applied with clearness and cogency. At the present day, certainly, there is far less danger of erring in the direction of religious severity, than in the direction of religious indulgence. . . . Conscience needs to become consciousness. . . .
>
> It is, therefore, specially incumbent upon the Christian ministry, to employ a searching and psychological style of preaching, and to apply the tests of ethics and virtue so powerfully to men who are trusting to ethics and virtue, as to bring them upon their knees. . . .
>
> These sermons run the hazard of being pronounced monotonous, because of the pertinacity with which the attempt is made to force self-reflection. But this criticism can easily be endured, provided the attempt succeeds. Religious truth becomes almighty the instant it can get *within* the soul; and it gets within the soul, the instant real thinking begins. . . . Men do not know themselves. The Delphic oracle was never less obeyed than now, in this vortex of mechanical arts and luxury. For this reason, it is desirable that the religious teacher dwell consecutively upon topics that are connected with that which is *within* man,—his settled motives of action, and all those spontaneous on-goings of his soul of which he takes no notice, unless he is persuaded or impelled to do so. Some of the old painters produced powerful effects by one solitary color. . . . sin, the one awful fact in the history of man, if caused to pervade discourse will always impart to it a hue which, though it be monochromatic, arrests and holds the eye like the lurid color of an approaching storm-cloud.[72]

And his sermons had the defects that he himself realized. They contained little illustration except some retelling of

[72] William G. T. Shedd, *Sermons to the Natural Man* (New York, 1871), iii, viii-x.

Bible narratives that pertained directly to his texts, or some brief rehearsing of details in Dante's Hell as prelude to urging the greater solemnity of the Bible Hell, or some description of mammalian cleverness as introduction to man's greater insight and thus to the further contrast between man's insight and God's. He also fell into some shortsightedness, as when he directed one of his sermons especially to youth and showed no awareness that there existed any kind except the sheltered middle-class young men in his congregation.[73] He also fell at times into mechanical arguments that gave lazy minds the chance to rest.

But even in those sermons in which he was most superficial, he adhered to his goal of an uncompromising psychologism. In preaching on the contrast in the fates of Dives and Lazarus (his text: "thou [Dives] in thy lifetime receivedst thy good things, and likewise Lazarus evil things: but now he is comforted, and thou art tormented") he gave a basic hellfire sermon, insisting that the evil who are enjoying life will get the punishment they deserve. His formal argument, aside from citations of scripture, amounted to little more than the idea that a man could not have his "chief pleasure" in both worlds: "Look at this as a *matter of fact.* Do not take it as a theory of the preacher. It is as plain and certain that you cannot lay up your treasure in heaven while you are laying it up upon earth, as it is that your material bodies cannot occupy two portions of space at one and the same time."[74] The bulk of his sermon, though, Shedd gave to stating the advantages that the worldling enjoys in the present life, advantages even psychological and moral. The worldly sinner enjoys his sin without any sense of "moral anxiety," but "the sins that are committed by a child of God are mourned over with a very deep sorrow. The

[73] On the sheltered quality in Shedd's work, note that R. H. Howard, "A Word about Extemporaneous Preaching," *Methodist*, Feb. 4, 1871, complains that Shedd failed to follow his own advice to preach one extemporaneous as well as one written sermon each Sunday.

[74] Shedd, *Sermons to the Natural Man*, 352.

longer he lives, the more odious does sin become to him, and the more keen and bitter is his lamentation over it. Now this, in itself, is an 'evil thing.' Man was not made for sorrow, and sorrow is not his natural condition. This wearisome struggle with indwelling corruption, these reproaches of an impartial conscience, this sense of imperfection and of constant failure of the service of God,—all this renders the believer's life on earth a season of trial, and tribulation."[75] This was stern and even morbid. He was in effect recommending a suicidal view: that the Christian accept a self-condemnation so intense that death would come as a release from anxiety.

Even in the course of a less graphic sermon, Shedd could see the intense relation between God and man in a way that would later turn up in some middling-serious popularizations of the analyst-patient relation. He was preaching on Isaiah: "Come now, and let us reason together, saith the Lord":

> In all our religious anxiety, we should *make a full and plain statement of everything to God. . . .* Even when the story is one of shame and remorse, we find it to be mental relief, patiently and without any reservation or palliation, to expose the whole not only to our own eye but to that of our Judge. For, to this very thing have we been invited. This is precisely the "reasoning together" which God proposes to us. God has not offered clemency to a sinful world, with the expectation or desire that there be on the part of those to whom it is offered, such a stinted and meagre confession, such a glozing over and diminution of sin, as to make that clemency appear a very small matter.[76]

Up to this point, the difference in tone between Shedd's intensity and Stephen H. Tyng's complacency is apparent, but the difference may not seem to reach explicit ideas. Tyng described the man on the street as not worrying about

[75] *Ibid.*, 344-345.

[76] *Ibid.*, 199.

sin, and Shedd seemed to say the same thing. But when Shedd dealt directly with the problem of self-knowledge, as he did in a pair of sermons, "God's Exhaustive Knowledge of Man," he achieved a position more complex than Tyng's. The two sermons were actually one long development of the text, "O Lord, thou hast searched me, and known me," from Psalm 139. He stated first that God knows all about a man that the man himself knows, including the painful self-accusing things. But, said Shedd, God knows also all that a man might but does not know about himself; and in the latter part of the development, Shedd used God's knowledge as an entry into the idea of unconscious thought. Man often failed in self-knowledge precisely because he did not subject actions to later recall, which could be a realistic and efficient way of forcing unpleasant material into awareness. "The re-exhibition of an action in memory, as in a mirror, is often accompanied with a distinct apprehension of its moral character that formed no part of the experience of the agent while absorbed in the hot and hasty original action itself." But God "knows that far larger part of our life which we have not yet subjected to the scrutiny of self-examination,—all those thoughts, feelings, desires, and motives, innumerable as they are, of which we took no heed at the time of their origin and existence, and which we suppose, perhaps, we shall hear no more of again." There was, of course, nothing particularly unusual in the idea that Hell consisted simply of terrible, self-accepted guilt, but Shedd was somewhat original when he read damnation as the total lifting of repression: "The Creator of the human mind has control over its powers of self-inspection, and of memory; and when the proper time comes He will compel these endowments to perform their legitimate functions, and do their appointed work. The torturing self-survey will begin, never more to end. The awful recollection will commence, endlessly to go on."[77] The total lifting of repression is of course a more hellish image to the twentieth-century imag-

[77] *Ibid.*, 63, 67, 70.

ination, trained as it has been to a full analytic conception of just what is under the lid. But one need not read full analytic notions back into the attitudes of 1870 in order to wonder what was happening to the thinking of a period that could find its popular preacher in the self-conscious, self-exploiting Beecher, and its best preaching intellect in the tentatively analytic Shedd.

There is, to be sure, an analogy between the Beecher-Shedd (or Moody-Shedd) pair and the Tennent-Dickinson (or Tennent-Edwards) pair. In each period the popular preacher was the man who could construct a rapid fire of images or illustrations that ticked off cues to material that was traditional or otherwise readily available to popular hearing. There needed to be little logical relation among the items within one sermon except a certain sharing of theme and a mounting or centripetal pattern of intensities. In each period, the larger intellect was the man who could engage his hearers in the process of facing the vulnerabilities, sudden contradictions, and painful implications within the same body of material that was readily available to popular response. Between the two periods there may have been no great change in the intellectual level achieved by intellectual preaching. Certainly the pathetically low taste of some of the illustrations used by preachers of 1870 should make one hesitate before claiming much for intellectual progress. The real shift that had plainly taken place was one in the larger structure of discourse from which all preaching took vocabulary and assumptions. The men of 1750 knew a world of theological propositions in terms of which they could symbolize and face the pains and complexities of human action. The men of 1870 could no longer use those propositions, except for routine statement and intellectual filler. They had to face human consciousness directly; or else they could shift the terms of discourse so that they faced rather the choice between social complacency and social criticism; or else—in the popular case—they could confront human consciousness in the symbol of the personality or celebrity. This relation between confrontation and the celebrity had been only partly foreshadowed during the earlier period, in the controversy over a "converted ministry."

Now all this may suggest that the change in intellectual climate, from an age of belief to an age of doubt, so far overshadowed any changes in popular learning that the shift in preaching styles can indicate little about what was happening to the American mentality. But neither Beecher nor Shedd accepted this view. Both were convinced that changes in popular knowledge and in popular mental sharpness had much to do with the way they preached and the way they advised others to preach.

Beecher, as always, saw the change in terms of his own experience. He recalled what preaching had been like fifty years before, in the early part of the century. For him, that preaching had meant especially the work of his own strong, intense, evangelical, orthodox father, or of men who worked in the same circles with the father and were suited to exchange pulpits with him. The son's resort to self as a sermon topic may have been a determined effort to protect his adult ego from the overwhelming example of Lyman Beecher. Whatever his motives, though, he did manage to take a patronizing tone toward the older techniques for building intellectual security and community: "The old-fashioned way of sermonizing affords us some amusement; but they did a great deal of good with those queer, regulation old methods of first, second, third, and then the subdivisions. I remember that, in my boyhood, the moment a man announced his text, I could tell pretty nearly as well as he could how he would lay it out, because I knew he must proceed according to certain forms."

The earlier preacher, by not concealing his intentions and his analysis, lost any advantage of suspense that he might have exercised over his listeners. And this advantage or power was what Henry Ward Beecher wanted. There were, he said, two different functions that a sermon might perform. It might, first, serve for the people's "broadening in knowledge"; but this kind of sermon had become less important, "because the people have so many other sources of knowledge, and so many other training influences are going on in the community." The remaining kind of sermon, on which the preacher should concentrate, sought "direct power on men's minds and hearts."[78] How should he achieve this? The minister, Beecher told the Yale students, should above all be a man and a soul, working to build the manhood and the souls of his hearers. Although Beecher was adopting the traditional view of rhetoric as persuasion, he paid little attention to the technical details of rhetoric, much more to the minister as personality and to the preaching strategy that he labeled "Personalism." The preacher must adapt himself to the modern advances that were sure to come in psychology. But what was he to do at the moment, when modern psychology had not yet arrived? And what was he to do if his congregation proved recalcitrant to his exertions of power? Beecher had answers. As a provisional system for classifying and understanding human nature, he recommended phrenology—even if one had to admit that phrenology was technically incorrect. And the preacher, he explained, should not challenge directly the feelings of any congregation; rather, he should practice "adaptation of one's self to others." The young minister, especially, should not worry too much about whether everything he said was right. "People . . . don't believe half that you say. The part that is nutritious they keep, and the rest they let alone."[79] If the minister wanted to say things that the people did not want to hear, he could use illustrations to "bridge difficult places." He recalled his own early efforts, preaching to a congregation just north of the Ohio

[78] Henry Ward Beecher, *Yale Lectures on Preaching* [1st series] (New York, 1872), 18.

[79] *Ibid.*, 49, 52, 87-90, 93-95, 146. On adaptation, compare George G. Lyon, "Ministerial Etiquette," *Christian Advocate*, XLV (1869), 114, 122, 130, 138, 146, 177.

River. He wanted to talk about slavery, but the people had Southern sympathies (and besides, Lyman Beecher, in the offing, did not approve of radical agitation). He therefore included, in sermons on other topics, illustrations in which were embedded concrete, somewhat disapproving references to slavery in places like Algeria. The congregation kept reacting with hostile expectation that he was about to launch into an all-out attack on their sensibilities, but he did not, and they gradually accepted his freedom to allude. To the Yale students, Beecher explained: "You may say that that was not the most honorable way, and that it was a weakness. It may have been so; but I conquered them by that very weakness."[80] But did he conquer in the cause of the slave or in that of Henry Ward Beecher?

Now in many things Shedd agreed with Beecher. He too talked more of personality than of piety; he too insisted that the object and test of a good sermon was "influence" over the congregation. Citing Buffon's maxim, "Le style, c'est l'homme," he said: "In the origination of the oration, there must be not only the co-agency of all the cognitive, imaginative and pathetic powers, but the presence and the presidency in and through them all of that deepest and most central power in which, as the seat of personality and of character, they are all rooted and grounded. The oration, in this view, is not so much a product of the man, as it is the man himself,—an *embodiment* of all his faculties and his processes."[81] But when he looked at the popular intellectual changes that had affected preaching, Shedd saw them in a way different from Beecher's. Beecher professed to believe that the growth in knowledge released the minister from some of his old tasks, released him into the career of a personality exercising power. Shedd, though, was not even sure that all the new knowledge was a good thing. It was "a rank growth of belles-lettres." It was "a crop of mushrooms." It

[80] Beecher, *Yale Lectures*, 1st series, 165-168.

[81] William G. T. Shedd, *Homiletics and Pastoral Theology*, 8th edn. (New York, 1873), 47, 53.

had issued into the "slender attempts of the modern naturalism" and "the light flutter of the current sentimentalism." But he gave the modern mind credit for knowledge, for quickness, even for an approach to the older Puritan ideal of intellectual plainness; and he recognized that all this imposed "higher demands."

> It is more difficult to make a permanent popular impression now, than it was fifty years ago. The public mind is more distracted, than it was then. It is addressed more frequently, and by a greater variety, both of subjects and of speakers. It is more critical and fastidious than formerly. It is possessed, we will not say of a more thorough and useful knowledge on a few subjects, but of a more extensive and various information on many subjects. . . .
>
> There is more call, consequently, in the present age, for a sermonizing that shall cover the whole field of human nature and human acquirements[,] that shall contain a greater variety and exhibit a greater compass, and that shall be adapted to more grades and capacities.

The popular intellect required power, but a kind of power different from what Beecher imagined:

> The greatest difference between the men of the present day and their forefathers consists in the greater distinctness, and rapidity, of their mental processes. They are not more serious and thoughtful than their ancestors, but they are more vivid, animated, and direct in their thinking than they were. They are more impatient of prolixity, of a loose method of arrangement, and of a heavy dragging movement in the exhibition of truth. Audiences a century ago would patiently listen to discourses of two hours in length, and would follow the sermonizer through a series of divisions and subdivisions that would be intolerable to a modern hearer. The human intellect seems to have shared in that increased rapidity of motion which has been imparted to matter, by the modern improve-

> ments in machinery. . . . Mental operations are on straight lines, like the railroad and the telegraph, and are far more rapid than they once were. The public audience now craves a short method, a distinct sharp statement, and a rapid and accelerating movement, upon the part of its teachers.
>
> Now the preacher can meet this demand successfully, only by and through a strong methodizing power. He cannot meet it by mere brevity. . . . The task, therefore, which the sacred orator of the present day has to perform, is to compress the greatest amount of matter into the smallest possible form, and in the most energetic possible manner. . . .
>
> But is such an ability as this a thing of spontaneous origin? Will it be likely to be possessed by an indolent, or an uneducated mind?[82]

Of course not. Beecher, too, would have insisted that the preacher had to prepare his intellect if he were to achieve the best results. But the difference in emphasis made all the difference. To Shedd, intellect was not just one qualification among others. Popular intellect required preaching power, and power required preaching intellect. The preacher should encourage the directness within popular taste, and discourage the superfluities and "light flutter," by determining to be plain himself. This, in turn, would lead him toward the cognitive equivalent of the self-examination that Shedd preached; the preacher would "not be able to read authors who do not understand themselves." He would "be impatient with a public speaker who does not distinctly know what he is saying." There was an element of excessive strain in all this. Shedd, in his own way, was one of the mental athletes of his period who recommended "intensity and positiveness" as a way to preserve conviction in the middle of doubt and controversy. But in him the intensity became an integral quality, and most so when he described the ideal

[82] *Ibid.*, 20, 21, 53, 55-57.

modern preacher: "He should be a plain, direct, terse, and bold orator. He must employ the rhetoric which Jael used upon Sisera, putting his nail to the *head* of his auditor, and driving it sheer and clear through his brain."[83] Whatever were Shedd's vices, "adaptation" was not one of them. Neither was a superficial or sentimental pity. The soul, in his view, pulled in two directions. One impulse, "earth-born," was a "constitutional love of ease." The other, which Shedd identified somehow with the "rational judgment," consisted of those "powers and motives which, when in action, will carry the human soul and body through scenes, and experiences, at which human nature, in its quiet moods and its indolent states, stands aghast." Within worldly culture, dramatic tragedy gave some support to these powers. It was the preacher's task, therefore, to make himself their full ally in pushing the soul to the "painful process of self-scrutiny and self-knowledge." Only at the brink of enforcing "everlasting despair" should the preacher show special consideration to the listening soul,[84] and even this consid-sideration was of a kind quite opposite to Beecher's "adaptation."

> It is not upright in a preacher, either from fear of man, or from a false kindness, to shrink, in the peroration, from a plain and solemn application of the subject of his discourse. He is in duty bound, to make the truth which he has established bear with all its weight, and penetrate with all its sharpness. [But:] The *spirit* with which he should do this, should be Christian. Let him not dart the lightnings, or roll the thunders, except with the utmost fear of God, the utmost love of the human soul, and the utmost solicitude lest he be actuated by human pride, or human impatience. . . . "Put the lust of *self*," says Coleridge, "in the forked lightning, and it becomes a spirit of

[83] *Ibid.*, 251, 252. Shedd, "The Fundamental Properties of Style," *American Presbyterian and Theological Review*, n.s. II (1864), 567.

[84] Shedd, *Homiletics and Pastoral Theology*, 279-280, 293.

> Moloch." Self, in all its phases, must be banished from a solemn application of an awful doctrine.[85]

If there had been many preachers who both exposed human corruption and indulged their own pride in the process, Shedd's warning against Molochism might have been to the point. Actually, he was probably one of the few who had the ability to work such a combination, and his warning may have been partly his own defense against pride and against justifiable intellectual arrogance. But, as social observation, his accusation joined the right elements in the wrong combination.

Preachers who said anything about the needs that shaped their work had been agreed since as early as the 1830s that the cultural impact on preaching was closely related to the new organizational needs that ministers had to serve. This sense of contrast between an older style and the new pressures was of course stated most sharply by men of conservative temperament, such as those who resisted the methods and influence of the revivalist Charles G. Finney, or those who fought the growing importance of bureaucracy and voluntary organizations within the churches. If they decried enthusiasm in general, they denounced especially enthusiasm for preaching on special occasions, or for preaching that served the ends of special organizations. They felt that such promotional work was of a piece with the growth of a popular periodical press. The age was given to light general reading; people were easily impressed by the apparently tasteful, the showy, the superficial. Ministers who consented to promote organizational interests, whether of church bureaucracies or of individual large city churches, were pushed to satisfy the tastes of a mass to whom the qualities of a great sermon were elegance, fine sound, oddness, and smartness. All this stood in supposed contrast to the situation of the man who preached to meet pastoral needs, who could give much time to thoughtful study and

[85] *Ibid.*, 207-208.

select reading, and who could build solid, instructive sermons that culminated in plain applications to the consciences of his particular congregation.

By about 1850, though, controversy over voluntarism had receded far enough that the shift in preaching needs could be stated in a way acceptable to most men of whatever denomination or whatever degree of evangelical temperament.[86] This was the device that both Beecher and Shedd used, of arguing that cultural change had shifted the old balance between the functions of instruction and persuasion. Within this point of view, it was quite easy for a man to argue that the new kind of preaching was a good thing, suited especially to building churches in new areas. Daniel Kidder, professor of homiletics at the Garrett Biblical Institute and the principal Methodist spokesman on homiletics in this period, insisted that special-occasion preaching, mainly to raise funds, was a necessity to which ministers should adjust themselves.[87] But the new kind of preaching, in men who accepted it without difficulty, was to be especially emotional, personal, earnest, individualistic. One favorable description of the new kind of preacher, printed in the staid *Princeton Review*, made him sound like

[86] Ashbel Green, "An Address Delivered to the Students of the Theological Seminary, at Princeton, at the Close of the Semi-Annual Examination, May 16, 1831," *Biblical Repository and Theological Review*, n.s. III (1831), 350-360. William R. Weeks, *A Letter on Protracted Meetings* (Utica, 1832). Eleazar Lord, "Means of Promoting Christianity," *Literary and Theological Review*, II (1835), 1-38. Leonard Withington, review of Jedediah Burchard, *Sermons* (Burlington, 1836), in *ibid.*, III (1836), 228-236. Edward W. Hooker, "The Spirit of the Ministry," *ibid.*, IV (1837), 595-621. Richard W. Dickinson, "Modern Popular Preaching," *ibid.*, V (1838), 235. John H. Avery, "Peculiar Fastidiousness of the Age in Respect to Ministers," *ibid.*, V (1838), 112-116. [Jabez Brown, comp.,] *The Pulpit Cyclopedia, and Christian Minister's Companion* (New York, 1847), 550. "The Manner of Preaching," *Biblical Repository and Princeton Review*, XXXV (1863), 177-206. J. Wheaton Smith, "The Dramatic Element of Pulpit Oratory," *Baptist Quarterly*, IX (1879), 96-97.

[87] Daniel P. Kidder, *A Treatise on Homiletics* (New York, 1864). 98-100.

a pious version of Renaissance man.[88] Writers in the more intellectual of the Methodist magazines urged the cause of naturalness and individual style in the preacher.[89] The preacher had to be earnest and sincere if he were to be effective; and naturalness was to come from easy expression of the "inner mood" of the preacher. Earnestness was also to be cultivated through activity in the pastoral side of the preacher's work, and by 1870 men were describing the pastoral function as one of emotionality and persuasion, in specific contrast to the thoughtfulness of the teaching function. In this point of view it became important for the preacher to prepare his self as an instrument of his work.[90]

Writers on both sides of the issue urged the importance of "manliness" in preaching, and the same commentator who advised that preaching, to be persuasive, should attend to the needs of listeners and not challenge their sensibilities, could also urge, "Manliness implies straight-forward simplicity, appreciation of the truths presented, and superiority to theatrical expedients."[91] On the other side, man-

[88] [Archibald Alexander,] review of *The Free Church Pulpit* (New York, 1848), in *Biblical Repository and Princeton Review*, XXI (1849), 94-95. [J. V. Campbell,] "The Church and the World," *Church Review*, IX (1856), 244-251. William Adams, "Completeness of Ministerial Character," *American Presbyterian Review*, n.s. VI (1868), 325-338.

[89] Caleb E. Wright, "Lesson from the Bar to the Pulpit," *Methodist Quarterly Review*, XLVII (1865), 400-412. Samuel Dunn, "Our Ministry," *ibid.*, XLIX (1867), 596-597. Thomas Wentworth Higginson's comparison of preaching problems to school-reading problems, quoted in "Unnatural Preaching," *Methodist*, IX (1868), 310. "Extempore Preaching," *Christian Advocate*, XLV (1870), 364. But compare the skepticism about defining "natural" in "The Natural Style of Public Speaking," *Methodist*, XV, Sept. 19, 1874, p. 8.

[90] "Sermon-Making," *Methodist*, XV, Aug. 29, 1874, p. 1. M. R. Vincent, "The Pulpit a Teacher," *ibid.*, IX (1868), 89. J. T. Crane, "The Early Methodist Ministry," *Christian Advocate*, XLIV (1869), 273. "Ministerial Success," *Methodist*, XIII (1872), 326.

[91] John Hall, *God's Word Through Preaching*, Yale Lectures on Preaching, 4th series (New York, 1875), 169. Compare "The Modern Pulpit," *American Quarterly Church Review*, XXIII (1871), 13; "A

liness became identified with intellectual independence, which was described as intellectual strength in the service of moral ends. Men ranging from E. L. Godkin among secular commentators, to a group in the Methodist press who worried the issue of plagiarism in sermon-making, pointed to fraud, time-serving, and insincerity as the evils threatening the quality of modern preaching.[92]

It was just here that those for adaptation and those for criticism were in agreement on a standard of excellence to be applied to preaching: on the importance of intellectual honesty understood in a sentimental or psychologistic sense as "sincerity." And it was here that the critics had the better argument, even in terms to which the adapters were committed.[93] The typical or popular American preacher was not —as he himself would have put it—in manly earnest. This does not mean that there was only one way in which he could be sincere, only one "line" by following which he

---

Cheerful Religion," quoted from *United Presbyterian* in *Christian Advocate*, XLIV (1869), 129; "The Physical Basis of Oratory," *Methodist*, XI (1870), 81; Hugh Miller Thompson, "*Copy*." *Essays from an Editor's Drawer, on Religion, Literature, and Life* (Hartford, 1872), 11-20, 72-77; Herrick Johnson, "Enthusiasm in Sacred Oratory," *Presbyterian Quarterly and Princeton Review*, n.s. IV (1875), 111. But compare also "Muscle versus Vitality," in *Methodist*, XIII (1872), 310.

[92] E. L. Godkin, "The Education of Ministers," *Nation*, XII (1871), 272-273. W. C. Wilkinson, "Bondage of the Pulpit," *Scribner's Monthly*, I (1870-71), 69-78, 437-448. "Patchwork Sermons and Original Sermons," *Methodist*, XIII (1872), 17. "Ministerial Insincerity," reprinted from *Gospel Messenger* in *ibid.*, XIV (1873), 261. "Pulpit Plagiarism," *ibid.*, XV, Jan. 24, 1874, pp. 1, 8. E. Wentworth, "Plagiarism," *ibid.*, Feb. 7, 1874, pp. 2, 8. E. E. Hale, "Insincerity in the Pulpit," *North American*, CXXXI (1880), 268-276. Richard S. Storrs, *Manliness in the Scholar* (New York, 1883).

[93] Note the lameness of the argument against Wilkinson, in Samuel W. Duffield, "The Freedom of the Pulpit," II (1871), 184-189. And compare the tension in Thomas Nichols, "Preaching to the Conscience," *Presbyterian Quarterly and Presbyterian Review*, n.s. IV (1875), 25, 26, which *condemns* preaching to the "manly instincts, the generous side of human nature," but at the same time condemns the preaching of "an emasculated gospel."

could prove his intellectual vigor. There were two general kinds of problems, one or the other of which a preacher usually posed for himself whenever he opened his mouth. One was the confrontation of social reality, in the form of the challenge posed to Christian ethics by industrial and urban life. The other was the confrontation of psychological reality, defined either in the language of traditional doctrine or in some emerging scientific language. Of the two, the psychological was that to which preachers were more strongly directed, both by evangelical tradition and by the kind of intellectual changes that were taking place in their audiences. Most preachers accepted the psychological emphasis, but only to the extent of accepting their own selves as the embodied instrument of congregational need. In treating self as a definite instrument to be used, rather than as something that had an interior to be questioned and examined, they acted consistently with the kinds of qualities they did often achieve—objectivity, definiteness, and distinctness. This was what one Methodist editor sought when he advised preachers to use simple, objective, illustrative language in talking to children, then added, "Preaching to children will be found to be one of the greatest helps to the formation of a simple and direct style of addressing adults."[94] But it was also what Shedd advised when he condemned speakers who did not know exactly what they intended to say.

Objectivity and distinctness were closely related to another, though different, quality: simplicity. One Episcopalian commentator of 1850, complaining that too many modern preachers still tried to follow the old sermon form, insisted, "The only *rule*, therefore, that is needed in order to give an air of earnestness to our discourse, is *to be* in earnest." But he took "comfort in the fact, that the operation of constructing a religious discourse, by which we mean the

[94] "Preaching to Children," *Methodist*, IX (1868), 300. Compare "The Pulpit and the Little Ones," *ibid.*, IX (1868), 292.

disposition of the beams and rafters of the edifice, is not so complicated as formerly."[95]

D. A Case in the Analytic: Bridge-Building

The analogy between the design of sermons and the design of roof trusses seemed reasonable to the churchly commentator of that generation. He may not have realized that the kind of partly practical, partly analytical thinking that went into structural design was also involved in the complex of attitudes and abilities that had to be enlisted in any process of intellectual growth on the part of the whole society. And this kind of quantitative, analytical thinking went through some of—but not all—the same transformations as did the verbal thought that was involved in popular preaching.

As of the middle of the eighteenth century, structural design in America had undergone a far more obvious regression and simplification than had the verbal culture that was embodied in preaching. "Practical" though Americans supposedly were, they had in some parts of life dropped the practical methods that Europeans had learned. This was another case of the effect of the new environment on the old culture. Even more, it was an illustration of the way the new environment exercised a selective effect on old culture, preserving some elements in a complex and sophisticated form even while letting others deteriorate. And this was not just a matter of the distinction between verbal and material culture. Even within the broad area of construction, the environment encouraged some activities and discouraged others. Americans lived along a narrow band of coastal settlement. Even most of the interior settlements could be reached by the wide rivers and estuaries that penetrated the continent at frequent intervals. Coastal shipping was the preferred means of transportation, and the American shipbuilding industry grew strong, then expanded in tech-

[95] Review of W. Greslay, *Ecclesiastes Anglicanus*, in *Church Review*, III (1850) 95, 106.

nique and style as it moved into the ocean trades. But because Americans had relatively little need for roads to connect one settlement with another, they did little to make overland travel simple and efficient. For river crossings they were willing to rely often on fords and ferries, even though these imposed detours or delays. In this situation, the typical bridge took one of two forms. It might be a very short bridge over difficult stream, in which case it could be a simple grouping of logs, perhaps braced by struts at either end. Or it might be a very long bridge over the marshland and the spreading waters near a river mouth where the failure to build a bridge might impose an unusually long detour upstream. These longer bridges were typically not built in deep waters, and the techniques used for constructing them were simple. A bridge might consist of platforms resting on pontoons, or it might consist of simple stringers, perhaps supported by struts, running between piers sunk at short intervals over a shallow bottom. The actual spans between pontoons or piers were limited in length by what a single horizontal beam would support. Only the simplest trussing and bracing were used to extend the practical length of spans.[96]

Most of the early American bridges were so unpretentious that no one bothered to record exact details of their form and shape. Travelers' complaints have left some information on the floating bridges that were put across the Schuylkill River during the Revolutionary War and then retained or rebuilt in later years.[97] Mrs. Knight, reporting

[96] Llewellyn Nathaniel Edwards, *A Record of History and Evolution of Early American Bridges* (Orono, Maine, 1959), 19-34. Edwards' book is especially useful for its reprinting of patent descriptions and other sources on bridge-building.

[97] Ellis Paxson Oberholtzer, *Philadelphia* (Philadelphia, n.d.), I, 337*n*-338*n*. Henman LeRoy Collins and Wilfred Jordan, *Philadelphia* (New York, 1941), III, 204, 273-275. John F. Watson, *Annals of Philadelphia*, enlarged by Willis P. Hazard (Philadelphia, 1879), III, 491. J. Bennett Nolan, *The Schuylkill* (New Brunswick, N.J., 1951), 250-251: David B. Tyler, *The Bay & River, Delaware* (Cambridge, Md., 1955), 57.

her tour along the coastal roads early in the eighteenth century, said that one of the larger bridges in the road northeast of New York was dangerous and high—by which she apparently meant that it was constructed in a spindly, insecure way, and seemed unusually high to the swaying traveler.[98] But the two bridges most important to the life of the New York area left nearly the best possible record: they survived into the period of nostalgic print-making and even photography. These were the King's Bridge and the Free Bridge, both connecting Manhattan Island with the mainland to the north. The King's Bridge was first built in 1693, then reconstructed in a new location in 1713. The Free Bridge (also called the Farmer's Bridge or Dyckman Bridge) was built in 1758 to undercut the toll at the older crossing. The two were similar: in general, at each site long causeways were built up over the low ground and the shallow water, then one crude stone pier was sunk in the water, then two short platforms, each about thirty feet long, were used to span the openings on either side of the pier. Height above water level was hardly more than ten feet; since the Harlem River would not be dredged through to the Hudson at Spuyten Duyvil until the 1890s, there was no problem with large boats wanting through.[99]

[98] As quoted in Charles W. Baird, *Chronicle of a Border Town: History of Rye* (New York, 1871), 142.

[99] John Thomas Scharf & al., *History of Westchester County, New York* (Philadelphia, 1886), I, 748-749. Ernest Freeland Griffin, ed., *Westchester County and Its People* (New York, 1946), I, 53. Arthur Everett Peterson and George William Edwards, *New York as an Eighteenth Century Municipality* (New York, 1917), 359-361. Isaac Newton Phelps Stokes, *Iconography of Manhattan Island* (New York, 1915-1928), chronological entries under 5 Jan. 1693, 1 July 1713, and 28 Dec. 1758. New York City Common Council, *Manual*, plates at 1857 f.p. 376, 1861 f.p. 508. Charles W. Baird, *Chronicle of a Border Town: History of Rye* (New York, 1871), 248. Christopher Colles, *A Survey of the Roads of the United States of America, 1789*, ed. W. W. Ristow (Cambridge, Mass. 1961), 2-56 *passim.* Randall Comfort and others, *History of Bronx Borough, City of New York* (New York, 1906), 17, 18, 19. Reginald Pelham Bolton, *Washington Heights,*

The rudimentary quality of standard bridge design was only accentuated by the daring innovations that a few American builders proposed in the latter part of the eighteenth century. By that time, overland transportation was becoming more important, since population was increasing in all areas, settlement was penetrating farther into the interior, and a period of wars and political troubles had made Americans think more of land travel as a safe and even loyal way of moving about. It became desirable to bridge some of the large rivers on which cities were located, or over which would pass major highways. This could not be accomplished simply by extending existing techniques, and builders drew ideas from outside American experience. Sometimes their proposals remained fanciful, as with Thomas Pope's "flying lever" bridge to span the Hudson. Other proposals were turned into actual bridges, as with several suspension bridges built by James Finley in the years after 1801. These bold innovations did not always have a happy outcome. Some of the suspension bridges fell under loads, and fire took others. The net effect of these turn-of-the-century innovations was to make plain the American reliance on rudimentary forms, and to impose a need that any further innovations stay in closer touch with traditional technique. The styles that had really belonged to American culture in the eighteenth century were the short platform bridges and the long pontoon or many-piered bridge. Either form was low and close to the element it was intended to span, simple in its technical means, and easily understood by anyone who used it or examined it. The longer form had in its arrangement of structural elements the same repetitious, reiterative quality as a Gilbert Tennent sermon. Some individual builders were certainly capable of the research and analysis necessary to produce bolder forms, but these did not take hold very effectively in the American scene.

Manhattan (New York, 1924), 215 and plates f. pp. 62, 66. [Moses] *King's Handbook of New York City* (Boston, 1892), 177-178.

In the same way that American preaching developed during the early nineteenth century as an effort to adapt traditional forms to the effects-seeking, Arminian spirit of revivalism, so bridge-building developed at first as an effort to combine familiar, safe techniques with ventures into the arching or extension needed to span greater distances. New bridge-building took two principal forms, both relying heavily on the carpentry skills that had remained fairly well developed in colonial houses, barns, and ships. One was the arch-truss of Theodore Burr combining a wooden arch built up out of beams with a truss composed of diagonal and rectilinear members. A heavy structure, it was to achieve security through avoiding reliance on any one structural concept (illustration 12). The other principal form was the lattice developed by Ithiel Town. It relied in general on the concept of the truss—that is, the principal that a properly arranged set of straight members would create a horizontal structure much stronger than any simple beam, yet so self-contained that it would simply rest on its piers, exerting vertical weight but no diagonal outward and downward thrust that would put unstabilizing strains on the piers themselves. But the Town lattice relied mainly not on any mathematical perfection of its arrangement but on the reduplication of carpentry devices: it consisted of many criss-crossing diagonal members bound rigidly at all the intersections by pegs or nails, and strengthened further by a few additional horizontal members extending the length of the span (illustration 13). The lumber-work was so thickly arranged that the bridge resembled a single oversized beam whose interior had been hollowed out for a roadway and whose walls had been pierced by holes to form a grille. It was a combination of the truss idea with some conscientious carpentry in order to create an oversized version of the old log stringer.

From about 1830, the more and more rapid building up of the transportation network created pressure for rapid, more simple bridge-building. Railroads, more modern construction on some canals, and the extension of roads around growing cities, all required more bridges, and often bridges that were planned in large numbers at once. Men who designed and built or promoted new bridge plans stripped away that overlay of elements that had obscured the simple truss device within the forms that had been popular earlier in the century. At first, as with the bridges designed by Stephen H. Long, these trusses included some diagonal braces that amounted to a compromise with the Burr method of adding an arch as an overlay to the truss in order to take diagonal thrust. Soon, though, even this was eliminated, and the typical bridge designs of the new generation were unbastardized trusses. For longer spans, Charles Ellet and then John Roebling promoted the suspension bridge; but this, though dramatic, did not amount to a major deviation from the developing style of the period. The suspension device was used for only a very small minority of all bridges built, and its mathematical clarity came across in the same spirit as the analytical clarity of the truss form. The idea that the ability of bridge members to take burdens could be analyzed in a definite, reliable way was an obvious element in the appeal that the new forms exerted to a wider public, not just to the designers themselves. Ithiel Town, earlier in the century, had advertised in a general way that the parts of his bridge were arranged to take account of the "tension strength" of timbers and the "thrust strain" placed on certain bridge members. Stephen H. Long then included in a prospectus for his bridges the statement that the strengths of various members could be specifically calculated—although he did not indicate just what the calculations were or how he had carried them out.[100] Up to this point the analytical ideas presented in early nineteenth-century French and British treatises on building, often reprinted or distributed in America, were clearly more precise than anything the American builders were saying.

[100] Edwards, *Record*, 39-63, 158-159.

These treatises were serving somewhat the same function for American bridge-building that was served for Anglo-American preaching by the popularization of those French seventeenth-century writers on homiletics, such as Fénelon, who had called for a simple, persuasive, unscholastic approach to preaching.[101]

But it was Americans themselves who provided the formal method for the new style of analytical simplicity. Working independently of each other, about 1840 and after, two engineers produced works in which they used simple trigonometric methods and the principle of the parallelogram of forces in order to analyze the stresses and strains in any truss that was compounded of triangular arrangements of beams. The more sophisticated of these men was Herman Haupt, a West Point-trained engineer who worked for the Pennsylvania Railroad. He not only presented the trigonometric analysis, but tried to cover the whole range of bridge-building problems, both by prescribing methods for many building details that were not subject to analytical treatment and by presenting approximate methods for calculating stresses in kinds of bridges that did not fit the trigonometric scheme.[102] Yet it was the less sophisticated of the two men, Squire Whipple of New York, who in some ways

[101] On the American use of E. M. Gauthey and Thomas Tredgold, see Tredgold, *Elementary Principles of Carpentry*, 1st American from 2nd London edn. (Philadelphia, 1837), viii; James Renwick, *The Elements of Mechanics* (Philadelphia, 1832), ix, 212-225; and Dennis Hart Mahan, *An Elementary Course of Civil Engineering*, 2nd edn. (New York, 1838), vii, 98-104, 136-168. On the dissemination of ideas about the classic French preachers, see: *The Pulpit Orator* (Boston, 1804); *The Charges of Jean Baptist Masillon, . . . Also, Two Essays, the One on the Art of Preaching, from the French of M. Reybaz, and the Composition of a Sermon* (New York, 1806); Ebenezer Porter, comp., *The Young Preacher's Manual* (Boston, 1819); and George Campbell, *Lectures on Systematic Theology and Pulpit Eloquence*, ed. Henry J. Ripley (Boston, 1832).

[102] "An Engineer" [Herman Haupt], *Hints on Bridge Construction* [n.p., 1842]. Haupt, *General Theory of Bridge Construction* (New York, 1851).

was more symptomatic of American life. Whipple had been educated in the common schools and then in a local academy of upstate New York. He was not a college man and had attended no institution for professional training. As an engineer he worked mostly on railroads in his own area, attempted no spectacular projects, and left as results of his work a large number of moderate-sized bridges in the rural areas of New York. But he also, using the intellectual equipment that his own study had added to the mathematics taught in academies, produced a handbook on the design of bridge trusses. He paid little attention to the many practical, nonanalytical problems that attached to the building of any bridge, problems in which he had presumably his own knowledge and skills. Rather, he confined himself to the triangular scheme and offered to other builders a way of reducing to definite numerical quantities the stresses and strains in any truss that could be handled within this scheme.[103] As Tocqueville remarked about Americans of that era generally, Whipple produced not mere practicality, but a ruthlessly simple abstraction by which practical men could achieve a sense of security within their operations (illustrations 14 and 15).

Over the following generation, the style of bridge-design that Haupt and especially Whipple stood for spread in America, reaching the peak of its acceptance about 1870. Britons and Europeans became conscious of the American style. Sometimes they damned it as naive and oversimple; sometimes they saw it as a solution to their own problems of building rapidly the large numbers of bridges they needed. European practice generally took whatever were the most solid and reliable methods of practical construction that had been developed in engineering workshops and at bridge sites, and adhered to these both for the sake of

[103] Squire Whipple, *Bridge-Building: Being the Author's Original Work, Published in 1847, with an Appendix, Containing Corrections, Additions and Explanation, Suggested by Subsequent Experience* (New York, 1869).

strength and for the sake of preserving techniques that were familiar to the workmen whom engineers supervised. Whether in stone or metal, such bridges were apt to be massive, using far more material than was necessary for bare safety; and the connections between members or elements of the bridge were made of heavy systems of riveting or welding. A truss built in that way could not be reduced for purposes of analysis to a simple set of triangles composed of members meeting at mathematically abstract points. It was, in the technical phrase, statically indeterminate. The American ideal, on the other hand, was to produce a statically determinate form, all the members of which could be calculated exactly. This was the style for which J.A.L. Waddell argued in 1885, when American and British bridge styles were competing for adoption on Japanese railroads (illustration 16). The determinate form had the psychological advantage of precisely calculated security. It had the economic advantage of permitting a much more exact statement of the minimum amount of material needed for any structure within whatever margin of safety the engineer adopted. In a country where metal was relatively more expensive than it was in Europe, this was important.[104]

The psychological motivation was in some ways more characteristic of the American style than was the economic motivation. In principle, the determinate form could not be used unless a bridge design was pared down to meet the mathematical assumptions made by the analysis. This paring down might actually discard many elements of practical strength, and the more doctrinaire of American builders in the generation after the Civil War took a Procrustean ap-

[104] *American versus English Methods of Bridge Designing Reprinted from the "Japan Mail"* [Tokyo, 1886]. L. Antoine Comolli, *Les ponts de l'Amérique du nord: étude, calcul, description de ces ponts: comparaison des systèmes américain et européen* (Paris, 1879). Edwards, *Record*, 104-105. For developments in the problem of static determinacy, see esp. Stephen Timoshenko, *History of Strength of Materials* (New York, 1953).

proach to their work. Determinate analysis assumed, in the first place, that bridge members met at points. Americans, therefore, espoused the system of putting eyes or loops at the ends of members, and bolting these ends to each other with pins about which the members could pivot. While they tried to argue that such a method of connection was actually more secure in a practical sense, it was clear that they adopted it mainly because it was dictated by theory. Similarly, the theory assumed that each truss rested independently on the piers of the bridge, with a pier at either end of the truss. If a bridge extended over several piers, then the railroad tracks that it bore might be continuous, but the trusses themselves should remain separate and independent. The difficulty with this was that a continuous bridge span, extending without break over the intermediate piers, would under proper arrangements distribute the burden of the load over a much larger number of members and would, therefore, be safer and more economical. But it could always be argued, and accurately, that a continuous bridge was subject to greater strain at *certain* points than was a series of discontinous spans; and the introduction of intermediate piers introduced analytical problems that could not be handled by simple trigonometric methods. The wavelike transmission of stresses across the fulcrum that was constituted by the central pier required the use of the higher mathematics in its analysis.[105] This did not simply alarm those engineers who wanted to use modest cookbook methods. Bridge inspectors working for the New York railroad commission, confronting bridges already built on the continuous plan, actually recommended that the continuities between the trusses be cut so that engineers could calculate the stresses in the members of each separate span.[106]

[105] Edwards, *Record*, 104, 112-115.

[106] New York Board of Railroad Commissioners, *Report . . . on Strains on Railroad Bridges of the State* (Albany, 1891), 258-259, 263, 784, 1076, 1112, 1126.

Two points should be noted in the addiction of American engineers to the ideal of simple calculability. First, it did not cover all the procedures and skills that went into bridge-building. Engineers had to perform many tasks in which experience and trained practical judgment were the main guarantees of reliability: the casting of individual bridge members, the making of connections between members that could not practically be joined by the pin-and-link method, the securing of railroad or roadway to the bridge, and the sinking of piers and other masonry structures that were needed to hold even the most abstractly designed metal truss. Within this range of considerations, for instance, there took place the whole evolution from wood to metal bridges, to meet especially the problem of fire. Within this range of practical problems there took place some of the important innovations in American bridge-building in this generation. Suspension bridges, for example, had been reintroduced by Charles Ellet in the 1850s. As far as abstract design was concerned, these relied always on the principle of the catenary as the curve naturally assumed by a hanging chain. But Ellet suffered some disastrous failures in his bridges, partly because no one yet knew how to calculate the stresses imposed by wind on a hanging bridge, partly because the cables that he used to support bridges were not strong enough. When John A. Roebling supplanted Ellet as the principal American designer of suspension bridges, he did so not on the basis of any theoretical innovation, but on the basis of practical improvements like his methods for building cables out of wires bound parallel to each other. Roebling was German by birth, nurture, and technical training; it may be that his concentration on the internal strengths of his structures was a European contribution to American practice.[107] But it is still true that no

[107] On the technical development generally see Edwards, *Record*, chapter 4. On Ellet and Roebling, see Charles Ellet, Jr., *Report on a*

practical building could proceed only on the basis of simple theory, and that American builders did keep up a level of practical technology to support their theory.

Second, though, the addiction to calculability had a double aspect. It was both actual and rhetorical. On the level of the actual, it did lead to such very concrete decisions as the recommendation to cut continous bridges into separate spans. More significant, the New York commission that made the recommendation decided to ignore any bridges that contradicted the basic assumptions necessary for calculability. Examining all railroad trusses in New York, in the years after 1884, and considering bridges that had been built during the whole period since the Civil War or earlier, it did try to calculate the stresses in every bridge it found. And it did find that about a fourth of all these bridges were demonstrably too weak for the loads being put on them (illustrations 13 and 15). It also complained that a few bridges were built on plans, such as the old Burr combined arch-truss, that made determinate calculation impossible, and it took that impossibility as one good reason for getting rid of those bridges. But those impossible bridges were almost all fairly old, and they were few. Although the commission did not require rigid adherence to the assumptions involved in static determinacy, such as the use of pin-and-link construction, it did impose some requirements, and it found that it had to ignore only the fairly recent plate-girder

---

Suspension Bridge across the Potomac, 2nd edn. (Philadelphia, 1854); John Roebling, *Final Report . . . to the President and Directors of the Niagara Falls . . . Bridge Companies* (Rochester, N.Y., 1855), 4-7; Roebling, *Report . . . to the President and Directors of the Niagara Falls . . . Bridge Companies, on the Condition of the Niagara Railway Suspension Bridge* (Trenton, 1860); *Annual Report of the . . . Covington and Cincinnati Bridge Company* (Trenton, 1867), 68-73; David B. Steinman and Sara Ruth Watson, *Bridges and Their Builders*, rev. edn. (New York, 1957), 206-208; Alan Trachtenberg, *Brooklyn Bridge: Fact and Symbol* (New York, 1965), 41-64.

bridges in order to bring "all" railroad bridges within its scheme of thought.[108]

On the level of the rhetorical, engineers whose own skills went beyond the simply analytical would use simpler analysis as a route of communication with the public. George Vose, who built bridges throughout the Northeast in the generation after the Civil War, and who made a special career for himself in the 1880s by campaigning against the improper building and inspection of bridges,[109] revealed this when he gave testimony on one bridge disaster near Boston. A bridge had fallen under a Boston-Providence passenger train, with much loss of life. Vose, like other engineers called in to testify, complained especially that certain key features of the bridge were asymmetrical in design and that the most dangerous member was concealed behind an ill-constructed joint where it could not be inspected. In response to the question whether he could calculate the strength of the asymmetrical member that appeared to have broken, he said: "I don't know whether I could tell what the strain on the different parts of that would be or not. It is going to be more on one side of the bar than it is on the other. It is not an easy thing to figure upon it. I am not prepared to say that I could figure upon it and give you an exact result. . . . I will, if you will give me Sunday to do it; only I may bring you in some differential calculus; I may bring you in the theory of probabilities. I will give you something you cannot understand. I will agree to do that."[110]

Even aside from the fact that Vose was not very happy about mucking around in calculus himself, he assumed that

[108] New York Board of Railroad Commissioners, *Report*, 3-6, 1025, 1118-1119, 1123-1124, 1414, 1461, 1484-1485, 1487, 1676-1677.

[109] George L. Vose, *Bridge Disasters in America: The Cause and the Remedy* (Boston, 1887), 3. Massachusetts Board of Railroad Commissioners, *Special Report . . . in Relation to the Disaster on Monday, March 14, 1887, on the Dedham Branch of the Boston & Providence Railroad* (Boston, 1887), 242-243.

[110] *Ibid.*, 262.

the kind of thought through which he could communicate to the educated men who were his questioners was not only technically confined to the trigonometric but more generally one in which exactness, clarity, and symmetry were the ideals.[111] And much the same thing was assumed by John Roebling when he came to communicate with a similar public. Just after his death in 1869, his son brought out a thin, profusely illustrated folio volume Roebling had prepared, entitled *Long and Short Span Railway Bridges.* It was clearly intended as what a later generation would call a "presentation," stating the case for Roebling's methods when he was just entering on his great project, the Brooklyn Bridge, and when he was also continuing to operate his bridge-building firm, which the Brooklyn Bridge would publicize and which would erect different kinds of bridges, not just suspensions. This brochure he organized around an idea that he stated prominently on the title page: "The greatest economy in Bridging can only be obtained by a judicious application of the Parabolic Truss."[112] He was, in effect, saying that the parabolic arch was the underlying simple form on which were built suspension bridges (which supposedly used the arch in an inverted form) and also new kinds of metal trusses that Roebling would build on the arch principle (illustration 17). This concept was not quite in the pattern of trigonometric calculability that was central to American bridge design, but it was in the same spirit: the insistence on a simple abstraction on which practical problems could be unloaded.

[111] For the fixation on trigonometry, rejecting calculus, see Edward Deering Mansfield, *A Discourse on the Utility of the Mathematics as a Means of General Education. Delivered before the Western Literary Institute and College of Professional Teachers, on the 8th of October, 1834* (Cincinnati, 1835), 14; "The Philosophy of the Science of Trigonometry," *District School Journal of New York*, VIII (1847-48), 81-82; and "Is the Higher Education Growing Unpopular?" *American Educational Monthly*, VII (1871), 35-36.

[112] John A. Roebling, *Long and Short Span Railway Bridges* (New York, 1869), 1-4, 49-50. Cf. Roebling, in *Annual Report . . . of the Covington & Cincinnati Bridge Company . . . 1867*, 67-68.

E. Interactions

Problems in the design of ships and bridges involved the same set of difficulties, those of creating a structure of considerable length that would remain rigid under shifting loads or shifting support, and under the impact of destructive weather. They both involved the production of highly visible structures that the public used and for which the public thought itself a knowledgeable audience.

Much of any gain in technique resulted simply from the stimulus of new needs. To this extent, increase in the active ability of builders or in the passive ability of the public was a matter of opportunity, exercise, and outlet. This simple gain was not trivial, since it was one form in which the population was experiencing the growth within the environment, and in which environmental change was imposing tighter discipline on mental behavior.

But the builders also worked out characteristic methods for solving problems, methods that amounted to cultural versions of the "learning strategies" that in some psychologies are crucial in the growth of intelligence. Among shipbuilders, the characteristic method was the lift model: among bridge-builders, it was determinate truss analysis. These methods may seem quite different in style, one appearing holistic and intuitive, the other partitive and analytic. Their similarity appears rather in contrast to British or European practice of the same time. British builders and engineers did make considerable use of models, both in ship design and in analyzing the effects of stress on the members of structures such as bridges, but their practice was essentially different from the American. When the Society for the Improvement of Naval Architecture conducted their tests in the 1790s, when William Fairbarn and Eaton Hodgkinson conducted their tests of structural members, when William A. Froude mounted his test-basin studies in the 1860s and 1870s, they were using tests to determine the internal properties of materials, the interactive behavior of quantities of water, or the motion of bodies in complex systems of conditions—none of which could be inferred from simple, unchallengeable propositions, at least then. They were using tests to extend their knowledge about the internal and interactive aspects of their problems. When Americans used models in building ships, they did so in order to avoid the difficulties of calculating final full-sized structures from plans, even though the methods for carrying out such calculations were known and used in other countries. When American bridge designers began to acquire greater mathematical competence, they still tried to keep the requisite skills as simple as possible by concentrating on determinate bridge-truss styles.

The American way with models and analysis favored a greater diffusion of these problem-solving techniques in the interested parts of the population, and it encouraged a wide connoisseurship about design. As long as ships or bridges were relatively small, and the loads put on them relatively light, this simplification and diffusion of techniques could only mean that the average level of successful problem-solving in the society was increasing.

Was this increase added to other abilities, or did it replace abilities that were being lost? Within ship- and bridge-building, there is little sign that earlier specific understandings were being lost, although it is possible that some details in the traditional crafts of the carpenter or shipwright were becoming irrelevant. Building in the mid-eighteenth century was too simple and too derivative for loss to mean much. It is more plausible that a real verbal ability and audience, such as was revealed in some eighteenth-century sermons, was giving way before a generally spatial or visual turn of thought. Since nineteenth-century verbal culture was copious, however vulgar, it may be that society's capacity for precision was shifting from the verbal to the spatial aspects of thought, while intuition and fluency were gaining on the verbal side.

This trend to simple calculation and superficial visualization, considered even apart from what was happening to the verbal culture, may have had emotional and demographic correlates. On this, contemporaries had a lot to say. They observed that Americans built light structures—houses, ships, steamboats, bridges—that Americans subjected these structures to intense, dangerous use, and that they did not seem to worry much when lives were destroyed by the failure of overstrained structures. In intellectual terms, this could be made to look good: it showed a willingness to seek the kind of stress that would bring a population into contact with novel, mind-developing problems. In moral terms, though, this willingness had no positive adventurous quality, suggesting rather a disregard for lasting values and even for human life. It was part of the taste for violence that the sensitive noted in American life. And to the conservative in temper, any abstract cognitive style was itself a violence, an insistence on eliminating many of the varied characteristics that gave substance to phenomena.

Repeatedly, observers who wanted to be sympathetic to the society explained American daring and flimsiness by the rapid growth of the population and its physical structures. Tocqueville noted this when he reported a workman's answer to his question why American ships were lightly built: shipping was expanding so rapidly that a vessel never needed to last longer than twenty years. This twenty years was close to the conventional figure of twenty-five years for the span within which the American population doubled. And the process of population growth helped to explain both the hasty construction of facilities and a relative indifference to violence. In analogy to the processes by which people coped with population growth, the abstract, simply calculating mode of thought takes on emotional as well as cognitive significance. Up until about 1840 the country had to work with an economy that was growing, but not at a rate that was dramatically or certainly greater than that of population growth. Often, if a particular family wanted to benefit from expansion, it could accomplish this only by doing some violence to its own growth in numbers—that is by forcing per capita income within the family up by limiting family size. For this, techniques of contraception and abortion were available, but even the mildest of them were looked on as immoral and unnatural. When they were used, people tended not to admit it, much as designers tried to exclude questions of internal stress from their calculations. To some extent, people did not resort to methods of restricting reproduction within the time-span of any family's existence, but instead simply postponed the age of marriage, thus restricting the size of the family by restricting its external bounds over time. In the elements of family life, just as in design, Americans accepted the terms of violence, as imposed by growth and expansion, but they tried to escape the consequences of growth through calculating and manipulating the external, uncontroversial features of the systems with which they dealt.

On the other hand, the geographical location of Roebling's great project points up the connection between structures and sermons, as symptoms of the mental change that Americans had achieved. The Brooklyn Bridge was needed because, in the urban growth then bursting throughout industrial America, the divisions between old municipalities were collapsing. Not only were suburbs growing and requiring the elaboration of new networks of transportation, but neighboring places that had once accepted their separation by waterways were now too involved with each other to rely on ferry travel. In the case of New York and Brooklyn, one of the most obvious features of this involvement was the popularity of Henry Ward Beecher, which drew congregations from a wide area. When the bridge was completed, it would make easier the road for visitors going to hear someone like Beecher, and it would fall into the same pattern of over-arching simplicity that Beecher insisted on in the structure of his own church. There he wanted only a bare podium, a spindly pulpit, and a hall free of ornament or supporting pillars, so that he could speak out to all his hearers in the most direct, personal way possible (illustration 18).[113] Roebling was the hero bridge-builder of his generation, Beecher the hero preacher, and there was an inner connection between the ideals of simplicity and personalism that they both embodied.

That connection rested ultimately in the importance of personal trust as a shortcut to the cementing of large-scale organization. Both Beecher and Roebling exploited an emotional quality in the popular reliance on them, although they both played the roles of great minds whose brilliant workings, beyond public comprehension, reached the public mainly through results produced. They differed mainly in that Beecher made a greater show of presenting the public with an inside view of the workings of his mind. Each man, in his own area of activity, served as the means of bringing organization to large social masses that were threatening to become amorphous—Roebling by the literal means of providing connections within the metropolitan area, Beecher by providing the personal attraction that would bring in large congregations, amass donations, and thus support a large church organization that would focus membership and attention in the new metropolis. The personal function that each man performed on a large scale had its counterpart in the function that was served by the simple, analytical techniques of professional performance that came within the abilities of lesser men.

In bridge engineering, the equivalence between personal trustworthiness and analytic clarity had been implied for years in the insistence with which builders' prospectuses had stated that the strengths of particular forms could be

[113] Lyman Abbott, *Henry Ward Beecher* (Boston & New York, 1903), 77-80. "The Pulpit and Preaching," *Christian Advocate*, XLIV (1869), 252, which also argues that intimacy between preacher and people is a function of large attendance, and "Pulpit Structures," *ibid.*, 276, which argues that excessive plainness of pulpit design can be a means to self-display by the preacher.

calculated exactly. It became explicit in the attitudes that were taken by the railroad commissions of New York and Massachusetts in the latter years of the century, when they came to assess the record that bridge-builders had made. The New York commissioners, as has been pointed out, were quite rigid in relying on formal calculation as the only means by which they could evaluate 2,500 bridges quickly, somewhat impersonally, and without raising nebulous internal questions about the history and composition of each structure; but even they found that analysis had to give way at times to personal contention. According to the commissioners' report, the authorities on most lines were willing to make the structural changes that the commission recommended. But the engineers for the Erie Railroad objected, claiming especially that the commission's engineers had assumed bridge loads heavier than were likely to be imposed in actual practice. This could not be resolved except as a question of whether the railroad officials were managing the line honestly, of whether they were imposing loads as limited as they said.[114]

In Massachusetts the investigation of the Bussey Bridge disaster brought out more clearly the way that analysis could substitute for personal reliability in the eyes of the men who represented the public or the railroad companies as users of bridges. The engineer who had won the contract to build the Bussey Bridge had guaranteed that the members of the bridge would be calculated to bear a certain designated load in pounds per square inch. No one in the investigation denied that this man had done what he promised, as far as basic truss design went. The problem was that he had been conducting a mere *ad hoc* bridge-building company, leasing some of the facilities of a larger company, and had failed to produce regular, examinable work in some of those connecting details that could not be sub-

[114] New York State, Board of Railroad Commissioner, *Report . . . On Strains on Railroad Bridges of the State* (Albany, 1891), 3-6, 1288-1292.

sumed under the analytic forms. But the analytic forms, embodied in and identified with a simple contractual relation, seemed to substitute for a personal reliability that the railroad company did not know how to secure—or did not want to take the trouble to secure, in the press and confusion of business.[115] One might rely on a Roebling to build a few spectacular bridges. One might even rely on a few of the less personalistic but conservative and reputable bridge companies to build many of the more important bridges. But bridges came in all types and sizes, and personal reliability inevitably gave way to analytic reliability at the supposedly lower levels of the range. Actually, both kinds of reliability were indispensable for any bridge, but there was a tendency for men to substitute one kind for another, depending on the circumstances.

Within preaching, the personal, organization-building charisma of a popular man had its substitute in the utilitarian simplicity toward which all preachers were pressed as they tried to raise money and build organizations. Such preaching for the sake of aggrandizement was hateful to men of a more aloof or nostalgic morality, but it was endorsed by Daniel Kidder, the Methodist homiletics professor who spoke for the interests of the newer America. In his view, the growth of "Christian enterprise," with its missions, its benevolent agencies, and its temperance movement, required that the minister not only take these needs into account in his formal sermons, but that he also preach or speak at the meetings arranged specially for such purposes. Although such addresses might range over a wide variety of topics from occasion to occasion, each particular effort required simplicity and unity of calculation: "Mere excellences of thought or elegancies of diction are of little value without strict relevancy to the object in view, it being essentially necessary to employ force of argument and expression with reference to practical and immediate results.

[115] Massachusetts Board of Railroad Commissioners, *Special Report*, 6-7, 22-23.

At this point Christian oratory gains some of the advantages which belong to judicial and forensic speaking, as well as to the demonstrative oratory of the ancients. An immediate practical issue is before both speaker and audience, and unless the issue is gained the address is a failure."[116] Between this style and that of a Beecher or Moody, there was a great apparent difference. Certainly the listener who disliked mere calculation and manipulation would be inclined to take refuge in the personalism that some men offered. But the two styles served essentially the same function, of providing the morale, the resources, and the sense of reliability that were needed to bind together the larger and larger units of people within a growing population. Since this population was also highly mobile, a simple fund-raising thought was useful in organizing prior, calculable niches for individuals in the various structures they might want to join. This mechanical style was of a pattern with both classical economics and determinate structural analysis. In larger situations or structures, though, the personalistic appeal offered individuals some reflection of their need for personal wholeness, texture, and security. In a way, too, Americans were already discovering what sociologists would later learn: that mere definite rules would not suffice for modern bureaucracies, within which the personal and the informal would always be a necessary factor in efficiency.

But neither the calculating mode nor the personal mode justified reliance. Over the previous generation, a series of moral scandals had afflicted at least two denominations in the New York area, the Methodists and Episcopalians. Almost always the scandals had furnished evangelical and churchly elements with charges to use in their warring against each other. Similar charges that one view or another encouraged moral irresponsibility ran through the arguments between Arminian and Calvinist groups, in other churches. When personalism became itself a vital preaching style, the moral integrity of the preacher became crucial

[116] Kidder, *Treatise on Homiletics*, 100.

and vulnerable. And in 1874 the Beecher-Tilton adultery case broke, throwing the New York public into contention over whether Henry Ward Beecher was guilty of the charges levied against him.[117] During the same years when this case was coming to a head, the analytic bridge style achieved its widest acceptance and was almost concurrently thrown into disrepute by a series of bridge disasters. Although the career of George Vose and the investigations conducted by state railroad commissions did later help to elucidate the ideas that underlay the analytic style, the bridge disasters of the 1870s set off these exposés and thus began the long transition to a different handling of the problems in bridge-building.[118]

There were, at the same time, two incidental features of the crises of the 1870s that suggested how the problems might reach out. First, the defenders of Beecher included one man who had a (for us) ambiguous relation and a (for him) possibly ambivalent relation to the central figure in mid-nineteenth-century ideas about child-raising. Lyman Abbott was one of the several sons of Jacob Abbott who went on to prominent or at least respectable careers in the professions and intellectual life. Lyman became a liberal Congregational preacher, successful especially in adapting evolution to a cautious but reformist social outlook. Like all the Abbott sons, he had been raised largely by female relatives, since their own mother had died young and since Jacob Abbott, besides marrying again, spent much time off traveling. Lyman, in his reminiscences of his father, said much about

[117] Lyman Abbott, *Henry Ward Beecher*, ch. xii. Paxton Hibben, *Henry Ward Beecher* (New York, 1927), chs., xxi-xxvii.

[118] Willard S. Pope, *Report . . . on the Falling of the Bollman Bridge at Zanesville, Ohio. Dec. 4, 1866* [Detroit, n.d.]; George L. Vose, *Bridge Disasters in America* (Boston, 1887); J.A.L. Waddell, "The Evolution of Art and Science in our Bridges: A Memoir," *American Scholar*, 1 (1932), 331-335. See also Massachusetts Board of Railroad Commissioners, *Special Report*, 369-372, for civil engineer Edward S. Philbrick's identifying of 1870 as the height and turning-point in the influence of the American style of bridge design.

his father's success in devising gentle, entertaining ways to communicate with his children, much especially about his father's ways with children after he had retired to a house in Maine late in life, but he said nothing to indicate that the father had also been one of the great exponents of imposing early and unconditional submission on children. Never believing the charges of adultery against Beecher,[119] he showed every sign of having transferred to Beecher's personality and personalism some of the attitudes that he felt for the gentler side of his father's life. And he seemed equally ready to repress or suppress the possibility of anything stern and disturbing in the lives of these men. For Lyman Abbott, possibly also for other people, to bring Beecher into question was to bring into question many of the basic educational ideas of that generation. No really clearcut decision was ever reached in the Beecher case. Although he was nominally vindicated, and though he continued to preach at the Church of the Pilgrims in Brooklyn, the hero-preacher was thenceforth an uncertain, tainted figure, no longer really useful in enabling people to personify rather than face their problems.

Second, the accidents that befell Roebling and his son in erecting the Brooklyn Bridge symbolized the inadequate preparation that that generation had for coping with the internal, textural aspects of problems, in contrast to its extensive mental equipment for dealing with the external, formal aspect. Of the two men, the father suffered a fatal injury when a ferry crashed into a pier where he was surveying for the bridge. The son met disaster while supervising work on one of the piers, in a caisson below the water level of the East River. Either he sacrificed precaution to the personal role of leading his men in construction, or he did not know how to deal with all the problems presented by pressure changes. He developed the bends, and never recovered. The latter years of work on the bridge saw him lying crip-

[119] Abbott, *Beecher*, ch. xii. Ira V. Brown, *Lyman Abbott*, 3-9, 15, 18-20, 68-69, 128-129.

pled in a room overlooking the site, using binoculars to supervise the continuing work. A complex, elaborately competent man, he became himself a monument to men's lack of ability to cope with inner, subsurface forces.[120]

Along with the intellectual and moral failures that beset American culture at this time, the character of that culture was beginning a transition to more complex, mature patterns. It would be tempting to say that Americans committed themselves to a certain level of culture in the form of a synthesis between the calculating and the personal, that failure then forced them to confront the inadequacy of that achievement, and that they responded to the confrontation by undertaking to learn new and more difficult lessons. In some ways, this actually happened. Men did engage in constant questioning in these years about why the pulpit was losing its influence. Although much of this questioning centered on ideological problems such as the rise of science, the techniques of preaching came in for their share of attention, and men both in and out of the ministry insisted that preachers should work for a more critical, informed style. The weaknesses and failures of bridges did lead men to discard the mere analytic mode as inadequate, first in the building of smaller bridges[121] and increasingly for all kinds of structures. In both areas, the proofs of inadequacy in the existing cultural achievement acted as some specific incitement to new effort. The same movement from failure toward new effort took place in other areas of American culture, as in the way that exposure of learning failures in the Quincy, Massachusetts, school system led to the calling of Francis W. Parker as superintendent of the town schools, and thus to Parker's work in promoting the "New Education."

[120] Alan Trachtenberg, *Brooklyn Bridge: Fact and Symbol* (New York, 1965), 94-96. D. B. Steinman, *The Builders of the Bridge* (New York, 1945), 319-320, 324-370.

[121] See Philbrick testimony, in Massachusetts Board of Railroad Commissioners, *Special Report*, 370.

Americans were seeking intellectual security through the specifics of intellectual discipline, such as better university and professional education. This latter search, especially as it took Americans to German universities, became more common during those years when the great failures in the calculating-personal synthesis were on the verge of breaking open. It touched many aspects of education. Parker's career took him from district schoolteaching to study in Berlin and then to the Quincy superintendency. And Mary Putnam's career took her from a dissatisfaction with the educational opportunities open to her as a woman, to a dissatisfaction with the opportunities in American medical education generally, to study in Paris, and then back to America, where she sought reforms in several areas of education: in the training of female medical students, in the kind of intellectual effort that the public believed women physiologically able to undertake, and most generally in the ways early education might prepare children for later intellectual discipline.[122]

But the actual shift was much more devious and slow than this apparent leap up from one cultural level to another. In one sense, it was a continuation of the old process by which Americans bound in a provincial culture reached out to grasp and assimilate the more subtle accomplishment of Europeans. Of a piece with that reaching out, but closer to the foreground, it was also a continuation of the process by which Americans, early in the nineteenth century, had begun going to Europe to fill out inadequacies they had found in their own experience.

From shortly before 1800 until about the middle of the new century, Americans undertook the risk of new experience in that aspect of thinking that would give them the

[122] Mary Putnam Jacobi, *Physiological Notes on Primary Education and the Study of Language* (New York, 1889). *Mary Putnam Jacobi, M.D., A Pathfinder in Medicine, with Selections from Her Writings* (New York and London, 1925), 349-356, 367-390. Mary Putnam Jacobi, *Life and Letters*, ed. Ruth Putnam (New York & London, 1925), ch. xi.

most immediate, unchallengeable, intuitable representation of problems: the visual and spatial. Confronted by the international competition of the post-Revolutionary years, and by the sudden need to build more or larger vessels than their facilities had often handled, shipbuilders in smaller New England ports took up new techniques of building from models. These techniques did more than make the subtleties of construction examinable by lay customers. They made it possible for new or overworked shipwrights to reproduce in full scale the lines given them. This means of rapid learning then suited the needs of New York during the years when that port was expanding from its torpor and partial closure during the Revolution. The same period saw much the same pattern in American acceptance of nonpractical, esthetic experience. As colonials, they had lived in ambivalence between aping and rivaling the forms and styles set for them by Britain. With independence and with participation in larger worlds of commerce and politics, the inadequacy of the provincial mode became obvious. While some then picked up verbal products from the European culture, many sought or encountered visual images. If these images were shocking to Puritan spirits because they conveyed too much, too directly, about the senses, imagery was also the easiest, least intellectual mode through which the inexperienced could approach a complex intellectual tradition. Visual novelty, to the callow but rapidly jaded mind, was the best shortcut to the facing of new problems.[123]

For the sake of wider, more effective functioning, men began looking at their world in ways that required less of formal, rationalistic discipline. The informal could reveal a more varied reality. In time this response became more common also in the verbal culture, as in the imagery and anecdotalism of sermons. If the visual and the verbal became confused in some areas, as in the sentimentalism of genre painting and popular print-making, this only indi-

[123] Neil Harris, *The Artist in American Society: The Formative Years, 1790-1860* (New York, 1966), chs. 1-2.

cated another aspect of the process: the synthesia, or mixing of sensory modes, that may accompany weakening in the ego's boundaries between categories of experience.

As shipbuilding developed during the first part of the century, it revealed only some of the complexities through which the visual could help advance the personalistic and the calculating. Models facilitated the intuiting and the measuring of hull problems. They contributed little, however, to actual decisions about hull form, a problem essentially like that of indeterminate structural analysis in bridge-building. Given the usual stability of the vertical dimension in land travel, a designer there could often make determinate assumptions. With the sea he could not, any more than an honest preacher could make determinate assumptions about the spirits of his parishioners. Concrete images provided a means by which the shipbuilder could transmit his skills to apprentices, or his reputation to the public. They gave him much less help when he ventured to analyze problems in quantitative detail. Then, even while he developed some skills that were analogous to the theology enjoyed in private among sophisticated clerics like Shedd, he had to rely more and more on personal reputation. Even aside from the scale of their accomplishments, men like Griffiths and the McKays were very much men of their time in their similarity to Beecher and Roebling.

At least in the two areas of preaching and bridge-building, this search was more than a mere reaction from inadequacy toward new learnings. In the same years that Roebling was stating a more "American," Beecheresque role than his own skills required, James Eads was building his great bridge across the Mississippi at St. Louis in a solid, conservative style, and with relatively conservative publicity. But Eads was a practical worker whose previous experience had been largely in boat-building, the raising of sunken boats, and the construction of river improvements, leading him into just those problems of pressure and underwater operation that incapacitated the younger Roebling.

At about the same time younger American engineers were beginning to advocate and explain the construction of continuous bridges, which violated the assumptions of determinate analysis.[124] On the side of preaching, the probing, internally analytic work of a Shedd had begun back in the 1850s, when he had been teaching in upstate New York. Though Shedd was in some ways the earliest of the neo-orthodox, he was also working in direct continuity with the psychological assumptions of eighteenth-century Calvinist orthodoxy and eighteenth-century Enlightenment disillusion. And even aside from the way that some individuals had begun making obvious efforts toward a more complex style during the very years that the calculating-personal synthesis was reaching its height, there remains the fact that Americans were ready to move toward the new learnings as soon as the great failures became obvious. The failures, rather than leaving a gap into which substance only afterwards flowed, simply provided the occasion on which what had been a minor and unpopular strain in American thinking could begin working toward greater influence.

The reorientation that took place after about 1870 had two main features. First, men in various fields paid increasing attention to the internal structure and composition of the units or materials with which they worked: metals, structural members, metal-connecting techniques, motives, learning processes, personalities, economic relations. Second, they gave increasing attention to the social guarantees and social structures by which they could ensure reliability in intellectual performance. The first of these developments was supported by men's efforts to learn techniques that they needed if they were to attend to the internal aspects of problems: more calculus for engineers (or at least, for the more routine operators, handbook formulas that reflected

[124] Steinman and Watson, *Bridges and Their Builders*, 170-192. Mansfield Merriman, *On the Theory and Practice of Continuous Bridges* (New York, 1876). Charles Bender, *Practical Treatise on the Properties of Continuous Bridges* (New York, 1876).

other men's work in the higher mathematics); more attention to the "contents of children's minds" by the teachers and psychologists of the child-study movement; more attention to the details of social problems by those preachers who were beginning to shift their casuistry toward what would emerge as the social gospel. The second of these developments took the form of stronger institutions to regulate professional training and practice: the gradual revival of examination and licensing in fields, such as medicine and law, that had done without serious entrance qualifications in the previous generation; the establishment or strengthening of prestige schools in various fields, providing a nationally understood scale of competence that could be applied to many practitioners; the creation of public regulatory bodies that advised or imposed new standards in certain task, such as the erection of works on which the public safety depended; and the continued growth of corporations and large economic complexes, within which personal performance could be governed by some kind of quality-control rather than by the formal but personal arrangements of individual contracting.

In the short range, some of earlier emphasis persisted from the synthesis of the calculating and the personal styles, not just in those persons who continued the old methods without much adjustment, but also in the patterns of the newer learnings. It is, to be sure, typical of the new patterns that a Wolcott Gibbs who was out of place and unappreciated at City College in the 1850s went on to become a leader in American science and mathematics at Harvard and during the latter decades of the century. But while the techniques of quantitative thought were being escalated up the scale of mathematical difficulty, the analytic, probing turn of mind remained bound to quantitative thought. If American preaching of the 1870s was much indication, any maturing of thought in verbal areas would probably have taken two lines of growth: that of social criticism, undertaken already by men like Washburn, and that of introspection and motivational analysis, represented by Shedd. In the long run, both of these did develop. Immediately, though, the second did not. Rather, after the early child-study movement had begun to implement the mode of psychological probing, that mode was diverted toward external problems. G. Stanley Hall continued through a long career to investigate motives in an uncritical, vacuum-cleaner way; even when he offered a welcome to Freud and Freud's ideas just before World War I, he made no significant adjustment in his own style of thought, whose miscellaneous character served as a virtual guarantee that it would not penetrate to anything obscure or difficult. More seriously, the American thinking about human nature took the direction shown by James and Dewey, with their tendency to think largely about external adjustments, but to shy defensively away from the problems to which psychoanalysis addressed itself. In preaching, the same pattern showed in the development of the social gospel and in the failure of Shedd's psychologism to win followers and fulfillment in that generation. Commonly, analytic thought about the human psyche took the mechanical route represented by Joseph M. Rice, Edward Thorndike, and the psychological measurements movement.

The culture that was produced by education and American life-patterns in the years around 1870 was marked in both its technical and its verbal reaches by a freezing of accomplishment at a superficial level, on which men could evade the difficulties of profound analysis or self-criticism. These intellectual evasions had their correlate and support in a social structure that seemed to rely on the formal, automatic relations of laissez-faire. Actually, of course, intellectual problems and social structure were alike already more complex than what could be coped with by the typical products of American culture. This disparity was reflected both in the self-improving efforts of some intellectuals and in the obvious cultural failures of the period. Americans began to correct the disparity by producing a more sophisticated quantitative culture, a more fully articulated social structure, and a verbal culture more sophisticated *in the direction of analyzing social life and scientific thought.* Growth was much less firm in those parts of the verbal culture that could not be tied to things social or quantitative.

The persistence of psychological evasion during the new learnings indicates that this evasion may well have been the focal weakness within the combination of competence and superficiality that marked American culture in 1870. But if that is true to any large degree, then it becomes valid to re-examine the mental spirit of the period as a whole, looking for coherences that extend over the range of problems from child-raising, through elementary learning, to the cultural products that intellectuals offered back to their society. And at this point it becomes possible to separate out the spirit of 1750, too. Although each particular level of mental problem developed continuously over the generation from the colonial period to an industrial society, the joining of these several kinds of problem makes it possible to abstract out a distinct pattern for 1750, another distinct pattern for 1870, and thus to say: Here is what American thinking accomplished during those years when it and American society were becoming developed and modern.

FIVE

WHAT DID HAPPEN; WHAT MAY HAPPEN

The training of human beings, up from infancy to participation in the culture around them, evolved during these years of American development, through many adjustments that flowed into each other. One kind of abstraction can take each phase in this training process and trace it separately as it changed from 1750 to 1870. This is what the preceding chapters have done with respect to child-raising ideas, the learning problems of children, and certain outcomes of learning. Another kind of abstraction, however, can pull back from the continuity of change and examine all the parts of the learning cycle as a bundle of processes operating around 1750, then as a bundle of processes operating around 1870. It is the comparison of these two abstract bundles that may define just how "learning" changed over this period.

On the surface, but only on the surface, the learning that bound together society in the middle of the eighteenth century looks like a stable though not primitive traditionalism. The elements of a "traditional society" appeared in the way that order and authority were accepted as essential ingredients in almost every social relation, including the relations of learning or intellectual expression. They appeared also in the confidence some men had that a large part of the population might share in a subtle intellectual life, through their response to the ideas that clerical intellects passed on to them as a basis for further discourse. In two of its official foundations—the "well-ordered family" and the articulated orthodox sermon—that culture might appear to have been a coherent whole, certainly too hierarchical and stable for the modern taste but comfortable, serious, and enabled by theological metaphor to accept an honest confrontation between thought and life. There may even have been a few communities that lived that way.

The difficulty was that the world of learning between those two apparent foundations was broken by fault-lines and gaps. These breaks began quite early, according to one observer, in the sense of emotional distance between parent and child even within the comfortable rural family. Because of this distance, many of the finer points of the culture were not transmitted to the young. Just as rural life had its own special cultural danger for adults—that they would sink into cloddish lethargy, neglecting to make explicit the learning with which they were in fact equipped—so it carried the danger that the young would prove backward in their encounters with polite social culture. Of a piece with this backwardness was the backwardness of Americans in furnishing their material culture with many of the forms of construction that had been familiar to their fathers.

There were beginning to appear a number of ideals of education or discourse that did not posit the kind of hierarchical, ordered sharing that had seemed a feature of the older intellectual life. The Lockean concept of a more absolutely paternal child-rearing was one of these ideals. Precisely by its absolute character, it sought to cut the bonds of authority quite early in the life cycle, leaving the individual free to move about under the guidance of an internalized, unconscious paternal standard. Another of these ideals was that of elegant, polished discourse, rising to fashionability over the older ideal of shared discourse. Elegant discourse in the form practiced by Tillotson or Addison or the American Samuel Johnson tended to assume in its hearers or readers a body of intellectual skill already acquired and finished. Such discourse often confined itself to persuading its audience of one single point that could be shown compatible with the rhetorical polish. It was largely indifferent to the patterning of contradictions and interior dialogue by which the older kind of discourse achieved a correspondence between the internal intellectual problems of the speaker and the external ties of the speaker-audience relation. In contrast to the ideal of polish, there were times when the older forms of culture simply diverged into stereotyped or degenerate forms: this was the case with many of the reiterative or text-chopping sermons of the period, and it may also have been true in the rudimentary bridge-building. Typically, though, the initiative in these years was held by men who were trying to create more formal places for training: King's College in New York, Queens in New Jersey, a variety of secondary and higher schools in Philadelphia, medical schools in both New York and Philadelphia.

This contrast between the older culture and the newer divergings was felt also by the individual who moved through the whole disjointed pattern. At the beginning of life, the "typical" American of 1750 encountered an apparently ordered family life, in which paternal discipline was forestalled and kept from running to excess by the compensatory workings of an unofficial maternal culture. But at about the age when the official side of that ordered family life was supposed to become more explicit the child began encountering an indifference to any real intercourse between adults and children. Slackness showed in a wide indifference to the actual learning problems of children. No one enforced any definite standard about what children were supposed to learn, or what constituted successful completion of such ill-organized elementary schooling as was available. From the point of view of twentieth-century efforts to re-establish ungraded instruction, the freedom of lower schooling from set standards may look like a blessing, but when higher schools were getting established in the middle provinces in the years around 1750 there were few standards of lower education that teachers could expect of entering students. The recruitment of students for higher and professional study had been split between two ways of proceeding, neither of which involved standards that were strictly part of the *local*, *public* life. One of these ways was the familial: especially for law and medicine, recruitment methods sometimes gave preference to the sons of existing practitioners. On the other hand, the more important failure to observe local, public standards in colonial New York was the dependence on recruitment or training from outside. Whether in Britain or New England or the Netherlands, many men took their professional training or licensing abroad. Finally, at least on the verbal side, the individual who passed through the whole sequence of educational stages available to the New Yorker as American ended up producing in a society in which intellectual performance was split between several standards. Some produced the older kind of shared discourse. Some produced stereotyped, degenerate versions of this structure. Others produced the newer Addisonian polish.

There were many points at which this pattern of learning was inadequate to the needs of a coherent society. Two general aspects of this pattern are significant when it is viewed as a form for the life cycle of individuals. First, there came quite early in life a break (partly a chronological break, partly simply a sense of disparity) from order to slackness, so that the individual was faced early with an open scene and with a lack of the direction that the official standards of the society might have entitled him to expect. Second, the intellectual product of the society—the content of its culture—was marked not only by contradiction between the ideal of shared discourse and the ideal of cultural polish, but also by a lack of the local social organization that could have maintained coherence in the face of diversity.

These two kinds of disparity reinforced each other, creating a pervasive pressure for men either to reinstate or to create some more coherent cultural cycle. This does not necessarily mean that the weakening of older paternal governing roles was the efficient force that led men to seek substitutes in the form of new kinds of cultural authority. But it does mean that when men began seeking ways to correct defects in their public intellectual life their efforts moved in consonance with needs that were strong in the earlier, "lower" phases of the life cycle. Their public efforts led to new formal educational institutions for the province, especially on the upper level: institutions on the American side of the water to maintain discipline and communication among men like physicians and preachers. Private efforts, on the other hand, led toward the Lockean standards in child-raising, adapted to the American need to fight familial, rural stolidity. Together, the public and private efforts worked toward a new resolution of the disparities that appeared throughout learning. The America of 1750 was already moving away from what was left of traditionalism in the training of individuals, toward a new paternalism and a new formalism that would serve as the base points for a more mobile life.

The new did not come for all men, and it certainly did not come all at the same time for those people who did take to it. For generation after generation, men who believed in the new adjustment would keep denouncing a slackness, stolidity, and indifference that were usually identified with rural familial ways. But the culture of the region was already the kind that could push its responsive, articulate members toward the new adjustment.

The mechanisms by which men took to the new adjustment seem to have been two. One, reflecting in part the fact that many men did *not* take to the new, was a drive to restore a sense of equilibrium in life. The "old" paternalism of the well-ordered family remained a controlling ideal for men, however often it proved an unfulfilled or violated ideal, and it was symptomatic that Americans who during the latter part of the eighteenth century described the Lockean approach were likely to combine it uncritically with elements of the well-ordered family. The second means by which men took to change was a drive toward status and polish, as defined partly by the British and European culture that overshadowed their provincial life. The polish that Americans attached to the Lockean ideal of learning could turn out to be quite superficial in practice, as was proved by much of the pretentious, *nouveau* quality of the Federalist society that emerged during the latter part of the century. But that pretentious society also relied on the stolid George Washington as one of its public symbols. The polish that some Americans wanted to create through a renewed attention by fathers to the training of their sons was a substitute for values that had disappeared from the older paternalism.

In these mechanisms these New York Americans were going through a process like that experienced by some semi-developed areas of the twentieth century. In their social and economic life, they were moving through a transition like that reported in Sicily from the Old Mafia to the New Mafia. Beneath the most trivial surface of British propriety, behind the ostensible controls of Calvinism, behind too the tendency for families to compose their differences through intermarriage, the political life of the early eighteenth century was marked by a spirit of vendetta, and the economic life was marked by a somewhat gangster-like identification of particular families with important sectors of the economy like the fur trade. By the end of the century the characteristic figure was, in the extreme case, an Alexander Hamilton, forming ties with older family interests but becoming himself the incorruptible politician who perceived and advocated more sophisticated, constructive kinds of economic life.

This social situation had its mental side. In the early and middle part of the century, Americans saw that an older life, in which the well-ordered family was partly identified with cultural organization, was in danger of degenerating into a familism that was unresponsive to outside ties, whether those ties were felt to be social, moral, or intellectual. The learning cycle presented men with high standards for the mental life, yet it was failing to provide developing individuals with the environing qualities of pace, discipline, and opportunity that would be needed to realize those standards. In testable intelligence, as it has emerged from twentieth-century procedures, the average eighteenth-century New Yorker would probably have tested quite low. The difference between eighteenth-century and later standards of achieved intelligence could well have been of the same order as that which the Army Alpha tests of World War I showed as a marked differential between Northern white and deep Southern white populations.

Of course, testable intelligence is an inadequate category here. Just how inadequate will appear by comparison with the life-and-learning cycle of 1870.

At almost every stage in his life, the "typical" learning individual of 1870 encountered different expectations and produced different responses than had the individual of 1750. At the outset, where the relation between paternal and maternal influence on the child had once been like the relation between overt culture and covert culture, these influences now worked in latent or open conflict. However much the everyday behavior of many families may have resembled the slack versions of the old well-ordered family, the Lockean ideal of strict paternal influence and early repression had become the official way, and was even a little old-fashioned. A strong ideology supporting maternal influence had developed, and its impact was evidenced by the greater ease with which Americans of the Civil War generation accepted Pestalozzian ideas after those ideas had penetrated only slightly into educational thought a few decades earlier. Both the Lockean and the pro-maternal ideas favored a relatively mild, uncoercive regime for the growing child, but they differed in how consciously they sought to equip the child with a controlled personality before he entered upon the mild regime. Both approaches, however, stood at odds with what they thought a hasty sloughing off of parental responsibilities.

At first, the contradictory demands put on children, and

the new uncertainty about sex roles had tended to weaken the position of rationalistic or analytic styles within the mentalities of developing individuals. In the face of this difficulty, which in an extreme form could have produced psychopathology, the population began to rely on intuitive, spatial symbols in dealing with problems. By the middle of the century this transitional mode was being codified in the object-teaching that was intended to resolve the tension between the maternal world of home and the impersonal world of organizations like the school.

Both the paternal-maternal opposition and the pressure on children to be up and moving had their parallels in the culture of the school itself. The learning problems of children seemed to show a definite split between the sexes, in what was by then the conventional distinction: girls did better in verbal tasks, boys less poorly at quantitative. Within both the verbal and the quantitative spheres, the kinds of problem that observers reported reflected a spirit of superficiality, of haste to get over the assigned material in a formal way and in the most obvious way available. Whatever their usual oral facility might have been, children showed themselves unable to read formal school material with naturalness and empathy; complaints about this failure persisted over a generation during which the selections in readers were being constantly revised to bring them closer to what were supposed to be the actual interests of children. On the quantitative side, observers noted that children were being continually trapped in the procedural rules of arithmetic and failing to develop ability at mental arithmetic or at the logical analysis of problems.

Even while observers complained that children failed to achieve naturalness or logical flexibility in handling school material, the schools and the society were developing formal schedules to define what they expected individuals to learn from the common-school education open to all. Schools in many cities developed syllabi detailing the desired attainments in each grade. The New York State Regents developed a test covering the major subjects of common-school education and used the granting of financial aid to academies as a way to enforce this standard on private schools as well as public. Within a few years, civil service systems were to begin giving examinations that quite closely resembled the New York Regents' examination. What was perhaps most important: even in school systems where administrators tried to provide flexibility of pace for individual students, pressure from parents and principals forced children through the syllabus toward the examination in a lockstep that emphasized all the most formal, examinable features of the new standard.

The contrast between formal standards and the superficiality of student understanding took a somewhat different form for those who did move on from common-school (or even secondary) education to higher or professional education. In this case, the proportion of the population operating at the higher educational level did not increase nearly so fast as did the number of colleges and formal professional schools available to teach them. This was the height of the period of proliferating colleges, law schools, medical schools, seminaries. At the same time, popular standards did not exact training at such schools as the condition for work in business or even in many professional positions. The opportunities to study for prestigious and intellectual occupations were becoming more widespread, yet the slack demand for such schooling prevented institutions from exacting high standards. Especially were they deficient in failing to supplement lecture-method instruction with opportunities for practical work in laboratory, office, or field. Like the elementary schools, they found it easier to offer formal standards than to give students naturalness, flexibility, and understanding.

The intellectual product that came out of the course of education displayed often a quality of mechanical calculation. That much was consonant with the character of the educational system. But, as if to compensate for the obvious deficiencies of the system, it also produced a charismatic personalism in which the style of the performer made up for any lack of intellectual drive. Both these outlets—personalism and a mechanistic calculation—served to relieve people of attention to the complex or bitter internal aspects of problems. A dishonest concentration on surface, at least in the way that intellectuals talked to other people, characterized the work that all too many professional men of the period turned out.

If the cultural world of 1750 seemed at first glance to be marked by its moorings in the well-ordered family and the ideal of shared discourse, the cultural world of 1870 seemed marked by contradictions at either end of the life cycle: by the cooperative antagonism between mother and father in child-raising, and by the split between personalism and calculation in intellectual work. The personalistic and the calculating modes of work seemed different in spirit and in the talents required, yet served much the same end of maintaining large and complex social organizations. But where the simple moorings of 1750 were misleading, the more complex moorings of 1870 gave real indication of what was happening in the minds of growing individuals.

Three general features marked the learning cycle of 1870. First, just as Americans often feared that they were slipping into the urban evils that had earlier plagued Europe, the prevailing attitude toward children was becoming more like what the English attitude had been in 1750. Observers complained that parents rejected children, through such proper means as pushing them into the world or through such brutal means as infanticide and abortion. This rejection, compensated for by sentimental humanitarianism, was the most important component in the complex of forces affecting child-raising. Second, and closely related to the first feature, a sense of pressure, haste, and superficiality appeared in many different phases of the learning cycle. Third, where standards (or confusions) about authority had defined many of the issues in learning in the previous century, standards (or confusions) about the relation of sex roles to learning characterized many of the issues of the late nineteenth century.

Mental ability, or what the twentieth century would come to see as testable intelligence, had almost certainly increased since the colonial years. Society was ready to accept a testing regime, and a spirit of pace and drive had appeared throughout the culture. But this rapid gain in "intelligence" was accompanied by adjustments in the style of learning that are difficult to abstract from any gain in mental efficiency. These changes in style and manner were the costs of change.

These costs included, first, the application to intellectual life of rigid, unrealistic distinctions between masculine and feminine role behaviors. The distinctions were, incidentally, a defense against feminist claims: women were beginning to demand a social and intellectual participation long denied them on the grounds that they were subordinate, vulnerable members of creation, and it now seemed easy to avoid this challenge by countering that women were perhaps not so much inferior as "different." The idea that verbalism is feminine and analysis masculine became a cliché in nineteenth-century assumptions about learning. The mind that could move back and forth between these modes of thought, in an inclusive "Renaissance" or "Jeffersonian" manner, was becoming discredited, and the specialization that was spreading in the economy had its counterparts in both the family sphere (with its sharpening cleavage between female household and male vocation) and the intellectual sphere (with its verbal-quantitative distinction). Much of this specialization, including the specialization as to intellectual style, was almost certainly necessary for the functioning of a more complex society. If it had been based on a sense of security about changing roles, intellectual productivity could have made major gains. But because the culture reacted with anxiety, change conduced more to efficiency than to creativity, and it tended to turn thinking away from that interplay between verbalistic hunches and quantitative evidence that inheres in much of real scientific procedure.

The costs of efficiency included also the spread of a repressive tone to many areas of life other than the child-raising functions where it was originally advocated as a reform. "Repressive" indicates, again, not so much the spread of authoritarian or censorship devices as the spread of an ability to remain unconscious of important areas of experience. Throughout the culture, attention was directed more and more to surface, to external structure, to what could be symbolized by wordless images, to what could be produced by observing form and rule.

Closely allied to this repressive tone was an additional cost: the resort to mechanistic thought-patterns in order to combat the very distrust that specialization might induce. Serious men were willing to cut back on the venturesome, the uncertain, or the difficult elements in what they undertook, because those elements could not be communicated. Intellectuals sometimes said that they were producing simplification for the sake of communicating to the general public, as if what was at issue were only the old Puritan plain style. In fact, they often accepted the simple and the regular and the squared-off for themselves as well.

America after the Civil War was in the position of an anxious mind, moving into intellectual maturity without having resolved what would be the function of the mental sets on which it had relied during the course of development. On the surface were the techniques of performance and communication that the society was then acquiring. Still active as less strenuous modes of understanding were the personalistic and merely analytic styles that had emerged just before the middle of the century. And through these worked a visual or spatial mode that had helped Americans move as far as they had. The earlier among these styles were not dead fact. They were to persist as an under-theme in thought, finding echoes in the techniques that would be used to simulate spatiality for a much later generation. The whittled and then segmented layers of the lift model demonstrated a procedure that would eventually be reversed in the computer languages of the twentieth century.

The culture relied on a pretense of wholeness. In its distortions, in the contrast between sentimentality or charisma and a pervasive withdrawal from awareness of inner aspects, and in its reliance on stereotyped mechanisms in order to insure communication, the process of learning was losing its primary function of introducing men to reality. Having changed in a way that allowed for one kind of growth in mentality, the learning cycle lacked its old ostensible anchors in stability, yet did not now encourage openness or depth in experience. There were many parts of life in which the culture fostered a confidence, vigor, and clarity of action that were wholly commendable. But every individual is an intellect as well as an agent. In his role as learner, the American of the generation around 1870 was cued to evasion, to a kind of dishonesty, even to disorientation and disturbance.

Consider, then, how change in the learner affects the teacher or performer who presents his own work to the demands and limitations of people around him. Intelligence may be a trait of a whole population, but reflects energy to a focus in the performer. The performer stands for the whole audience. We are supposed to know, in matters of present-day mental development, what a Four does and what a Seven does. But what does "A 1750" do? And what, "An 1870?"

The 1750 is, say, a preacher, riding out from town to give an ordination sermon at a country church in the next county, going over his outline, wondering whether the sermon will instruct the people in the way that he intends. The main points of his argument he has used a couple of times with his own people, even though he hasn't used the same text or quite the same arrangement. He wants to warn the people against the evils of listening to wandering ranters and make them realize, if they don't already, how fortunate they will be to have a pastor of their own. He himself feels blessed in having found a new text on which to build his urgings: the passage in which God orders the reluctant preacher to go proclaim the truth in a far country. This will alert the congregation to anything he may say about wandering preachers, but he will be able to hold them first while he applies the text to the ordination: point by point, he will go over the things that make up the commission that the Lord gives to any preacher when he sets out on his duty in this world. This will include some of the hard things, such as the duty of presenting hypocrites with the scandal that is Grace, or the duty of challenging complacent peoples with the sins of which they are really guilty, things that some of the ranters have been trying to claim as their own message. It will even include the preacher's duty to go wherever the Lord sends him. With that, the congregation will be ready to receive the particular point he has planned: that the particular "wherever" to which God sends most men now is the parish to which each man is called as pastor. It is his duty to go there, and then the people's duty to attend to him. This argument should bind the congregation's consent. And yet—? There may be difficulties. Did his own congregation understand when he was making some of the same points? They seemed a little stolid when he got down to applying his ideas to the present temptation. Just to make sure, he took the trouble to do something that his own father had done every Monday night: he called his sons in and questioned them about the main points of the sermon. Their answers touched on most of the main tags but somehow lacked comprehension, and he did not want to press the matter. Perhaps the next time he plans a sermon on these ideas he should compose a very simple final section, stating in the plainest language just what he was saying. But such an explanation should be nicely finished, so that he would not offend anyone who disliked crudeness. There is not time to compose such an extra piece now. Some other time, perhaps. That might please his own congregation, but he can't be sure about this congregation out here. They are a simply schooled people, a little slow-moving. They were used to taking their lessons from well-worn books. It really isn't polish that they need, but familiarity. They might take any hard exhortations as long as there is something about them that is so familiar that the ideas don't rub too harshly. They only need rousing—as perhaps he does himself in his ride out. And at about this point in his rehearsals, he may get to the bridge over the river into the next county. The central section of the bridge, where there is a mechanism for pulling the section aside to accommodate boats, is a little shaky and alarming. But then there comes the causeway that extends over the marsh and meadow up to dry ground. He relaxes, thinking partly about the sequence of main points that he has sketched out for the day's sermon, partly about the way his own congregation has responded to the sequence of points in a similar sermon. There, too, they seemed not quite to understand what he was saying in his final application, but there was a real if decorous feeling of rousing as he came to each point. He thinks over the points as he rides. The horse will strike a solid sound as it walks over each pile that is sunk in the marsh, then will strike a higher-pitched, more hollow sound as it walks over the boards to the next pile. The sound falls and rises and falls, and the roadbed over the causeway is lower or higher in the same rhythm. Each new point in his rehearsal comes to fit a new sound and feel of security underfoot, and he feels some reassurance that he will be able to get across to the people who will be listening. They might not understand all they receive, but there should be plenty of time for the ideas to settle and find firm ground.

And the 1870? He might be an engineer, contemplating the same river crossing where the 1750 found his own reminder of familiarity. The old bridge and causeway have been replaced by a bolder wooden arch-truss, and that has been paralleled by a railroad bridge. The railroad bridge has long since been outmoded by heavy engines, and the engineer is now planning to submit plans and estimates for the new bridge that the railroad company is going to put up. The job will be profitable enough, but the site is annoying. It seems wasteful to have both a railroad and carriage bridge here, and the engineer can imagine the larger structure that might carry both in one span from dry ground to dry ground. The combined structure would work, but persuading the company and the local governments to collaborate on it would be nearly impossible, and the common road traffic is not important. Crowds may cross the bridge to see the impressive new preacher in the next town up the coast, but well-planned excursions will get most of the traffic for the railroad, and the preacher himself will soon be transferred into the city. The engineer sees that the design for a combined bridge would have to be complex and might puzzle those people, officials as well as ordinary passengers, who cross bridges all the time and therefore think that they know something about how structures should look. Such people would glance out the window as they rush over a bridge, and decide from its general appearance whether it was sound. To make the necessary designs acceptable to such people, he would have to engage in stunts of self-dramatization, building up a sense of confidence in him, to outweigh what such people think was their own judgment. The prospect disgusts him. It would make him a little unclean, like the popular preacher he knows who is drawing crowds by taking them into his confidence, or like the palavering female teacher who is professing to keep his small sons in line by tricking up ways to get them interested in their work. She is wasting time: his boys have sound minds, and can work to learn any facts in proper order, without gush. They can stick to plain facts and plain relations between facts—why, even they could cross over a bridge and make some judgment on its soundness. They are at least as bright as some of the adult bridge-builders he has dealings with. If good clear arrangement of bridge members would reassure those men it would surely make its points to his boys, too. And the kind of analysis that goes into such design is reassuring to the father as well. He has several bridges he wants to estimate and build for this railroad company and it will be convenient to use the same basic plan for all of them. No one will give much acclaim, but they should not complain, either. Even some of the insolent clerks who ride the excursion trains will think they know enough of technology to justify their looking critically as they pass over. But they will not see anything to disturb what they think they know, and will not look a second time. The railroad can go about its business, not worrying about passenger complaint. And the engineer can proceed to his next job, sure that neither the public nor the company will worry. There is work to do, and the knowledge that it can proceed is reassuring.

The first of these types of the performer imagining his audience is not what might come from a true "undeveloped" society, and the change from the first to the second is not a full course of "development" or modernization. The American of 1750, even the American on the frontier, had an elaborate culture that he had inherited. This culture included a kind of performer-audience relation that might often stand in abeyance but that could be reorganized and activated at any time out of the elements of parental example and tradition. Within that potential, though, the quality of prevailing intelligence was one of need for activation. And the primary means by which audience responses would be renewed was a ritualistic use of what was retained from the fuller culture. The *stolid* and the *incantatory* were the crucial qualities in American intelligence.

But by 1870 the salient qualities of thought had changed. What had been the stolid was now the *driven*, the sense of movement under pressure. What had been the incantatory element in performance appeal was now split between the *picturesque* and the *calculating*. Americans had gained, and gained heavily, in those qualities of intelligence that produce standardized results. In large measure they had found those qualities by the technique of disjoining mental activities that in earlier times had flowed together. Disjunction reinforced a mood of distrust, creating a kind of intellectual anxiety at odds with the surface optimism of American feeling. Yet disjunction meant also that men sought to ease distrust with methods themselves disjoined, methods that operated on the separate tracks of personalism and of a determinate rule-mindedness.

Since then, the ways mentality has changed in the twentieth century include the methods Americans used to resolve this disjunction. On one line of development, they succeeded in increasing the seriousness, discipline, and complexity with which various population groups operated. More people were exposed to the urban environment. More people reached more advanced levels of professional expertise, so that advanced audience behaviors became more common. More children progressed further through grammar school. And more families adopted a conception of child-raising (this time in the version offered by Holt and Watson) intended to produce orderly, unsentimental, self-reliant minds. This is the pattern of changes that by the 1920s produced an American mind ready to give formal, bookish, classifying responses to word-association tests.

But just as the prosperity of the 1920s concealed serious inequalities in the distribution of goods, so the advancing levels of competence and expertise concealed a lack of audience community among the intellectual strata of the population, especially a lack of shared experience between intellectual producers and intellectual consumers. This persisting disjunction pushed American thought processes toward a second line of development: the creation of techniques and languages by which experts could *simulate* whole, memorable images for audiences that were more interested in the results of speed than in the ways by which speed was achieved. In one kind of case, these speed-consumers might be the general audience of television; in another, they might be the medical diagnosticians using real-time computer results.

But ask: what within this happened to the three elements that marked the mental solutions of the mid-nineteenth century—the visual shortcut, the personalism, the determinate rule-mindedness? None disappeared, though each was reinterpreted and intensified. In a way, the culture returned to a somewhat more unified version of the mental habits of a century earlier, thus revealing its own stability.

Yet there were differences. Any cult of celebrity in twentieth-century television was certainly less solemn, taken less seriously, than the analogous cult centered on Mr. Beecher. And rule-mindedness had become less a substitute for understanding, more simply a technical procedure for making communication sharp over a wide audience: though there was no correct number of screen-lines embedded in any Platonic or school-marm's ideal of television, transmitter and receiver had to use the same number if an image was to result. And no notions of propriety dictated that each user of a computer language follow exactly the syntactical rules of that particular language—only the need to have the system work at all in producing its high-speed results. Furthermore, *some* of the procedures and rules that were required to produce high-speed results could be mastered by most individuals within the society, while even those most expert in the new techniques and languages needed to act sometimes as mere consumers of high-speed products. The practical gap between the precise, expert producer and the open-eyed consumer was certainly wide enough to define intellectual castes, but the logic of the situation (in which both roles were widely distributed through the society) meant more potential for participation and less for sentimentality.

But there were dangers, not so much that wicked communicators would deceive passive audiences as that the whole communicating audience would deceive itself. A society in which communicator and audience roles were shared by all might be one in which every person feared to throw the first criticism. If the mental difficulties of 1870 were somewhat analogous to the psychopathology of the compulsive, with his drive to observe rules and idealize the rule-giver, the mental difficulties of 1970 were analogous to the pathology of the classical hysteric, with her ability to simulate concrete realities out of assumed need and then to trust those realities as guides to action. Given this capacity for mental hysteria, one of the deficiencies in the culture had its compensations: despite all the gains that had been made in diffusing both the communicator's expertise and the viewer's credulity, enough people remained outside this synthesis to constitute a real force of emotionally based criticism. This critical spirit of the outsider often resembled the scepticism of those individuals who were more involved in producing images than in seeing them.

And in that there lay possible policy—both for the mental elevation of the society and for its emotional health. Perhaps the attempt to teach outsiders first how to be good consumers of culture was wrong-headed as well as time-wasting. Perhaps their more efficient potential was that for moving directly into the undeceived work of making and analyzing. Whatever the virtues of specialization, there were many males who had been *defined* outside the verbal culture. And females who had been defined outside the quantitative culture. And blacks, of both sexes, who had been defined into the role of colonials. When the good bureaucratic society took pride in the number within its audiences who could step into performer roles, it ignored the variety of ways in which it froze out people's thinking. Of course the contented "intelligent" consumer, when he moves into producing, may become a nice performer of other men's work. But the excluded consumer may produce theory and art.

APPENDIX

AGE AND EDUCATIONAL DEVELOPMENT: DUTCHESS COUNTY, NEW YORK, 1850

THE 1850 Census was the first to collect enough information on individuals to permit detailed analysis of educational conditions. In execution, that Census still did not achieve the quality that the twentieth century would like. Definitions of categories like literacy were often vague, interpretation by census-takers seems to have varied from district to district, and the published tables did not break data down in ways that would answer some educational questions. The tables reported the distribution of the population into age groups: it reported numbers of illiterates in each district, numbers of workers of various occupations, numbers of students attending school, and numbers of persons born in different states or countries. They did not cross-analyze these categories against each other, as, for example, by breaking school-attendance and literacy down by age; they also did not do much with family size and structure, on which the schedules did collect extensive data. The raw data for such analyses are available in the manuscript census returns. Execution of the tabulation, even on a significant *selection* of towns or counties, would require a large investment in clerical work (the subsequent computer processing would be relatively inexpensive).

For the purposes of this essay the returns for selected towns in Dutchess County, New York, have been retabulated to show: (1) the time perspective for literacy, and (2) the relations of family structure and economic conditions to school attendance. The towns, making about half the population of the county, are Fishkill (a commercial and manufacturing town), Rhinebeck (a large, prosperous, mainly agricultural town, with few families who had migrated in from outside the state), and six smaller, less prosperous agricultural towns (Stanford, Red Hook, Pine Plains, Union Vale, Pawling, and La Grange).

The logic used in the analysis of literacy was stated in studies by the Census Bureau late in the nineteenth century and applied later by international agencies. If a population is broken down by age groups, the literacy rate of each group reflects the efficiency of the country's or district's elementary-education system at the time that group was eligible for schooling—when it was about ten years old, to take a specific year—together with the extent to which adult education reached illiterates. Both these effects showed in the literacy rates of United States Negroes after the Civil War. Both, but mainly the state of elementary education, showed in the literacy rates for eastern European countries at the end of the nineteenth century; then the backward projection of rates for different ages produced curves with increases and plateaus corresponding to the course of school reform in each country.

The general hypothesis "tested" in the analysis of school attendance is that pressures from the crowded conditions of large American families were one element in the drive to expand and modernize schools in the nineteenth century.

On both these subjects, some tentative inferences have been presented in the body of the essay. The tables below give the relevant details, plus some other information whose relevance the reader might get ideas about. All this material is highly tentative in character, since the representative character of the towns selected is plausible, not provable, and since the numbers of individuals in separate cells of tables is sometimes small.

A. LITERACY

TABLE 1. LITERACY BY AGE AND TOWN

Age:	*20-29*	*30-39*	*40-49*	*50-59*	*60-69*	*70-79*	*80-89*	*90+*	*Total*
Fishkill									
Literate	1,979	1,206	961	648	299	148	38	5	5,284
Illiterate	268	201	146	89	42	20	11	2	779
% Illiterate	11.9	14.3	13.2	12.1	12.3	11.9	22.5	28.6	12.9
Rhinebeck									
Literate	460	348	295	200	121	67	16	1	1,508
Illiterate	2	2	5	3	4	1	0	0	17
% Illiterate	0.4	0.6	1.7	1.5	3.2	1.5	0	0	1.1
Smaller Towns									
Literate	2,081	1,552	1,020	720	476	195	59	13	6,116
Illiterate	86	77	71	59	40	26	3	0	362
% Illiterate	4.0	4.7	6.5	7.6	7.8	11.8	4.8	0	5.6
Total Group									
Literate	4,520	3,106	2,276	1,568	896	410	113	19	12,908
Illiterate	356	280	222	151	86	47	14	2	1,158
% Illiterate	7.3	8.3	8.9	8.8	8.8	10.3	11.0	9.5	8.2

TABLE 2. LITERACY BY AGE AND SEX, ALL TOWNS

Age:	*20-29*	*30-39*	*40-49*	*50-59*	*60-69*	*70-79*	*80-89*	*90+*	*Total*
Male									
Literate	2,200	1,597	1,146	793	457	199	49	5	6,446
Illiterate	128	121	97	75	38	17	6	1	483
% Illiterate	5.5	7.0	7.8	8.6	7.7	7.9	10.9	16.7	7.0
Female									
Literate	2,319	1,508	1,130	773	439	211	64	14	6,458
Illiterate	228	159	125	76	48	30	8	1	675
% Illiterate	9.0	9.5	10.0	9.0	9.9	12.5	11.1	6.7	9.5

TABLE 3. LITERACY BY AGE AND RACE, ALL TOWNS

Age:	*20-29*	*30-39*	*40-49*	*50-59*	*60-69*	*70-79*	*80-89*	*90+*	*Total*
White									
Literate	4,416	3,027	2,228	1,546	876	404	111	19	12,627
Illiterate	284	220	173	104	63	33	6	0	883
% Illiterate	6.0	6.8	7.2	6.3	6.7	7.6	5.1	0	6.5
Black									
Literate	89	62	39	18	12	5	2	0	227
Illiterate	64	52	48	45	23	13	8	2	255
% Illiterate	41.8	45.6	55.2	71.4	65.7	72.2	80.0	100.0	53.0
Mulatto									
Literate	15	16	9	4	8	1	0	0	53
Illiterate	8	7	1	2	0	1	0	0	19
% Illiterate	34.8	30.4	10.0	33.3	0	50.0	–	–	26.4

TABLE 4. LITERACY BY AGE AND SELECTED BIRTHPLACES, ALL TOWNS

Age:	*20-24*	*25-29*	*30-39*	*40-49*	*50-59*	*60-69*	*70-79*	*80-89*	*90+*	*Total*
New York (White)										
Literate	1,833	1,743	2,500	1,883	1,343	787	356	99	15	10,559
Illiterate	57	79	126	130	87	55	31	6	0	571
% Illiterate	3.0	4.3	4.8	6.5	6.1	6.5	8.0	5.7	0	5.0
New England, New Jersey, Penna., Del., Ohio										
Literate	112		94	83	75	46	27	7	1	445
Illiterate	1		4	3	1	0	1	0	0	10
% Illiterate	0.9		4.1	3.5	1.3	0	3.6	0	0	2.2
Ireland										
Literate	250	228	232	123	51	13	6	1	1	906
Illiterate	63	64	72	28	12	7	0	0	0	246
% Illiterate	20.1	21.9	23.7	18.5	19.0	35.0	0	0	0	20.5

TABLE 5. LITERACY BY AGE AND SELECTED OCCUPATIONS OF FAMILY HEAD

Age:	*20-29*	*30-39*	*40-49*	*50-59*	*60-69*	*70-79*	*80-89*	*90+*	*Total*
Farmers and Gentlemen									
Literate	1,482	1,145	912	728	416	188	49	10	4,930
Illiterate	58	44	43	34	16	5	1	0	201
% Illiterate	3.8	3.7	4.5	4.5	3.7	2.6	2.0	0	3.9
Major Professions									
Literate	89	76	49	39	14	5	3	0	275
Illiterate	1	0	0	1	0	0	0	0	2
% Illiterate	1.1	0	0	2.5	0	0	0	—	0.7
Manufacturing, Cloth									
Literate	165	92	81	44	9	5	1	0	397
Illiterate	13	6	9	3	0	1	0	0	32
% Illiterate	7.3	6.1	10.0	6.4	0	16.7	0	—	7.5
Mfg., except Cloth									
Literate	770	524	323	190	95	32	5	0	1,939
Illiterate	21	10	15	3	4	3	1	0	57
% Illiterate	2.7	1.9	4.4	1.6	4.0	8.6	16.7	—	2.9
Servants and Laborers									
Literate	1,022	595	426	211	111	38	9	1	2,413
Illiterate	195	187	121	74	29	17	5	1	629
% Illiterate	16.0	23.9	22.1	26.0	20.7	30.9	35.7	50.0	20.7

B. SCHOOL ATTENDANCE

TABLE 6. SCHOOL ATTENDANCE BY AGE AND SEX, ALL TOWNS

Age:	*Under 1*	*1*	*2*	*3*	*4*	*5*	*6*	*7*	*8*	*9*
Male										
Attended	2	1	4	11	66	166	222	245	261	234
Did not	298	329	324	314	290	180	102	76	73	52
% did	1	0	1	3	19	48	69	76	78	82
Female										
Attended	3	1	4	14	47	142	197	225	255	201
Did not	274	308	334	336	282	174	119	75	56	49
% did	1	0	1	4	14	45	62	75	82	80
Total										
Attended	5	2	8	25	113	308	419	471	516	435
Did not	572	637	658	636	572	354	221	151	129	101
% did	1	0	1	4	16	47	65	76	80	81

Age:	*10*	*11*	*12*	*13*	*14*	*15*	*16*	*17*	*18*	*19*	*20+*	*Total*
Male												
Attended	260	185	242	179	172	97	85	47	34	19	29	2,561
Did not	63	59	101	96	146	148	212	240	240	224	7,058	10,625
% did	80	76	71	65	54	40	29	16	12	8	0	19.4
Female												
Attended	247	200	225	155	144	86	48	24	8	9	23	2,258
Did not	86	74	106	103	175	204	258	293	324	272	7,348	11,212
% did	74	73	68	60	45	30	16	8	2	3	0	16.8
Total												
Attended	507	386	467	334	316	183	133	71	42	28	52	4,821
Did not	149	133	207	199	321	352	471	509	565	497	14,411	21,845
% did	77	74	69	63	50	34	22	12	7	5	0	18.1

Age:	*3*	*4*	*5*	*6*	*7*	*8*	*9*	*10*	*11*	*12*	*13*	*14*	*15*	*16*	*17*	*18*	*19*
N.Y.-born Whites																	
Attended	24	101	290	389	438	481	409	460	365	432	313	296	177	124	69	41	25
Did not	572	520	318	192	125	103	78	117	109	159	152	267	295	383	431	443	401
% did	4	16	48	67	78	82	84	80	77	73	67	53	37	24	14	8	6
N.Y.-born Non-whites																	
Attended	1	8	6	11	12	14	9	12	7	15	4	3	3	4	1	0	0
Did not	29	28	17	16	14	18	11	15	11	17	17	17	20	29	25	22	18
% did	3	22	26	41	46	44	45	44	39	47	19	15	13	12	4	0	0
Ireland-born																	
Attended	0	0	3	7	8	10	5	10	3	6	3	4	1	0	0	0	0
Did not	10	9	8	3	5	3	7	8	8	15	12	20	21	29	31	68	48
% did	0	0	27	70	62	77	42	56	27	29	20	17	5	0	0	0	0
U.S. born, but some of family born abroad																	
Attended	4	6	30	38	29	45	30	28	16	27	5	15	7	2	0	0	1
Did not	69	43	32	14	11	3	2	16	5	15	10	20	17	17	9	11	9
% did	5	12	48	73	73	94	94	64	76	64	33	43	29	11	0	0	10
N.Y.-born, but some of family born other U.S.																	
Attended	2	12	7	21	13	15	11	18	18	16	14	10	4	4	0	2	0
Did not	20	21	8	4	6	8	4	5	3	4	5	7	14	7	10	13	7
% did	9	36	47	84	68	65	73	78	86	80	74	59	22	36	0	13	0

TABLE 8. SCHOOL ATTENDANCE BY AGE AND SELECTED FAMILY SIZES, FISHKILL, N.Y.-BORN WHITES

Age:	*4*	*5*	*6*	*7*	*8*	*9*	*10*	*11*	*12*	*13*	*14*
Nuclear Family Size											
4											
Attended	1	4	3	22	14	4	14	10	8	9	6
Did not	20	7	4	2	5	3	6	4	13	5	13
% did	5	36	43	92	74	57	70	71	38	64	32
5											
Attended	6	11	24	17	16	10	18	17	23	17	15
Did not	38	20	6	5	5	5	6	4	9	7	19
% did	14	35	80	77	76	67	75	81	72	71	44
6											
Attended	8	21	29	22	33	32	23	26	24	9	12
Did not	33	23	10	6	5	5	5	3	8	13	15
% did	20	48	74	79	87	86	82	90	75	41	44
7											
Attended	3	20	28	36	27	40	36	16	28	29	21
Did not	34	34	13	13	7	8	5	11	10	11	13
% did	8	37	68	73	79	83	88	59	74	73	62
8											
Attended	5	25	25	32	30	26	40	20	30	27	12
Did not	27	17	5	9	3	4	4	7	9	11	21
% did	16	60	83	78	91	87	91	74	77	71	36
9											
Attended	4	7	20	19	26	19	32	22	22	20	16
Did not	31	13	13	3	3	2	6	3	5	4	12
% did	11	35	61	86	90	90	84	88	81	83	57
10											
Attended	1	10	11	16	17	18	19	16	12	7	11
Did not	11	8	8	3	4	1	3	7	8	9	13
% did	8	56	58	84	81	95	86	70	60	44	46
11											
Attended	2	2	5	9	8	8	7	4	4	5	4
Did not	8	5	6	3	1	1	2	2	5	4	9
% did	20	29	45	75	89	89	78	67	44	56	31

TABLE 9. SCHOOL ATTENDANCE BY AGE AND SELECTED FAMILY SIZES, SMALLER TOWNS, N.Y.-BORN WHITE

Age:	*4*	*5*	*6*	*7*	*8*	*9*	*10*	*11*	*12*	*13*	*14*
Nuclear Family Size											
4											
Attended	0	8	7	14	16	11	12	14	15	14	21
Did not	14	12	4	4	1	2	10	9	7	12	14
% did	0	40	64	78	94	85	55	61	68	54	60
5											
Attended	3	16	14	28	24	20	22	13	15	21	14
Did not	49	23	11	6	10	5	6	7	15	11	14
% did	6	41	56	82	71	80	79	65	50	66	50
6											
Attended	17	23	36	35	29	32	25	29	40	11	16
Did not	44	39	32	18	10	6	9	8	12	7	17
% did	28	37	53	66	74	84	74	78	77	61	48
7											
Attended	9	26	31	38	37	37	31	28	34	12	26
Did not	43	23	16	9	14	8	7	8	9	10	8
% did	17	53	66	81	73	82	82	78	79	55	76
8											
Attended	7	14	21	24	24	20	21	31	15	20	14
Did not	25	20	13	10	12	9	9	6	11	4	19
% did	22	41	62	71	67	69	70	84	58	83	42
9											
Attended	1	8	15	9	22	18	23	19	21	15	15
Did not	22	12	9	10	2	8	3	3	4	5	8
% did	4	40	62	47	92	69	88	86	84	75	65
10											
Attended	3	9	11	11	18	14	19	13	21	13	15
Did not	16	10	13	5	10	2	5	5	7	5	7
% did	16	47	46	69	64	88	79	72	75	72	68
11											
Attended	1	3	4	4	9	2	8	5	7	7	4
Did not	7	3	3	2	3	1	3	2	1	4	3
% did	13	50	57	67	75	67	73	71	88	64	57

BIBLIOGRAPHIES

In some parts of these essays, the footnotes suffice as selective bibliography to the topics treated and emphases explored. For certain subjects, though, the essays draw on research materials and primary sources rather more diffuse than what bears on any particular passage: for the development of child-raising ideas in the eighteenth and nineteenth centuries, for the development of the school system as a setting where children act and teachers observe learning problems, and for the largely more recent articulation of ideas about the relations between child development and intelligence levels.

I. Child-Raising Attitudes before 1900

Abbott, Eloise Miles, *Personal Sketches and Recollections* (Boston, 1861).

Abbott, Jacob, *Congo; or, Jasper's Experience in Command* (New York, 1857).

———, *The Corner-Stone, or A Familiar Illustration of the Principles of Christian Truth* (Boston, 1834).

———, *The Duties of Parents, in Regard to the Schools Where Their Children Are Instructed* (Boston, 1834).

———, *Early Piety* (New York, 1834).

———, *Every Day Duty* (London, 1837).

———, ed., *Fire-side Piety, or The Duties and Enjoyments of Family Religion* (New York, 1834).

———, *Gentle Measures in the Management and Training of the Young; or The Principles on Which a Firm Parental Authority May Be Established and Maintained, Without Violence or Anger* (New York, 1871).

Abbott, Jacob, *Harlie's Letter; or, How to Learn with Little Teaching* (New York, 1864).

———, *Jasper; or, The Spoiled Child Recovered* (New York, 1857).

———, *A Lecture on Moral Education, Delivered in Boston, before the American Institute of Instruction, August 26, 1831* (Boston, 1831).

———, *The Little Learner, Learning about Right and Wrong* (New York, 1857).

———, *Parental Duties in the Promotion of Early Piety* (London, 1836).

———, *Prank, or The Philosophy of Tricks and Mischief* (New York, 1855).

———, *The Rollo Code of Morals; or, The Rules of Duty for Children* (Boston, 1841).

———, *Rollo Learning to Read; or, Easy Stories for Young Children* (Boston, 1835).

———, *The Sea-Shore; or, How to Plan Pic-nics and Excursions* (New York, 1863).

———, *The Way to Do Good; or The Christian Character Mature* (Boston, 1836).

———, *The Young Christian; or A Familiar Illustration of the Principles of Christian Duty* (Boston, 1835).

Abbott, John S. C., *The Child at Home* (Boston, 1834).

Alcott, William A., *The Young Mother, or Management of Children in Regard to Health*, 17th edn. (Boston, 1849).

Alexander, James W., and others, *The Man of Business, Considered in His Various Relations* (New York, 1857).

[Allestree, Richard], *The Ladies Calling* (Oxford, 1673).

Ambrose, Isaac, *The Well-Ordered Family* (Boston, 1762).

Bakewell, Mrs. J., *The Mother's Practical Guide in the Early Training of Her Children* (New York, 1843, from 2nd London edn.).

Barnard, John, *A Call to Parents, and Children* (Boston, 1737).

Bass, Benjamin, *Parents and Children Advised and Exhorted to Their Duty* (Newport, R.I., 1730).

Baxter, Richard, *A Christian Directory* (London, 1678).

Blackwell, Elizabeth, *Counsel to Parents on the Moral Education of Their Children* (New York, 1880).

Brackett, Anna C., and others, *The Education of American Girls* (New York, 1874).

Buchan, William, *Family Medical Library* (Cincinnati, 1843).

Bulkeley, H. W., *A Word to Parents, or The Obligations and Limitations of Parental Authority* (Philadelphia, 1858).

Burr, Aaron, *A Discourse Delivered at New-Ark, in New-Jersey, January 1, 1755. Being a Day Set Apart for Solemn Fasting and Prayer, on Account of the Late Encroachments of the French* (New York, 1755).

Cadogan, William, *An Essay upon Nursing and the Management of Children, from Their Birth to Three Years of Age* (London, reprinted Boston, 1772).

Carll, M. M., "Motives to Obedience on the Part of Children," *District School Journal*, VII (1846/47), 56, reprinted from his *Essay on Moral Culture* (Philadelphia, 1833).

Carr, Walter L., "Early Regularity in Diet and Sleep," *Babyhood*, III (1886/87), 334-336.

Chavasse, Pye Henry, *Advice to a Wife and Advice to a Mother on the Management of Her Own Health and on the Treatment of Children*, 20th-century edn. (New York, [ca 1907]).

Cobb, Lyman, *The Evil Tendencies of Corporal Punishment as a Means of Moral Discipline in Families and Schools* (New York, 1847).

The Countryman's Lamentation, on the Neglect of a Proper Education of Children; with an Address to the Inhabitants of New-Jersey (Philadelphia, 1762).

[Craik, Dinah Maria], *Sermons out of Church* (New York, 1875).

Defoe, Daniel, *The Family-Instructor* (Philadelphia, 1792).

Doddridge, Philip, *Sermons on the Religious Education of*

Children, Preached at Northampton, 4th edn. (Boston, 1763).

Dwight, Theodore, *Travels in America* (Glasgow, 1848).

Edgeworth, Maria, *Early Lessons*, 5th edn. (4 vols.; London, 1824).

"Ethics of Marriage and Divorce," *National Quarterly Review*, XXXVII (1878), 27-49.

The Family Book; or, Instructions Concerning All the Relations of Life (New York, 1835).

Fénelon, François, *Some Advice to Governesses and Teachers* (New York, 1799).

Fernald, James C., *The Home Training of Children* (New York, 1898).

Foster, James, *The Married State; Its Obligations and Duties. With Hints on the Education of a Family*, 3rd edn. (New York, 1845).

Fowler, Orville S., *Phrenology and Physiology Explained and Applied to Education and Self-Improvement, Including the Intellectual and Moral Education and Government of Children* (New York, 1842).

———, *Self-Culture, and Perfection of Character, Including the Management of Youth* (New York, 1848).

———, *Sexual Science; . . . as Taught by Phrenology* (Philadelphia, 1870).

Friends, Society of, *Advice and Caution from Our Monthly Meeting at Philadelphia, Held the 25th Day of the Sixth Month, 1732, Concerning Children and Servants* [Philadelphia, 1732].

Hampshire Northern Association, *Sermons, on Various Important Doctrine and Duties of the Christian Religion; Selected from the Manuscripts of Several Ministers, Members of the Northern Association, in the County of Hampshire* (Northampton, Mass., 1799).

Harker, Ahimaaz, *A Companion for the Young People of North-America. Particularly Recommended to Those within the Three Provinces of New-York, New-Jersey, and Pennsylvania* (New York, 1767).

Hinkley, Susan H., "The Spirit of the Age in Education," *Babyhood* XI (1894/95), 268-271, 299-302.

Holt, L. Emmett, *The Care and Feeding of Children*, 1st edn. (New York, 1895); 3rd edn. (New York, 1904).

———, "The Feeding of Older Infants and Young Children," *Babyhood*, III (1886/87), 122-128.

———, "How Infants Should be Housed and Fed," *Babyhood*, IV (1887/88), 331-333, 359-363.

Hopkins, Erastus, *The Family a Religious Institution; or Heaven Its Model* (Troy, N.Y., 1840).

The Instructor (10 numbers; New York, 1755).

James, John Angell, *The Family Monitor or A Help to Domestic Happiness*, 1st American edn. (Boston & New York, 1829).

Keagy, John Miller, *An Address on Early Education* (New York, 1833).

Locke, John, *Some Thoughts Concerning Education*, in *Works* (London, 1823).

Mellen, John, *A Discourse Containing a Serious Address to Persons of Several Ages and Characters* (Boston, 1757).

Meyer, Bertha, *Aids to Family Government; or, From the Cradle to the School, According to Froebel. . . . To Which Has Been Added an Essay on the Rights of Children and the True Principles of Family Government, by Herbert Spencer*, tr. from 2nd German edn. (New York, 1879).

Mosher, Martha B., *Child Culture in the Home: a Book for Mothers* (New York, 1898).

New York State Convention of County Superintendents, May 1843, Minutes, *District School Journal*, IV (1843), 49-64.

Orcutt, Hiram, *The Parents' Manual; or, Home and School Training* (Boston, 1874; new edn. Boston, 1892).

Pemberton, Ebenezer, *Advice to a Son. A Discourse at the Request of a Gentleman in New-England, upon His Son's Going into Europe* (London, 1705).

Phelps, Almira Lincoln, *Christian Households* (New York, 1860).

Phillips, Samuel, *Children Well Imployed, and, Jesus Much Delighted* (Boston, 1739).

The Poor Orphans Legacy: Being a Short Collection of Godly Counsels and Exhortations to a Young Arising Generation. . . . By a Minister of the Gospel (Philadelphia, 1734).

Rankin, Francis H., *Hygiene of Childhood: Suggestions for the Care of Children after the Period of Infancy to the Completion of Puberty* (New York, 1890).

Rapson, Richard L., "The American Child as Seen by British Travelers, 1845-1935," *American Quarterly*, XVII (1965), 520-534.

Rich, Ezekiel, "Objects of Early Education," *Monthly Educator* (Rochester), I (1847), 14, 29-30, 61; II (1848), 13-14.

Sedgwick, Elizabeth Buckminster, *A Talk with My Pupils* (New York, 1863).

Sigourney, Lydia Huntley, *Letters to Mothers* (New York, 1839).

Sizer, Nelson, *Forty Years in Phrenology* (New York, 1891).

———, *How to Teach According to Temperament and Mental Development; or, Phrenology in the Schoolroom and the Family* (New York, 1877).

Smith, Hugh, *Letters to Married Ladies, to Which is Added, a Letter on Corsets, and Copious Notes by an American Physician*, 3rd edn. (New York, 1832).

Smith, J. Lewis, "The Feeding of Infants," *Babyhood*, II (1885/86), 42-45.

Smith, Josiah, *The Young Man Warn'd: or, Solomon's Counsel to His Son. A Discourse Delivered at Cainboy, in the Province of South-Carolina* (Boston, 1730).

The Son Unguided His Mother's Shame; *and the Social Position and Culture Due to Women. Two Addresses before the Maternal Association of the Amity-st. Baptist Ch., N. Y.* (New York, 1847).

Spencer, Herbert, *Education, Intellectual, Moral and Physical* (New York, 1861).

Spring, Gardiner, *Hints to Parents: a Sermon on the Religious Education of Children* (New York, 1833).

Steele, David, and a friend, *A System of Moral Philosophy, Adapted to Children and Families, and Especially to Common Schools* (Boston, 1847).

Taylor, John, *The Value of a Child; or, Motives to the Good Education of Children. In a Letter to a Daughter* (Philadelphia, 1753).

[Terhune, Mary V.], *Our Baby's First Year* (New York, 1886).

Townsend, Shippie, *A Practical Essay* (Boston, 1783).

[Vanderheyden, J.D.E.], *An Essay on the Intellectual, Moral, and Religious Instruction of the Youth of This State, by Means of Common Schools: . . . Read before the Troy Lyceum* (Troy, 1834).

Wadsworth, Benjamin, *The Well-Ordered Family* (Boston, 1719).

Waldstein, Louis, *The Subconscious Self and Its Relation to Education and Health* (New York, 1897).

"Walking Baby to Sleep," *Babyhood,* I (1884/85), 89.

Watts, Isaac, *Christian Discipline; or the Character of a Polite Young Gentleman* (Boston, 1759).

Whitman, Jason, "Home Preparation for School," *District School Journal,* IX (1848/49), 51-57, 67-72.

Wiggin, Kate Douglas, *Children's Rights; a Book of Nursery Logic* (Boston & New York, 1892).

Winterburn, Florence Hall, *Nursery Ethics* (New York, 1899).

Witherspoon, John, *A Series of Letters on Education* (New York, 1797).

Wright, Henry C., *The Unwelcome Child; or, the Crime of an Undesigned and Undesired Maternity* (Boston, 1860).

II. School Development

For all the topics under this heading, the indispensable first sources are the school reports and educational periodicals that many agencies in New York published during the nineteenth century. They do have the defect, though, that they began quite early to pick up cues from a standard line of thought that was being pushed by promoters and bureaucrats. Despite this screen, much authentic observation slipped into the two main sources:

the *District School Journal of the State of New York*, published in Albany from 1840 to 1852;
and the *Annual Report* of the Superintendent of Public Instruction of the State of New York, published under varying titles from 1855 on.

The *District School Journal* included not only signed articles but revealing advertisements, pointed bits of news, and selected statistics. The Superintendent's *Report* included not only comments, recommendations, and statistics from his own office, but excerpts from reports sent in by county and district superintendents. Although these local reports often reflected the pedagogical orthodoxy being retailed by school agencies (such as the *District School Journal*), they sometimes spilled over with an authenticity hard to find in other sources. Many local boards or school superintendents also published their own reports, which sometimes spoke free from the screen of educational orthodoxy. So, too, did the reports from some private schools. From the following places and schools, reports proved particularly useful for the years indicated:

Adelphi Academy (Brooklyn), 1864-1869, 1872, 1876.
Albany, 1870, 1877.
Albany Academy, 1865/66-1880/81.
Brooklyn, 1867, 1875.
Kingston, 1865-1868, 1871, 1872.
New York City and County, 1856-1880.
Packer Collegiate Institute (Brooklyn), 1857, 1870, 1876.
Rochester, 1844, 1852, 1872, 1877/78.
Saratoga Springs, 1874, 1880-1884.

Schenectady, 1856, 1873.
Syracuse, 1852, 1855-1873.
Utica, 1868-1870.

1. Organizational Problems

Adams, Francis, *The Free School System of the United States* (London, 1875).

Benezet, Anthony, *Some Necessary Remarks on the Education of the Youth in the Country-Parts of This, and the Neighbouring Governments* [Philadelphia, 1778?].

Bourne, William Oland, *History of the Public School Society of the City of New York* (New York, 1870).

Cabot, J. E., Review of Packard, *The Daily Public School in the United States* (Philadelphia, 1866), in *North American Review*, CIII (1866), 291-302.

Dwight, S. E., *The Life of President Edwards* (New York, 1830).

Finegan, Thomas E., *Free Schools: A Documentary History of the Free School Movement in New York State* (Albany, 1921), including Robert Francis Seybolt, "The Evening Schools of Colonial New York City," 630-652, and Seybolt, "New York Colonial Schoolmasters," 653-669.

Fraser, James (assistant commissioner, School Inquiries Commission of Great Britain), *Report . . . on the Common School System of the United States and of the Provinces of Upper and Lower Canada* (London, 1866).

Free School Society, *Manual of the Lancasterian System, of Teaching Reading, Writing, Arithmetic, and Needle-Work, as Practised in the Schools of the Free-School Society, of New-York* (New York, 1820).

Friends' Academy, Union Springs, N.Y., *Catalogue of the Officers and Students of Friends' New York Yearly Meeting Boarding School* (Auburn, 1866).

"German-American Citizens," *The System of Public Instruction in the State and City of New York. A Memorial, Addressed to the State Legislature and the School Authori-*

ties by the German-American Citizens of the City of New York (New York, 1869).

Hall, Baynard R., *Teaching, a Science: The Teacher an Artist* (New York, 1848).

Hinsdale, Burke Aaron, *Our Common Schools: A Fuller Statement of the Views Set Forth in the Pamphlet Entitled, "Our Common-School Education," with Especial Reference to the Reply of Superintendent A. J. Rickoff* (Cleveland, 1878).

Katz, Michael B., *The Irony of Early School Reform* (Cambridge, Mass., 1968).

Kemp, William Webb, *The Support of Schools in Colonial New York by the Society for the Propagation of the Gospel in Foreign Ports* (New York, 1913).

Kiddle, Henry, T. F. Harrison, & N. A. Calkins, *How to Teach; a Manual of Methods for a Graded Course of Instruction* (New York, 1874).

Livingston, William, and others, *The Independent Reflector*, ed. Milton M. Klein (Cambridge, Mass., 1963).

Miller, George Frederick, *The Academy System of the State of New York* (Albany, 1922).

Mount Pleasant Academy, a Select Boarding School for Boys, at Sing Sing, Westchester County, New York. Maj. W. W. Benjamin, Superintendent (New York, 1865).

New York City and County, Board of Education, *Discussion before the Joint Committee on Studies, &c., of the Board of Education, (Appointed February 19th, 1868,) in Reference to Modifications of the Course of Studies, &c. 1868* (New York, 1868).

Northend, Charles, *Obstacles to the Greater Success of Common Schools* (Boston, 1844).

On the Establishment of Public Schools, in the City of New-York (New York, 1825).

Orcutt, Hiram, *Hints to Common School Teachers, Parents and Pupils; or Gleanings from School-Life Experience*, rev. edn. (Rutland, Vt., 1859).

[Packard, Frederick Adolphus]. *The Daily Public School in the United States* (Philadelphia, 1866).

Passy, Paul, *L'instruction primaire aux États-unis: rapport présenté au ministre de l'instruction publique* (Paris, 1885).

Pratt, Daniel J., *Annals of Public Education in the State of New York from 1626 to 1746* (Albany, 1872).

Public School Society, *An Account of the Free-School Society of New-York* (New York, 1814).

Public School Society, *An Address to the Parents and Guardians of the Children Belonging to the Schools under the Care of the New-York Free-School Society, by the Trustees of the Institution* (New York, 1819).

R., E., "Notes on Teaching," *Monthly Educator* (Rochester), I (1847/48), 83.

Rice, Joseph Mayer, *The Public-School System of the United States* (New York, 1893).

Rickoff, Andrew J., *Past and Present of Our Common School Education. Reply to President B. A. Hinsdale* (Cleveland, 1877).

Schneider, Herbert and Carol, *Samuel Johnson, President of King's College: His Life and Writings*, 4 vols. (New York, 1929).

Tweed, B. F., *"The Public-School System a Failure." A Reply to Richard Grant White. A Paper Read before the Massachusetts Teachers' Association, December, 1880* (Boston & New York, [1880?]).

Vaughan, Mary C., "Julian Gurdon: Schoolmaster," *American Educational Monthly*, III (1866), 24-30, 63-68, 104-108, 141-145, 185-189, 229-233.

[Wellington, O. H.], *Some Principles and Methods, Adopted and Imperfectly Tried Twenty Years Ago, in an Ideal School. Prepared at the Request of Mrs. Elizabeth Thompson* (New York, 1879).

White, Richard Grant, "The Public-School Failure," *North American Review*, CXXXI (1880), 537-550.

Whitney, Barney, *Fifty Years a Teacher* (Syracuse, 1902).

Willson, Marcus, and others, "Report of the Committee to Whom Was Referred the Consideration of the Subject of Recommending the Adoption of a Systematic Course of Common School and Academical Education," *New York Teacher*, III (1854/55), 52-61.

2. Examination Systems

Blake, Sophia Jex, *A Visit to Some American Schools and Colleges* (London, 1867).

Boston, School Committee, *Report on the Public Schools, and the Systems of Public Instruction in the Cities of New York, Philadelphia, Baltimore and Washington* (Boston, 1867).

Burked, S. G., *The Examiner; Designed for Teachers and Students Preparing to Teach* (Chicago, 1865).

Comstock, J. M., *The Civil Service in the United States* (New York, 1885).

Edward Danforth, "The Condition of Education," *American Educational Monthly*, IX (1872), 413-418.

Gifford, Walter John, *Historical Development of the New York State High School System* (Albany, 1922).

Hathaway, B. A., *1001 Questions and Answers on the Theory and Practice of Teaching* (Cleveland, 1886).

Hoose, James H., "The Arithmetical Preparation Necessary to Commence the Study of Algebra," in New York Regents, *Annual Report*, 80th (1867), 621-628.

Kiddle, Henry, and Alexander J. Schem, *Cyclopaedia of Education* (New York, 1877).

New York Regents, *Annual Report*, 49th-85th (1836-1872).

Phelps, William F., *The Teacher's Handbook, for the Institute and Class Room* (New York, 1874).

Pratt, Daniel J., "Annals of Public Education in the State of New York. . . . 1664-1746," in New York Regents, *Annual Report*, 83rd (1870), 617-692.

Stone, Isaac, *The Elementary and Complete Examiner; or, Candidate's Assistant. Prepared to Aid Teachers in Securing Certificates from Boards of Examiners, and Pupils in Preparing Themselves for Promotion* (New York & Chicago, 1869).

Swett, John, *Questions for Written Examinations: an Aid to Candidates for Teachers' Certificates* (New York, 1872).

Werner, Adolph, "The Examinations of the New York Free Academy," in New York Regents, *Annual Report*, 78th (1865), 376-381.

Williams, James Watson, *Annual Report of the Superintendent of Schools of the City of Utica: An Historical Address* (Utica, 1868).

3. Learning Problems

A. COMBINED TOPICS

Abercrombie, John, *Inquiries Concerning the Intellectual Powers and the Investigation of Truth; with Additions and Explanations to Adapt the Work to the Use of Schools and Academies, by Jacob Abbott* (Boston & Philadelphia, 1835).

Abbott, Jacob, *The Teacher: or, Moral Influences Employed in the Instruction and Government of the Young* (Boston, 1836).

———, *Timboo and Fanny; or, The Art of Self-Instruction* (New York, 1855).

Barnard, Henry, *Papers for the Teacher*, 1st series (New York, 1860).

Blackwell, Elizabeth, *The Laws of Life, with Special Reference to the Physical Education of Girls* (New York, 1852).

C., W. C., "Brains—How to Get Them," *American Educational Monthly*, II (1865), 236-238.

D., D., "Elementary Education," *American Educational Monthly*, IX (1872), 561-562.

DeGraff, Esmond V., *The School-Room Guide, Embodying the Instruction Given by the Author at Teachers' Institutes*, 2nd edn. (Syracuse, N.Y., 1879).

Fowle, William B., *Teachers' Institute; or, Familiar Hints to Young Teachers* (Boston, 1847).

Fowler, Orson S., *Fowler on Memory: or, Phrenology Applied to the Cultivation of Memory, the Intellectual Education of Children, and the Strengthening and Expanding of the Intellectual Powers*, 2nd edn. (New York, 1842).

———, *Hereditary Descent: Its Laws and Facts Applied to Human Improvement* (New York, 1848).

Greenwood, James M., *Principles of Education Practically Applied* (New York, 1887).

Hammond, Felicia A. D., "A Woman's Opinion of Women Teachers," *New York Teacher and American Educational Monthly*, VII (1870), 321-323.

Hecker, John, *Scientific Basis of Education Demonstrated by an Analysis of the Temperaments and of Phrenological Facts* (New York, 1868).

Holbrook, Alfred, *The Normal; or, Methods of Teaching the Common Branches*, 4th edn. (New York & Chicago, 1859).

Hughes, James Laughlin, *How to Secure and Retain Attention* (Syracuse, 1884).

Jacobi, Mary Putnam, *Physiological Notes on Primary Education and the Study of Language* (New York, 1889).

Kingsbury, John, "On Failures in Teaching," in American Institute of Instruction, *Lectures*, 1848, 1-24.

Klemm, Louis Richard, *Educational Topics of the Day. Chips from a Teachers' Workshop* (Boston, 1888).

L., E. A., "Intellectual Development," reprinted from *Practical Educator* in *District School Journal*, VII (1847/48), 144-145.

Lamborn, E., *The Practical Teacher, or Familiar Explanations and Illustrations of the Modus Operandi of the School Room* (Lancaster, Penna., 1855).

Lewis, Tayler, "Methods of Teaching, with Special Reference to What is Called Memoriter Instruction," in New York Regents, *Annual Report*, 78th (1865), 404-423.

Mansfield, Edward Deering, *American Education, Its Principles and Elements* (New York, 1851).

Mayhew, Ira, *Popular Education: for the Use of Parents and Teachers and for Young Persons of Both Sexes* (New York, 1850).

New York City and County, Board of Education, *Report of the Select Committee of the Board of Education in Relation to the Propriety and Expediency of Establishing a Free Academy for Females* (New York, 1849).

Orcutt, Hiram, *Reminiscences of School Life* (Cambridge, Mass., 1898).

Page, William P., *Common Schools; the Necessity of Their Improvement* (Geneseo, 1838).

Phelps, Almira H. L., *The Female Student* (New York & Boston, 1836).

Potter, Alonzo, and G. B. Emerson, *The School and the Schoolmaster* (New York, 1842).

Prince, John T., *Courses and Methods. A Handbook for Teachers of Primary, Grammar, and Ungraded Schools* (Boston, 1886).

Public School Society of New York, *A Manual of the System of Discipline & Instruction for the Schools of the Public School Society of New York, Instituted in the Year 1805* (New York, 1850).

Randall, Samuel Sidwell, *First Principles of Popular Education and Public Instruction* (New York, 1869).

Shepard, Edward Morse, *The Work of a Social Teacher, being a Memorial of Richard L. Dugdale* (New York, 1884).

Siljeström, Per Adam, *The Educational Institutions of the United States, Their Character and Organization*, tr. Frederica Rowan (London, 1853).

Stearns, John, *Philosophy of Mind* (New York, 1840).

Taylor, John Orville, *The District School* (New York, 1834).

———, *The First Lecture on Popular Education. The Sec-*

ond Lecture. . . . The Third Lecture. . . . (New York, [ca. 1842]).

Tenny, Mary B., "Essay on Thoroughness in Teaching," *New York Teacher*, II (1853/54), 231-234.

Wickersham, James Pyle, *Methods of Instruction* (Philadelphia, 1865).

"Woman's Work as Teacher, and Her Preparation for It," *American Educational Monthly*, IX (1872), 496-501.

B. OBJECT-TEACHING

"The Artificial Production of Stupidity in Schools," reprinted from *Massachusetts Teacher* in *American Educational Monthly*, X (1873), 445-451.

Barnard, Henry, *Pestalozzi and His Educational System* (Syracuse, N.Y., 1881).

Batchelder, J. P., *Thoughts on the Connection of Life, Mind, and Matter; in Respect to Education* (Utica, 1845).

Brothers of the Christian Schools, *Teaching: Its Theory and Practice. A Course of Notes* (Westchester, N.Y., 1884).

Calkins, Norman Allison, *Primary Object Lessons . . . A Manual for Teachers and Parents*, 7th edn. (New York, 1863).

Carll, M. M., *Mother's Manual and Infant Instructer; Designed for Infant or Primary Schools, and Familes*, 4th edn. (New York, 1845).

Chapman, John L., and James Scott, *First Thoughts; or, Beginning to Think* (New York, 1853).

"The Education of Idiots," *New York Teacher and American Educational Monthly*, VI (1869), 169-176.

Edwards, Richard, and John Russell Webb, *Analytical First Reader* (New York, 1866).

Hailmann, William N., *Outline of a System of Object-Teaching* (New York, 1867).

Holbrook, Alfred, *School Management* (New York & Chicago, 1872).

Keagy, John M., *The Pestalozzian Primer; or, First Steps in*

Teaching Children the Art of Reading and Thinking (Harrisburg, Penna., 1827).

May, Samuel J., *Lecture on the Education of the Faculties, and the Proper Employment of Young Children* (Boston, 1847).

"Object-Teaching According to the Oswego Method," *New York Teacher and American Educational Monthly*, VI (1869), 443-446.

Schoolmaster of the Nineteenth Century. Tr. from the German. A Full Guide for the Natural Development of the Mental Powers of Childhood, Adapted to the Wants of American Classes in the Primary Department (New York, 1880).

Sheldon, Edward A., *Autobiography* (New York, 1911).

———, *A Manual of Elementary Instruction*, 6th edn. (New York, 1869).

———, comp., *Lessons on Objects* (New York, 1863).

Wells, William, "The Influence of Pestalozzi," *Christian Advocate*, XLIV (1869), 321.

C. READING

Abbott, Jacob & Charles E., *The Mount Vernon Reader, a Course of Reading Lessons, Selected with Reference to Their Moral Influence on the Hearts and Lives of the Young* (New York, 1835).

B., "Learning to Read," *New York Teacher*, V (1855/56), 258-264.

Brooks, Edward, *Suggestions for Instruction in Language in the Elementary Schools* (Philadelphia, 1900).

Buckingham, Henry B., *Hand Books for Young Teachers. Number 1, First Steps* (Syracuse, N.Y., 1881).

Calkins, N. A., "Primary Reading," *New York Teacher and American Educational Monthly*, VII (1870), 34-35.

Clark, Solomon Henry, *How to Teach Reading in the Public Schools* (Chicago, 1899).

Corson, Hiram, "Vocal Culture in Its Relation to Literary Culture," *Atlantic Monthly*, LXXV (1895), 810-816.

Dewey, O., "On Reading," *Christian Examiner*, XXVII (1839), 1-18.

Duco, E., "Teaching to Read," *New York Teacher*, VI (1856/57), 367-368.

Dwight, Theodore, Jr., *The School-Master's Friend* (New York, 1835).

Edwards, Richard, *Analytical Fifth Reader* (Chicago, 1867).

Emerson, Benjamin Dudley, *The Third-Class Reader. Designed for the Use of the Younger Classes in the Schools of the United States* (Philadelphia, 1838).

Foster, Charles M., *Reading in the District Schools. A Paper Read Before the St. Louis Society of Pedagogy, on Saturday, December 18th, 1886* (n.p., n.d.).

Fuerst, Sidney Marsden, ed., *Reading and Literature*, New York Teachers' Monographs, IV, no. 2 (June 1902).

Hill, Thomas, *The Four Ways of Teaching to Read* (Cincinnati, 1856).

Hume, R. W., "Elocution," *New York Teacher and American Educational Monthly*, VII (1870), 373-375.

J., W. B., "Reading," *New York Teacher*, IX (1859/60), 131-160.

Kellogg, Eva D., ed., *Teaching Reading in Ten Cities* (Boston, 1900).

L., W. W., "Aids to Science—Reading," *New York Teacher*, IX (1859/60), 316-318.

Laing, Mary E., *Reading: a Manual for Teachers* (Boston, 1901).

Leavitt, Joshua, *Easy Lessons in Reading; for the Use of the Younger Classes in Common Schools* (Keene, N.H., 1829).

———, *Easy Lessons in Reading. For the Younger Classes in Common Schools* (Leavitt's Reading Series, Part II: Boston, 1849).

Loomis, Burt Weed, *The Educational Influence of Richard Edwards* (Nashville, Tenn., 1932).

Lyman, Walter C., "Hints on the Education and Use of Gesture," *New York Teacher and American Educational Monthly*, VII (1870), 19-24, 62-68.

New York State Normal School, Executive Committee, *Report* (N.Y. State Senate Doc. No. 32, January 27, 1846).

"The Old and the New in Education," *American Educational Monthly*, I (1864), 20-21.

Potter, H.L.D., *Manual of Reading, in Four Parts: Orthophony, Class Methods, Gesture, and Elocution* (New York, 1873).

"Primary Instruction. III. Reading," *American Educational Monthly*, I (1864), 133-134.

Randall, Samuel Sidwell, *Randall's Fourth Reader* (Albany, 1856).

Reeder, Rudolph Rex, *The Historical Development of School Readers and Method in Teaching Reading* (New York, 1900).

Russell, William, *A Manual of Instruction in Reading* (Andover, 1852).

S., G. H., "How Shall We Make Good Readers?" *New York Teacher*, IX (1859/60), 206-207.

Sigma, Omega, "The Use of Rules in Elocution," *New York Teacher*, VII (1857/58), 323-327.

Smith, Nila Banton, *American Reading Instruction: Its Development and Its Significance in Giving a Perspective on Current Practices in Reading* (New York, 1934; rev. edn., Newark, Del., 1965).

Stone, T.P.D., "Reading in Common Schools," in New York Regents, *Annual Report*, 83rd (1880), 529.

Thayer, Gideon, "Letters to a Young Teacher," *American Journal of Education*, IV (1857), 219-228.

W., A., "Elocutionary Instruction—Fitzgerald's Exhibition Speaker," *New York Teacher*, VI (1856/57), 313-314.

Webb, John Russell, *Webb's Normal Reader, No. 1. A New Method of Teaching Children to Read: Founded on Nature and Reason*, rev. edn. (New York, 1855).

———, *Webb's Normal Reader, No. 4. Designed to Teach Correct Reading, to Improve and Expand the Mind, and to Purify and Elevate the Character* (New York, 1856).

Willard, Emma, "Address on the Time and Teaching of Little Children," *New York Teacher*, II (1853/54), 139-140.

D. ARITHMETIC

A., E. S., "The Study of Arithmetic," *New York Teacher*, I (1853), 176-178.

Abbott, Jacob, *The Mount Vernon Arithmetic. Part II. Vulgar and Decimal Fractions* (New York, 1847).

Abbott, Jacob & Charles E., *Abbotts' Addition Columns, for Teaching the Art of Adding with Facility and Correctness from the Mount Vernon Arithmetic* (New York, 1847).

Brockett, Dr., "The Old School House and the New; or, Fifty Years Ago and To-Day," reprinted from *Educational Record in American Educational Monthly*, VIII (1871), 473-486.

Brooks, Edward, *The Course of Study in Arithmetic for the Public Schools in Philadelphia* (Philadelphia, 1898).

———, *The New Normal Mental Arithmetic: A Thorough and Complete Course, by Analysis and Induction* (Philadelphia, 1873).

———, *The Philosophy of Arithmetic as Developed from the Three Fundamental Processes of Synthesis, Analysis, and Comparison* (Philadelphia, 1876).

C., G. R., "Female Education," *American Educational Monthly*, IX (1872), 124-30, 170-175.

Clark, Josiah, *The Parent's Monitor: or, An Address to Parents and Teachers, Concerning the Education of Youth in Several Particulers* [sic] (Boston, 1794).

Colburn, Warren, *Observations on the Method of Teaching Numbers, Proposed in the Following Sheets* (n.p., n.d.).

———, "On the Teaching of Arithmetic," in American Institute of Instruction, *Lectures*, 1830, 279-298.

Davies, Charles, *Arithmetic Designed for Academies and Schools; Uniting the Inductive Reasoning of the French with the Practical Methods of the English System* (New York, 1848).

———, *The Common School Arithmetic* (New York, 1833).

———, *Elements of Written Arithmetic* (New York, 1870).

———, *First Lessons in Arithmetic, Combining the Oral Method, with the Method of Teaching the Combination of Figures by Sight* (New York, 1849).

———, *Grammar of Arithmetic; or, An Analysis of the Language of Figures and Science of Numbers* (New York, 1850).

———, *Intellectual Arithmetic; Being an Analysis of the Science of Numbers, with Special Reference to Mental Training and Development* (New York, 1868).

———, *School Arithmetic*, rev. edn. (New York, 1865).

Dodd, James B., *An Essay on Mathematical Text-Books, and the Prevailing System of Mathematical Education* (New York, 1859).

———, *Strictures on Greenleaf's Arithmetic; with Comparisons between That and Dodd's Arithmetic* (Philadelphia, 1859).

Eggleston, George Cary, *How to Educate Yourself* (New York, 1874),

Greenwood, James M., and Artemas Martin, *Notes on the History of American Text-Books in Arithmetic* (Washington, 1899/1900).

Johnson, Clifton, *Old-Time Schools and School-Books* (1904, reprinted New York, 1935).

Monroe, Walter Scott, *Development of Arithmetic as a School Subject* (U.S. Bureau of Education, *Bulletin*, 1917 no. 10).

Olney, Edward, "Arithmetic," in Henry Kiddle and Alexander J. Schem, *Cyclopaedia of Education* (New York, 1877), 40-45.

Peterson, Ellis, *Arithmetic in the Public Schools* (Boston, 1887).

Preston, John, *Every Man His Own Teacher; or, Lancaster's Theory of Education, Practically Displayed; Being an Introduction to Arithmetic* (Albany, 1817).

Robinson, H. N., "Educational Reform," *American Journal of Education and College Review*, III (1857), 77-84, 235-240.

"Schools as They Were in the United States Sixty and Seventy Years Ago," *New York Teacher*, XIII (1863/64), 281-287.

"A Seasonable Talk with Teachers," *American Educational Monthly*, IX (1873), 106-109.

Smith, David Eugene, *The Teaching of Elementary Mathematics* (New York, 1900).

Smith, Henry Lester, and Merrill Thomas Eaton, *An Analysis of Arithmetic Textbooks*, 4 vols. (Bloomington, Ind., 1942/43).

Smith, Roswell C., *Arithmetic on the Productive System* (Hartford, 1842).

———, *Practical and Mental Arithmetic*, "99 ed." (Auburn, N.Y., 1844).

Soldan, Louis, *Grube's Method. Two Essays on Elementary Instruction in Arithmetic* (Chicago, 1878).

Walker, [Francis Amasa], *Arithmetic in Primary and Grammar Schools* (Boston, 1887).

Willard, Emma, *Letter, Addressed as a Circular to the Members of the Willard Association, for the Mutual Improvement of Female Teachers; Formed at the Troy Female Seminary, July, 1837* (Troy, N.Y., 1838).

III. Intelligence Levels and Emotional Development

Altus, William D., "Birth Order and Scholastic Aptitude," *Journal of Consulting Psychology*, XXIX (1965), 202-205.

Anastasi, Anne, ed., *Individual Differences*, (New York, 1965).

———, "Intelligence and Family Size," *Psychological Bulletin*, LIII (1956), 187-209.

———, and C. de Jesús, "Language Development and Nonverbal IQ of Puerto Rican Preschool Children in New York City," *Journal of Abnormal and Social Psychology*, XLVIII (1953), 357-366.

Arnheim, Rudolf, *Visual Thinking* (Berkeley & Los Angeles, 1969).

Arthus, Henri, *Le village, test d'activité créatrice; une psychologie virtualiste* (Paris, 1949).

Ausubel, David P., H. M. Schiff, and M. Goldman, "Qualitative Characteristics in the Learning Process Associated with Anxiety," *Journal of Abnormal and Social Psychology*, XLVIII (1953), 537-547.

Bagley, William C., "Educational Determinism," *School and Society*, XV (1922), 373-384.

Barclay, A., and D. R. Cusumano, "Father Absence, Cross-Sex Identity, and Field-dependent Behavior in Male Adolescents," *Child Development*, XXXVIII (1967), 243-250.

Barron, Frank, *Creativity and Personal Freedom* (Princeton, N.J., 1968).

Baumrind, Diana, and Allen E. Black, "Socialization Practices Associated with Dimensions of Competence in Preschool Boys and Girls," *Child Development*, XXXVIII (1967), 291-327.

Bayley, Nancy, "Research in Child Development: a Longitudinal Perspective," *Merrill-Palmer Quarterly*, XI (1965), 183-208.

Bayley, Nancy, and Earl S. Schaefer, "Correlations of Maternal and Child Behaviors with the Development of Mental Abilities," Society for Research in Child Development, *Monographs*, XXIX, no. 6 (1964).

Beston, W. H., W. Heron, and T. H. Scott, "Effects of Decreased Variation in the Sensory Environment," *Canadian Journal of Psychology*, VIII (1954), 70-76.

Bieri, James, "Parental Identification, Acceptance of Authority and Within-Sex Differences in Cognitive Behavior," *Journal of Abnormal and Social Psychology*, LX (1959), 76-79.

Bieri, James, W. M. Bradburn, and M. D. Galinsky, "Sex Differences in Perceptual Behavior," *Journal of Personality*, XXVI (1958), 1-12.

Bing, Elizabeth, "Effect of Child-Rearing Practices on the Development of Differential Cognitive Abilities," *Child Development*, XXXIV (1963), 631-648.

Bloom, Benjamin S., *Stability and Change in Human Characteristics* (New York, 1964).

Bowlby, John, *Maternal Care and Mental Health*, with Mary D. Ainsworth and others, *Deprivation of Maternal Care* (New York, 1966).

Brim, Orville, G., Jr., Richard S. Crutchfield, and Wayne H. Holtzman, *Intelligence: Perspectives 1965* (New York, 1966).

Brodbeck, A. J., and O. C. Irwin, "The Speech Behavior of Infants without Families," *Child Development*, XVII (1946), 145-156.

Brody, Sylvia, *Passivity: A Study of Its Development and Expression in Boys* (New York, 1964).

Bronfenbrenner, Urie, "Early Deprivation in Mammals: a Cross-Species Analysis," in Grant Newton, ed., *Early Experience and Behavior* (Springfield, Ill., 1968).

Brown, Roger W., and Eric H. Lenneberg, "A Study in Language and Cognition," *Journal of Abnormal and Social Psychology*, XLIX (1954), 454-462.

Bruner, Jerome S., "The Cognitive Consequences of Early Sensory Deprivation," *Psychosomatic Medicine*, XXI (1959), 89-95.

———, ed., *Learning about Learning: a Conference Report* (Office of Education, Cooperative Research Monograph No. 15, 1966).

Burt, Cyril, *Intelligence and Fertility: the Effect of the Differential Birthrate on Inborn Mental Characteristics*, Eugenics Society, *Occasional Papers*, No. 2 (London, 1946).

———, "The Trend of National Intelligence," *British Journal of Sociology*, I (1950), 154-168.

———, "The Trend of Scottish Intelligence," *British Journal of Educational Psychology*, xx (1950), 55-61.

———, and Margaret Howard, "The Multifactorial Theory of Inheritance and Its Application to Intelligence," *British Journal of Statistical Psychology*, ix (1956), 95-131.

Calvin, Allen D., P. B. Koons, Jr., J. L. Bingham, and H. H. Fink, "A Further Investigation of the Relation between Manifest Anxiety and Intelligence," *Journal of Consulting Psychology*, xix (1955), 280-282.

Catell, Raymond B., "The Fate of National Intelligence: Test of a Thirteen-Year Prediction," *Eugenics Review*, xlii (1950), 136-148.

———, "Theory of Fluid and Crystallized Intelligence: A Critical Experiment," *Journal of Educational Psychology*, liv (1963), 1-22.

Chomsky, Noam, *Language and Mind* (New York, 1968).

Cicirelli, Victor G., "Form of the Relationship between Creativity, IQ, and Academic Achievement," *Journal of Educational Psychology*, lvi, (1965), 303-308.

———, "Sibling Constellation, Creativity, IQ, and Academic Achievement," *Child Development*, xxxviii (1967), 481-490.

Coleman, James S., and others, *Equality of Educational Opportunity* (Washington, 1966).

Coopersmith, Stanley, *The Antecedents of Self-Esteem* (San Francisco, 1967).

Corah, Norman L., "Differentiation in Children and Their Parents," *Journal of Personality*, xxxiii (1965), 300-308.

Cronbach, Lee J., "Year-to-Year Correlations of Mental Tests: a Review of the Hofstaetter Analysis," *Child Development*, xxxviii (1967), 283-289.

Cross, Herbert J., "The Relation of Parental Training Conditions to Conceptual Level in Adolescent Boys," *Journal of Personality*, xxxiv (1966), 348-365.

Dahlke, Arnold E., and Richard H. Dana, "Intraindividual Verbal-Numerical Discrepancies and Personality," *Journal of Consulting Psychology*, xxvii (1963), 182.

Dearborn, Walter Fenno, *Intelligence Tests: Their Significance for School and Society* (Boston, 1928).

de Groot, A. D., "Effects of War Upon the Intelligence of Youth and Children," *Journal of Abnormal Psychology*, XLIII (1948), 311-317.

Di Vesta, Francis J., "Developmental Patterns in the Use of Modifiers as Modes of Conceptualization," *Child Development*, XXXVI (1964), 185-213.

Dockrell, W. B., ed., *On Intelligence: the Toronto Symposium on Intelligence, 1969* (London, 1970).

Douglas, J.W.B., *The Home and the School: a Study of Ability and Attainment in the Primary School* (London, 1964).

Drews, Elizabeth M., and John E. Teahan, "Parental Attitudes and Academic Achievement," *Journal of Clinical Psychology*, XIII (1957), 328-332.

Duncan, Otis Dudley, "Is the Intelligence of the General Population Declining?" *American Sociological Review*, XVII (1952), 401-407, with reply by Frank Lorimer, XVII, 770-771.

Eells, K., A. Davis, R. J. Havighurst, V. E. Herrick, and R. W. Tyler, *Intelligence and Cultural Differences* (Chicago, 1951).

Emmett, W. G., "The Trend of Intelligence in Certain Districts of England," *Population Studies*, III (1950), 324-337.

Ervin, Susan M., "Changes with Age in the Verbal Determinants of Word-Association," *American Journal of Psychology*, LXXIV (1961), 361-372.

Escalona, Sibylle K., and G. M. Heider, *Prediction and Outcome: a Study in Child Development* (New York, 1959).

———, and Alice Moriarty, "Prediction of Schoolage Development from Infant Tests," *Child Development*, XXXII (1961), 597-605.

Farnham-Diggory, Sylvia, "Cognitive Synthesis in Negro

and White Children," Society for Research in Child Development, *Monographs*, xxxv, No. 2 (1970).

Fitzgerald, Maureen P., "Sex Differences in the Perception of the Parental Role for Middle and Working Class Adolescents," *Journal of Clinical Psychology*, xxii (1966), 15-16.

Floud, Jean, and A. H. Halsey, "Intelligence Tests, Social Class and Selection for Secondary Schools," *British Journal of Sociology*, viii (1957), 33-39.

Freeberg, Norman E., and Donald T. Payne, "Parental Influence on Cognitive Development in Early Childhood: a Review," *Child Development*, xxxviii (1967), 65-87.

Fromm, Erika, and Lenore Dumas Hartman, *Intelligence, a Dynamic Approach* (Garden City, N.Y., 1955).

Getzels, J. W., and P. W. Jackson, "Family Environment and Cognitive Style: a Study of the Sources of Highly Intelligent and of Highly Creative Adolescents," *American Sociological Review*, xxvi (1961), 351-359.

Gladwin, Thomas, *East is a Big Bird: Navigation and Logic on Puluwat Atoll* (Cambridge, Mass., 1970).

Gleser, Goldine C., Louis A. Gottschalk, and Watkins John, "The Relationship of Sex and Intelligence to Choice of Words: a Normative Study of Verbal Behavior," *Journal of Clinical Psychology*, xv (1959), 182-191.

Grimes, Jesse W., and Wesley Allinsmith, "Compulsivity, Anxiety, and School Achievement," *Merrill-Palmer Quarterly*, vii (1961), 247-271.

Haan, Norma, "Proposed Model of Ego Functioning: Coping and Defense Mechanisms in Relationship to IQ Change," *Psychological Monographs*, lxxvii, no. 8 (1963).

Halsey, A. H., "Genetics, Social Structure and Intelligence," *British Journal of Sociology*, ix (1958), 15-28.

Harris, Irving D., *Emotional Blocks to Learning: A Study of the Reasons for Failure in School* (New York, 1961).

Harvey, O. J., David E. Hunt, and Harold M. Schroder, *Conceptual Systems and Personality Organization* (New York, 1961).

Harwood, B. Thomas, "Some Intellectual Correlates of Schizoid Indicators," *Journal of Consulting Psychology*, XXXI (1967), 218.

Hayes, Keith J., "Genes, Drives, and Intellect," *Psychological Reports*, X (1962), 299-342.

Haywood, H. Carl, "Novelty-seeking Behavior as a Function of Manifest Anxiety and Physiological Arousal," *Journal of Personality*, XXX (1962), 63-73.

Hebb, D. O., *The Organization of Behaviour: a Neuropsychological Theory* (New York & London, 1949).

Heilbrun, Alfred B., Jr., Helen K. Orr, and Samuel N. Harrell, "Patterns of Parental Childrearing and Subsequent Vulnerability to Cognitive Disturbance," *Journal of Consulting Psychology*, XXX (1966), 51-59.

Helson, Ravenna, "Personality of Women with Imaginative and Artistic Interests: the Role of Masculinity, Originality, and Other Characteristics in Their Creativity," *Journal of Personality*, XXXIV (1966), 1-25.

———, "Sex Differences in Creative Style," *Journal of Personality*, XXXV (1967), 214-233.

Helvétius, Claude Adrien, *A Treatise on Man; His Intellectual Faculties and His Education* (2 vols.: London, 1810).

Hess, Robert D., "Early Experience and Socialization of Cognitive Modes in Children," *Child Development*, XXXVI (1965), 869-886.

———, and Roberta Meyer Bear, eds., *Early Education: Current Theory, Research, and Action* (Chicago, 1968).

Himmelweit, H. T., "Intelligence and Size of Family: Their Relationship in an Adult Group of High Educational Standard," *Eugenics Review*, XL (1948), 77-84.

Hoffman, Lois Wladis, and Martin L. Hoffman, eds., *Review of Child Development Research*, vol. II (New York, 1966).

Hofstaetter, Peter R., "The Changing Composition of 'Intelligence': a Study in T-Technique," *Journal of Genetic Psychology*, LXXXV (1954), 159-164.

Holzman, Philip S., and Riley W. Gardner, "Leveling and

Repression," *Journal of Abnormal and Social Psychology*, LIX (1959), 151-155.

———, and George S. Klein, "Cognitive System-Principles of Leveling and Sharpening: Individual Differences in Assimilation Effects in Visual Time-Error," *Journal of Psychology*, XXXVII (1954), 105-122.

Honzik, Marjorie P., "Developmental Studies of Parent-Child Resemblance in Intelligence," *Child Development*, XXVIII (1957), 215-228.

———, "Developmental Study of the Relations of Family Variables to Children's Intelligence," *American Psychologist*, VII (1952), 527-528.

———, "Environmental Correlates of Mental Growth: Prediction from the Family Setting at 21 Months," *Child Development*, XXXVIII (1967), 337-364.

———, "A Sex Difference in the Age of Onset of the Parent-Child Resemblance in Intelligence," *Journal of Educational Psychology*, LIV (1963), 231-237.

Horan, Edmund M., "Word Association Frequency Tables of Mentally Retarded Children," *Journal of Consulting Psychology*, XX (1956), 22.

Horton, Donald, and R. Richard Wohl, "Mass Communication and Para-social Interaction," *Psychiatry*, XIX (1956), 215-229.

Hudson, Liam, ed., *The Ecology of Human Intelligence* (Harmondsworth, Eng., 1970).

Hunt, J. McVickar, *Intelligence and Experience* (New York, 1961).

Hurley, John R., "Maternal Attitudes and Children's Intelligence," *Journal of Clinical Psychology*, XV (1959), 291-292.

———, "Parental Acceptance-Rejection and Children's Intelligence," *Merrill-Palmer Quarterly*, XI (1965), 19-30.

———, "Parental Malevolence and Children's Intelligence," *Journal of Consulting Psychology*, XXXI (1967), 199-204.

Hymovich, Bernard, "The Effects of Experimental Variations in Early Experience on Problem Solving in the Rat,"

Journal of Comparative and Physiological Psychology, XLV (1952), 313-321.

Jackson, Brian, and Dennis Marsden, *Education and the Working Class* (London, 1962).

Jackson, Philip W., Jacob W. Getzels, and George A. Xydis, "Psychological Health and Cognitive Functioning in Adolescence: a Multivariate Analysis," *Child Development*, XXXI (1960), 285-298.

Jenkins, James J., and Wallace A. Russell, "Systematic Changes in Word Association Norms: 1910-1952," *Journal of Abnormal and Social Psychology*, LX (1960), 293-204.

John, Vera P., "The Intellectual Development of Slum Children: Some Preliminary Findings," *American Journal of Orthopsychiatry*, XXXIII (1963), 813-822.

Jordheim, G. D., and I. A. Olsen, "Use of a Non-verbal Test of Intelligence in the Trust Territory of the Pacific," *American Anthropologist*, LXV (1963), 1122-1125, with reply by A. Richard King, LXVI (1964), 640-644.

Kagan, Jerome, ed., *Creativity and Learning* (Boston, 1967).

———, and others, "Information Processing in the Child: Significance of Analytic and Reflective Attitudes," *Psychological Monographs*, LXXVIII, no. 1 (1964).

———, and Marion Freeman, "Relation of Childhood Intelligence, Maternal Behaviors, and Social Class to Behavior During Adolescence," *Child Development*, XXXIV (1963), 899-911.

———, and Howard A. Moss, *Birth to Maturity: a Study in Psychological Development* (New York, 1962).

———, and Howard A. Moss, "Parental Correlates of Child's IQ and Height: a Cross-Validation of the Berkeley Growth Study Results," *Child Development*, XXX (1959), 325-332.

———, and Howard A. Moss, "Stability and Validity of Achievement Fantasy," *Journal of Abnormal and Social Psychology*, LVIII (1959), 357-364.

———, Howard A. Moss, and Irving E. Sigel, "Conceptual

Style and the Use of Affect Labels," *Merrill-Palmer Quarterly*, VI (1960), 261-278.

———, L. W. Sontag, C. T. Baker, and V. L. Nelson, "Personality and IQ Change," *Journal of Abnormal and Social Psychology*, LVI (1958), 261-266.

Kaswan, Jaques, Sally Haralson, and Ruth Cline, "Variables in Perceptual and Cognitive Organization and Differentiation," *Journal of Personality*, XXXIII (1965), 164-177.

Kennedy, Wallace A., *A Follow-up Normative Study of Negro Intelligence and Achievement* (Tallahassee, Fla., 1965).

———, and Herman Willcutt, "Youth-Parent Relations of Mathematically Gifted Adolescents," *Journal of Clinical Psychology*, XIX (1963), 400-402.

Kent, Norman, and D. Russell Davis, "Discipline in the Home and Intellectual Development," *British Journal of Medical Psychology*, XXX (1957), 27-34.

Koff, Robert H., "Systematic Changes in Children's Word-Association Norms 1916-63," *Child Development*, XXXVI (1965), 299-305.

Kogan, Nathan, and Michael A. Wallach, *Risk Taking: a Study in Cognition and Personality* (New York, 1964).

Kohlberg, Lawrence, and Edward Zigler, "The Impact of Cognitive Maturity on the Development of Sex-Role Attitudes in the Years 4 to 8," *Genetic Psychology Monographs*, LXXV (1967), 89-165.

Korner, Anneliese F., and Rose Grobstein, "Visual Alertness as Related to Soothing: Implications for Maternal Stimulation and Early Deprivation," *Child Development*, XXXVII (1966), 867-876.

Kubie, Lawrence S., *Neurotic Distortion of the Creative Process* (New York, 1967).

Lantz, De Lee, and Eric H. Lenneberg, "Verbal Communication and Color Memory in the Deaf and Hearing," *Child Development*, XXXVII (1966), 765-779.

———, and Volney Stefflre, "Language and Cognition Revisited," *Journal of Abnormal and Social Psychology*, LXIX (1964), 472-481.

Lee, Everett S., "Negro Intelligence and Selective Migration: A Philadelphia Test of the Klineberg Hypothesis," *American Journal of Sociology*, XVI (1951), 227-233.

Levy, David M., *Maternal Overprotection* (New York, 1943).

Lipsitt, Lewis P., and Charles C. Spiker, eds., *Advances in Child Development and Behavior*, I (New York, 1963).

Liverant, Shephard, "Intelligence: a Concept in Need of Re-Examination," *Journal of Consulting Psychology*, XXIV (1964), 101-109.

Lorimer, Frank, "Trends in Capacity for Intelligence," *Eugenical News*, XXXVII (1952), 17-24.

Maccoby, Eleanor E., and Lucy Rau, *Differential Cognitive Abilities* (Stanford, 1962).

MacKinnon, Donald W., "The Nature and Nurture of Creative Talent," *American Psychologist*, XVII (1962), 484-495.

———, "Personality and the Realization of Creative Potential," *American Psychologist*, XX (1965), 273-281.

Maddi, Salvatore R., and Naomi Berne, "Novelty of Productions and Desire for Novelty as Active and Passive Forms of the Need for Variety," *Journal of Personality*, XXXII (1964), 270-277.

McNemar, Quinn, "Lost: Our Intelligence? Why?" *American Psychologist*, XIX (1964), 871-882.

Mitchell, Ida, I. R. Rosanoff, and A. J. Rosanoff, "A Study of Association in Negro Children," *Psychological Review*, XXVI (1919), 354-359.

Milton, G. A., "The Effects of Sex Role Identification upon Problem Solving Skill," *Journal of Abnormal and Social Psychology*, LV (1957), 208-212.

Moss, Howard A., and Jerome Kagan, "Maternal Influences on Early IQ Scores," *Psychological Reports*, IV (1958), 655-661.

Munday-Castle, A. C., "Electrophysiological Correlates of

Intelligence," *Journal of Personality*, xxvi (1958), 184-199.

Murphy, Gardner, *Human Potentialities* (New York, 1958).

Mussen, Paul H., "Long-Term Consequences of Masculinity of Interests in Adolescence," *Journal of Consulting Psychology*, xxvi (1962), 435-440.

Neff, Walter S., "Socioeconomic Status and Intelligence: a Critical Survey," *Psychological Bulletin*, xxxv (1938), 727-757.

Nichols, Robert C., "Parental Attitudes of Mothers of Intelligent Adolescents and Creativity of Their Children," *Child Development*, xxxv (1964), 1041-1049.

Nisbet, John, "Family Environment and Intelligence," *Eugenics Review*, xlv (1953), 31-40.

Nisbet, John D., "Level of National Intelligence," *Nature*, clxx (1952), 852.

———, and N. J. Entwistle, "Intelligence and Family Size," *British Journal of Educational Psychology*, xxxvii (1967), 188-193.

Oldfield, R. C., and J. C. Marshall, eds., *Language: Selected Readings* (Harmondsworth, Eng., 1968).

Palermo, David S., "Word Associations and Children's Verbal Behavior," in Lewis P. Lipsitt and Charles C. Spiker, *Advances in Child Development and Behavior* (New York & London, 1963), i, 31-68.

———, and J. J. Jenkins, "Superordinates, 'Maturity' and Logical Analyses of Language," *Psychological Reports*, x (1962), 437-438.

———, and J. J. Jenkins, *Word Association Norms: Grade School through College*, xxx (Minneapolis, 1963).

Peck, Robert F., "Family Patterns Correlated with Adolescent Personality Structure," *Journal of Abnormal and Social Psychology*, lvii (1958), 347-350.

Penrose, Lionel S., "Genetical Influences on the Intelligence Level of the Population," *British Journal of Psychology*, xl (1950), 128-136.

———, "The Supposed Threat of Declining Intelligence,"

American Journal of Mental Deficiency, LIII (1948), 114-118.

Peterson, Joseph, *Early Conceptions and Tests of Intelligence* (Yonkers, 1925).

Piaget, Jean, *Biology and Knowledge: An Essay on the Relations between Organic Regulations and Cognitive Processes* (Chicago, 1971).

Pine, Fred, and Robert R. Holt, "Creativity and Primary Process: A Study of Adaptive Regression" *Journal of Abnormal and Social Psychology*, LXI (1960), 370-379.

Pressey, Sidney L., and Raymond G. Kuhlen, *Psychological Development through the Life Span* (New York, 1957).

Price-Williams, D. R., ed., *Cross-Cultural Studies: Selected Readings* (Harmondsworth, Eng., 1969).

Raup, R. Bruce, and others, *The Improvement of Practical Intelligence: the Central Task of Education* (New York, 1950).

Reeves, Joan Wynn, *Thinking about Thinking* (New York, 1965).

Rosen, B. C., "Family Structure and Achievement Motivation," *American Sociological Review*, XXVI (1961), 574-585.

Rosenthal, Robert, and Lenore Jacobson, *Pygmalion in the Classroom* (New York, 1968).

Rubinstein, Judith, "Maternal Attentiveness and Subsequent Exploratory Behavior in the Infant," *Child Development*, XXXVIII (1967), 1089-1100.

Schachtel, Ernest G., *Metamorphosis: on the Development of Affect, Perception, Attention, and Memory* (New York 1959).

Schafer, Roy, "Regression in the Service of the Ego: the Relevance of a Psychoanalytic Concept for Personality Assessment," in Gardner Lindzey, ed., *Assessment of Human Motives* (New York, 1958), 119-148.

Schroder, Harold M., Michael J. Driver, and Siegfried Streufert, *Human Information Processing: Individuals and Groups Functioning in Complex Social Situations* (New York, 1967).

Scottish Council for Research in Education, *Social Implications of the 1947 Scottish Mental Survey* (London, 1953).

———, *The Trend of Scottish Intelligence; a Comparison of the 1947 and 1932 Surveys of the Intelligence of Eleven-Year-Old Pupils* (London, 1949).

Shaw, Merville C., and Donald L. White, "The Relationship between Child-Parent Identification and Academic Underachievement," *Journal of Clinical Psychology*, XXI (1965), 10-13.

Silverman, Julian, "Scanning-Control Mechanism and 'Cognitive Filtering' in Paranoid and Non-paranoid Schizophrenia," *Journal of Consulting Psychology*, XXVIII (1964), 385-393.

Skodak, Marie, *Children in Foster Homes: a Study of Mental Development* (Iowa City, 1939).

Solley, Charles M., and Gardner Murphy, *Development of the Perceptual World* (New York, 1960).

Sommer, Robert, "Rorshach *M* Responses and Intelligence," *Journal of Clinical Psychology*, XIV (1958), 58-61.

Sontag, L. W., C. T. Baker, and Virginia L. Nelson, "Mental Growth and Personality: a Longitudinal Study," Society for Research in Child Developnent, *Monographs*, XXIII (1958).

Stott, L. H., and Rachel S. Ball, "Infant and Preschool Mental Tests: Review and Evaluation," Society for Research in Child Development, *Monographs*, XXX (1965).

Strodtbeck, Fred L., "Family Interaction, Values and Achievement," in D. C. McClellan and others, *Talent and Society* (Princeton, N.J., 1958).

———, "The Hidden Curriculum in the Middle-Class Home," in John D. Krumboltz, ed., *Learning and the Educational Process* (Chicago, 1965).

Thomson, Godfrey, "Intelligence and Fertility: the Scottish 1947 Survey," *Eugenics Review*, XLI (1950), 163-170.

Thomson, Godfrey, "The Trend of National Intelligence," *Eugenics Review*, XXXVIII (1946), 9-18.

Thompson, J. W., "Genetics, Social Structure, Intelligence and Statistics," *British Journal of Sociology*, XI (1960), 44-50.

Thompson, W. R., and W. Heron, "The Effects of Restricting Early Experience on Problem-solving Capacity of Dogs," *Canadian Journal of Psychology*, VIII (1954), 17-31.

Thorndike, Edward L., and others, *The Measurement of Intelligence* (New York, 1927).

Torrance, E. Paul, *Education and the Creative Potential* (Minneapolis, 1963).

Trumbull, Richard R., "A Study of Relationships between Factors of Personality and Intelligence," *Journal of Social Psychology*, XXXVIII (1953), 161-173.

Tuddenham, Read D., "Soldier Intelligence in World Wars I and II," *American Psychologist*, III (1948), 54-56.

Vernon, Philip E., "Ability Factors and Environmental Influences," *American Psychologist*, XX (1965), 723-733.

———, *Intelligence and Cultural Environment* (London, 1969).

Walker, C. Eugene, and James Tashmirian, "Birth Order and Student Characteristics," *Journal of Consulting Psychology*, XXXI (1967), 219.

Wallach, Michael A., and Nathan Kogan, *Modes of Thinking in Young Children: a Study of the Creativity-Intelligence Distinction* (New York, 1965).

———, and Nathan Kogan, "A New Look at the Creativity-Intelligence Distinction," *Journal of Personality*, XXXIII (1965), 348-369.

Watson, Godwin, "Some Personality Differences in Children Relative to Strict or Permissive Parental Discipline," *Journal of Psychology*, XLIV (1957), 227-249.

Wechsler, David, *The Measurement and Appraisal of Adult Intelligence*, 4th edn. (Baltimore, 1958).

———, "The Non-intellective Factors in General Intelligence," *Journal of Abnormal and Social Psychology*, XXXVII (1943), 100-104.

Wellman, Beth L., "Our Changing Concept of Intelligence," *Journal of Consulting Psychology*, II (1938), 97-107.

Whipple, Guy Montrose, ed., *Intelligence: Its Nature and Nurture*, National Society for the Study of Education, *Yearbook*, XXXIX, 2 vols. (1940).

Wild, Cynthia, "Creativity and Adaptive Regression," *Journal of Personality and Social Psychology*, II (1965), 161-169.

Wiseman, Stephen, ed., *Intelligence and Ability: Selected Readings* (Harmondsworth, Eng., 1967).

Witkin, H. A., and others, *Personality through Perception* (New York, 1954).

Wright, John C., and Jerome Kagan, eds., *Basic Cognitive Processes in Children*, Society for Research in Child Development, *Monographs*, XXVIII, no. 2 (1963).

Yarrow, Leon J., "Research in Dimensions of Early Maternal Care," *Merrill-Palmer Quarterly*, IX (1953), 101-114.

Young, H. B., and others, "Influence of Town and Country upon Children's Intelligence," *British Journal of Educational Psychology*, XXXII (1962), 151-158.

Ziman, J. M., *Public Knowledge: an Essay Concerning the Social Dimension of Science* (Cambridge, 1968).

Zubin, Joseph, and George A. Jervis, eds., *Psychopathology of Mental Development* (New York, 1967).

INDEX

FIRST SERIES.—No. 12.

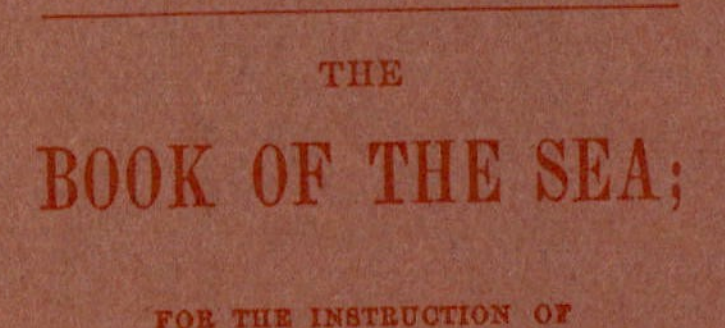

THE

BOOK OF THE SEA;

FOR THE INSTRUCTION OF

LITTLE SAILORS.

NEW YORK:
KIGGINS & KELLOGG,
123 & 125 William St.

THE SAILOR.

Sailors pass most of their time on the water. They become so used to living on the water, that when they are on land they sometimes do not know what to do with themselves to pass away their time. And after a few days or weeks they are very glad to be on board their ship again, and on the wide, blue sea. Sailors are kind and brave; and if you are kind to them they will do everything in their power to show that they feel it, and will repay it. They are a class of men who are very much needed, and do us great good by going

THE BRIG.

The brig is next in size to the ship. It has but two masts —but is otherwise like a ship. The ship and the brig are called square-rigged vessels because nearly every sail is square. Like the ship, the brig too is used mostly in long voyages.

SCHOONER AND SLOOP.

The schooner has two masts, and the sloop but one. The sail is fastened at the bottom to a long stick, called the boom, to the mast at the side, and to the gaff at the top. The vessel in the picture is a sloop.

upon the sea, and risking their lives in storms, to bring us the good things of countries afar off. They amuse one another on long voyages by telling long stories. This they call spinning yarns.

THE SHIP.

The ship is the largest kind of vessel that sails upon the water. It has three masts, made of the trunks of pine trees, that have pieces of timber called yards put across them on which are spread the sails. Ships are used for long voyages, being often months out of sight of land.

THE SKIFF.

The skiff is a small boat, made of boards or thin planks. It is used about rivers and on ponds and lakes, and is pushed through the water with a paddle, like a canoe. The canoe is made sometimes out of the trunk of a tree, and sometimes out of bark or skins.

N. HOWLAND

Like prisoned eagles sailors pine
On the dull and quiet shore;
They long for the flashing brine,
The spray and the tempest's roar.

To shoot through sparkling foam,
Like an ocean bird set free—
Like the ocean bird their home
They find on the raging sea.